Edward Thomas Booth, E Neale

Rough notes on the Birds observed during twenty-five years shooting and collecting in the British Islands

Edward Thomas Booth, E Neale

**Rough notes on the Birds observed during twenty-five years shooting and collecting in the British Islands**

ISBN/EAN: 9783742864925

Manufactured in Europe, USA, Canada, Australia, Japa

Cover: Foto ©ninafisch / pixelio.de

Manufactured and distributed by brebook publishing software (www.brebook.com)

Edward Thomas Booth, E Neale

# Rough notes on the Birds observed during twenty-five years shooting and collecting in the British Islands

## CONTENTS OF VOL. II

| | |
|---|---|
| Wood-Wren | Phylloscopus sibilatrix. |
| Willow-Wren | Phylloscopus trochilus. |
| Chiffchaff | Phylloscopus collybita. |
| Dartford Warbler | Sylvia provincialis. |
| Wren | Troglodytes vulgaris. |
| Golden-crested Wren | Regulus cristatus. |
| Wood-Pigeon | Columba palumbus. |
| Stock-Dove | Columba œnas. |
| Rock-Dove | Columba livia. |
| Turtle-Dove | Columba turtur. |
| Pheasant | Phasianus colchicus. |
| Capercaillie | Tetrao urogallus. |
| Black Grouse | Tetrao tetrix. |
| Red Grouse | Lagopus scoticus. |
| Ptarmigan | Lagopus mutus. |
| Common Partridge | Perdix cinerea. |
| Red-legged Partridge | Perdix rufa. |
| Quail | Coturnix vulgaris. |
| Stone-Curlew | Œdicnemus crepitans. |
| Golden Plover | Charadrius pluvialis. |
| Dotterel | Charadrius morinellus. |
| Ringed Plover | Charadrius hiaticula. |
| Kentish Plover | Charadrius cantianus. |
| Grey Plover | Squatarola helvetica. |
| Peewit | Vanellus vulgaris. |
| Turnstone | Strepsilas interpres. |
| Sanderling | Calidris arenaria. |
| Oyster-Catcher | Hæmatopus ostralegus. |
| Heron | Ardea cinerea. |
| Bittern | Botaurus stellaris. |
| White Stork | Ciconia alba. |
| Spoonbill | Platalea leucorodia. |
| Curlew | Numenius arquata. |
| Whimbrel | Numenius phæopus. |
| Spotted Redshank | Totanus fuscus. |
| Redshank | Totanus calidris. |

## CONTENTS OF VOL. II.

| | |
|---|---|
| Green Sandpiper | Totanus ochropus. |
| Wood Sandpiper | Totanus glareola. |
| Common Sandpiper | Totanus hypoleucus. |
| Greenshank | Totanus canescens. |
| Black-tailed Godwit | Limosa melanura. |
| Bar-tailed Godwit | Limosa rufa. |
| Ruff | Machetes pugnax. |
| Woodcock | Scolopax rusticula. |
| Snipe | Scolopax gallinago. |
| Jack Snipe | Scolopax gallinula. |
| Curlew Sandpiper | Tringa subarquata. |
| Knot | Tringa canutus. |
| Little Stint | Tringa minuta. |
| Temminck's Stint | Tringa temminckii. |
| Dunlin | Tringa alpina. |
| Purple Sandpiper | Tringa maritima. |
| Land-Rail | Crex pratensis. |
| Spotted Crake | Porzana maruetta. |
| Water-Rail | Rallus aquaticus. |
| Moorhen | Gallinula chloropus. |
| Coot | Fulica atra. |
| Grey Phalarope | Phalaropus fulicarius |

# LIST OF PLATES TO VOL. II.

GOLDEN ORIOLE. Adult male, summer.
HOOPOE. Adult male, summer.
BLACK REDSTART. Male adult and male in last stage before assuming adult plumage.
WHEATEAR. Large variety and ordinary form. Males.
WILLOW-WREN. Northern variety and ordinary form.
ROCK-DOVE. Female and young.
CAPERCAILLIE. Adult male, winter.
BLACK GROUSE. Adult male.
RED GROUSE. Adult male and female.
PTARMIGAN. Summer plumage.
PTARMIGAN. Autumn plumage.
PTARMIGAN. Winter plumage.
STONE-CURLEW. Heads of male and female during breeding-season.
DOTTEREL. Male, female, and brood.
HERON. Male and young.

SPOONBILL. Adult male.
COMMON SANDPIPER. Adult and immature.
BLACK-TAILED GODWIT. First autumn plumage.
RUFF. Male, breeding-plumage. Adult males in autumn plumage. Female, breeding-plumage. Adult female and immature in autumn plumage.
WOODCOCK. Summer plumage.
WOODCOCK. Winter plumage.
SNIPE. Adult male, winter.
CURLEW SANDPIPER. Adult males, summer and winter plumage.
KNOT. Adult male, summer.
MAP OF BREYDON MUDFLATS AT LOW WATER.
LITTLE STINT. Adult, summer, and immature.
TEMMINCK'S STINT. Adult, summer.
TEMMINCK'S STINT. Adult male, winter, and immature.
GREY PHALAROPE. Autumn plumage.

# MISSEL-THRUSH.

## *TURDUS VISCIVORUS.*

---

But few notes concerning the occurrence of the Missel-Thrush in the more northern counties of Scotland are to be found in my journals; a pair or two were, however, observed in the densely wooded strath through which the Beauly river runs down towards the coast. I also recognised the species near Dingwall, on the islands of Inverness, and in the neighbourhood of Dunkeld and a few of the adjacent glens. According to my own experience this fine Thrush is decidedly local to the north of the Tweed. During a residence of a couple of years in East Lothian a few scattered birds were occasionally noticed late in autumn about the plantations in the vicinity of the coast; these were, without doubt, migrants from across the North Sea working their way towards the south. Throughout England the Missel-Thrush is well known in every locality where a sufficient amount of cover is to be found.

Numbers of this species occasionally join in flocks before the close of summer: on August 5, 1876, shortly before dusk, I remarked some fifty to sixty circling in company round some of the beech-plantations on the Downs near Brighton; these birds had collected to roost among the thick cover, and were probably all reared in the district. In Cornwall several flocks passed over the country between the Lizard and Penzance, flying west, during October 1880. On November 3, the day being fine, with a cold north-east wind, numbers of Missel-Thrushes were resorting in small parties to the shelter of the cliffs between the Logan Rock and the Land's End; the afternoon sun rendered the spot they had selected warm and bright, and flitting, when disturbed, from one patch of moss-grown rock to another, they carefully avoided the keen and wintry blasts: Swallows and Martins were also skimming backwards and forwards in the sunshine, while Blackstarts and a few Pipits were to be seen on the same ledges as the Thrushes.

From the accession to their numbers frequently observed during the latter part of autumn and early winter, it is evident that considerable numbers of Missel-Thrushes must reach our shores from the north of Europe. What track the migrants follow I am unable to state, though in all probability the majority make the land towards the more northern portions of the British Isles, but two or three having been secured on the light-ships off the east coast during the seasons I was in correspondence with the crews. Early in April 1873 a couple of wings were received from the 'Lynn Well;' these had been taken on board during the latter part of the winter.

The Missel-Thrush is well able to withstand the rigour of our winters, unless the weather should prove unusually severe. On December 9, 1882, a pair of these birds settled to some food provided for the Blackbirds and Thrushes in our garden, and kept the starving pensioners, for whom the feast was intended, at bay till their own hunger was appeased. It appears at all times a bold and forward bird; its jaunty and upright mode of progression on a lawn at once proclaims the species, even if the clear and well-defined markings on the breast are not sufficient guide.

The note of this Thrush is wild and remarkably attractive, being frequently heard when every other songster

## MISSEL-THRUSH.

is cowering from the ............... I repeatedly noticed these birds early in ...............
on some lofty ...............
utterance to a few loud notes, ............... at ............... of food. ...............
1880, my attention ............... near ............... in the ...............
and singing while on ............... the drop was by no ...............
that of the ............... On ...............
time ............... the air, ............... the ...............
was a ...............

The nest is usually placed at some height in a commanding forest tree, at times in a Scotch fir, or even in close proximity to a dwelling in an apple- or pear-tree. Being for the most part constructed before the leaves have opened, it is artfully concealed in a cleft among the branches or against the main stem, and is rendered still less ............... by the ............... to its exterior of tufts of moss and lichen gathered from the tree itself. ............... spring of 1878 in a damp alder-car at Ludham, in ............... of ............... built in a small stunted bush within three feet of the ground. I ............... an elevation; and in this instance it could not have been for ............... size were growing over the identical bush in which the nest was placed. ............... probably chosen by the old birds as not so exposed to the attacks of ............... unchecked in the district.

The eggs of the Missel-Thrush are too ............... usually vary but slightly; some thirty years ago, however, I took, for four or five successive seasons, one or two clutches of a most singular variety in the east of Sussex. In shape they were far rounder than the usual type, and were of a pale uniform blue, similar in colour to those of the Starling; now and then one exhibited a few scrawls of a darker blue or ...............

I could ............... this species in the Highlands; indeed in many glens it appeared to ............... In the broad-district of the east of Norfolk it is known as ............... or "Deo ............... correspond with that of the Dove. In East Sussex ...............

In hard ...............

# FIELDFARE.

## *TURDUS PILARIS.*

It is usually supposed that the numbers of Fieldfares visiting the British Islands vary considerably according to the weather. As a rule, in open winters but few are noticed for a time, though a sharp frost or a heavy fall of snow at once brings thousands under observation. In mild weather I have frequently remarked large flocks of several hundreds harbouring about various remote parts of the country, where a combination of large woods and cultivated land afforded suitable quarters; here they will resort for weeks, if not months, till a sudden change causes them to move onward, their course in the first instance being held for the south. On reaching the coast-line, the large flights that have by this time collected pursue their journey towards the west. Should the winter continue open, it is quite possible that in many districts not a single Fieldfare will put in an appearance. During such seasons remarks are frequently made by local observers in the pages of ornithological publications concerning the absence of the Fieldfare.

Early in January 1880 two or three reports to this effect appeared; and up to that date, though almost daily driving along the coast between Brighton and Shoreham since the first week in the previous December, not a single specimen had come under my notice. On the 17th of January, after a sharp white frost in the early morning, rain fell without intermission during the day, and at dusk a flock of from forty to fifty Fieldfares were discerned through the mist making their way to roost in a plantation on the downs. Half a dozen that I bagged to ascertain their condition were as fat as butter, proving that the quarters they selected had been suited to their wants. But small numbers were seen during the remainder of the winter or early spring in the vicinity of the south coast, though on the 10th of March, when about a dozen miles inland in the well-wooded country near St. John's Common, I discovered the haunts the birds had taken up since their arrival in the south; from five to seven hundred were busily feeding on the ploughed ground, betaking themselves, when disturbed, to the large timber, many trees being perfectly covered by the swarms settling on the branches. These Fieldfares, I learned, on making inquiries, had been for many weeks in the district. On visiting the spot a fortnight later the greater number had taken their departure.

When gunning on the north-east coast of Scotland, I repeatedly remarked large arrivals at the usual season during autumn, though should the weather prove open but few reach the southern counties of England. From observations obtained during several years, I am of opinion that much the same numbers annually land on our shores, though in mild winters their presence may escape the notice of ornithologists; a severe storm, however, puts the large flocks in motion, and during their flight from north to south or east to west they are certain to attract attention.

The 16th of September, 1869, is the earliest date on which I noted Fieldfares in the Highlands: small parties then continued making their way south across the hills near Tain for several days. The main bodies, as a rule, do not reach our coast till a somewhat later date, though I have detected them as far south as Cornwall soon after the middle of October. On the 19th, weather at the time cold and stormy, a party of eight or nine Fieldfares were noticed near Rinsey (a few miles east of Penzance) flying towards the north-west.

... little doubt that between the beginning of ... the North Sea, either to or from our coasts. ... entry in my notes:—
"November 27. ... wind from ... by the spray. Pigeons and Fieldfares in immense numbers continued flying ... of the day; with the last of the light they were still passing over." It is probable that the whole of these birds were migrants from the north of Europe. On making inquiries of the light-ships shortly after, I received the wings of two or three Fieldfares taken on board the 'Lynn Well' during the last week in November. From April 1873 till the end of May two birds were taken on each of the vessels—' Lynn Well,' ' Hasbro',' and ' Newarp.'

In January 1867 immense flights of Fieldfares passed from east to west for several consecutive days: though the frost was severe and the wind bitter from the north-west, the travellers appeared to suffer but little from the effects of cold and hunger. The storms early in December 1874 greatly reduced this hardy species, numbers being found dead after the breaking up of the frost. The mortality during this gale was, however, slight compared with the terrible losses inflicted on all our small feathered visitors by the hurricane of January 18, 1881. While shooting in Pevensey level, at the time of the heavy storm of January 1867, I noticed Fieldfares on several occasions basking in the interior of the wreaths of snow that had formed round and, in some instances, over the thorn-bushes alongside of the marsh-dykes. When the sun struck down warm the birds were often to be seen stretching themselves out towards its rays, their snug snow shelter open towards the south affording protection from the cutting north-west wind. As a rule, large bodies of Fieldfares do not show themselves with the first fall of snow; the less hardy birds, such as Larks, Thrushes, and Blackbirds, are the advanced guard of the approaching hosts.

I have never seen it mentioned that this species roosts among the stems of the reed (*Phragmites communis*). In March 1871 I put up on two occasions large flocks of these birds, which, in company with Redwings, had taken up their quarters for the night in the large reed-beds at Somerton Broad, in the east of Norfolk.

In parts of the eastern counties I occasionally heard Fieldfares termed "Felts," though by far the commonest name for this species among the country people of the east of Norfolk is the "Fulfer" or "Jay Fulfer." White or pied varieties of the Fieldfare are by no means so frequently recorded as those of many other species; I, however, clearly identified and closely examined by means of the glasses a very fine specimen, perfectly white, which resorted for a couple of days to the marshes adjoining the river Adur, between Shoreham and Beeding, during the severe weather of January 1870.

# REDWING.

## TURDUS ILIACUS.

Though apparently good evidence has been obtained concerning the nesting of the Redwing in the British Islands on more than one occasion, I have entirely failed to meet with the species during the summer months. Towards the end of April 1877 a pair were repeatedly seen resorting to the garden of a shooting-lodge in the Island of Lewis, the birds being exceedingly fearless, merely withdrawing to the shelter of a few stunted bushes overhanging a rocky burn when disturbed. As they appeared to have taken up their quarters so contentedly, the male singing gaily whenever a gleam of sunshine lighted up the dreary and well-nigh deserted glen, I was in hopes they might remain and breed in the district. Unfortunately, on the 1st of May, the cock was killed by a Merlin, and a few days later the feathers of his mate, who had also evidently been destroyed by a Hawk, were found near the same spot. On but one or two other occasions were Redwings observed so late as May, even in the more northern counties of Scotland.

I have but seldom met with any number of this species in the south of England till November. The earliest entry in my notes concerning their arrival on the north-east coast of Scotland is under date of September 16, 1868, large flights on that occasion passing south over the Ross-shire hills. Though the southern parts of Great Britain are usually deserted at an earlier date, stragglers may frequently be seen in the north till well on in April, and (as previously stated) a bird or two has come under my notice in May.

A considerable difference of opinion exists concerning the note of the Redwing, some writers comparing the song to that of the Nightingale, while others hold its vocal powers in but slight estimation. During the last week in December 1879 a fine male took up his quarters in a small plantation in our own garden near Brighton. For several weeks he daily made his appearance under the windows to claim his share with the regular pensioners. After a time a strange note was frequently heard; and watching closely, I detected the Redwing perched on a birch tree, uttering a low and somewhat plaintive warble. The bird remained till March, taking his departure during the second week; its song appeared to increase in power as the weather grew warmer.

At roosting-time Redwings usually repair to the shelter of woods and plantations where the timber is of no great height, also to dense hedgerows and shrubberies in the vicinity of dwellings; when the wind blows cold a sheltered and lowly situation is chosen, though in mild and open weather they perch at a higher elevation. Numbers are at times taken in bat folding nets; but a keen and wintry blast is necessary to insure success. While returning from flight-shooting on Somerton Broad, in the east of Norfolk, during March 1871, I disturbed on two consecutive nights immense numbers that, in company with Fieldfares, had taken up their quarters in a large bed of reeds and flags. Since that date I have not met with these birds in a similar spot, though by day flocks were repeatedly watched searching about among the reeds in the water-dykes in Pevensey Level during the cold weather in January 1867. Whether food or simply shelter was their object in creeping among the stems of the plants it was impossible to ascertain, the naturalist to whom some specimens obtained were sent having neglected to make the necessary examination.

From the entries in my notes concerning the numbers of Redwings captured on the light-ships off the east coast, it is evident that, with the exception of some eight or ten weeks in the early part of the year, an almost constant stream must be passing over the North Sea from October till the end of April. Since no wings were obtained in September during the years I was in communication with the vessels, it is probable that the first arrivals make their way direct towards the coast of Scotland. Redwings and Starlings almost invariably cross the North Sea at or about the same time, both species following a similar course. Though the Starlings captured on the light-ships are by far the most numerous, I remarked that it seldom happened that any quantity fell on board without one or two Redwings being taken. On the 13th of January, 1873, I received from the 'Lynn Well' floating light two Starlings and one Redwing; these three unfortunates, with the exception of a Gull which had settled on deck, were all that had been secured since the beginning of November. Though large numbers of small birds came in contact with the lights, the wind had continued blowing strong while the flights were passing, and those striking had fallen clear of the vessel.

# THRUSH.
## *TURDUS MUSICUS.*

This well-known songster is widely dispersed over the British Islands, the nature of the country, however, having less suited to its haunts in the south; it is not so abundant in many of the wild districts of the Highlands. On the flat lands of Sutherland and Caithness, Thrushes are for the most part conspicuous by their absence; they do by no means seem to frequent parts of the Hebrides.

Late in May 1877 I noticed several frequenting the walls and banks near the roadside on the track leading from Stornoway to Harris. The birds appeared more numerous in the vicinity of the scattered collections of shealings, placed for the most part near the shores of the saltwater lochs; in the wild or more deserted portions of the country but few were met with. It is stated by ornithological writers that the Thrushes of the Hebrides are a smaller as well as a darker race; and though no specimen was shot had I at once remarked this distinction. Till examined through the glasses, I was almost at a loss to identify a pair or two keeping company with a few small parties of Starlings, but little difference being made between the two species in the dull light of a West-Highland drizzle.

As autumn advances a large accession to our native Thrushes may be noticed on the north-east coast of the Highlands. While Partridge-shooting on the Hill of Tarlogie, near Tain, on the 15th and 16th of September 1868, I found the turnip-fields perfectly swarming with various species of small feathered migrants, which must have recently landed on the coast; Blackbirds and Thrushes were strongly represented in their ranks, the whole body being evidently intent on working their way towards the south. Though a few continued in the district for a week or two, the majority shortly disappeared and but the usual residents remained. As I did not meet with any considerable quantity of wings of this species among the contributions received from the light-ships off the east coast during the seasons of 1872 and 1873, I am of opinion that the course followed by this species when on the southward journey is most frequently towards the north-east coast of Scotland.

The parties that arrive on the shores of Ross-shire and the more northern counties early in the autumn probably distribute themselves over the country for a few months previous to undertaking a further journey. I have seldom noticed any considerable additions to the Thrushes in the southern or eastern counties of England till frost and snow have set in. The more severe the weather the greater the number that pass along in company with countless Larks, Redwings, and other small birds. On the Norfolk coast a few straggling parties were making their way south during the storm that occurred late in November 1879; and the following week I observed them working west along the shores of the channel in Sussex. From these dates till early in February I have watched them pursuing the same course on many occasions. The heavy fall of snow that broke over the country in January 1867 brought to the south coast myriads of all the species commonly seen under similar circumstances; for a week at least, with but slight intervals when the weather moderated, the fugitives continued following a course from east to west. Thrushes, I have repeatedly remarked, are the first of the feathered tribe to exhibit signs of succumbing to the hardships encountered during their passage; they may frequently feathers puffed out like a ball, under banks and hedges, while Blackbirds, are able to retain their ordinary condition. When suffering from snow, I have often noticed Thrushes hopping about in search of food with one leg concealed in their plumage for warmth, a change from one foot to the other being ..... Wherever I take up my quarters a copious supply of scraps is always provided for the swarms ..... pensioners that gather round the house in severe winters: hundreds may occasionally be seen awaiting and eventually quarrelling over their long-expected dole. On the 21st of January 1881, the terrific hurricanes and snow-drifts which had prevailed for several successive days greatly exhausted the whole of the smaller land-birds on the south coast, and, in the neighbourhood of Brighton, Blackbirds and Thrushes were utterly unable to stand: without the slightest power in their legs, the unfortunate birds fluttered slowly with drooping wings to the food, and falling on their breasts fought ravenously over every morsel. Thousands of many species were found dead for several weeks as the snow slowly melted and revealed the sheltered corners into which they had crawled to die.

Thrushes were ............................................. breed on the Bass. This ............ been the case; but ................................................. Blackbirds were at ...................................................................................... Numbers of Thrushes, however, ........................................................................................ cracks and ............................................................................................ the fortifications ..............

............ neatly built nest of ...................................................... in .......... of a .................................................................................................. on the ground itself. ...................................................................................... buildings, disused saw-pits, and, ...................................................... resorted to. On the 28th ........................................................................... evergreen oak in a garden near Brighton, on .................................. young, the male arrived and, alighting on the side of the nest, thrust his bill ............ upward movement of the head which forced her immediately to withdraw to the ................ young and took his departure, the female at once resuming her former position. ................... man bestowed on his spouse to induce her to vacate the ....................................... unnecessary violence.

To note down accurately the food of this useful bird is almost impossible. Snails, flies, spiders, and many insects that are injurious to the gardener are liberally consumed. A few minutes' observation of the actions of a Thrush while hunting for a breakfast on a lawn in the early morning will speedily give a notion of the number of worms devoured. The berries of privet, hawthorn, and barberry (*Berberis Darwinii*) are also swallowed, and the fruit having been separated from the stones the latter are cast up. On July 22nd, 1882, I noticed a Thrush repeatedly settling on a barberry-bush, and rapidly bolting ten or a dozen berries, with which it flew off at once to supply its young. There is no denying the fact that many fruits, if unprotected, may suffer from their attacks; but the means of keeping them at a distance are now so well known that little damage need be feared during the short season the trees can suffer from their depredations. When starving in severe weather scraps consisting of raw meat, bones, bread, and vegetables are eagerly

.................................................................... be heard at all times of the year. Under ................................................................... south-west, fog and light rain; Thrushes ............................................................ in a season. Should the weather be mild young may be seen by the middle of March; and on August 9th, 1883, I came across a nest near Brighton in which the eggs were just on the point of hatching.

Young birds brought out early in the season may not unfrequently be observed supplying food to juveniles younger and more helpless than themselves. Thrushes are seldom quarrelsome unless pressed by want; and more than once I have seen them show a disposition to put a stop to the pugnacious habits of their smaller feathered companions. On one occasion late in April, while watching a furious battle between a couple of Sparrows on a lawn, a Thrush, who was quietly searching for worms at a short distance, happened to become aware of the dispute; regarding the combatants intently for a moment, he puffed out his feathers and went at them full tilt, knocking both out of time and effectually putting a stop to the fight.

To the casual observer there is little difference between the male and female. The markings on the breast of the male, however, are somewhat brighter and more distinct, while the bird is also slightly larger.

# BLACKBIRD.

## TURDUS MERULA.

A RESIDENT in every part of the country where suitable woods or cover can be found, the Blackbird is common from north to south. Large numbers of migrants from across the North Sea also reach our eastern coasts early in the autumn, and continue to land for several months. I have observed the fields in the east of Ross-shire perfectly alive with freshly arrived birds about the middle of September; and from the information gleaned from the crews of the light-ships, it is probable that Blackbirds pass over the North Sea, one way or the other, during most months of the year.

In my notes for 1872 I find the following entries concerning the capture of Blackbirds on the light-ships off the east coast:—On the 20th of November I boarded the 'Newarp,' and learned that one female Blackbird had been secured during the gale that commenced on the 11th and continued almost without intermission till the 16th. On the 11th the wind blew in furious gusts, with squalls of rain from north-north-east. On the 12th the wind was east-north-east; 13th east; 14th east-north-east with hail-squalls; 15th, after a lull in the early morning, it came on to blow harder than ever from the east-north-east; on the 16th blowing hard from east-south-east, with occasional blinding snow-squalls. But few birds had flown during this storm, six only having fallen on board, two of which were Petrels. During November and December, and up to the end of January 1873, but one Blackbird alighted on the 'Leman and Ower.' Early in March a single bird was captured on the 'Dudgeon;' and during this month and the first week in April two more were taken on the 'Lynn Well.' On visiting the 'Newarp' again on August 9th, I found on board the wings of five Blackbirds, being the total number that had struck the lights since the end of March.

I did not recognize the Blackbird on the Outer Hebrides; but on the Bass Rock and the Isle of May several have come under my notice. To the May, I believe, the birds are only occasional visitors; but on the Bass there are in some seasons a nest or two among the old fortifications or the broken face of the cliff on the east side. When carefully searching the crumbling walls, known to the frequenters of the rock as the ruins of the Governor's house, to ascertain if Thrushes had bred there, I came across the remains of at least half a dozen Blackbirds' nests in the summer of 1874: having been built in sheltered nooks and crevices of the masonry, several years would probably elapse before the old structures fell to pieces. On one occasion, while watching a fine old male conveying food among the buildings, I discovered his nest snugly placed in an old chimney.

In a garden near Brighton I noticed, in 1880, two Blackbirds (they could scarcely be termed a pair) construct no less than five nests during the season. In every instance the nests were placed in a thick bush of *Cupressus macrocarpa*. The first brood, when about a week old, early in March, were dragged out and killed by a cat. On Saturday, May 1st, the second brood died in the nest through exposure to the cold east winds, and on the following Monday the third nest was commenced. On the 12th the old male was unfortunately caught in a cat-trap (set for their especial preservation), and so badly nipped that death must have been instantaneous. The female, however, was not inconsolable, and within a day or two, without the slightest intermission to her family arrangements, a new mate was found. All went smoothly for the future, and three broods were now successfully reared. It is, however, a fact that when on one occasion the newly acquired husband had by some strange fatality taken up his position to roost on the identical limb on which the late lamented had been accustomed to perch on, her mistress, her feelings appeared to be aroused, and quitting her nest she administered not only an exceedingly rosy lecture, but a well-intentioned thrashing into the bargain. The cause of this strange proceeding I was unable to account for; I merely relate what occurred.

It is, at times, exceedingly amusing to watch closely the actions of a party of Blackbirds, gaining thereby a slight insight into their manners and customs. A group consisting of an adult male and female together with a couple of immature females attracted my attention while disporting themselves on a lawn on November 11th, 1883. A young male was also present; he kept, however, somewhat in the background, his demeanour while in the company of the elders being decidedly retiring. The old gentleman was apparently desirous of paying his respects to one of the juvenile females; with upraised tail and drooping wings, his feathers also at times puffed out to the fullest extent, he hopped constantly in attendance—halting for a few seconds occasionally, stretching forward his head and jerking his tail in the most absurd manner, evidently endeavouring to show himself off to the greatest advantage. The old female, while this performance was taking place, flew hither and thither, exhibiting plainly the utmost annoyance. At last her anger could no longer be restrained: dashing suddenly at the offender she struck him instantly to the ground. Lying flat and helpless on his back with outspread wings, she perched on his breast and vented her rage by pecking in the most savage manner at his head for ten or fifteen seconds; she then relinquished her position, when, without the slightest signs of resentment, he sneaked quietly off to some place of security beneath the evergreens".

After the same manner as Thrushes, I have repeatedly noticed young Blackbirds supplying food to birds of their own species, evidently only just out of the nest. Whether youngsters exhibiting such care are brothers or sisters belonging to an earlier brood, or simply neighbours, it is impossible to say. At times, however, these precocious nurses are apt to play tricks with the juveniles they profess to take charge of. On the 10th of August, 1882, two helpless mites had managed to hop from beneath the shrubs to the edge of the lawn unattended by either of their parents. A lively young female, who was actively searching for food on the grass, at once approached and picking up in her bill a dried leaf of that hardy evergreen the broad-leafed *Euonymus*, popped it into the widely opened mouth of the nearest fledgling. With a shake of the head the unpalatable morsel was immediately rejected, when it was seized again and thrust down the throat of the second innocent, who likewise refused to swallow it. This performance was repeated five or six times with similar results, till the arrival of an old bird on the scene broke up the party.

In their earliest stages, as soon as the feathers have opened, the males are distinguishable from the females while still in the nest. The longer feathers of the wings do not moult the first autumn, and this portion of the plumage of the males will be found on close examination considerably darker than that of the females. Varieties pied or sporkled with white are not unfrequently met with. A male showing a perfectly white head and shoulders took up his quarters for some time in the gardens round the outskirts of Brighton. On two different occasions I was summoned by residents in the district to inspect the rarity that had invaded their territories. At last, early in July 1879, this conspicuous wanderer made his appearance in an out-of-door fernery in our own garden: here he caused such extensive and widespread destruction, by dragging down the moss from the stones while searching for grubs, that at least a couple of barrow-loads of fragments, torn down from the upper parts, were lying at the foot of the rocks. Though it was possible the work at which he was engaged would have to be undertaken at some future time to check the ravages of the insects, it was necessary to put a stop to his proceedings. In order to administer a lesson, a small trap baited with one of the grubs of which he had been in quest was carefully set, the teeth being wrapped round with flannel to prevent severe injury. In spite of the precautions, a couple of toes were unfortunately broken when the bird was captured. That he did not suffer greatly, however, was evident, as on the following morning he was noticed singing, balancing himself on one leg, the crippled foot being slightly raised. The lesson concerning the moss was nevertheless sufficient, as for the future it remained unmolested.

In the choice of a site for its nest the Blackbird greatly resembles the Thrush, though perhaps the position, as a rule, is more carefully concealed. According to my own experience it is seldom, if ever, seen at the elevation to which the Greybird* aspires to place its cradle in some of the covers of the southern and eastern counties. Early in March 1883, I examined a Blackbird's nest built on a pot, hanging in a fernery, containing a fine root of *Lastrea Filix-mas*: the nest, which was one of the largest and most substantially constructed I ever saw, completely filled the pot, being placed on the crown of the fern, and causing the fronds to droop over the edges.

Though this species is decidedly more hardy, and consequently able to bear exposure to frost and cold with far greater ease, than the Thrush, a protracted gale at times causes them to suffer excessive hardships. Towards the end of January 1881, I noticed numbers of Blackbirds that were searching for food so severely cut up as to be incapable of making the slightest use of their feet or legs. Early in the following April the long-continued and cruel east winds greatly affected the survivors of the winter storms; many broods also perished through want. The old birds might be watched by the hour seeking carefully though hopelessly over the dried grass for worms and grubs for their starving young, the parched turf being at the time as likely to supply a meal as the surface of a turnpike-road. Notwithstanding the straits to which they were driven, they declined to make use of scraps of meat (both raw and cooked) placed out on the spots they frequented.

The disposition of the Blackbird is decidedly noisy and demonstrative. Throughout the broad country in the east of Norfolk they may commonly be seen "mobbing" some of the numerous Cuckoos frequenting that watery district. Their well-known alarm-note in the coverts as soon as the sun disappears also proclaims the departure of the Long-eared Owl from the shelter in which it has rested during the day. Many a prowling member of the cat family owes its death to my attention having been attracted while covert-shooting by the warning "chuck chuck" of two or three old birds exasperated at the sight of their natural enemy. There is no doubt that a wandering pussy is the worst of poachers, and few suffer more from its attacks than our familiar friend the Blackbird: the parent birds are often killed on the nest, the young being dragged out and carried off.

No complaint can, with justice, be brought against the Blackbird by either the farmer or gardener. Like its constant companion the Thrush, this species will doubtless prey on wall-fruit and berries if left unprotected; very simple precautions, however, render its attempts at robbery utterly futile. Their partiality for insects, maggots, and such like frequently leads the unfortunate birds into trouble, many being taken in vermin-traps while exploring the fly-blown baits in search of food. Though dozens of Blackbirds have come under my observation captured in this manner, I never noticed a Thrush in a like predicament.

In my opinion the song of the Blackbird is decidedly superior to that of the Thrush. Though the note is by no means so striking in the depth of winter, it may frequently be heard at that season.

* The country people in the east of Sussex almost invariably term the Song-Thrush the "Greybird."

I am ignorant whether this species usually pairs and nests at the age of one year. In an instance where there was every chance for observation, I remarked that a young male did not pair till the third year. A nestling taken from our own garden and reared in confinement, proved, when full-grown, so exceedingly wild, that all hopes as to his becoming reconciled to captivity having failed, he was at length released. When once at liberty his nature appeared thoroughly changed, and taking up his quarters in a small shrubbery in close proximity to the kitchen windows, he came daily and called with a low and plaintive cry for food. When twelve months old he did not pair, indeed the poor fellow appeared rather frightened at the presence of a female that invaded his haunts, being seen on more than one occasion beating a hasty retreat and the lady in full pursuit. A year later he took unto himself a wife, and a brood or two were reared, our old friend remaining as familiar as formerly, though the female was by no means so confiding. Both birds still resort to their old quarters, the female becoming bolder in severe weather, and approaching like her lord and master to tap the windows when their accustomed supply of food has been forgotten. The young broods are not allowed to remain for any length of time in the small domain over which the old bird has now assumed the rule. His efforts about roosting-time on a cold winter's evening to prevent the few Yellow Hammers that make their way in off the downs from gaining the shelter of some dense bushes of *Cupressus* are at times most amusing, the unfortunate birds being driven from one spot to another till after daylight has disappeared.

# RING-OUZEL.

## *TURDUS TORQUATUS.*

to our numbers during the breeding-season young in several English counties—pages of those I am acquainted with. Sussex is not included in the lists the nests discovered, though I possess the best evidence that a pair reared their young, of 1865, the lower branches of a stunted thorn bush in a sloping hollow in the South Downs between Portslade and the Dyke Hill, the juveniles being seen near the same spot, attended by the birds, a week or so after they were observed in the nest. My informant (who was well acquainted with this species at that time, held a situation as gardener at the Manor House, Portslade, and is now at our place near Brighton) also stated that the previous year a shepherd had told him that a bird resembling a Blackbird with a white ring round the throat (which he soon ascertained to be a Ring-Ouzel) had taken up its quarters in a ruined hovel in one of the valleys among the hills near Hangleton, the nest having been placed on the wall-plate in the space left where one of the rafters had fallen away. Though the Ouzel is generally well known in this part of Sussex, a few being seen annually in spring while on the passage towards the north, and numbers frequenting the hills about Falmer, Patcham, and Portslade during the latter end of autumn, I failed to learn of other instances of this species remaining during summer in the county.

These birds reach our shores towards the end of April or early in May; while fishing on the broads and rivers in the east of Norfolk about that date or a week or so later, I usually observed a few alighting on the marsh-walls and flying to the fields in quest of food. At that season they seldom remained any time in the district, appearing eager to resume their passage; the course they held was invariably due northeast, as if bound for the coast. It was seldom before the end of the second or third week in May that we noticed any Ouzels in Glenlyon: numbers, however, frequented the corries and sheltered gullies on the rough hillsides, their nests being placed for the most part on the ledges or in the cracks or crevices among the broken slabs of rock that are to be found here and there on the steeper portions of the moors.

Ouzels appear to suffer occasionally from the attacks of the various predatory species, as a nest or two that had been deserted was now and then noticed; Peregrines or Sparrow-Hawks in all probability were the culprits. Though Merlins have been accused of destroying these birds, I was unable to bring any charges against the few pairs that frequented our ground. The shell of an Ouzel's egg that had been sucked was discovered in the nest of a pair of Crows (the one black and the other grey), plainly indicating that these plunderers were by no means averse to varying their usual diet of Grouse eggs with those of smaller species. While engaged in killing down the vermin in the spring of 1866 on one of the hills to the south of the Lyon in Perthshire, a fine old male was taken in a clam set for a stoat in the ruins of an antiquated shealing. The bird must have had some difficulty in forcing its way up the narrow track that was left open, as we had taken out several large stones and built up the trap, together with a rabbit recently shot, in the centre of the dry-stone wall *. It was improbable that the bait had proved the attraction, as, being fresh, it could not yet have produced maggots, often so fatal under similar circumstances in the south to Blackbirds and Thrushes. There was little doubt that the bird must have been forced to seek shelter among the cracks in the ruins to escape the swoop of a Falcon or a Hawk. Peregrines from the wild rocky cliffs further up the glen occasionally swept over the moors, and a Sparrow-Hawk now and then dashed out from the Meggernie woods, dealing death in his course while in search of prey; one or other of these pitiless freebooters was without doubt the cause of the mishap to the unfortunate Ouzel.

The Ring-Ouzel is evidently astir betimes in the morning; while driving between Gairloch and Dingwall on the 17th of May, 1868, we entered the Glen Docherty Pass, that lies a mile or so to the east end of Loch Maree, an hour and a half after midnight, and during the time spent in climbing the steep and dangerous track cut in the rugged mountain-side these birds never ceased their plaintive calls till we had reached the high ground, though it was then not fairly daylight.

* A wall built without mortar, the stones being cleverly fitted together and held in their places, when necessary, by chips inserted in the gaps.

# GOLDEN ORIOLE.

## ORIOLUS GALBULA.

---

Though abundant in some parts of the continent, and formerly of more frequent occurrence in the British Islands, this species is now only a rare visitor to our shores, and the reception given to those that make their appearance renders a lengthened stay almost an impossibility. Several pairs have been known to nest during the last thirty years; but the numbers of these summer residents have lately decreased, and the majority of their old haunts are now entirely deserted. From personal observation, I can say but little concerning these attractive and interesting birds, about half a dozen specimens being all that have come under my notice.

In the summer of 1852, a pair of Golden Orioles constructed their carefully built cradle in a large garden near Norwich, and an egg I was enabled to obtain from this nest still remains in my possession. The bright-coloured male proved exceedingly mindful concerning his own safety, though occasionally showing himself more conspicuously in early morning shortly after daybreak. The nest was placed among the dense foliage on the wide-spreading and drooping limbs of a weeping ash, at the height of about ten or twelve feet from the ground. On April 12th, 1854, I caught sight of a male and female flying across the garden at Catsfield House, near Battle, in Sussex, and noticed them alighting for a few minutes in a large bushy thorn tree. Though a careful watch was kept around the adjacent woods and plantations by all our keepers and gardeners for several days, in order to learn if the strangers had taken up their quarters in the district, we could gain no further tidings concerning their movements.

For over twenty years I never obtained a glimpse of an Oriole, and it was not till the 18th of April, 1872, while driving between Shoreham and Lancing, that a fine male was observed in the act of perching on the thorn-hedge along the old road running close to the coast-line and now partly washed away by the encroachment of the sea. The bird shortly moved on and kept steadily making his way from the west towards the east; after a flight of a hundred yards or so he would settle again on the hedge. Though repeatedly disturbed by carts and persons on foot, he still held a line along the coast, returning, after having been diverted from the course he followed, by a short circuit to the quick-set by the roadside, and again resuming his journey towards the east. After following and watching his movements for over a mile, I got a chance for an easy shot, and obtained this very handsome wanderer as a specimen.

During the next few years, though none came under my own observation, two or three males were seen and a couple shot within half a dozen miles of Brighton. One of these was followed by a friend, who thought I wanted a specimen of a male, for several hours about the hedges near Hatchington, while he sent a message to summon me to the spot. Being absent on the downs between Falmer and Lewes, I only learned too late what had occurred; and a day or two after, the bird was shot by a policeman and, after having been brought up for my inspection, was sold to a dealer. The last Oriole I met with was a female that attracted my attention in April, a few years back, while flying from the trees in the Swiss Gardens at Shoreham to a fence between two grass-fields. The bird was lost sight of as I was making my way to the spot, and a close search to ascertain its whereabouts proved unavailing.

The male in spring gives utterance to a loud clear whistle, which if once listened to can scarcely fail to attract attention and is sure to be recognized. When not alarmed, the flight of this species is by no means rapid, being somewhat undulating and not unlike that of the Green Woodpecker.

There are statements in several ornithological works to the effect that the males of the Golden Oriole occasionally pair and breed before assuming full adult plumage. Only two pairs have come under my observation in this country, and in both I remarked that the males were of the most brilliant colouring.

# HOOPOE.

### *UPUPA EPOPS.*

---

If we may credit the writings of ornithologists who lived in days gone by, and they appear perfectly trustworthy, the numbers of the Hoopoe that visit the British Islands at the present time are gradually becoming less year by year; a singular appearance is sure to attract attention, and the unfortunate Hoopoe, rendered conspicuous by his colouring and crest, suffers in consequence. Though I have never had a chance of observing these birds engaged in breeding-operations in the British Islands, there are many instances recorded of their having remained and constructed their nests in various parts of the country where they were free from persecution.

How abundant Hoopoes were in some parts of Sussex about thirty after their first arrival in spring, may be judged from the fact that seven were shot in the head keeper at Ashburnham Park. The estate on which these birds were killed adjoined the my father hired for sporting-purposes, and his keeper, who was exceedingly energetic when in of rarities, usually obtained one or two every season. Early in May 1856 I observed a Hoopoe round on a wide stretch of furze-clad down, termed the horthy field, on which Normanhurst now stands: my gun having, however, been laid down while engaged with the keeper in setting traps for vermin and searching for nests, the chance of a shot was lost. In the spring of 1858, while Snipe-shooting on a portion of Pevensey Level known as Harnborn Ponds, I marked a Hoopoe down into a high and spreading thorn tree on the marsh-bank, and had just come up within range when the bird dashed out, but was dropped before it had gone a couple of yards, the charge also bringing down a second, which must have been for some time concealed among the branches.

Though many were heard of on different parts of the South Downs, it was not till the 28th of April, 1882, that I again fell in with the species; a friend, over whose ground I had liberty to collect specimens, then rode over to Brighton, and reported that in the early morning a Hoopoe had risen from the roadside as he passed, and taken up-hill to a plantation near Saddlescombe. Starting at once for the gap in the hills through which the road he indicated was cut, the bird was soon discovered, sheltering from a gale, among the small patches of stunted thorn-bushes on the steep sloping sides of the downs; here, after due consideration, I came to the conclusion that it would be utterly impossible to obtain a shot. Shortly after, however, he took a flight, carried off, I believe, by the force of the wind, which was blowing strong from the west with fitful gusts, to the open country on the summit of the hills, where the ground had been lately turned over by the plough. Here he alighted, and commenced hopping about and pecking along the ridges; as the spot he had selected was bare and open, without a vestige of cover near at hand, there was obviously no chance of approaching within range. At a loss as to what was next to be done, I withdrew behind a large circular bed of furze at the distance of about a hundred yards, and paused to watch his actions and ascertain, if possible, the course he would next follow. After busily investigating the rough surface of the soil for about a quarter of an hour or twenty minutes, elevating and drooping the feathers of his crest from time to time, he rose at last on wing and came with a slow and deliberate flight straight towards the furze behind which I was concealed, disappearing from sight as he darted down on the opposite side of the bush. Silently making my way round with the utmost caution not to break a twig or cause a sound, he sprung up from the long rough grass surrounding the furze, within four or five yards, and offering an easy chance as he crossed the open, in the attempt to regain his old quarters on the low ground, fell on the unbroken downs at the distance of about five-and-twenty yards, his feathers unruffled by a single shot-mark.

The colours of the soft parts of this specimen, which proved to be a fine male in very handsome plumage, were as follows:—Iris dark hazel. Upper mandible black at the point and dark horn-tint towards the base; lower mandible horn-colour at the point and a pale flesh hue towards the base. Legs and toes a dark horn-tint. The stomach of the wanderer, who had probably but lately reached our shores, contained scarcely any nourishment—a few small beetles, a spider or two, and some other tiny insects being all that was found on an examination being made.

# HEDGE-SPARROW.
## *ACCENTOR MODULARIS.*

There are few parts of the British Islands, with the exception of the more remote and barren moorlands or far-spreading rush-grown swamps, where this familiar and confiding species has not come under my observation. Though partial to the immediate vicinity of dwellings, the Hedge-Sparrow occasionally strays to distant solitudes when sufficient cover is obtainable. While searching for the nest of the Dartford Warbler on the summit of the breezy downs of Sussex, far from human habitation, I have often disturbed a pair or two of these birds. If merely a glimpse is caught of the tiny stranger skulking through the dense undergrowth or darting rapidly across an opening in the furze, it is by no means easy to form an opinion as to which species the individual belongs, the tints of their plumage being almost precisely similar and the difference in size exceedingly small.

These birds have been described by several writers as of a retiring disposition and by no means quarrelsome; when asserting their own rights, however, I have repeatedly seen them square up to Sparrows and other small birds, with such pluck that the aggressor was always compelled to leave the field.

Hedge-Sparrows commence their nesting-operations at an early date; soon after the beginning of the year the male may be seen shuffling round the female and showing himself off for her admiration. On the 2nd of January, 1884, I noticed a pair going through the singular antics often indulged in by this species, when a House-Sparrow settled on the grass near at hand, and approaching in a threatening manner was immediately attacked and driven from the spot by one of the pair.

Macgillivray asserts that these birds "seem to pair in the quietest possible manner." The Scotch naturalist was a most accurate observer, though I can scarcely agree with these remarks. Having carefully watched the actions of these birds throughout the winter, I am of opinion that when once paired they invariably remain together till death divides the partnership. There is, however, a very marked courting early in the year; this is carried on, in open weather, all through January and the greater portion of February, the nests being occasionally built towards the end of the month, though more commonly in March. The past winter having been extremely mild, I noticed a couple of nests containing eggs before the end of February.

It is stated by several writers that these birds are not gregarious, and on no single occasion have I met with flocks of any number. I remarked, however, that four individuals have kept company in our garden all through the winter, showing themselves conspicuously on the lawn, the whole party invariably chasing and driving one another in such a manner that it is impossible to mistake them for the quiet and sober pairs that frequent the same spot. At the present time, within a few days of midsummer (1884), they have not yet separated, and may still be seen performing their monotonous evolutions on the green turf in early morning and again towards evening.

The particles of food on which this species subsists must be exceedingly minute, these birds having been frequently watched feeding on a grass-plat, pecking at almost every step, though even the most powerful glass failed to reveal the prey secured. I possess, however, good proof that this species is beneficial on a well-kept lawn, having observed an old bird, followed by one of her young brood, searching out with immense success the grubs of the crane-fly, or daddy-long-legs. Having satisfied the wants of the first juvenile, which was then carefully conducted beneath the shade of the adjacent evergreens, she shortly after emerged from the cover with the second fluttering eagerly after her towards the same spot. While providing for her querulous offspring, I remarked that she dragged out the caterpillars of the destructive insects with almost the rapidity of Starlings. I find this fact first recorded in my notes under date of April 14, 1881; on several subsequent occasions the birds have also been watched engaged in the same manner.

# REDBREAST.
## ERITHACUS RUBECULA.

The ………… increase in numbers appear to have exercised the minds ………… declare that the old birds drive off their young, and others ………… are credited with a share in the work of extermination ………… in straggling parties, large quantities leave our shores as autumn draws to a close, ……… make their way to distant climes, from which few, if any, return, the gourmands of the south of Europe and the birds of prey that frequent their supposed winter haunts accounting satisfactorily for those that reach so far on their journey. Possibly there is some truth in these statements, though Robins, according to my own observations, only appear inclined to pick quarrels with those intruding on their domains; that the old and young engage in strife has also entirely escaped my notice. Cats, I am well aware, are merciless marauders, and I fully believe in the bad characters ascribed to the whole feline tribe. With regard to the migratory habits of our familiar friends, I have nothing to say gathered from personal experience, not a single specimen having ever been seen while on passage over the North Sea or the English Channel. I also failed to gain the slightest information concerning their movements from the crews of the light-ships off the east coast. The utter disregard of danger evinced by Robins and their disposition to enter dwellings prove injurious to them, and assist in keeping down their numbers; the situations chosen for nesting-purposes are also often undesirable to those whose precincts they intrude on, and their nests not unfrequently being destroyed tends to keep down the numbers of young that are reared. How relentlessly these birds persist in driving off those who find their way by accident or design into their own particular quarters, and with how little pity for a fallen foe they conduct their battles, may be judged from the following lines extracted from my notes for 1884 :—" November 27. The Robin that resorts to the indoor fernery was seen this morning in the act of pitching into one of those from the garden that had entered the building and been detected regaling himself on some food deposited on the rocks. The outsider was speedily driven off and retreated into the corner of one of the conservatories, where he first sought refuge in the foliage of some of the larger plants, and finally among the rows of flower-pots, gaining shelter for a while from his active pursuer. Though left in peace for a time, whenever attracting attention he was viciously attacked, and at last, when utterly disabled and helpless to offer resistance, was only saved by his persecutor, who was evidently bent on putting an end to his existence, being driven off. After being rescued and returned to the garden, the poor little bird presented a piteous spectacle, having barely sufficient strength to secrete itself among the bushes. Repeatedly, after attacking and punishing his victim, the Robin had mounted on the top of one of the open doors and sang sweetly for a few minutes, as if to celebrate his victory, jerking his tail and bowing his head to show himself off to the greatest advantage." During the following spring I remarked that no nest was commenced at the usual date by a pair annually resorting to an outdoor fernery in the garden, and I also remarked the absence of the male, who had invariably been in the habit of making his appearance to welcome visitors to his quarters. After making inquiries I learned from the gardeners that one of the Robins in the indoor fernery had been observed driving an interloper about the place a week or two before and piteously attacking him when down. The men declared that the little savage pecked furiously at the helpless victim while endeavouring to seek shelter among the crevices of the rocks. In consequence of this information, a search was made, and we soon discovered his mangled remains floating in a small pool near the waterfall. The flesh had been literally torn from portions of the breast and neck, and the greater part of the head was devoid of feathers, showing the barbarous treatment to which he had been exposed. This evidence is corroborated by the following lines, which appeared in the 'Field' of October 25, 1884:—"*Pugnacity of the Robin.*—On Sunday last I saw two Robins fighting under my dining-room window in such a fierce manner that they astonished me. I watched them until one actually killed the other, and then, like a game-cock, continued to peck his victim. I then went out to examine the poor bird, and found both eyes out and his skull quite bare, and the victor flew on a branch close to me, and began to sing in the sweetest notes. I then left the dead bird where I found it, and before I could get into the house he was at him again, pulling him about and standing on him, and he actually pecked a hole in his side. I have often seen dead Robins about the grounds, but had no idea they would kill one another, though I knew they were most pugnacious.—JOHN WORTHINGTON (Fishguard)."

For the last six or seven years I have, when at home in the south of England, carefully watched three pairs that breed round the house, notes also being received with reference to their proceedings during my absence. One pair annually construct their nests among the rocks in an enclosed fernery, secure from cutting winds and safe from the attacks of cats; these in every instance have succeeded in rearing a couple of broods. Two pairs, one resorting to an outdoor fernery and the other to an ivy-clad wall, have in only one instance brought out both broods—cats, cold winds, and the loss of eggs (for which, I believe, both rats, mice, and Starlings must be held responsible) having caused them repeatedly to desert their nests. That no increase in numbers takes place is certain, more than three pairs having never nested on the grounds; a few young may be observed till well on in autumn, after which the old birds only are seen, each emerging from its usual haunt when called, and looking down in expectation for what they like best, viz. a small lump of butter.

I am unable to offer any opinion as to the length of life of this species; witnesses, however, whose statements ought to be reliable, have informed me that these birds have been known to frequent one spot for from fifteen to twenty years. My own acquaintance with any individual has never extended over between seven and eight years. On every occasion when driving through a beech-plantation on the South Downs, between May 1872 and January 1880, a Robin came regularly to welcome us to his quarters. Bobby was a fine old bird in full song when his acquaintance was first made; our conveyance drawn up for lunch under a spreading beech having attracted him to the spot, crumbs and fat meat at once found favour in his sight. In course of time he grew more familiar; no sooner were the wheels heard descending the rough hill-track, than Bobby, even if his haunts had not been visited for several months, was on the look out some three or four hundred yards from where we usually pulled up. Flying at once to meet the conveyance, he perched on any convenient part and, singing from time to time, rode for the remainder of the way. While lunch was being unpacked he usually explored the interior of the nose-bag with which the horse was provided, and regaled himself with a few oats. The fat of ham, beef, or mutton was the delicacy he relished most, though butter or even a humble crumb of bread proved acceptable at times. His wife and, on two or three occasions, their family were seen; these, however, never ventured within the distance of two or three yards, and after snatching a mouthful or two, at once sought the brambles. It is now over four years since poor Bobby was last seen, and no ............ near the spot he frequented; stoats and weasels were by no means ............ on the rough hill-side, and on one occasion I plainly detected a marten in the ............ our old friend fell a victim to one of these marauders. It is exceedingly ............ fascination exercised over small birds by such animals: on the 10th of September, ............ driving along the coast-road between Shoreham and Lancing in Sussex, my attention was first attracted by four Wheatears perched two and two in the middle of the road intently regarding with outstretched necks the antics of some diminutive creature rolling over and over at the side of the track; the birds appeared helplessly spell-bound, turning their heads at every movement with the regularity of clockwork. A Whitethroat was hovering at the same time directly over, while safe on his perch on a twig in the thorn hedge a Robin quietly, though with evident suspicion, looked down upon the proceedings. Having ascertained that a young weasel was the cause of the excitement, I put a stop to his designs with a charge of shot, before he had obtained a chance to secure any of the deluded and infatuated spectators.

A weakly or wounded Robin is a sad spectacle, the poor bird usually draws near to one who seems interested in its welfare and claims assistance. Towards the end of last January an unfortunate with its beak broken off at the base took up its quarters in our indoor fernery, and in a piteous manner looked up when approached, evidently in hopes of obtaining assistance. Soaked bread, sponge-cake, and chopped worms were provided, but after lingering a few days the sufferer succumbed. To cool the base of its beak, on which a fungoid growth was forming, the bird was constantly dipping its head in water and rubbing it on the stones. A Robin with a club-foot was known for several years to frequent the grounds of the Manor House at Portslade near Brighton; during the day he constantly attended the gardener, and after dark, if forgotten, his tap at the window was soon heard; when admitted he speedily sought his accustomed roosting-place on the ............ of an old oak clock. At tea-time in winter he usually joined the party in the kitchen, helping ............ to what he fancied best and showing a predilection for the currants in a fresh cut cake, which ............ dexterously extracted while perched on the dish.

While eagerly searching to provide food for their earlier broods the Robins that resort to our ferneries are more confiding than at any other season of the year; they will take butter, worms, or insects when offered on a fork. It is seldom that such familiarity is exhibited during summer; on the 28th of June, 1884, however, while I was examining a caterpillar of the scalloped oak, *Crocalis elinguaria*, which the gardener had brought for identification on a sprig of willow, the insect relaxed its hold and dropped. No sooner had it reached the ground than one of the Robins, who was watching the proceedings from a bush close at hand, darted down and seizing his prize in triumph carried it off to some full-grown young to whom he occasionally supplied food, the dry weather having rendered the work of procuring sustenance almost too severe for the inexperienced juveniles. There are few insects that come amiss to Robins; they destroy vast quantities of caterpillars that are injurious to plants and vegetables. On a few occasions I have seen the grub of the crane-fly, or daddy-long-legs, in their beaks; they also prey upon both centipedes and earwigs, moths and flies of every description, as well as small worms. On the 10th of June, 1883, I watched a Robin creeping, after the manner of a Woodpecker, up the bark of an old alder-stump on one of the Norfolk marshes. Remarking that the bird halted at one particular spot and pecked for a few moments with great vigour, I closely examined the trunk of the tree and discovered the empty cocoon from which he had evidently just extracted the ............ large moth. In September 1883 immense quantities of the wings of moths ............ *Phlogophora meticulosa*), as well as those of a few butterflies, were found ............

and also in some pots hanging in one of the outdoor ferneries. At first I was of opinion that Bats had caught the insects, which numbered at least two or three hundred; shortly after, however, a Robin was seen perched among the ferns with a moth in its beak. These birds are especially fond of wheat, six or eight grains being the utmost they consume at a time; a few will take oats, but none I have watched attempted to swallow barley, which is doubtless unsuitable for digestion. On the 11th of August, 1883, I noticed a young Robin with a partially red breast hovering over a barberry-bush and seizing the ripe berries in his beak. After securing one or two he retired to the shelter of some of the adjoining shrubs to rest, returning shortly for a further supply; the prickly stems and leaves of the plant probably rendered it impossible for the bird to settle on the branches.

Some years back, at a farm in the east of Sussex, I was shown a most elaborately constructed cradle which a Robin had built in the corner of a coop in which a hen was confined with a brood of chickens, the two families appearing to agree in the most satisfactory manner. Though the Robins that resort to our ferneries have the option of building in most comfortable quarters, the spots they select are at times exceedingly singular. On one occasion a nest was placed on the bare ground below the spreading fronds of a large root of *Scolopendrium*. The young would doubtless have escaped undetected had not a strong volume from the hose, while watering the ferns, induced them to turn out somewhat prematurely. Early in the present season a pair of birds gave themselves the trouble to scrape out the mould from a small crevice in the rockery in which to place their nest, though far more suitable quarters surrounded them on all sides. Large quantities of mould and sand were scratched out and a round stone weighing over a couple of ounces was loosened and then dragged from its position, several pieces of broken brick being also removed. For ten days or a fortnight from the 26th of February they were busily employed in this needless undertaking, and, owing to the confined space, when their work was accomplished the female while sitting appeared exceedingly cramped, the tail being doubled up at right angles to her body. The brood having been hatched in due course, the five youngsters so completely blocked up the space that one or two were forced out of the aperture on to the ledge outside. Profiting by past experience, the old birds selected for their second nest a much more extensive cavity among the blocks of stone. Another pair having attempted to build in the drooping tendrils of a creeping rock-plant, eventually discovered that their nest was too heavy for its supports to bear the weight. Undaunted by their first failure, a second nest was commenced in an adjoining plant, and to this structure they built up a foundation from the sprouting fronds of a strong root of *Lastrea Filix-mas*. The mass of dead leaves and moss they had gathered together measured just over fourteen inches in height and occupied the birds a week to collect. Though a fortnight or three weeks often elapses from the time of the commencement of their nest till eggs are laid, Robins, when pressed for time, can be far more expeditious. A few weeks back a pair had just completed their second nest on a shelf in a summer-house when the removal of a hair broom into which one side of their edifice had been entwined gave offence, and another nest was begun in a coil of rope (the stays of a lawn-tennis net) on the same shelf, and only a few feet distant from the previous one. This was commenced soon after midday on the 27th of April, and an egg was laid on the following day. The materials were certainly somewhat scanty, though the cradle was carefully lined, the coil of a rope assisting to form a sufficiently substantial exterior.

Though beneficial to a certain extent in the ferneries, the Robins take great delight in detaching small pieces of moss from the stones; at times a concealed grub may offer an excuse for these attacks, though I fully believe the pure love of mischief prompts them in most instances to commit these depredations.

Occasionally after dark the male that frequents our indoor fernery approaches the entrance to the rooms in the house and, selecting a perch to which the glare of the lights penetrates, will continue singing for some time: I have repeatedly listened to him as late as a quarter past nine. The Robin is also one of our earliest songsters, being heard not unfrequently before the day has fairly broken; his plaintive note also proves especially attractive in the depth of winter, when almost every other bird is sheltering from the cutting blasts.

# REDSTART.
## RUTICILLA PHŒNICURA.

 to the British Islands. The Redstart first week in April; and all departure before the end of . The latest entry in my
 species of September 11, 1871, on which day a female pitched bunch of fowl on the deep water at the upper part was carried out in a workmanlike manner.

This known over the greater portion and Scotland. I have met with but few in the most Highlands, though in certain parts of Inverness-shire and Perthshire it is in fact, than in any other county I am acquainted with. As might be from habits, it is only found in the wooded portions of the country. In the greater number of the southern counties of England, the Redstart is more numerous at the seasons of migration, those that are met with being for the most part either on their way towards their summer quarters or returning south for the winter. In Norfolk it is not uncommon; I remarked the birds especially numerous in the vicinity of Norwich. My attention has been attracted on several occasions during the summer months by the bright colours of a male perched on a garden-wall or tree in some private grounds in the outskirts of the city. I met with a few in some of the more timbered portions of Yorkshire and Cumberland; though it can scarcely be described as rare in these localities, it is decidedly local.

By the middle of August these birds commence to gather down towards the south coast. I am aware of none breeding in the immediate neighbourhood, though I have repeatedly observed a few young ones in my own garden near Brighton soon after that date. During the last week in August 1882 an immature bird, which had been noticed on several previous occasions, darted out from under some bushes, and hopped off with a grape which had been flung to a brood of young Blackbirds, who, together with other pensioners, usually collected at certain hours in quest of what might be provided for them.

The nesting-habits of the Redstart have been so accurately described by numberless writers that it will be sufficient to state that, as a rule, it makes use of holes in trees or old walls, though at times it rears its young in somewhat eccentric situations. Some years back I noticed a pair were building in the foundation of the Osprey's nest on the old castle of Loch-an-Eilan, in Inverness-shire. At that time the rightful owners of the structure had been banished by frequent persecution. I am ignorant whether the Redstart still resorts to the same situation since the return of the Ospreys to their old quarters.

The fact that the nest of the Fishing-Eagle had been again tenanted was recently proclaimed in print, in order, as the writer stated, to incite large landed proprietors in the north to afford more effectual protection to these and other interesting birds of prey. Though this information was doubtless given in the hopes of adding to the chances of the Ospreys bringing off their brood, I fear it may only result in inducing some unscrupulous individual to make a raid in the district, and lead to the "lifting" of either the eggs or young. This eiry has been plundered repeatedly in days gone by; and the chances are that the robbery may be again accomplished. Some years ago I heard a lively account of the exploit from one who carried off the eggs from the nest. In order to effect his purpose he was forced to swim out to the island, as the boat which was usually kept on the loch had been removed from the water. It was scarcely daybreak when he started from the shore; but by the time he returned to the bank it was fairly light, and snow was falling heavily. As he emerged from the water in the garb of Adam before the fall (bar the blue bonnet on his head which contained the spoil), he was surprised by a piercing shriek; and on looking up he saw the forester's wife rush towards her house and slam the door. It seems that the woman (whose husband was known to be absent) had been attracted by the screams of the birds, when she was startled by the strange apparition slowly appearing from the water. Ever after she entertained a firm belief in the existence of that fearful being the "water-kelpie."

# BLACK REDSTART.
## RUTICILLA TITHYS.

There is, I am of opinion, little doubt this species is frequently overlooked. The number of the Black Redstarts that annually make their appearance on certain parts of our shores varies considerably. It is, however, seldom that our southern coast-line is not visited, during the latter part of October, by a succession of these birds gradually working their way towards the west. According to my own observations, the old and young pursue a somewhat different course when passing along the coast of Sussex during their migration. The adults keep, as a rule, to the cliffs along the sea-shore, while the immature birds often penetrate some distance inland.

The chalk cliffs near Hastings and Fairlight were regularly resorted to by this species some years ago; but of late I have not had an opportunity of searching the locality. Along the precipitous range from Eastbourne to Brighton I have repeatedly recognized this Redstart in the face of the cliffs, and also at times flying down to the rocks on the beach. In the west of Sussex I failed to identify more than two or three specimens. The sheltered coves and steep ravines among the rocks on the Cornish coast appear admirably suited to the requirements of these birds. I observed them flitting about the outskirts of several of the villages near the shore, and on one occasion noticed an immature bird perched on the esplanade at Penzance. The cliffs about Rinzey and Trewartas, and again from the Logan Rock to the Land's End, are a favourite resort; numbers may be seen on the warm and sheltered ledges when the wind blows strong from the north or east. On November 3, 1880, I counted eight or ten immature birds within less than a mile of the Tol-pedn penwith; and doubtless there were others, scattered over the inaccessible portions of the cliffs, which I failed to detect.

In pursuit of insects, which appear to form the greater part of their food, I have watched these birds closely searching the cracks and crannies in the chalk cliffs of Sussex. At times they would mount upwards to the grass on the summit, and occasionally extend their flight to some neighbouring wall or farm-buildings, any heaps of refuse or manure being sure to attract them. I have remarked them darting out on the shingle banks at the foot of the cliffs, and occasionally inspecting the sea-weed and decomposing rubbish washed up by the tide.

To the best of my knowledge, I never observed a perfectly adult male at any distance inland; the immature birds and females, however, are to be met with in considerable numbers within a mile or two of Brighton during the latter end of October and November. The dust-heaps, which contain the sweepings of the streets as well as all the rubbish collected from the town, are generally their favourite resorts. They may also be found in the small allotment gardens perching on the old palings and sheds, and carefully searching any ground newly manured or turned. I learn, on referring to my notes, that these birds were remarkably plentiful in the neighbourhood of Brighton in the autumn of 1875, three or four specimens not unfrequently being in view at the same time. Since that season we have been visited by no great numbers, though a few might generally be detected by closely watching their accustomed haunts at the date of their passage. The wind and weather, I expect, have much to do with the points at which they break their journey while travelling on towards the west. But one or two have come under my notice in the spring: it is probable these Redstarts follow a different course when returning to their breeding-quarters.

The bird occasionally referred to as the Grey Redstart (*Ruticilla cairii*) is without doubt the immature of this species. At what age the perfectly adult plumage is assumed appears, from the observations I made, somewhat doubtful. I have remarked males showing a small quantity of black feathers about the head and breast as early as the latter end of October, and numbers without any signs of such marking were procured through the greater part of November. In 1873 and the two following years I shot several of these birds in the endeavour to learn their various changes. Though males were obtained in four distinct states of plumage, I could form no decided opinion as to the ages of the two intermediate stages.

The young males of the year appear in much the same dress as the females. Some I procured were of a more uniform grey tinge.

The second stage was in almost similar plumage, but exhibited a slight indication of the black feathers about the head and breast.

The third stage showed the same amount of black as the adult males; but the white feathers on the wing were wanting.

The old males with the perfect black markings and a well-defined white patch on the wing were by far the most scarce. I never detected a single specimen with white on the wing, unless in the dress of the perfect adult male. I conclude this species must be at least two or three years in attaining the full plumage.

The Plate shows an adult male, shot along the chalk cliffs near Rottingdean, on October 13, 1873; also a male in what I take to be the last stage before assuming the perfect plumage: this specimen was obtained near the same spot ten days later.

# STONECHAT.
## SAXICOLA RUBICOLA.

From north to south the Stonechat is well known throughout the British Islands, a few pair remaining here and there in their usual haunts during the winter months. Fresh arrivals, however, make their appearance in the spring; and a certain number take their departure before the approach of winter. Whether the migrants are the young or old, or both, I am unable to state.

The furze-clad downs of Sussex are a favourite haunt of the Stonechat, and here this sprightly bird may be met with in greater numbers than in any other district I am acquainted with. It is also to be seen along rough country-lanes where the surrounding fields are divided by broad hedgerows of no great height, or where a portion of the land is unreclaimed. In Norfolk a few frequent the neighbourhood of the broads at all seasons of the year. The Stonechat, with the exception of the Reed-Pheasant and Pick-cheese*, was almost the only small bird I used to find among the marshes and broads when wildfowl-shooting, during the winter months, in the east of Norfolk. One of these birds may not unfrequently be observed to rise some height above the reeds and remain hovering in the air for nearly half a minute. At any considerable distance it would be difficult to distinguish this species, while fluttering in this manner, from the Kingfisher, as both species exhibit the same habit.

In Perthshire, Ross-shire, and Sutherland I have remarked this species at almost all seasons. I believe, however, during severe weather the birds desert the exposed hill-sides and come down into the sheltered glens and corries, and at times even to the vicinity of houses and gardens. I noticed a pair or two nested in the rough herbage among the sandbanks on the "fendom," a remarkably flat district to the east of Tain.

During autumn and winter the male Stonechat is by no means so showy as in his summer plumage; but though his dress is sober-coloured, his lively actions as he flits from twig to twig along the roadside or over the open moor are sure to attract attention. I have occasionally remarked that a few of these birds take up their quarters for a portion of the winter within a short distance of the sea-shore. Early in November 1882, two pairs made their appearance on the ridge of shingle between Shoreham and Lancing. They usually frequented the upper part of the banks, where plants of dock, chamomile, sea-beet, and sea-poppy were numerous; at times, however, they showed themselves on the breakwaters, and settled now and then on the lumps of seaweed cast up by the tide. I noticed that each pair confined themselves to a regular beat, seldom straying beyond the distance of three or four of the sea-groyns.

This species commences its nesting-operations at an early date in the southern counties, being one of the first of our small birds to build on the Sussex Downs. It usually selects a spot among low furze and coarse grass, or at times in a lump of rubbish or trimmings lying on the ground. The female sits close; and the nest is by no means easy to find. In the more northern counties I noticed the Stonechat was at least a month later in nesting.

* Norfolk name for Bearded Tit and Blue Tit.

# WHINCHAT.

## SAXICOLA RUBETRA.

The Whinchat is a migrant, arriving on the south coast about the middle or latter end of April, and gradually working its way towards the north. It occasionally happens that but few show themselves till the first or second week in May; I have seen the largest gatherings of fresh comers in the vicinity of the Sussex shingle-banks on the 6th and 8th of the month. It is seldom that these birds, after landing, remain long in the vicinity of the coast; in general they rapidly disperse to their haunts in the neighbourhood, or betake themselves inland on their way towards the north.

I never received word of this species or the Stonechat being taken on the light-ships off the east coast. I, however, on two or three occasions, remarked a number of Whinchats on the Denes on the Norfolk coast during squally weather, at about the season when they prepare for a move towards the south. As there is usually a considerable addition to the residents in the southern counties shortly before their time of migration on the return journey to the continent, it is, I imagine, probable that the greater number of the summer visitors to the northern and eastern portions of the country make their way inland towards the south, and then cross the channel from the coasts of Kent and Sussex. What course may be followed by the birds from the western counties I have not had an opportunity of judging.

Though I find but few notes in any of my journals concerning this species, I met with it in most of the northern counties of the Highlands. I cannot call to mind a single instance of having come across the Whinchat in the Outer Hebrides, though a few pairs were noticed during the breeding-season on the west coast of Ross-shire. In Sussex and Norfolk, where I have had frequent opportunities for studying the habits of this species, it breeds in much the same localities as the Stonechat, though in slightly different situations; I have repeatedly found the nest of the Whinchat in far more open spots than would be resorted to by its congener.

By the middle of          numbers of                              in                          plumage,
                                        along the                                    the south coast. Soon after

# WHEATEAR.

## SAXICOLA ŒNANTHE.

Almost every portion of the open districts in the British Islands is visited by the Wheatear. The first arrivals usually make their appearance on the south coast about the end of March or early in April. As these pass on towards the north, or take up their quarters on the hills in the neighbourhood, a continued stream of fresh comers may be noticed on favourable mornings in the vicinity of the shore. The birds that remain during the summer on the downs of Sussex are, I believe, among the first to show themselves on the coast. I have noticed a few flitting round their well-known haunts among the sheltered hollows on the hills whenever I passed through these localities early in April. The warrens and sandbanks on the east coast, and the sheep-walks and moor-lands of the north, are each tenanted in succession—the latest arrivals (from observations I have made during many seasons) passing on towards the northern counties, and eventually taking their departure to still more distant breeding-grounds. To the best of my knowledge, it is usually well into April before the Wheatear is seen in Ross-shire, Sutherland, or Caithness, the 10th, 13th, and 15th of the month being the dates on which I have first remarked this species when daily on the hills or along the coast.

On the return journey, the first detachments usually reach the marshes in the vicinity of the south coast about the beginning of August, a few stragglers being occasionally seen at an earlier date. From this time they continue to arrive daily throughout the month; and their numbers do not fall off till about the middle of September. A few single birds may not uncommonly be met with for several weeks later; but I never yet detected any remaining during the winter months in the British Islands. The last stragglers met with in the season of 1882 were a pair I noticed chasing one another on the downs a few miles west of Brighton on the 18th of October.

The Wheatear breeds in almost every district I have explored where the nature of the country is suitable to its habits. In the south, though plentiful on the downs, these birds are not so numerous during the summer as in many of the northern counties. The nest is more frequently placed in a rabbit-burrow than in any other situation They also resort to cracks and crevices among rocks and stones, and, at times, holes in banks and pits. The earliest date at which I have come across the nest containing eggs was on April 15th. In this instance the bird had selected a disused burrow in a warm and sheltered valley near the Dyke hill in Sussex. The greater number of the residents in this locality have, I believe, their full complement of eggs before the end of the first week in May. At this time fresh travellers from the continent may still be observed on the beach and in the fields along the coast.

The student in natural history, who takes up the works of our various authors, must, I should imagine, be somewhat perplexed to reconcile the conflicting reports that he may chance to light upon concerning the habits of this species. One writer tells us that the Wheatear "not unfrequently perches on trees and bushes," while possibly the next referred to declares "the Wheatear does not perch on trees and bushes." Such contradictory statements doubtless arise from the fact that two forms of Wheatear frequent the British Islands. In addition to the bird that arrives on our coasts in March and early in April, a larger variety makes its appearance at a somewhat later date. This form is seldom seen before the middle of April, and continues to land till the end of the first or second week in May[*]. It is perfectly correct that the common Wheatear seldom, if ever, perches on trees or bushes, though the large form if disturbed usually makes its way to a commanding position, either on a twig, on a hedgerow, or even on the topmost branches of some lofty tree. I have repeatedly remarked this habit in the vicinity of the south coast, as well as on the downs, and also on the moors in the Highlands. In Glenlyon, in Perthshire, I carefully watched this form in the first week in June. A pair or two frequented a steep hill-side, where I imagined they must be engaged in nesting-operations. When closely approached they almost invariably retreated to the upper branches of a clump of tall spreading beech trees. As these birds entirely disappeared after the 5th or 6th of the month, I came to the conclusion they had passed on towards more northern breeding-quarters. With regard to the nesting of this form or variety within the limits of the British Islands, I can only state from personal observation that I have not clearly ascertained a single instance. Though a considerable amount of time was spent in many parts of the country, I never succeeded in discovering the nest of the large Wheatear; I have, however, been assured, by persons well acquainted with the variety, that these birds breed on the South Downs at times, in rabbit-burrows, after the fashion of their smaller relatives. The eggs are described as being slightly marked with rusty blotches or spots. This information concerning their nesting I give for what it is worth, my own opinion being that this form only passes over the British Islands on its way to the far north. According to my own experience, there is little or no difference between the two forms, with the exception of size. I have never been guilty of slaughtering any great numbers for the sake of comparison; but after a careful examination of several fresh-killed specimens of both forms, I consider the larger seldom attain a state of plumage where the tints are so clearly or brightly defined as on a few of the earlier arrivals of the smaller race. I have frequently remarked that the first Wheatears met with along the south coast at the commencement of their migration exhibit the most conspicuous colouring. With regard to the habits of the two forms, they may be described as similar, with the exception of the far later date at which the larger form reaches our shores, and its predilection for perching on bushes or trees.

A male of each form is depicted in the Plate, figured side by side in order to convey an idea of the relative sizes. The smaller specimen, shown on a fragment of drift wreckage, was obtained during the first week in April; the larger bird a month later, shortly after his arrival on our shores. As the Plate represents the two forms life-size, any description is rendered unnecessary.

The nestling-plumage of the Wheatear is dull and far less showy than the dress of the adults; a short inspection, however, of the actions of the juveniles, as well as the conspicuous white bar across the tail, would speedily convince those who are not thoroughly acquainted with the species in all its variations that they are undoubted chips of the old block. Before the movement towards the south is commenced, the young have completely assumed their autumn dress, and at a short distance can scarcely be distinguished from the old birds.

Considerable numbers of Wheatears must at times pass over the North Sea. While conversing with

[*] I find in ...... that a ........ shot on the beach near Shoreham on ...........

the mate of one of the light-ships off the east coast concerning the birds that flew on board his vessel, I learned that the most frequent captures had lately consisted of Larks, Starlings, and Shepherds[*]. During 1872 and 1873, when I received the wings of the birds that fell on the light-ships off this coast, I did not find any sign that a single Wheatear had been taken, though Starlings and Larks were by far the most numerous. I conclude it is only during thick hazy weather at the seasons of their migration that these birds get out of their reckoning and come to grief in this manner.

The Wheatear was in former days in great request for the table, and immense numbers were captured by the shepherds on the South Downs. The ingenious snares they employed for the purpose have been so frequently and accurately described by writers, that any remarks I could make on the subject would be superfluous. It will be sufficient to state that, from inquiries made during the autumn of 1882, I was unable to learn that any birds now finding their way to the Brighton market are taken by these means. The season of 1878 was the last in which the poulterers received a supply from the shepherds; and the quantity then captured was exceedingly small compared with the hundreds of dozens formerly sent in. On examining the books of one of the game-dealers in which the daily takes of each shepherd were recorded, I discovered their whole season's catch did not amount to more than from two hundred to four hundred birds per man. The manager of one of the leading firms assured me that some thirty years ago they have had as many as sixty dozen brought in by the carriers in a single day. The supply occasionally considerably exceeded the demand; and one of my informants described, with evident signs of regret, the stupendous pies that not uncommonly fell to their share in those days. The farmers have now put a stop to the formation of the traps by the shepherds. The sheep-walks have become so contracted by the land falling under the plough, that they doubtless consider the encroachment on the pasture, caused by the displacement of the turf, to be by no means beneficial to their interests. The birds now reaching the market are furnished by the professional bird-catchers, who capture them by clap-nets. The neighbourhood of the race-hill near Brighton is a favourite set, one or two men or boys being employed in driving the birds over the net. The numbers taken are but small, from a dozen and a half to a couple of dozen being considered a fair morning's work. This brings in to the catcher about one and six pence a dozen, and an equal profit to the poulterer.

[*] On certain parts of the east coast the Wheatear is known as the Shepherd.

# GRASSHOPPER WARBLER.

## SALICARIA LOCUSTELLA.

The Grasshopper Warbler has been traced, I believe, to various parts of Scotland; further north than Norfolk, however, I have been unable positively to identify a single specimen. In that county it is numerous, though local; and the same remark as to its distribution might apply to Sussex and others of the southern counties.

Although a considerably earlier date has been assigned to the first arrivals of this migrant, it is seldom, according to my own experience, that any number show themselves till the first week in May. There is little doubt these Warblers, as a rule, make the passage of the Channel in small scattered parties, after the manner affected by others of the family; still I have, on two separate occasions, met with large numbers in the immediate vicinity of the south coast. When shooting in the Nook at Rye, in Sussex, early one morning in May 1868, I found the samphire and other small salt-water weeds growing on the mudbanks completely swarming with Grasshopper Warblers. These birds had apparently just reached the coast, and were on the point of making their way inland. There must have been several hundred in a small patch of weeds of a dozen or twenty acres. There were probably other denizens of the marshes among them; but the half-dozen birds secured by two shots which I fired into the cover were all of this species. Again, during the first week in May 1868 it was evident that a large flight must have reached the shore a short distance west of Brighton, many of the hedgerows in the district being thickly tenanted with these Warblers as well as other members of the same family. It was late in the day before the whole of the travellers had worked any distance inland; but on the following morning they had all taken their departure.

Though frequently found in the neighbourhood of water, this Warbler is by no means so aquatic in its habits as the more common Reed- and Sedge-Warblers. Several pairs breed round many of the broads in the east of Norfolk, frequenting the tangled bushes and rough cover round the marsh-walls. I have also discovered their nests under the shelter of long coarse grass in hay-fields and on bramble-covered banks in the more southern counties.

The nest, usually concealed with the utmost care, is composed of the dried strands of various grasses and plants. The architects, whether inhabiting the moist flat districts of the eastern counties or the dense hedgerows and rough banks of Sussex, appear to make use of much the same materials. The eggs have a dull white ground (with a pinkish tinge when fresh) thickly speckled with fine spots of light red.

The curious note of this species has frequently attracted my attention in localities where I had no notion the bird was to be met with. It is useless, in these pages, to attempt to describe this singular performance, not inaptly denominated by several authors the "trill." Words, indeed, can scarcely convey an idea of the strangely deceptive sounds as they rise and fall in the still morning air, the movement of the head of the bird producing a mysterious uncertainty as to the direction from which the note is uttered. Though very difficult to catch a glimpse of during the day, these Warblers may generally be observed about daybreak singing on some high reed or branch of a tree. The topmost spray of a bush or the summit of a tall reed is their favourite perch throughout the fen or broad-district. In the south I have watched them on two or three occasions at an elevation of from twelve or fifteen up to even twenty feet in the branches of an oak. If undisturbed during fine still weather, the monotonous note is frequently continued with but slight intermission for the first two or three hours after daybreak. The slightest sign of danger is sufficient to cause them to drop like a stone into the thick cover, where they quietly remain creeping about like a mouse till the place is again quiet.

# SEDGE-WARBLER.

## SALICARIA PHRAGMITIS.

Like the rest of the family, ............... Islands, arriving in April, and taking its departure from our ............... towards its haunts, and also on its return in ............... plantations, ............... numbers ............... that ............... a sufficient amount of ............... through ............... or ............... of ............... the nosy ............... quarters are reached.

From north to south the Sedge-Warbler may be found, if searched for, in almost every locality adapted to its habits and requirements. I have repeatedly met with this species nesting in Sussex within a few miles of the coast, and also round the edges of the rush-grown lochs in the north of Caithness. The bird seems as clamorous and as much at home in the solitude that reigns supreme round the remotest Highland lochs as when observed in close proximity to the constant traffic of steamboats, wherries, and yachts on the rivers and broads of Norfolk and Suffolk.

The attractive cackling note of this species may be heard at almost all hours of the night. If silent for a time, should their haunts be invaded and the birds disturbed, they will at once commence "noising"* on all sides. Though the song of the Reed-Wren (according to my own experience) is for the most part uttered among the stems of the reeds, the Sedge-bird occasionally deserts its usual quarters and may be noticed assiduously pouring forth its cheerful though somewhat monotonous ditty while perched on the twigs of a thick bush or even on the branches of an oak, an alder, or any greenwood tree growing near the water-side. These birds not unfrequently rise from the cover of the reeds or sedge and, flying or rather floating through the air, continue their song on wing. At times, while so engaged, they alight high in the foliage of some dense tree, from which the descent is effected with the same curious wavering flight to their accustomed lowly haunts. When viewed at a short distance, their downward course much resembles the drop of the Titlark as, with quivering and expanded wings, it makes its way towards the ground.

The nest is generally placed at no great distance from water, either among the roots of the sedge on a rough bank, or against the stump of a tree. The egg of *S. phragmitis* differs considerably from that of *S. strepera*. To describe them briefly, it may be said that the eggs of this species are of a dull brownish-yellow tint, thickly speckled with a darker brown, and occasionally scrawled here and there with a few fine black lines, while those of the Reed-Warbler have a pale greenish-blue ground with dull grey and brown blotches and spots. The juveniles of this species and also the Reed-Warbler, while in their first feathers,

* "Noising" is the term given by the Norfolk marshmen to the noise of several species of birds frequenting their entire swamps. They

bear a close resemblance to the adults. Should a family party come into view among the reeds or sedge-plants, there is little difference to be detected in the whole group, save the brighter appearance of the feathers of the youngsters and their shorter tails. In the same manner as in the rest of the tribe, the plumage of the old birds becomes considerably soiled and worn by the middle of summer.

I am well aware many of the Sedge-Warblers landing on the Sussex coast in the spring are only on their way towards the more northern counties, having frequently noticed them during their overland passage in all sorts of uncongenial situations. It is, however, evident that a few must make their way to the British Islands across the North Sea, as the wings of a couple of these birds were received from the 'Lynn Well' light-ship during the summer of 1873, and on making inquiries I learned that both came on board the vessel early in May.

# REED-WARBLER.

## *SALICARIA STREPERA.*

For some years scientific naturalists were of opinion that another Warbler, much resembling the species, occasionally made its appearance in certain parts of the British Islands. To this form the name of Marsh-Warbler (*Salicaria palustris*) has now been given, and the bird is considered by more than one writer to be of far from uncommon occurrence. This species has hitherto escaped my notice.

Up to the present I have never observed our noisy and familiar summer visitor the Common Reed-Wren taking up its residence in any spot where the reed (*Phragmites communis*) was not to be found in larger or smaller quantities. Shortly after landing on our shores, and while passing over the country to or from their haunts, the birds may be detected settling for a time in any green cover, though such quarters are speedily deserted when rest or food have been obtained. It is only among the stems of the reeds that I have seen the nest; the fact, however, that this species occasionally resorts for breeding-purposes to osier-beds, lilac bushes, and other similar situations has been frequently recorded by trustworthy authorities.

The Reed-Wren is scarcely so early in making its appearance as the Sedge-Warbler, and is by no means so widely distributed over the country. I never identified a single specimen in Scotland, though one locality in the south-east, where the presence of the bird had been recorded, was most carefully watched. The neighbourhood of the larger broads in the eastern counties is probably the headquarters of this Warbler in Great Britain. In some of the more southern counties there are several well-known haunts; but from recent observations, I have come to the conclusion that the species is far less numerous than it was twenty years ago.

Like their neighbours the Sedge-Warblers, these birds are remarkably noisy, though far from melodious songsters. During the day both species confine themselves for the most part to an occasional cackling note, evidently reserving their harmony for the evening concert, which usually commences as soon as the sun gets low. Hickling Broad in the east of Norfolk is one of the spots where this may be heard to perfection any fine evening early in June. The din that is caused by several hundreds of these birds singing and chattering at the same time, together with the croaking of the frogs, the jarring of the Nighthawks, and the drumming of the Snipes, is perfectly deafening, and would never be credited by those who have not heard it. By about 11 p.m. the greater number of the performers are quiet; but the slightest sound, even the splashing of a large pike on the look-out for his supper, is enough to make them break out again in full chorus.

During cold and stormy weather these birds remain remarkably silent, hardly a sound, except the occasional scream of a Coot or Moorhen, being heard through the swamps to break the monotony of the sighing of the wind through the reed-beds and the splash of the rain on the open water.

The nest is usually attached to three or four stems of the reed; and if rocking is a luxury to the young birds they must certainly during rough weather have a particularly happy time of it, as their cradle sways backwards and forwards with every gust of wind. I have found this species breeding in the small straggling patches of reeds that fringe the edges of the marsh-dykes in various parts of Sussex. In Norfolk thousands resort to the dense reed-beds in the neighbourhood of the larger broads. In these localities the Cuckoo frequently selects the Reed-Warbler as a foster-parent for its troublesome offspring.

The immense quantities of minute insects that abound throughout the moist and rush-grown districts frequented by this species afford an endless supply of food. When brought up in a boat fishing in some quiet corner of the broads, I repeatedly remarked these Warblers flitting across the water, carrying in their mouths the wingless bodies of a pale buff-coloured moth. On shooting one or two of the birds, it was discovered that the remains of the insect somewhat resembled the species captured by the Dartford Warblers for their young. It is probable, however, that the moth belonged to some other genus of the Leucanidæ, possibly *Nonagria cannæ*.

# NIGHTINGALE.
## PHILOMELA LUSCINIA.

According to my own observations, the range of this favourite songster is decidedly limited over the British Islands. I have only met with it in the southwestern counties, and have been unable to identify a single specimen further north than the parishes of Norfolk.

The males of this species make their appearance on the south coast at least a week or ten days in advance of the females, the earliest arrivals being usually noticed during the second week in April. The song is then continued for a month or six weeks, after which it is heard no more, the bird simply giving notice of its presence by a curious croaking note of warning to its young.

Hundreds are annually taken in traps on their first appearance in the spring, though but a small number of these wretched captives survive for any length of time. One fourth at least, under even the most favourable circumstances, or possibly more than half should a delay occur before the newly caught birds receive attention, pine away and die during the process of "meating off"[*]. Strong, healthy, and early-caught birds are meated off in three days; the majority of those requiring a longer time grow thin, and of those but few recover. Dealers state that about four fifths that outlive the first week of their captivity usually break out in song in a fortnight, the note being continued in some instances for five or six weeks. A few, I suppose, occasionally become thoroughly reconciled to confinement should they happen to fall into the hands of those acquainted with their habits and willing to afford the constant care and attention that is necessary. All, however, that have come under my observation were such wretched mockeries of the birds in the state in which I have been accustomed to watch them as to be positively painful to behold.

A meal-worm is a bait this species is unable to resist; and by means of one of these insects impaled on a pin in a spring-trap of the very simplest construction, the unfortunate birds are enticed to their doom. The quantities captured in the neighbourhood of London, Brighton, and other parts of the south would appear incredible to any one who has not watched the proceeding, and noted the ease and rapidity with which almost every bird either seen or heard can be secured. There are certain spots, well known to the professionals who follow this occupation, where Nightingales are sure to be met with the first fine morning after their arrival. Even if the note is not audible (and this seldom occurs) an experienced catcher speedily detects the exact positions the birds have taken up. Carefully noting every movement among the branches, their whereabouts is at once ascertained when they fly down from the covert or hedgerow to search for a few moments for food in the ditch round the wood-side, or a yard or two out in some grass-field. The red feathers in the tail attract attention in the bright sunlight at a considerable distance, even if their actions were not unmistakable to experienced eyes. A trap having been placed within view of the perch where the bird has

---

[*] Among professional catchers a bird is termed "meated off" as soon as it will feed itself. Almost any fresh-caught Nightingale will ravenously devour living meal-worms; but no little care and experience is needed to induce them to take of their own accord the scraped beef, yolk of egg, and other preparations with which they are supplied.

been discovered singing, or on the spot where it was seen, but few minutes usually elapse before the capture is effected. At times, when dull weather or a passing cloud renders this shy and wary species unwilling to move, a certain amount of judicious driving is resorted to. Some years back, while inspecting the proceedings of two worthies who were working a couple of traps, I remarked, on one occasion after shifting their ground, that a prisoner was struggling in each net before they had been placed in position above a couple of minutes. From a dozen to a score of males is, I believe, considered a good morning's work by the birdcatching fraternity. In order to insure success, a warm, still, sunny morning is indispensable. A cold wind not only affects the birds, causing them to skulk in the cover, but also rapidly chills the meal-worms. A torpid bait is by no means so effective as a lively writhing insect, whose contortions are supposed to be the most attractive part of the performance. Nightingales invariably resort to the warmest and most sheltered side of the wood or hedgerow where they are enabled to enjoy the rays of the sun.

I have repeatedly remarked that shortly after their arrival, and before the females have made their appearance, Nightingales sing almost continuously during the early morning, the note being heard with scarcely a moment's intermission from 6 till 9 A.M. There are certain districts in the interior of Sussex where the country is interspersed with numerous plantations, the large timber mostly consisting of oak, with an abundant undergrowth of hazel and ash. The hedgerows are of thorn, and for the most part broad and thick and allowed to grow in the old-fashioned style, the very brambles being also, as a rule, untrimmed. Though this locality would scarcely find favour in the sight of some of our advanced agriculturists, it attracts an immense number of Nightingales. On warm bright mornings towards the end of April I have listened to at least half a dozen singing at the same time, the notes being heard on all sides almost incessantly. Shortly after the arrival of the females, the numbers seem to decrease, at all events the birds are less frequently seen or heard. As it is hardly possible that Nightingales could be snared in this district, I conclude that they are fully engaged in making preparations for nesting during the early hours of the morning.

The nest is somewhat rough and unfinished in appearance, dead and decayed leaves being freely used in its construction. It is usually placed at a very small elevation, and at times on the ground, either close to the stump of a tree or in some thick prickly bush.

The young in their first feathers are spotted with pale yellowish markings, being not altogether unlike young Robins. The tint of the tail-feathers, however, is the same as in the adults, though scarcely so conspicuous.

# BLACKCAP.

## CURRUCA ATRICAPILLA.

This well-known songster, whose note almost rivals that of the Nightingale, is distributed over the majority of our English counties, being found, according to my own experience, more plentifully in the southern and eastern portions of the country. The Blackcap is stated to have been observed, in suitable localities, as far as the north of Scotland by many competent witnesses; this is doubtless the case, though the bird has but seldom come under my notice in the Highlands. When busily occupied in studying the habits or endeavouring to obtain specimens of the larger birds of prey, or some scarce member of the Wader or Wildfowl family, it is quite possible such small fry would escape unnoticed; this, I conclude, is the reason I have failed to recognize one or two of the Warblers and other diminutive wanderers that have been reported by certain observers. Some years back I remarked a few scattered birds in East Lothian in a warm sheltered valley at no great distance from the coast; as it was then towards the close of summer, I was ignorant whether these Warblers had been bred in the locality (which was in every respect adapted to their habits) or were working their way southward from some more northern haunt.

The Blackcap arrives on the south coast of England about the second week in April. My attention was attracted a few years ago by two remarkably fine males that had taken up their summer quarters within what appeared an exceedingly short distance of one another: the spot they had selected was situated in the wooded district a few miles north of the range of the South Downs in Sussex. These two birds were watched on several occasions during three or four days (April 15th to 18th) feeding on ivy-berries in the most amicable manner, almost side by side. Not a glimpse of either of the females was obtained, and it is doubtful whether they had at that date reached our shores. I can find no entry in my notes referring to the earliest date at which the eggs of this species have been seen. The young birds in my collection were obtained on the 8th of July, when just on the point of quitting the nest; this was evidently a late brood (the first nest having probably been robbed), as I have repeatedly remarked young birds appearing in the woods and coverts within a few miles of the south coast shortly after this date.

In company with Garden-Warblers, these birds may regularly be seen every autumn feeding greedily on fruit in gardens near the coast just previous to their departure, their heads, beaks, and breasts being at times deeply stained by the juice of the elder-berries, for which they appear to entertain an especial fancy. Insects and caterpillars also afford a large proportion of the food of these birds. I repeatedly watched both old and young taking the green caterpillars from plants and flowers. Bird-catchers are well aware that the meal-worm is a bait this species is unable to resist.

Though usually concealed with considerable care, I have on more than one occasion met with the nest of this species in a ridiculously conspicuous position; this, however, has only occurred when the site chosen was more elevated than that commonly selected, and where a perpetual dark shade was thrown over the whole of the immediate surroundings by the dense foliage of lofty overhanging timber. The cradle constructed for the expected brood, though coarsely put together, is compact, and yet sufficiently serviceable to perform its required duty; the accommodation for the juveniles, however, when compared with that provided by various other small birds, can only be described as second class.

The eggs vary greatly, and to describe them in a few words is almost hopeless. The ground is usually of a pale yellowish or dirty white tint, scrawled, spotted, or blotched with irregular markings of dark red and yellowish brown. I have occasionally come across a nest where the whole of the clutch of four or five eggs closely resembled variegated brown marble.

In the nestling plumage the young are similar to the female; the general tint of the feathers, however, is somewhat more dingy.

# GARDEN-WARBLER.
## *CURRUCA HORTENSIS.*

Unless its note is detected, the Garden-Warbler rarely intrudes itself sufficiently to attract observation. In several of the southern counties this species is by no means uncommon, though its presence is seldom or never noticed by the natives of the district. When making inquiry in any remote locality concerning the various species of Warblers, I have invariably found, with the exception of any exceedingly abundant local variety, such as the ... this family was less known than any class of birds.

At the time of its arrival, which usually takes place towards the latter end of April, though prolonged by stragglers till well on in May, this species may be met with along rough hedgerows, and also in gardens and plantations, in the neighbourhood of the south coast. By the end of the second week in May, all but the residents have passed on towards their inland quarters. During the summer months this species frequents situations where thick cover abounds in woods and tangled thickets, extending its rounds only so far as the shelter is dense and enables it to creep about without any considerable exposure to view.

The Garden-Warbler is one of our most pleasing songsters; the note, however, is scarcely so attractive as that of the Blackcap or Nightingale, and few but close observers of bird-life are acquainted with either the species or its note.

The nest, which much resembles that of several others of the family, is usually well concealed in brambles or low bushes, though the bird at times is true to its name, and rears its young among cultivated shrubs, or even the straggling roots of fruit-plants in gardens. The eggs correspond to a certain degree in colouring with those of the Blackcap; the markings, however, are by no means so distinct and bright, or the tints so rich; they have, in fact, a more washed-out or faded appearance.

I never positively identified the Garden-Warbler beyond the Scotch border, though repeatedly expending considerable time and trouble in endeavouring to obtain a satisfactory view of any of the family that came under my notice in the sheltered valleys near the coast of East Lothian. In certain parts of Yorkshire this Warbler is by no means uncommon, though retiring (as usual) and but little known. I met with several pairs in the east of Norfolk, and also in Suffolk. In the southern counties the bird is perhaps more numerous than in any other part of the British Islands.

When collecting previous to its departure in the autumn, the Garden-Warbler is at times exceedingly abundant for a few days in the vicinity of the south coast. The earliest arrivals make their appearance by the latter end of July or the beginning of August, and for several weeks a constant succession of these birds may be noticed frequenting any gardens where fruit can be obtained. For elder-berries they have a particular fancy; I have at times remarked their beaks and plumage deeply stained by the juice of the ripe berries. The majority of Warblers of this genus may be attracted by hanging small bunches of fruit among bushes or the lower branches of trees. By this means it is possible to gain an insight into their habits, and a chance of watching the actions of these usually retiring birds, as well as identifying some rare species.

# WHITETHROAT.

## CURRUCA CINEREA.

---

We are informed by several writers that this species makes its appearance in Great Britain towards the end of April. This is certainly correct as regards the first comers, though the greater number of our visitors do not arrive till the first or second week in May, and it is probably near the end of the month before the last stragglers have reached us shores. Having carefully taken note the dates on which I met with large numbers in the country during my stay at the southcoast, I am able to mention the period over which their spring migration extended.

The Whitethroat is common in most parts of England where the country is suited to its habits. I remarked several pairs in various districts in Scotland; but, except in certain localities, it is far less numerous than in England, and, according to my own experience, is not observed in the northern counties.

These lively little migrants soon make their arrival known, showing themselves, singing and chattering on the top of the hedges, shortly after they reach our shores for their summer visit. They appear happy enough when once they have made the land; but I have noticed them very hard pressed during a fresh north-west wind in the channel. These birds seem to fly low, possibly in order to escape the force of the wind; and this unfortunately leads to their being struck down by the spray when some unusually heavy sea happens to break right in front of them. I believe the smaller birds of passage seldom attempt to cross in the face of a gale; but that they will occasionally make a mistake in the weather there is good proof, as I have picked up several (particularly of this species) floating dead on the water a few miles off the south coast. Under the date of May 17, 1872, I find in my notes the following entry:—"Strong breeze with drifting rain from the north-east. Swallows were again crossing the channel. There was, in fact, a constant stream of small birds, Whitethroats and other Warblers forming the majority; I also remarked one or two Spotted Flycatchers. Many of these travellers could barely hold their way in the face of the frequent squalls and heavy rain; and the greater number of those we noticed, ten or a dozen miles off the land, must have had hard work to make the shore." On the following day (May 18) I was again in the channel. The wind had dropped, and there was scarcely a breath of air, the sea, for several hours, being as still as a mill-pond. I did not notice any Warblers on passage; but several Whitethroats were met with floating dead on the water, also one Flycatcher and two Willow-Wrens. It is probable, if any of the small migrants had made the attempt to cross during the early morning, that the still weather had enabled them to complete the journey at their usual hour. With the exception of the Swallow tribe, who appear to fly with somewhat less regularity, I believe the most of our small summer visitors that cross the English Channel arrive during the first three or four hours of daylight. A sudden shift of wind, accompanied by heavy squalls of drifting rain, of course delays their passage and is frequently fatal to hundreds, if not thousands.

Though I have little doubt that by far the greater number of these birds land on the south coast of

England, a few occasionally come to grief on the light-ships off the east coast. Early in June 1873 I received the wings of two or three Common Whitethroats which had fallen on board the "Lynn Well" floating light during the first or second week in May. Unless some of our visitors reach this country by crossing the German Ocean, I am at a loss to understand what could have caused their presence on the stormy North Sea at that season.

At their first arrival on our shores, Whitethroats are particularly neat and handsome birds, their feathers soft and glossy, the males especially exhibiting a conspicuous pale rosy bloom on their breasts. By the end of summer they are completely changed in appearance, their feathers worn and ragged, and the bright colours faded into a general dirty grey tint.

For several weeks previous to their departure these Warblers may be noticed collecting in considerable numbers in the neighbourhood of the south coast. They are to be met with along broad hedgerows, and also frequenting gardens and plantations, usually preferring those spots where they are able to find an abundance of thick cover. On September 12th, 1882, I remarked a couple of young birds busily engaged in capturing the green caterpillars of the small White Butterfly (*Pontia rapae*) on a bed of mignonette. Hopping below the plants, these interesting juveniles carefully inspected the upper portion of the flower; and on an insect being detected they fluttered upwards, and, hovering for a moment, seized their prey on the wing.

The nest is by no means an elaborately finished structure, dead blades and stems of various grasses being used in its composition. Though well concealed during summer, its position is generally exposed to view when once the foliage on the brambles and thorn bushes has been cut up by frosts. The number of old nests of this species that can be counted in the hedgerows in almost any rough locality clearly indicates how extensively the Whitethroat is distributed over the country. The eggs might almost be described as a mass of yellowish-brown streaks and spots, marked here and there with darker lines and dots, the small amount of ground tint is visible being usually of a dirty white tint with a shade of greenish yellow.

I have noticed several of the provincial names of this species recorded by various writers; but I cannot call to mind having met with that of "Hayjack." The bird is commonly known by this title to the marsh-men in the east of Norfolk.

# LESSER WHITETHROAT.

## CURRUCA SYLVIELLA.

The notes I have compiled in my journal with reference to this species are necessarily scanty in the extreme. It is just possible the Lesser Whitethroat may be more or less common in the north of England, but in the Southern Journals it is not common; and I cannot at the present moment call to mind a single instance. The country between Oxford and Birmingham, in the south of Yorkshire, appears to be the most northern locality in which this neat and elegant little bird has attracted my attention. In Sussex, Kent, and Middlesex the species, though local, is by no means uncommon during the breeding-season. It is also to be met with in Norfolk, Suffolk, Cambridgeshire, and a few of the adjoining counties, though in smaller numbers than in the south.

I never recognized this Whitethroat on passage. The birds may be noticed, on their first arrival, on the south coast, frequenting for a day or two the thick hedges in the vicinity of the shore. In Sussex none remain during the summer within four or five miles of the coast; I am of opinion that the whole of those observed to the south of the downs shortly betake themselves to inland haunts. In the well-wooded district immediately north of this range of hills the country is admirably adapted to their habits; and here several pairs take up their summer residence, usually appearing at a rather later date than their relative the Common Whitethroat.

The nest of this species is a particularly light and finely interwoven structure, being just sufficiently strong to carry the weight of the young brood, and at the same time so slightly built with dry and seasoned materials as almost to convey the impression of being old and deserted. It is usually concealed in an artful manner, though the situation in which it is placed is by no means unapproachable owing to the denseness of the cover. A spot is often selected among the stems of creeping brambles, or in stunted bushes of blackthorn, at no great height from the ground; indeed it is seldom seen at a greater elevation than two or three feet. On one occasion I detected no less than five nests of this species along a low broad hedgerow (at most two hundred yards in length) dividing a couple of grass-fields in the Harrow country, about ten miles north of London. The eggs are slightly smaller than those of the Common Whitethroat; the tint of the ground-colour is purer (at times approaching a pale bluish white), marked with yellowish-brown blotches and spots on the larger end.

For some weeks previous to their departure these birds may be noticed in small numbers in gardens and sheltered plantations within a short distance of the south coast. I conclude that the majority of our visitors reach this country by crossing the English Channel, and also depart by the same route, as I never received a single wing from the light-ships off the east coast.

# WOOD-WREN.

## *PHYLLOSCOPUS SIBILATRIX.*

According to my own observation, Wood-Wrens are either decidedly less numerous throughout the British Islands than Willow-Wrens or Chiffchaffs, or they betake themselves to their summer quarters more speedily than their relatives, but few being met with in the vicinity of the coast at the time of their arrival. I have seldom noticed many of these birds till the first week in May; and in Scotland it is usually a week or so later before their presence is recognized.

Though exceedingly local, this species may be found, if carefully sought for, in most counties in England and Scotland. I remarked several pairs in Glenlyon in Perthshire, and also heard numbers singing in the plantations on the south side of Loch Maree in Ross-shire. About Lairg and Altnaharra, in Sutherland, they frequented the groves of larch in the vicinity of the lochs, and appeared by no means scarce in some of the sheltered glens about Berriedale, in Caithness. I did not meet with the species in the neighbourhood of the shores of the Pentland firth; but as plantations increase I have no doubt they will, in time, reach that locality. In Sussex the Wood-Wren appears to have a partiality for woods containing high trees, especially beech, the fine old timber in Stanmer Park being one of the favourite haunts of this bird. Occasionally I have observed this species frequenting plantations of elm and oak; I remarked this fact in both Middlesex and Norfolk. But a single specimen came under my notice in the broad-district on the east coast; and I believe the species is scarce in that part of the country. In Yorkshire I detected a few in the sheltered glens and corries down which the mountain-streams run towards the east coast. As it was late in the summer, it is possible these birds were only working their way towards the south, as a second search for them in the same locality proved fruitless. The west of Perthshire contains, in many of the wildest glens, a quantity of large timber almost exclusively composed of beech. In some spots these fine trees cover a considerable amount of ground on the lower slopes of the mountains, or are scattered in small clumps at intervals along the river-banks or road-sides. In such localities Wood-Wrens are to be heard in numbers, their song being particularly attractive during fine summer weather. In a sheltered birch-wood through which a hill-burn dashed down towards the Lyon, I remarked several Wood- and Willow-Wrens keeping up a continued concert, the murmur of the falling water, as it splashed over the rough stones, apparently inciting them to an additional display of their vocal powers. In the more northern counties these birds are forced to put up with the stunted birch or fir that alone contrive to exist in several of the rocky glens they frequent. I have repeatedly distinguished their note in plantations of larch of only six or eight feet in height. As millions of small trees have, during the last few years, been planted on several estates, it is probable this species may shortly become more generally distributed throughout the Highlands.

Towards the end of summer these birds may be noticed gathering in the woods and plantations near the south coast previous to their departure across the channel. I have seen a few in gardens in the vicinity of towns (though they usually prefer a more rural district), eagerly searching for insects among the trees and bushes. The countless varieties of small insect life that in their various stages infest vegetation appear to furnish the whole of the food of this useful and harmless species. Though frequently seen flitting through the branches in close proximity to both Willow-Wrens and Chiffchaffs, the excessive brightness of their plumage renders it impossible to confuse them with those birds.

The nest of the Wood-Wren has come under my observation in many localities in both England and Scotland. In every instance it has been placed on the ground, or, at most, at an elevation of only a few inches. Owing to the effect which much of the timber, beneath which this species places its nest, produces on vegetation, it is not unfrequently found in situations where the immediate cover is somewhat scanty. Though there are, of course, many exceptions, the Willow-Wren and Chiffchaff for the most part conceal their nests with greater care, at times in rank grass with a small mouse-like track to the entrance. I have now and then come across the nest of a Wood-Wren built almost openly on the bare ground, merely sheltered by a few straggling tufts of herbage or some twining plant in which a few dead leaves have caught and lodged. If cautiously watched, the birds may now and then be detected dropping like stones from one of the overhanging branches to the immediate vicinity of the nest.

The cradle itself is domed, with a side entrance, resembling, to a certain degree, the nests of the Willow-Wren and Chiffchaff. It is, however, seldom so elaborately worked up, the construction of the exterior being looser, and the lining of the interior, which is devoid of feathers, being for the most part less finished. The eggs, which are a shade larger than those of its relatives, are of a beautiful pinkish white ground, thickly marked with rich warm brown spots. Like the eggs of all the family, they lose their beauty soon after incubation commences. Those seen in the cabinet of the collector bear also but a faint resemblance to the appearance they presented when fresh laid.

NORTHERN VARIETY & ORDINARY FORM

# WILLOW-WREN.

## *PHYLLOSCOPUS TROCHILUS.*

---

............... of our ............ ............ ... ... over ............ in the spring, and the ............ ............ ............ ............ ............ ............ ............ own observations, Willow-............ ............ ............ ............ ............ ............ ............ my note-books show that stragglers ............ ............ ............ ............ ............ ............ ............ 10th of May. On one occasion I received ............ ............ ............ ............ ............ ............ to the conclusion belonged to this species, from one of the ............ ............ east ............ ............ ............ the birds came on board during the first week in May.

Though the difference between the Willow-Wren and Chiffchaff is obvious to most scientific observers when the bird is fresh-killed, I doubt if many who have written pages on their history could point out each species when first landed on our shores. It may possibly be easy to distinguish separately the two species while flitting up a hedgerow or eagerly searching for insects in the herbage on the shingle-banks; but I must confess I would not undertake to successfully accomplish this task myself until their accustomed haunts were reached. The Wood-Wren can scarcely be confounded with the Willow-Wren or Chiffchaff; its brighter colours are particularly conspicuous when the sun is shining, and though measurements prove there is little difference in the size, it has always the appearance of a longer and altogether larger bird. Not unfrequently Willow-Wrens as well as Chiffchaffs resort to situations in which the timber is smaller and the undergrowth more dense than in the usual haunts of the Wood-Wren; I have remarked this fact in many parts of the country. The nests of Willow-Wrens and Chiffchaffs may occasionally be seen in such spots as a ditch in a hay-field, with simply a thorn-bush and a few brambles for shelter, or on a rough sloping bank beneath an overhanging hedgerow. The Wood-Wren evidently prefers the shade of larger and more spreading timber. There is, however, no certain rule, since, in England as well as in Scotland, I have detected the Willow-Wren and Wood-Wren breeding within a short distance of one another and in localities almost precisely similar.

When once at home in their summer quarters there is little or no chance of confusing the Willow-Wren and Chiffchaff. In many localities among the woodlands and coverts of Sussex and other southern counties the actions, song, and breeding-habits of the two species can be studied and compared from the same spot. I am unable to draw attention to any striking dissimilarity in the actions of the two birds. As they flit from leaf to leaf or hover for a moment in quest of an insect, it would, I am of opinion, be difficult to point out which was which, when, as is often the case, both species may be noticed on the limbs of the same tree. The note, however, which is repeatedly uttered, at once proclaims the species of the songster—that of the Willow-Wren consisting of a short and somewhat plaintive warble, while the Chiffchaff merely gives utterance to a monotonous repetition of the syllables from which its English name is derived.

The localities selected for nesting-purposes are frequently so exceedingly similar, that I consider it hopeless to attempt to point out any difference in this respect. A thick tuft of grass in a hedgerow, or a convenient shelter below some creeping bush in a plantation or wood, is frequently made use of by both species. The Willow-Wren at times resorts to situations in which to rear its brood considerably out of character with those usually selected. Early in June 1867 I discovered a nest placed in a cavity among some rough stones that had been built up like a wall to strengthen the crumbling bank below a hill-road in Glenlyon, in Perthshire. The structure, which was externally composed of the usual materials, such as dried strands and blades of grass, looked somewhat singular among the grey and weather-beaten slabs of rock. It was located at least four feet from the level of the ground, a tuft or two of short grass, a trailing bramble, together with a few ivy-leaves being the sole signs of vegetation in the immediate vicinity. The absence of suitable cover could hardly have been the cause of such an exposed site being chosen, as within the distance of a few yards a straggling grove of alder and hazel, with abundant undergrowth, stretched down to the banks of the Lyon. The hill-side above the road was also densely wooded, beech and larch forming the chief of the larger timber. Here I have repeatedly noticed both Willow- and Wood-Wrens, and have also detected their nests on several occasions. In many of the wild glens in this part of the country I found Willow-Wrens excessively numerous in the plantations of silver birch among the hills, their notes being heard on all sides during still weather in the early summer. In every instance where the nests came under my observation they were carefully concealed in the same description of herbage to which the birds resort in England, and frequently at no great distance from the rugged stem of one of the drooping birches. Though the position, construction, and form (domed, with a side entrance) of the nests of the Willow-Wren and Chiffchaff differ but slightly, the eggs vary considerably, and at once point out the species to which they belong. The egg of the Willow-Wren has a pinkish-white ground, blotched with spots of light red towards the larger end; while the markings on that of the Chiffchaff are of a claret-colour, and generally more diffused over the surface, the ground-tint being of the same beautiful and transparent hue.

The Willow-Wren is probably the commonest of the family, and on the whole more generally distributed over the British Islands than either the Wood-Wren or the Chiffchaff. I do not, however, consider this species so abundant as the Wood-Wren in the counties to the north of Inverness, where I have as yet been unable to detect the Chiffchaff. Early in the autumn these birds may be seen making their way towards the south coast. I have frequently remarked considerable additions to the natives of the locality in the neighbourhood of Brighton by the beginning of August. The first detachments, I believe, take their departure across the channel shortly after they have made their appearance in the district. For several successive days at this season I have remarked the haunts lately alive with recent arrivals totally deserted, till, with a change of weather, their places were filled by fresh comers. On fine still mornings (especially with a light westerly breeze, succeeding rain and heavy weather) these small migrants may be noticed working their way slowly from cover to cover, steadily advancing towards the      . As many as ten or a dozen, or even a score, may now and then be in view at one time in the           a short distance of the sea-shore, the whole party eagerly searching for insects on the plants and                           being one of their favourite hunting-grounds. Doubtless Willow-Wrens and Chiffchaffs           at this season, though the task of naming each individual specimen as it flits through the leaves would, I am afraid, puzzle even our greatest authorities. During the spring a newly killed                   identified by the colour of the tarsi, those of the Willow-Wren being of a                       while      legs and feet of the Chiffchaff are considerably darker. Towards the                                        juveniles, this distinction is by                           I have seen young birds whose identity it appeared impossible to determine by a cursory glance. Although, as         writers inform us, the general colouring of the plumage of the Willow-Wren is brighter than that of the Chiffchaff, it would, I believe, be close investigation, be discovered that there is many an exception to this rule. The plumage of young birds of this species is of a decidedly warmer tinge of yellow than the adults; immature Chiffchaffs also exhibit this heightened colouring.

Almost every writer on ornithology has drawn attention to the pleasing note of this lively species; and although I fully agree with them on this subject when the song is heard in bright and sunny weather, I have often remarked how excessively monotonous this frequently repeated ditty becomes if listened to in the depths of some dense wood when black clouds and a leaden sky foretell an impending storm. With the exception of its relative the Chiffchaff, whose constant performance, under such circumstances, is still more irritating, the voices of almost the whole of the feathered tribe are now hushed, though possibly some pugnacious old cock Pheasant may give vent to a loud and startling crow in response to the rumble of a distant clap. As the gloom increases, and while scarcely a leaf is seen to stir in the sultry air, unless disturbed by one of these irrepressible Warblers as it flits from twig to twig, their wearisome notes continue to break out on all sides. The heavy rain-drops as they patter on the leaves, and the peals of thunder echoing far and near, always appear a decided relief, the tiresome melody of these persevering birds being either completely drowned in the general downpour, or the musicians themselves forced to seek shelter till the storm has passed over.

There is no more harmless species than the Willow-Wren among our British birds. Though it has been reported that these Warblers occasionally feed on fruit, I am of opinion this is a mistaken statement. According to my own observations, insects of various kinds form almost if not the whole of their insect diet. When watching their habits during the early summer in some of the northern forests where fir and birch are intermixed, I remarked that these Warblers almost exclusively confined their attentions to the larch, the particular insects they were then in quest of appearing to resort exclusively to the latter. Numbers of small birds, consisting principally of Coal and Blue Tits, with occasional Goldcrests, and here and there a wandering Crested Tit, might also be met with; but these, for the most part, were to be seen closely investigating the limbs of the fir. From an entry in one of ............ under date of June 24rd, I find that quantities of Willow-Wrens resorted to a garden in the ............ in order to feed on the green aphides on the currant-bushes. .................................................... in clearing off this swarm of insects.

Scientific ............ inform us ........ in the ........ regions ...... Willow-Wren (*Phylloscopus trochilus*) loses all traces ........................ in its ............. To this form, viz. the Arctic Willow-Wren, I conclude a specimen I shot ........................ May ........ be ascribed[*].

The Plate shows this ........................... with an ordinary individual (obtained in the spring) for comparison, and renders all .........................................

Before shooting the bird I had little or no opportunity of observing it, the weather being exceedingly blusterous. The note, which appeared to resemble that of a Whitethroat, first attracted my attention, when I fired at once, being at the time engaged in procuring a few small birds for a tame Owl. Owing to a heavy shower it was impossible either to see clearly or hear distinctly; so I do not pretend to describe the note accurately; I merely state my first impression.

---

[*] This is the opinion of naturalists who have examined the bird

# CHIFFCHAFF.

## *PHYLLOSCOPUS COLLYBITA.*

We are informed by several writers that the Chiffchaff occasionally winters in the British Islands. This, however, has entirely escaped my notice. The majority of these birds, I believe, arrive on our shores shortly in advance of the Willow-Wren, though I have seldom detected their presence at the early date frequently assigned to them. The latest straggler that ever came under my observation in the autumn was seen in a plantation near Brighton about the middle of October. A Hedge-Sparrow (usually the most retiring of the feathered tribe) evidently considering the small visitor, who was certainly cut up by a drifting rain and a cold wind, somewhat out of place at this season, attacked it with the utmost fury and forced it to seek the shelter of some evergreen shrubs.

In the southern counties this species appears very generally distributed. I have remarked it more abundant to the south of London than in any other part of the British Islands. In the north of England I met with but few, and up to the present date entirely failed to identify the Chiffchaff in Scotland. Two or three close observers of birds assured me that in certain localities it may be found every summer. In order to satisfy myself that this species advanced so far north, I undertook some years ago, while collecting specimens in the Highlands, a journey of several miles across the hills; and although the object was not accomplished, a short and condensed extract from my notes concerning the expedition may not be out of place, as it will serve to indicate the style of country the bird is stated to resort to in that district.

"Shortly after pulling up at the ―― Inn, I recognized an old acquaintance from the braes of Rannoch, frequently encountered during my wanderings in the Highlands. The man was a good authority on the birds of this district; and while giving an account of the rarities lately seen, he happened to mention the fact that a pair or two of Chiffchaffs were this season nesting in a wild glen to the north. My informant was a curious character; but I was well aware Duncan was perfectly acquainted with the species when he once made an assertion to that effect, as he had formerly assisted me on several occasions in Scotland, and had also visited the south of England, where he had picked up his knowledge of the bird as well as its note. Being anxious to satisfy myself as to the presence of this Warbler so far north, I determined to search the locality. To reach the spot it was necessary to make our way over some thirty miles of rough hill-roads, in places almost impassable to any ordinary vehicle. The conveyance in which I was travelling was a large and heavy four-wheel waggonette, and utterly useless for this purpose; so I allowed Duncan to borrow a machine from some accommodating friend in which we could perform the journey. I must confess I was somewhat doubtful as to how far we might be carried on our way when the rickety old shandridan was first pulled up at the door for my inspection. As my attendant, however, was able and willing to bear the whole amount of baggage in the event of a breakdown, I decided to make the attempt on the following morning. The sky, at daybreak, was gloomy and overcast; there was, however, every prospect of fine weather when we started from the inn. A stock of provisions and liquor had been laid in, as I anticipated that the bill of fare at the shealing to which we were bound would prove exceedingly limited. After mounting a steep brae, up which it was necessary to walk in order to ease the beast, we descended by an unpleasantly rough track to a fairly level road, and the next ten miles were speedily passed over. So far but little of interest in the bird way had been met with. Grey Crows I noticed at intervals hunting the open moors and also perched by the wayside. These mischievous brutes are not treated as vermin in a forest; and this fact doubtless accounted for the utter contempt with which they regarded us. Here and there a Stonechat fluttered from bush to bush in front of the trap as we passed along the open ground, while beneath the shade of the large and spreading pines an occasional glimpse of a Redstart was obtained as it darted into the cover on our approach. Several of these birds, and the usual numbers of Willow-Wrens and Coal Tits which are to be met with in almost every Highland glen where fir and birch abound, composed the greater part of the small fry that came under observation. A stray Pipit, a Lark or two, and some Blue Tits showed themselves within a short distance of the roadside; but it was not till we pulled up for a rest near the shores of a small wooded loch that any thing of note came in view. The wants of the quadruped having been attended to, we sat down in a cosy nook to refresh ourselves. Before our meal was half completed, a Crested Tit made its appearance, hopping from twig to twig in a small fir immediately above my head; in a few moments the inquisitive little fellow was down among the heather-stalks within a yard of our feet, and next disappeared in a juniper bush, where he was shortly joined by another. Here I noticed them creeping among the lower portions of the stems, where they appeared busily engaged for some moments, when they again made their way to the pines. The spot we had selected for our midday halt was a slight clearing in a patch of straggling Scotch firs by the side of the hill-track we had followed. A few scattered birches interspersed with dense bushes of juniper stretched down to the shores of the loch, while here and there a lofty pine raised its crest above the surrounding undergrowth. A burn swarming with small trout, which were darting in countless numbers hither and thither in the eddies, and ultimately disappearing among the red stones, rolled down from the hills within a short distance of where we were encamped. Among the waving leaves of the birch trees, Willow-Wrens were moving on all sides; and the unmistakable note of a Wood-Wren was detected in some thick cover a short distance up the burn-side. Arming myself with an extra-strong pair of field-glasses, I made my way into the plantation, and choosing a dry spot beneath a thick fir, sat down to keep a watch for whatever might come into view. Before many minutes had elapsed, an Osprey, evidently a male, passed along the loch-side. The bird was sailing round in large circles at the height of perhaps fifty or sixty feet above the water, and was shortly out of sight. I was considerably surprised at the appearance of the Fishing-Eagle at this season, as the nearest eyry I was acquainted with was distant at least thirty miles as the Crow flies. The first to approach my place of concealment was a Goldcrest, followed a few minutes later by a Tree-Creeper, whose frequent visits to an old rotten stump revealed the spot where his newly hatched brood was snugly hidden. Willow-Wrens were repeatedly in view; but still the long-expected Chiffchaff remained invisible. Though the early hours of the day had been occasionally dull and threatening, the weather was now fine and bright; and a pleasant breeze keeping those unbearable pests the midges at bay, I was in little hurry to resume our journey. While almost dozing, a low whistle caught my ear. At first I imagined it was Duncan attempting to draw my attention to something he had noticed; but an immediate repetition revealed the fact that the note proceeded from the nearest edge of the loch. For some moments, though it appeared familiar, I was at a loss to account for the sound, when I remembered the call of the female Goosander to her brood, frequently heard the previous year while collecting specimens in another locality. Though I had watched many broods, the male, at this season, had invariably escaped observation; and being anxious to ascertain his state of plumage, I determined to crawl down to the water's edge in order to obtain a view of the party in case a Drake might happen to be on the loch. While proceeding with the utmost caution through the cover (there were dead and rotten limbs on all sides, and to snap a twig would have been good-bye to my chance of obtaining a view of the brood), I caught a momentary glimpse of a single bird, apparently belonging to this species, swimming some twenty or thirty yards from the shore. Considering it most probable, from what I had already learned concerning their habits at this season, that the male, if present, would be keeping his own company at some distance from the family, I came to the conclusion that this might possibly be the bird of which I was in want. Returning at once to our encampment, an air-gun, which I had brought in order to obtain any specimens of small birds, was rapidly put into working order. The barrel having travelled among the rods and the stock in the lunch-hamper, the weapon had escaped the notice of Duncan, who was evidently somewhat surprised at its appearance. His astonishment increased when the movement of a spring disclosed an aperture on the top of the barrel into which a bullet was dropped. As I fully expected to be able to crawl within about thirty yards of the fowl a bullet from the rifled barrel of this weapon would be quite as effective for procuring a single bird, as the charge of an ordinary gun, without disturbing the neighbourhood, which I was anxious to avoid. An antiquated Highlander, who was plodding along the road with a home-made rod on his shoulder, had been detained by my watchful companion by an inviting wave of the bottle, as he imagined the old body might alarm the birds by showing himself at the next turn of the road. Enjoining the strictest silence, I started again for the loch, and had reached within some twenty yards of the shore, when a Warbler, which passed within a few feet of my head, settled among the foliage of a birch. I was unable to detect any note; but the view I obtained almost satisfied me the bird was a Chiffchaff; its constant movements, however, among the drooping leaves of the birch rendered a shot with a single bullet almost hopeless. Unfortunately my weapon was only breech-loading for ball, and the shot and ramrod had been left where we had lunched. In a few moments the bird had worked its way across the burn; and as it would have been necessary to return some hundreds of yards if I wished to cross dry-footed, I determined to proceed first in quest of the Goosander family, anticipating little or no difficulty in again finding the Warbler when provided with small shot. On reaching the extremity of the cover, and carefully scanning the surface of the loch, I could detect no signs of the single fowl. An old female Goosander was paddling slowly to windward with a brood of six or eight, the young ones following close in her wake. While watching the retreating brood through the glasses, a few heavy drops of rain gave warning that the hills to the south were obscured by mist and heavy squalls approaching. Rapidly retracing my steps, I soon reached the spot where Duncan was awaiting my return. Though the delay that occurred was short, a drifting rain was upon us before I had obtained the shot and implements required. As it seemed useless to start in search of so small a bird during the continuance of such unfavourable weather, I determined to collect our impedimenta and start at once for the bothy where we were to pass the night. I was in hopes we should still find the Warblers either where my informant first had heard them, or on our return in the plantation in which I had just lost sight of the doubtful bird. After collecting and packing our scattered property, which was somewhat mixed and confused (rods, guns, and creels having all been got ready for use), we were soon off for the next stage. On leaving the loch-side our course lay through a wooded glen; and as large stones and rocks encumbered the track and rendered locomotion decidedly rough, we were forced to proceed on foot for at least a couple of miles. The country became at last more open; and a high brae clear of timber was shortly reached. From this point barren and treeless moors stretched in every direction, though belts of dark and gloomy pines were in sight at some elevation on the hill-sides. We were now travelling due north, and consequently avoided the unpleasant effects of the squalls of drifting southerly rain. There was, unfortunately, every appearance of a dirty night: a dense mist was sweeping along well down the mountain-slopes; and the tops and higher ranges were all invisible. At length, during a break in the showers, when the clouds had rolled somewhat further up the hills, I noticed the country appeared to wear a familiar look, and soon discovered we were entering a glen I was well acquainted with. The road was now more even, and mounting the trap, we spun along downhill at a pace that promised to bring us to our destination before nightfall. Not a bird, with the exception of two or three Grey Crows and a Peregrine, had come under observation since leaving the loch-side. In an old weatherbeaten fir in one of the pine forests, I well remembered that, when last in the district, an Eagle used to nest regularly. On inquiring of my companion if the bird still resorted to the same spot, he replied, after some slight hesitation, that in the preceding season the nest had been 'tampered with,' and, to the best of his belief, it was now untenanted. It was quite evident that Duncan knew more than he chose to relate concerning the robbery of the eggs; but, from previous knowledge of his character, I was well aware that there was more chance of hearing the true story concerning the fact by assuming an utter indifference to the subject. Consequently the next few hundred yards were passed in absolute silence. We were now slowly climbing a steep rise; and by the number of times he turned his head towards the wood, I could see poor Duncan was anxious to unburden his conscience of any participation he might have had in the crime. At length, after a good deal of beating about the bush, he remarked that, early in the spring of the previous year, he felt an irresistible inclination to become the possessor of an Eagle's egg—to use his own words, uttered in a most deprecating manner, 'just to take an egg to myself.' In order to accomplish this object, and also to avoid being recognized in the locality, he crossed the country by a hill-track instead of following the usual road, and, descending into the glen soon after dusk, reached the vicinity of the nest shortly before midnight. The weather was fine and clear, and, being well acquainted with the country, he made his way rapidly through the wood, scarcely turning to the right or left till he stood within some sixty or seventy yards of the tree. On casting his eyes upwards he was excessively startled on beholding close to the nest the dark figure of a human being clearly defined against the eastern sky. Hastily withdrawing into a deep shadow cast by a large slab of rock, he watched the actions of the unknown slowly descending limb by limb from the tree. At last the descent was accomplished and the identity of the culprit at once revealed, as, while retracing his steps he passed within three feet of the spot where my informant was in hiding. I shall not weary my readers by a long recital of Duncan's indignation while moralizing on the wickedness of this reprehensible individual, who turned out to be a character I was well acquainted with, and who, if current reports were to be credited, could scarcely be looked upon as having too much loyalty on his mind.

The wind shifting and which ever since we reached the low ground, and the wind rising rapidly in fitful gusts, partly indicated that it would be useless to wait any time in searching some very likely cover we were then passing, on the chance of meeting with Warblers. By the time our quarters were reached the fine rain had increased to a steady downpour, which continued till after sunset. The spot where the birds had been seen was only about a mile distant, and, hoping for finer weather the following morning, we made no more ado but turned in by 9 p.m.

During the night the wind grew still more boisterous, but on turning out it was evident that all chance of success was hopeless. After wasting an hour or two the pony was put to, and we made the best of our way to the spot by the loch-side where we had halted on the previous day. Though remaining here for three hours, I failed to recognize more than two or three Warblers in even the most sheltered parts of the woods. A couple that I shot being unable to distinguish the species among the waving branches, turned out to be a Willow-Wren and a Wood-Wren. Before reaching our journey's end we again pulled up, and I closely examined some small birds noticed by the roadside; but, although Willow-Wrens were again met with, my search for the Chiffchaff proved an utter failure."

In order that the nest and eggs, the **situations** resorted to for breeding-purposes, as well as the note and general **habits of** this species might be compared with the manners and customs of the Willow-Wren, I have briefly referred to those subjects under the heading of that Warbler.

# DARTFORD WARBLER.

## SYLVIA PROVINCIALIS.

---

Though scarcely to be considered rare, the present species is decidedly local. I have only met with it in the south-eastern counties.

A few years back, Dartford Warblers were to be found in many of the large patches of furze scattered over the South Downs; but the constant demand for their nests and eggs by collectors and dealers has, as might have been expected, at length thinned down their numbers considerably, and many of their former haunts are now deserted. There are, however, still colonies to be met with, as on the only occasion I closely searched one of their favourite resorts among the hills, during the season of 1882, I noticed three separate pairs, and doubtless there were others in the district. Being remarkably shy, these birds are liable to escape observation, as on the slightest signs of danger they immediately seek the shelter of the densest bushes. In order to gain an insight into the habits of many of our small birds, it is necessary to reach the localities they frequent shortly after daybreak. Before the sun is fairly up, several species, whose very existence would never be recognized during a midday visit to their quarters, may, if care is exercised, be closely watched and their actions studied. In the early morning the note of the male, which somewhat resembles that of the Whitethroat, may be constantly heard, the bird mounting at short intervals to the topmost twigs of the furze and flitting from bush to bush.

In the winter, though they perform no ................................................ a roving disposition. I have repeatedly come across a pair or ................................. thorn bushes and straggling furze on the beach between Eastbourne and Pevensey; ............... rabbit-shooting further inland, stray birds were occasionally driven out by the beagles from cover where the species was seldom, if ever, found during the summer months. To the best of my recollection, I have never seen the Dartford Warbler at any considerable distance from furze; I mention this fact, as some accounts published concerning the localities in which these birds have been met with would almost lead to the belief that the Hedge-Sparrow * has been mistaken for this species.

The nest, which is constructed of dried grass and roots, is usually placed in a thick furze bush, and is by no means easy to discover, unless the old birds are carefully watched. If deprived of their first nest, one pair will continue attempting to rear a brood till late in the season, even after having been robbed of three or four sets of eggs. By the end of summer the male and female have in most cases worn their plumage considerably. A pair shot in July would present a very different appearance to specimens obtained in April, before the cares of providing for their families had removed the gloss from their feathers. I remarked the young were repeatedly fed on the bodies of moderately sized buff or pale yellow-coloured moths. The wings of these insects had been removed, but I am of opinion they belonged to the species known as *Leucania pallens*. I particularly noticed that the birds hunted for their prey among the lower portions of the stems of the old dead furze.

* One of these birds moving stealthily through cover or darting rapidly across a track much resembles this Warbler.

# WREN.
## *TROGLODYTES VULGARIS.*

There are few parts of the British Islands in which this diminutive species is not well known. The name of Jenny Wren is almost as familiar in most localities as that of Cock Robin. Like the latter, the Wren (in England and Scotland at all events) is exempt from the persecution that is not unfrequently inflicted on other small birds. Even the juvenile members of the population appear to have a respect for their nests; and it is but seldom that their eggs or young are molested. In some country districts, particularly in East Sussex, I remarked it was considered unlucky even to touch their nest, the general impression being that if only a finger was inserted the structure would be deserted.

I have now and then recognized this active little bird in the most exposed situations, where I should never have looked for or even expected to find it unless I had accidentally become aware of its presence. On a rough and stormy day early in June 1878, I made an attempt to cross the hills from Inverness-shire into one of the neighbouring counties, but, owing to the force of the wind, which had rapidly increased into a perfect hurricane, was compelled to turn back before half the journey was accomplished. While sheltering from a blinding squall behind some slabs of rock near the entrance of the pass, my attention was attracted by the shrill notes of the consequential little songster, who was strutting up and down on a large block of stone. Heavy drops of rain and sleet pattered on the rock; but for a time he kept his position in defiance of the storm. At last a furious gust of wind, which, as it howled through the crags near the summit of the cliffs, dislodged several massive splinters of granite, came roaring down the glen, and literally swept the tiny mite from his perch. A few minutes later, when the main force of the squall had passed over, he was singing again as gaily as ever on the dripping stones. The loudness of the notes and the distance at which they were audible were somewhat astonishing considering the size of the performer. On other occasions I have found this species located far up among the hills, where heather, coarse grass, and a few moorland plants were the only covering to the steep mountain-side. On the approach of winter, I believe these birds betake themselves to more sheltered quarters on the low ground. I cannot call to mind having noticed a single specimen at any elevation on the hills when the country was covered with snow.

During the cold nights of winter, Wrens commonly collect together at roosting-time for warmth. Shortly before dusk I have repeatedly watched as many as eight or ten flying, one after another, into a hole in a haystack or the thatch of an outhouse.

The habits of this species, as well as its manner of nesting, have been so accurately described by several writers, and are so generally well known, that any description I could give would be superfluous.

# GOLDEN-CRESTED WREN.

## *REGULUS CRISTATUS.*

---

The Golden-crested Wren is distributed over the British Islands from north to south, occurring perhaps most abundantly in the neighbourhood of extensive fir-plantations. Though this familiar and lively little bird remains with us as a resident throughout the year, I have noticed in several counties that fresh arrivals take place in autumn; and such being the case, it is reasonable to suppose a corresponding number leave in spring.

In the Highlands this species may be described as decidedly local, the large tracts of barren moorland being rarely visited, though I have on more than one occasion remarked a small party in some straggling belt of firs on the mountain-side. I never detected these birds at any considerable elevation on the hills, even though the tops were well wooded.

There is not the slightest doubt that immense flights at times reach this country from across the North Sea during the autumn. Early one morning, about the middle of October 1863, I discovered a plantation of Scotch firs near North Berwick, on the coast of East Lothian, literally swarming with these birds. On numberless trees, especially in the more sheltered parts of the wood, they were clustered thickly on the lower branches, eagerly searching for food. As they took not the slightest notice of the presence of several observers, it is probable these tiny travellers had but recently made the land, famished and worn out by the length of their journey. When once their strength is regained, the birds forming these gatherings soon disperse, and move onward to some fresh locality. On reaching the spot the following morning, provided with a supply of dust-shot and powerful field-glasses, in order to learn if any Firecrests were in their ranks, I was unable to detect a single specimen of either species. Considering it most probable the birds might be met with in some of the neighbouring fir-woods, I turned westward and thoroughly searched several plantations without success. As a large flight was reported on the coast of Northumberland immediately after this date, it was evident the army of Goldcrests had proceeded in an easterly direction, and followed the coast-line towards the south.

Judging from my own observations, and also by the information received from fishermen and others engaged in the North Sea, I conclude there is little doubt that when few are noticed on our coasts contrary winds and prolonged storms have claimed their victims and the birds have perished at sea. With the exception of some five or six individuals, I have never personally met with this species while crossing the North Sea during the autumnal migration; though on one occasion the remains of a dozen at least were detected, together with a few unfortunate Tree-Sparrows and Chaffinches, drowned and draggled in the water in the bottom of a smack's boat, in which they had probably taken refuge on the previous night to escape the force of the drifting squalls. Several fishermen well acquainted with the bird have assured me that, about the height of the herring-voyage, scores have occasionally settled on the luggers to rest. One man in particular, who had repeatedly watched their movements, stated that they would roost all night in any shelter they could find, some even creeping into the blocks, where he remarked they would remain "weeping*" all night," and in the morning fly down and pick about on the corks and other portions of the nets that were out of water. A cold wind and the spray of the breaking seas would often prove fatal to those already exhausted, and numbers were at times discovered either utterly helpless or dead. As it appeared that these birds were known to the men by the name of "Herring-Spink," I was particular in inquiring whether they referred to the Chaffinch (a frequent visitor to the boats during October), and was at once satisfied they were well acquainted with that bird. During the seasons I was in communication with the light-ships off the east coast, I could gather but little information concerning the Golden-crested Wren from any of the crews of those vessels. I, however, received a wing from the "Lynn Well" early in the spring of 1873, which would tend to prove that a few at least return towards the north of Europe after passing the winter on our shores.

Though there is a general movement southward as winter approaches, I never either met with or received information concerning one of the immense flights of Goldcrests except in the vicinity of the coast and during autumn. As early as the beginning of October I have remarked considerable additions to the residents in Sussex, small parties being noticed in all parts of the county flitting along the hedgerows in the open, as well as roaming through plantations with dense and rank undergrowth. At this season they frequently make their appearance in gardens, climbing over the shrubs and plants and closely investigating all likely spots where insects are concealed. Occasionally for a short time they join in company with Blue or Coal Tits and other small birds. In order to capture minute insects, such as gnats and flies, situated on the under surface of the foliage, I have repeatedly observed these birds hovering below the spot and snapping up their prey while on wing. The singular actions of a brightly tinted male, one of a small flock of ten or a dozen, particularly attracted my attention as the party were working their way through a garden near Brighton in the autumn of 1882. After carefully searching the bark of several trees, the bird reached a somewhat faded and dilapidated willow, and immediately darting at the leaves, he seized them one after another in his bill, tugging apparently in the most desperate manner, each leaf evidently passing completely between his mandibles. I noticed this performance repeated at least twenty times within three or four yards of where I was standing. For some weeks previous to this date (October 10th) the stems of the willows had been infested by swarms of black aphides, which had produced a dark and glutinous secretion on the foliage immediately below where they were located. Possibly the flavour of this nastiness was grateful to the palate of the tiny Kinglet; I can imagine no other cause for his eccentric behaviour. Several of these Wrens while climbing up the stems of the willows halted for a moment and after intently regarding the heaving mass of aphides, immediately passed on without further delay. I never detected one of the feathered tribe feeding on the black aphis, though the green is eagerly sought after by several of our Warblers.

In December 1884 I observed a wandering party of five or six Goldcrests, together with as many Blue Tits, flitting from stem to stem through the reeds on Heigham Sounds in Norfolk. As soon as a few stunted alders along the bank were reached, the Wrens made their way towards a neighbouring plantation, while their former companions continued hunting for insects among the reeds and rushes. This is the only occasion on which I have noticed the species frequenting the reed-beds over the water, though they commonly resort to the neighbouring woods and plantations.

I never detected any large gathering of the Golden-crested Wren in the early spring, at which date they would be supposed to start on their return journey towards the north. Though I spent two or three seasons almost daily along the shores of the Firth of Forth (where the vast swarm was met with in

* This does not imply that the birds uttered any sounds of lamentation; it is simply the best manner of describing a low and plaintive note

October 1863), I remarked no accession to the usual inhabitants of the district. I also failed to notice any quantity of these birds in early spring on the Norfolk coast.

The elaborately constructed and beautifully finished pendent nest of this species is well known to all who take an interest in bird-life, being frequently seen in the various descriptions of yew and ornamental fir in gardens and pleasure-grounds. In the Highlands this species appears to entertain an especial fancy for plantations of Scotch fir of from ten or twelve to fifteen years' growth. I have repeatedly remarked this fact in the counties of Ross, Inverness, and Perthshire.

# WOOD-PIGEON.

## COLUMBA PALUMBUS.

THE destruction of birds of prey, combined with the larger extent of ground of late years devoted to plantations, is supposed to account for the rapid increase in the numbers of the Wood-Pigeon. During 1863 and the following year, while studying farming in East Lothian, I met with ample opportunities for observing the immense gatherings of these birds occasionally witnessed in autumn and early winter. The loss caused by the countless swarms in various parts of the country could not be serious, though had *** been a ***, *********** *** ******, **** **** *** **** *** * ***** ********* **** **** ******* **** ***** ** *** *** ******** ** ****** * ***** ********. In order to scare the flocks it was the custom in *** ***** ** ****** ** *** armed with some antiquated fowling-piece and a supply of powder; wee laddies, **** *** ***** ** *** farm, were not unfrequently entrusted with the work, and the value of their services in protecting the crops from plunder may readily be estimated. Though invariably on the alert awaiting the arrival of the Doos * while the farmer or the grieve † were in sight, these precocious youths, having provided themselves with shot, passed most of their time in endeavouring to circumvent the hares or Pheasants that strayed from the coverts.

The high standard of farming in this locality does not permit the presence in the corn-crops of the rank weeds that prove so attractive to the Wood-Pigeon in many less favoured districts, consequently the agriculturists, having few chances of ascertaining its redeeming qualities, failed to appreciate the species, and made strenuous efforts to reduce its numbers. As far as I was able to judge, the thousands that were stated to have been killed by the association formed for their destruction appeared to have but slight effect in checking the evil.

In the south of England I have heard but few grave charges brought against these birds by the farmers, and it is obvious that much of their sustenance consists of worthless seeds and berries. The beech-plantations on the chalky downs of Sussex are a favourite resort for this species, and flocks varying from fifty to one hundred may occasionally be seen, though, according to my own experience, the birds are never met with in this locality in anything approaching the numbers observed in the south of Scotland. Shortly before harvest Wood-Pigeons may often be seen flying in small parties to the fields of wheat or barley; after wheeling round for a time the birds will disappear from view in the standing corn. An examination of the state of the ground on which they were lost sight of would doubtless cause astonishment to those who imagined that the birds were in pursuit of grain: on reaching the spot it would be discovered that for a considerable space the crop was exceedingly scanty, completely choked, in fact, by a mass of weeds rank and strong, whose seeds, well nigh ripe, had proved the sole attraction.

A small tribute, however, is annually levied on the field-peas shortly before they are carried, and turnip-

---

\* Wood-Pigeons are always spoken of as Doos by the natives of this district.
† The farm-bailiff is known by this title in East Lothian.

greens suffer considerably in winter when food is scarce. Cabbage-plants are also attacked; I remarked the birds feeding greedily on the leaves about the end of June in the neighbourhood of Brighton in 1881.

On the extensive shingle-banks lying between Shoreham Harbour and the coast-line luxuriant beds of wild tares have gradually formed; here, towards the end of the summer, when the pods are ripe, numbers of Pigeons are attracted to feast upon the seeds. During fine weather a constant stream of birds may be seen crossing and recrossing the harbour from the woods on the downs, the flight being continued from shortly after daylight till well on in the afternoon. Small parties frequently alight at the brackish pools in the salt-water marshes and also on the shore itself; in all probability drink (of a saline nature) rather than food is the object of their visits to such spots.

Though but few attractions are offered to this species on the barren moorlands of the Northern Highlands, the more extensive glens, which usually contain a certain amount of timber, along the river-side, as well as scattered plantations, afford ample shelter during the nesting-season to large numbers of Pigeons. To the wild and wooded gorges in the valley of the Beauly many pairs resort, their nests being placed for the most part in firs, though I met with one or two in the drooping moss-grown birches that overhang the course of the river. In autumn, when shooting on the moors in the west of Perthshire, I frequently drove out small parties of ten or a dozen Pigeons from the cover of the stunted birch bushes that fringe the mountain-burns at a considerable elevation on the hill-sides; little if any inducement (except the berries of some hardy plant) could be found to account for the presence of the birds in such remote and desolate spots.

It is probable that Wood-Pigeons arrive on our north-east coasts in considerable numbers during autumn and early winter from across the North Sea. Early in November 1863 I remarked on two occasions large flights that had apparently only recently made the land, worn and weary by the length of their journey, fluttering along the links and about the fir-plantations on the sea-coast near North Berwick in East Lothian. Doubtless also migrants occasionally make the land along the whole of our eastern coasts. My notes for 1872, while shooting in the east of Norfolk, contain the following lines:—

"Nov. 27. Heavy gale of wind from south-west. Scarcely possible to work punts on the open broad, being almost swamped by the spray. Pigeons and Fieldfares in immense numbers continued flying west during the greater part of the day; with the last of the light they were still passing over."

As the Pigeons were in company with Fieldfares and holding the same course, it may reasonably be supposed that both species had only recently arrived from the north of Europe.

The scanty collection of sticks prepared by the Wood-Pigeon for the accommodation of its anticipated brood is too well known to need description. As a rule, in Sussex, the nests are placed in fir, beech, or other forest-timber at a considerable elevation; occasionally, however, I have noticed them at the height of only six, eight, or ten feet in thorn bushes or stunted beech trees in the valleys on the South Downs. Their familiarity during the breeding-season has been referred to by most ornithological writers; for nesting-purposes these birds frequently resort to the immediate vicinity of houses. In the neighbourhood of Brighton I have repeatedly watched the female sitting on her nest on the limb of a Scotch fir, stretching immediately over a highroad, utterly regardless of the constant traffic.

# STOCK-DOVE.

## COLUMBA ŒNAS.

---

The Stock-Dove is exceedingly common in some of the southern and eastern counties of England, becoming less abundant towards the north, and appearing to be but little known in the north. Flocks numbering from twenty up to fifty, and even more, may often be seen feeding in the fields in the neighbourhood of Shoreham, near Brighton; many pairs also breed in Stanmer Park. In 1870 I found them exceedingly common on the Potter Heigham marshes in the east of Norfolk, being attracted to the locality by the newly sown fields of peas. But few came under my notice while residing in East Lothian, though in the beautifully wooded glen through which the Beauly runs near Eilean Aigas, and again in the valley of the Dhruim, I recognized several pairs. When seen from the hill-side above, as they skimmed up and down the course of the river, or perched on the moss-grown drooping birches, the contrast between this bird and the Wood-Pigeon, both species being within view in the same tree, was very marked, and at once attracted my attention, as I had been formerly led to believe that Stock-Doves were not residents in this part of the country.

This species is by no means fastidious when choosing its nesting-quarters, almost any site on which eggs might be laid appearing to be adapted to its requirements. I did not get much chance for observation, or make a search for their breeding-places, in either Norfolk or Inverness, but met with many opportunities for ascertaining their habits in Sussex within a few miles of Brighton. In May 1874, a keeper pointed out a nest in Stanmer Park on a small limb near the top of a spruce fir, at the height of about 20 feet from the ground. This structure, which was somewhat more carefully put together than that of the Wood-Pigeon, contained two young birds, in order to reach them, as I was then in need of specimens at this age, it was deemed expedient to make use of a ladder, the upper portion of the tree being too weak to admit of climbing. When taken, it was discovered that the youngsters were not sufficiently advanced for preservation, and it was necessary to rear them for a week longer; on a diet of green peas, however, they thrived rapidly, and soon acquired the desired condition of plumage. In the large elms in the same park there were also several birds sitting on eggs in the hollows formed where the stems had rotted away; in most instances no attempt had been made to form a nest, the soft dust of the decaying wood probably affording a sufficiently luxurious accommodation. The rabbit-burrows in the chalky soil on the slopes of the South Downs were also resorted to, and I noticed several pairs breeding in the face of the cliffs in the chalk-pits at Beeding and Offham. While in quest of the young of a Tawny Owl in a large wood adjoining Balcombe Forest, we alighted on a brood of juvenile Stock-Doves in a squirrel's drey on the limbs of an antiquated oak standing in a dense thicket.

# ROCK-DOVE.

## COLUMBA LIVIA.

There can be little doubt that several writers have confused the Stock-Dove, which is now well known to resort to cliffs, with this species. The situations in which the nests of the Rock-Doves in Gould's beautifully executed plate in his work on the 'Birds of Great Britain' are placed, viz. open ledges in the face of a steep cliff, plainly indicate that some breeding-place of the Stock-Dove must be represented. According to my own experience, it is only in caves—small occasionally, but for the most part deep, dark, and gloomy—that the Rock-Dove rears its young. On more than one occasion I have been assured that these birds were to be found during the breeding-season frequenting some of the Sussex chalk-pits on the downs, on visiting the spot, however, I ascertained in every instance that the presence of a few pairs of Stock-Doves had led to the mistake. The east and west caves at the Bass were also said to be tenanted by Rock-Doves, though the only Pigeons I ever observed about the rock were birds that had escaped from the large "Doocot" near ............ and had taken up their quarters in hundreds among the ruins above the entrance to the old castle. ........ birds harboured about the coast-line as far as the rocks extended towards Seacliff, and ................ a flight out to the Bass; I was, however, unable to learn that they had ever made .................... rock.

Numbers of these birds breed in the caves in the ................ overlooking the Moray Firth, their nests being placed on the ledges and in the crevices in the ........ parts of these fantastically formed caverns. I remarked repeatedly that the birds issued from fissures in the rock to which not even a ray of light appeared to penetrate. In addition to the Blue ................ were a few buff-tinted birds frequenting the caves; these were all similar in colouring, ............... escaped from some of the farm-buildings near at hand or merely varieties I had no ................... as they kept at a respectful distance, and I was unable to procure one for examination. There was .. difficulty in securing a fine pair of the Blue Doves as specimens at one of the caves, after which I allowed them to fly in and out unmolested; my visits to the locality having been made during May and June, the birds were all engaged in attending to their young. The Doves, we ascertained, were not the only occupants of the caves, as in those nearest the entrance to the Cromarty Firth we came across frequent tracks of otters.

The young Rock-Doves that are figured in the Plate were taken in a small cave on the west coast of Ross-shire, almost opposite the island of Fura, on the 27th of May, 1868. Being well in sight from below, we ascertained they were nearly full-fledged and of the age required; but how to get at them was at first a puzzle. At last we hit upon a plan that proved successful; a couple of tall sturdy Highlanders having taken their station at the foot of the rock, a third then mounted on their shoulders, after which, by the help of the mast of our fishing-boat which had been brought ashore, I managed to climb above the men and, assisted by the inequalities in the slabs of broken rock, to reach the young birds and nest.

The lodge on which their cradle was placed proved to be in an exceedingly filthy condition, Rock-Doves evidently disregarding all sanitary precautions.

Dried stalks of heather, with a few of the finer twigs and fibres of roots, had been used in the construction of the nest, which, after the manner of the surroundings, was smeared with dirt and highly odoriferous. The beaks of the juveniles were of a dull livid lead-tint, with small white knobs showing at the base; the legs and feet a livid flesh-tint. The plumage, including the markings on the wings, resembled that of the adults, but of course without the gloss on the feathers and the bright metallic tints, the white rump being especially conspicuous. A quantity of yellow hairy bristles or down showed among the scanty feathers on the head, neck, and throat, the latter being almost naked.

# TURTLE-DOVE.

## *COLUMBA TURTUR.*

---

The Turtle-Dove is one ........................................... Islands, the first week in May having usually arrived ........................................... But a short season is passed in this country, the majority taking their departure ........... September, not a single individual having come under my observation after the end of that month.

In Sussex the Turtle-Dove is exceedingly plentiful, nesting in most of the wooded districts, as well as in considerable numbers in the sheltered valleys of the South Downs. In Surrey and Middlesex it appears equally abundant; when at school at Harrow I frequently noticed the birds breeding in the woods and plantations in the neighbourhood. The broad-district of Norfolk does not appear to offer any great attraction to this species; a few pairs, however, may occasionally be found where a sufficient quantity of timber exists to meet their requirements. In the summer of 1881 I remarked an old bird, accompanied by a couple of young ones which had evidently just left the nest, in a damp and swampy alder-car near Ludham. Early on the morning of May 31, 1871, several small parties of Doves were observed flying over Breydon mud-flats, bending towards the north-west; one or two I shot were in an exceedingly bright state of plumage. Judging by their movements, it is most probable, though late in the season, that these flocks were still on their way to more northern quarters. In the neighbourhood of Doncaster, in Yorkshire, I remember shooting a few Turtle-Doves many years ago during autumn; the keepers, however, were unacquainted with the species, which possibly did not breed in the district. With the exception of a pair seen flying along the rocks between Canty Bay and Seacliffe, on the shores of the Firth of Forth, early in May 1864, I never met with the Turtle-Dove in Scotland. As far as I was able to ascertain, the bird was unknown to either keepers or gillies among whom inquiries were made in the Highlands.

A few of the complaints brought against the Wood-Pigeon as to damage inflicted on the crops are also laid to the charge of this species; in no part of the country, however, is the bird sufficiently numerous to render its presence objectionable. From frequent observations on their habits, I am fully convinced that our handsome summer visitors make ample reparation for the small amount of plunder that falls to their share; this is more especially the case in those parts of the country, unfortunately too numerous, where the farming operations are somewhat slovenly. There is little doubt that the seeds of numberless rank and injurious plants are consumed by Doves; the grain also littered in the harvest-fields goes a considerable way towards making up their humble bill of fare. In company with Wood-Pigeons I have frequently seen these birds, shortly before harvest, resorting to those portions of the corn-fields where a profusion of widely spreading weeds had choked the grain and caused a failure in the crop.

Doves often make their way to the sea-shore on the coast of Sussex during the heat of summer; constant flights may also be seen crossing the marshes towards the rivers up which the tide flows. As numberless dykes are passed at which their thirst might be appeased, it is doubtless the salt in the water that proves the attraction to such spots. The wild tares on the Shoreham shingle-banks draw large numbers of birds from the wooded part of the country many miles inland. Though repeatedly alarmed and put to flight by the local gunners, Doves, as well as Wood-Pigeons, invariably return to the abundant store of seed furnished by the heavy crop that annually springs up on this otherwise barren waste.

The nest of the Turtle-Dove resembles in construction that of the Wood-Pigeon, though for the most part of somewhat lighter build. After the manner of all the Pigeon tribe, the aspect of the squabs when newly hatched is by no means inviting: a livid and cadaverous hue pervades the naked skin; the wrinkled neck, bare head, and sightless eyes are repulsive in the extreme; while here and there, falling off by degrees as they advance in age, a yellow, straggling, hairy down in the first instance spreads over the sprouting quills.

# PHEASANT.

## *PHASIANUS COLCHICUS.*

---

have                    this country from various parts of Asia Minor, though the date at which its                         have taken place is so far back that no duly authen-
                                                                informed, however, in the fourth edition of Yarrell,
         it                                                by the Roman conquerors, who naturalized the Fallow
                                    this              is said to be derived from the Phasis, in Colchis, the banks of
                                                             attempt had been made to transport these handsome
         distant countries.
                                         in most of the English counties where protection is afforded them by an
                                                    is well wooded and the surrounding fields sufficiently
            suit                       In the            greater attention is paid by sportsmen to
                                        the nature of the country is but little fitted for rearing a large stock of

                                                    and best-patronized battues are made, incredible
                                                    out into the adjoining woods and coverts when
                                    The tremendous slaughter that has occasionally taken place at some
                          termed, during the battues has now and then raised the animosity of
                                        their         by giving a somewhat exaggerated account of the
                                                    even at times in the comic papers. I never witnessed one of these big shoots, and                     to say much on this subject, but fail to understand how any one taking an interest in real sport could assist in the destruction of hundreds of hand-reared birds as tame as farmyard chickens. When the outlying nests of eggs liable to be robbed are taken, and the young hatched and turned out in time to get used to the country, good sport may be obtained where a fair stock of wild birds is also kept up.

In the summer of 1876 I ascertained quite by chance the manner in which these birds are occasionally reared in the north, and the arrangements entered into between the master and his keepers; as they differ from the usual custom, it may not be out of place to refer to the subject. While in quest of specimens in the northern counties, I had gone, on a Sunday afternoon early in June, to lunch with a well-known sportsman and large land-owner whose woods and moors I was about to explore the following week. Having finished our repast, he proposed that we should go and have a look at the young Pheasants now being reared in a field close at hand; on reaching the spot a large number of coops were observed spread out over the open ground, and the head keeper soon made his appearance. Two of his assistants, armed with guns, concealed under some large trees in a hedge-row bordering the field, soon caught the master's eye and he at once gave orders for the weapons to be laid aside for the day; an explanation from the keeper, however, changed these instructions and the men were allowed to remain on guard. No less than three or four small Hawks, in all probability Sparrow-Hawks and Kestrels, were to be seen sitting among the branches of the highest trees, waiting for an opportunity to sweep down and carry off some of the young. The birds in their present state were the property of the head keeper, who had procured the eggs, and reared and protected the downy mites during their first stages; he was entitled to no remuneration till a price was paid for them when fit to be turned out, and consequently it would have been a great loss to him to have them carried off by the Hawks. I learned on my arrival on Monday that, owing to the constant watch kept on Sunday evening, the guns were not brought into use that day; but the following morning a couple had been killed, and during the remainder of the week the whole of the marauders were, I believe, cleared off.

Many years ago my father rented the shootings of Catsfield, near Battle, in Sussex, and caring little for the sport of knocking down hand-reared birds, his keeper seldom reared above twenty or thirty broods from eggs rescued from outlying or exposed nests that would otherwise have been robbed; the coops were placed out on an open part of the wild heath-grown stretch of land close by the spot on which Normanhurst now stands. While at home from school for the holidays my whole time was generally spent either shooting or fishing, according to the season, in company with one or other of the keepers, and I had many opportunities for becoming well acquainted with the preservation of game. The vermin that gave most trouble were Rats, Crows, Magpies, and Jays, and for these traps were constantly set and kept in working order: stoats and weasels also were destroyed whenever a chance was obtained, but they were for the most part shot when detected on the open ground hunting for prey. While the coops were out with young Pheasants and a few Partridges that were also reared the keeper had a busy time, and it was necessary for him to be constantly on guard. A couple of noisy terriers were also kept in barrels near the coops, to give warning of impending danger, and it was seldom any of the young birds were lost; a few, however, had been missed one summer, and a closer watch was necessary. On a fine bright Sunday morning I had succeeded in evading the usual routine, and, provided with a strong shooting-double, had constructed a comfortable shelter among the bushes growing near the coops on one side of the open ground, while the keeper was on the look out on all parts where sufficient concealment could be obtained. After waiting a couple of hours I crept stealthily from my station into the cover close at hand to take a look over the furze-clad slopes on the open ground, to ascertain if any of the predatory species were in sight in that quarter. While crossing a ride * a view of the coops was obtained and a savage growl and low cries from the terriers caught my ear. On rapidly making my way down towards the spot I was in time to see a large black-and-white dog roll over to a shot, while an instant later a second report was heard and another almost similar in colouring came in view, evidently badly wounded, but continuing its course towards the ride through which I was now proceeding. Drawing at once into the shelter of the bushes I quietly awaited its approach, and a charge of No. 3 shot behind the shoulder settled the matter, the poor beast having been previously hard hit. On reaching the open ground I made my way to where the keeper was standing, admiring a beautiful black-and-white setter lying dead. He stated that his attention had first been attracted by the excitement of the terriers, and then he had observed the dogs snapping up some young birds which had not yet retreated to the shelter of the coops. His first barrel, as I was well aware, had done its work successfully; but the second animal at which he fired had been, he asserted, at a longer range and had carried off the charge, though evidently suffering from the effects of the shot. Having reported my share in the work, we quickly made our way to the spot where the second had fallen, and assistance having been summoned, the offenders were at once put under ground. We were well aware of the kennel to which this brace of setters belonged; but how they had managed to escape from the care of [...] never solved. [...] the head keeper nor any of his [...] in such a manner, and during [...] in the British Isles since [...] I have never met with a similar [...]

I frequently remarked that cock Pheasants answer the reports of artillery or distant thunder by crowing loudly: in the woods about Catsfield they were particularly noisy on the afternoon of March 11, 1850, immediately after the blow-up of the Hounslow powder-mills. The birds continued uttering their calls for some time after the explosion, which was plainly heard, though the distance must have been over sixty miles. The weather happened to be particularly fine and still for that time of year, and this may possibly account for the fact of the sound being conveyed so far.

Pheasants when flying over water occasionally get as perplexed as Partridges, and on falling seldom succeed in reaching terra firma again, but perish by drowning. While fishing on Heigham Sounds on the 21st of June, 1871, a male and female (the latter in pursuit of the former) were noticed dashing rapidly over the water from one bank to another, the distance being about a quarter of a mile. The birds were soon lost sight of behind a high and widely spreading reed-bush; but a wherry passing a few minutes later, the owner called out to us that two Pheasants were swimming in an open pool among the reeds he had just sailed by and that they appeared unable to make the shore. As the fish were biting well we did not care to disturb the spot where the boats were brought up by moving, and took no more notice of the matter for the present. Later in the day, when the fish had ceased to feed after several hours' good sport (a couple of perch weighing 3½ lbs. and four 2½ lbs., with many of smaller size, having been taken), we pulled in the direction indicated by the wherry-man and discovered both birds floating dead on the surface of the water within a short distance of each other. Other instances of these birds being picked up drowned on the Norfolk broads and meres have been reported by the natives; the Partridges, however, that incur the same fate in this marshy district number at least ten to one compared with this species.

While living at Ferrygate, near North Berwick in East Lothian, in 1863, for the purpose of studying agriculture, I discovered a nest with sixteen eggs in the thick tangled grass in a small plantation of young trees only a short distance from our farm-house. The eggs evidently belonged to Pheasants and Partridges, each species having contributed about the same number; for a week or more I visited the nest daily, but never identified the sitting bird. Unfortunately before she had hatched out the young I was obliged to leave that part of the country for a few weeks, and could only ascertain on my return, by the mass of broken shells, that the whole of the eggs had proved prolific.

About thirty years ago a hen Pheasant selected a strange situation for her nest in the railway-cutting near Battle great wood, on the line between Tunbridge Wells and Hastings. An unusually large cavity under one of the sleepers on which the rails were laid had been detected by the bird; this she had deepened by scratching and then constructed the nest for her eggs. Utterly regardless of the deafening uproar caused by the passing trains, she sat closely and in due course brought off her brood, having been carefully watched during the time of incubation by the plate-layers constantly passing up and down the line, who were well acquainted with the position of the nest.

# CAPERCAILLIE.

## TETRAO UROGALLUS.

The few remarks I give concerning the last survivors of our native Capercaillies and the introduction of foreigners from Norway and Sweden, with the reports as to how they flourished in their new quarters, are taken from 'The Capercaillie in Scotland,' a work lately written by Mr. J. A. Harvie-Brown, which contains an immense amount of valuable information concerning this species.

The final extinction of the original stock of this species may be considered to have taken place about the year 1760. There have been, however, several other records of a considerably later date that are supposed to be properly authenticated. While engaged in making observations in the Highlands, in Strath Glass and the adjoining glens in Inverness-shire, a few years back, I found the keepers asserted that this district had been the last stronghold of the native breed of the Capercaillie*. The cause of their disappearance is somewhat strange when all things are considered; immense fir-woods cover the slopes of most of the rugged hills in this locality, which appears in every respect suitable to supply all their requirements as to food and shelter, and render them almost entirely free from persecution. Possibly the birds could not procure their proper food among these stupendous pines, as I remarked in the woods on Logierait Hill, in Perthshire, that they appeared to prefer the young Scotch-fir trees, of about eight or ten feet in height, off which they nibbled the topmost shoots and put an end to all chance of further growth. There is one question respecting this species to be considered which may not strike those who have not thoroughly examined their haunts. Did the birds in former days consume or destroy all the young sprouting shoots of the small-growing trees on which they fed and then perish from want of sustenance, or were the owners of the forests exasperated on detecting the tops of their young fir trees that were progressing favourably torn to pieces and ruined, and then attempted to mend matters by making a general clearance of the depredators?

As to the restoration of the Capercaillie in this country it is stated that between 1837 and 1839 numbers were brought from Sweden and turned out about Taymouth and a few near Dunkeld. In 1863 the birds in the woods on the Taymouth estate were estimated to be nearly two thousand in number; they increased rapidly all along the valley of the Tay as far as Dunkeld, where the nature of the country was most suitable to their habits—the proprietors on whose estates they had been turned out (the Duke of Athol and Lord Breadalbane) having had immense quantities of larch, Scotch fir, and spruce planted

---

\* Since writing the above, I turned to the last page in 'The Capercaillie in Scotland' and found the following in the Appendix:—"Mr. Peter, Lord Lovat's factor at Beauly, informs me that 'one of the old native breed of Capercaillies was trapped at Struy (?) about 50 or 60 years ago. None have been seen since that time.'" This date would be placed at from 1819 to 1829. I wrote for further particulars and more exact dates, but have not received any up to the date of going to press." This seems to corroborate the statements of the keepers as related to myself. Mr. Harvie-Brown appears doubtful as to the whereabouts of Struy, which is situated close to Erchless Castle, at the entrance to Strath Glass, in Inverness-shire, in the vicinity of which I have often collected and also been in communication with several of the keepers.

on the hill-sides, which afforded the birds both food and cover. Of late years much of this wood has been cut down, and it now seems that the Capercaillie, though still abundant, has much decreased in numbers. Mr. Roderick Anderson, of Dunkeld, is of opinion that at the present time there are not half the birds on the Athol estates that there were twenty years ago. There is an entry in Mr. Harvie-Brown's book on the Capercaillie, stating that in 1844 this species became established at Logierait, fourteen miles from Taymouth, in Perthshire: this is the only locality in which I have as yet had an opportunity of meeting with the Capercaillie, and at the time of my visit in the spring of 1878 there must have been some hundreds still remaining in the immediate neighbourhood.

The following extract from 'The Capercaillie in Scotland' will show the numbers that have been bagged in the Highlands in one day since the restoration of the species:—"The greatest number I have heard of killed in one day was 36 at Ladywell plantation, Pitnacree, near Dunkeld, in 1865. This is part of the Athol estates, upon which are at least 10,000 acres of suitable woods. At Banff, in the east of Perthshire, 25 were shot in one day in 1877—area 2000 acres. At Dunkeld 23 were shot in one day."

A few charges have been brought against this species for persecuting Blackgame, but the accusations do not seem to be backed up by any evidence worth recording. Mr. Harvie-Brown, however, says that he has many statements from correspondents bearing out the truth of the assertion. I give one extract from page 120 of his work:—"The same correspondent adds that they drive away Blackgame 'by driving off the old birds and killing the young'; and he states that he has seen battles between the species in 'clucking-season.' He also saw a Capercaillie and a Greyhen with their broods coming in contact, when a terrible battle ensued. 'The Capercaillie succeeded in driving away the Greyhen, and then killed the most of her brood.'"

Under the heading of "Damage to Forests" in Mr. Harvie-Brown's book I discovered that some grave charges are brought against the Capercaillie; and as these assertions indicate that there was some reason for the question I asked at the end of the second paragraph on the preceding page, it will not be out of place to give a few extracts.

"Extensive damage done by Capercaillies to woods and forests is another sad thorn in many proprietors' sides. To hear some speak of the awful destruction going on might almost lead one to suppose that in bygone days the evil deeds of the species brought its own punishment; that, in fact, the Capercaillie exterminated the forest-growth over large areas of Scotland and that this extermination exterminated them in turn. In many parts of the area at present inhabited by the birds, on this account alone, they are shot down upon all occasions, in the endeavour to reduce their numbers; or, at all events, no encouragement is given them to increase. Twenty years ago, when Capercaillies appeared on an estate, the greatest care was taken to foster them. Now, it is usually different; and, where at all plentiful, they are shot, both sexes indiscriminately; and in some places, as we have seen in a former section, very heavy bags are often made. I have, however, sufficient faith in the robust character of the species to prevent my becoming anxious, lest a second extermination should ever take place, if fair means only be used to keep its numbers in check.

"I have in this connection endeavoured to collect independent testimony from the best sources as to the nature and amount of damage done. Mr. Malcolm Dunn (who has specially studied, and who read a paper on the subject before the Botanical Society of Edinburgh: see 'Zool.' 1875, p. 4338) writes to me as follows:—'In reference to the damage done to plantations by both Capercaillie and Blackgame, the proof is too strong to admit of the slightest doubt. Where either exist in large numbers, in, or in the neighbourhood of, young plantations of larch and Scotch fir, they do a vast amount of injury to the young trees, by eating the young buds, leaves, and shoots of the trees: and, in the case of the Scotch fir especially, at a season of the year when there are no insects of any kind upon them—I here refer to beetles, caterpillars, or aphides; coccus ............ may be upon the trees, but not on the wood or leaves eaten by the Capercaillie. ..... is the ...... of all my correspondents who have paid any attention to the matter, ............ by ... own experience. Of the very many 'crops' of the Capercaillie which I have .......... and ......... examined, none contained any traces of the bird having fed upon insects. In ......... the ...... are usually entirely filled with the leaves, buds, and young shoots of the Scotch fir. The ........ of one 'crop' of a male bird, which I examined in November 1873, were as follows:—203 points of shoots of Scotch fir, with the leading buds entire, some of the shoots being fully 3 inches long; 11 pieces of young wood, 1½ to 2½ inches long, having leaves attached but no terminal buds; and 52 buds—making in all 266 shoots and buds, besides a large handful of single leaves, of the Scotch fir, which the birds had devoured at one meal. The whole were quite fresh and green, were to all appearance selected from a very healthy tree, and showed no trace whatever of ever having been attacked by the pine-beetle (*Hylurgus pinaperda*) or any other insect; and most certainly there were no other insects in the crop. The contents of the crop I presented to the Edinburgh Botanical Society, and they can now be seen in the Museum of the Society in the Botanic Gardens. In another crop, which I examined in April 1874, I found the contents to be wholly the young shoots, leaves, and buds of larch. I counted the extraordinary number of 918 buds alone in the 'crop,' besides the bits of shoots and leaves, which formed by far the bulkiest part of the whole. There were but a few bits (three) of silvery lichen amongst the contents, but nothing else; these pieces of lichen no doubt were picked up along with the other contents of the crop, and do not form a part of the regular food of the bird. These are given as fair samples of many crops I have examined, received chiefly from Perthshire, Mr. Brown having sent me about a score in 1874. In none of them did I ever meet with a pine-beetle, or any other insect that would lead me to suppose that the bird preys upon insects, or had a preference for shoots which were infected by them. In fact, I should maintain that the bird prefers clean, healthy, fresh food, and has no taste for damaged or decaying vegetation of any kind. I have never examined the crop of a young bird taken out of the nest; but I have analysed the crops of several birds of the same year in July and August, and failed in every instance to find any insects, so that, although I am aware that it is said in books that they are fond of insects, especially when young, I am unable to corroborate the assertion. The nature and habits of the birds do not in any way lead me even to suppose it feeds on insects; but in other parts of the world—in Norway for instance—it may feed on different matter to what it does in Scotland. Since I made my investigations anent the injury done by the Capercaillie, &c., to forest trees, I have also investigated the injury done by insects. The injury done by the pine-beetle to the Scotch firs is in no ways analogous. The beetle does its injury internally by eating the pith of the shoots and the heart of the buds; the Capercaillie 'lops' the shoots, buds, and leaves clean off, and the one cannot by any possibility be mistaken for the other; besides the injury is done by the beetle in the middle of summer, and the most serious injury is done by the bird in the winter, when the beetles are hybernating in, or on, dead wood on the ground. The beetle attacks almost any pine tree, sick or healthy, any size or any age; only, as it climbs from the ground to the branches, small trees, say under 25 years of age, are those commonly attacked. Capercaillies, on the other hand, attack only healthy trees of any size or age, and will, in some instances, return to the same tree for days continuously, till it is completely stripped of its buds or growing points, and, of course, most seriously injuring it, and rendering it perfectly useless for timber. If the bird is kept within due limits (in numbers), the injury they do is immaterial to the general welfare of our forests, but if they become very numerous, they will certainly play havoc with the pine and larch plantations in their neighbourhood, especially young plantations. Blackgame at certain places are just about as injurious to young pine and larch trees.' The above remarks by Mr. Dunn were evoked by special queries which I put to him regarding the possibility existing of the buds affected by the pine-beetle being those chosen by the Capercaillie. As has been seen, Mr. Dunn is of opinion that the bird prefers 'clean, healthy, fresh food' and has 'no taste for damaged or decaying vegetation of any kind.' He does not consider that insects of any kind form part of their food, but he at the same time states that he 'never examined the crop of a young bird taken out of the nest.' I have quoted Mr. Dunn's letter fully, as it is perhaps the letter, amongst many others I have received, which places the damage done in the strongest light. I am still of opinion, however, that the final results exhibited in certain young trees are just as likely to have been caused by beetles as by the Capercaillies. If the buds are destroyed, whether by beetles internally or by Capercaillies, whether in summer or in winter, I believe the results will be the same, viz.—as will be seen further on—the trees becoming bushy, branchy, and stunted."

Here are a couple more extracts :—"A correspondent in Perthshire writes as follows: 'From the 1st of November up to the end of May the Capercaillie lives principally on Scotch-fir sprigs. Then, from the 1st of June to the end of October, he lives greatly on insects, digs deep into ants' mounds* in search of food, and strips the bark of rotten trees in search of worms and beetles.' Fancy hundreds, yes and thousands, of Capercaillies thus employed. Do they do no good?"

"Mr. J. B. Hamilton, of Leny, amongst others, informs me that he has seen abundant evidence of their work and mischief, and adds, 'on Scotch firs of twenty to thirty years old. My own impression is that they are not so injurious to young Scotch-fir plants of a foot or two in height as Blackgame, which are very fond of the leading buds in these, and are one of the causes of that tufty appearance in these that you allude to.'"

It seems that these birds have a better character in the north of Europe than in this country, as Mr. Harvie-Brown gives the following :—"Mr. Robert Collett, of Christiania, in reply to inquiries I made of him regarding destruction done to forests in Norway and Sweden, writes: 'In Norway there is not any trace of destruction to the forests done by the Capercaillie. Certainly they do live in winter almost exclusively on the leaves of the fir (*Pinus sylvestris*), but they only take some shoots here and some there; for the most part from old—or at least not young—trees.'"

The following lines by Mr. Harvie-Brown so exactly describe the damage I witnessed on the hill at Logierait in the spring of 1878 that it supplies all deficiencies in the remarks I made concerning the effect on the trees :—

"Becoming interested in the subject of destruction of forest-plants and trees, I rented, in January 1878, a piece of ground fourteen acres in extent, or thereabouts, situated in the midst of old pine wood of different ages, and which had been planted six years previously with pine seedlings on the above-mentioned estate. In one corner, facing the sun and the south and protected on the north and west by older growth, the damage which the young trees had suffered was perhaps most apparent. Upon this estate Capercaillies are tolerably abundant, as many as four having been shot in one day by a party in 1877, and I have myself estimated the numbers seen in one day as at least sixteen. Blackgame are scarce, and have been so for a number of years; but I have seen Blackgame driven out of the adjoining covers, and once rising out of the above enclosure. The stunted, bushy, or tufty young trees were pointed out to me, and I clearly saw where the central buds of the leaders had been picked out—or had dropped off!—resulting in side shoots taking the place of the leaders, and thus deforming the trees. This was affirmed to be the damage done solely by the Capercaillie, which birds were stated to stand upon the ground and pick out the buds from the leading shoots, when the trees were perhaps four or five years old, and had been planted perhaps three years. After reaching this age the trees are

* Lloyd directs that ants' eggs be provided for the young birds when rearing them by hand (*op. cit.* p. 32).

considered ... as they ... too high ... to ... ... ... from the ground, and the
... ... ... ... ... ... and ... ... and ... ... ... ... of the bird. Becoming
... ... the ... ... ... ... beyond the ... of the ... when it stands upon the
... ... It ... ... ... that the trees, in ... of this treatment when young, were
delayed in ... growth, and that ... ... ... ... useless."

The foregoing quotation ... ... ... in ... ... ... ... ... for the deterioration of the Scotch fir in the Highlands.

"There seems to be considerable diversity of opinion amongst those inimical to the Capercaillie as to the ages of the wood attacked. On the other hand, I have the following opinion from Sir Robert Menzies, which I quote in full:—'Neither do I blame them for being destructive to the plantations, a fault that is frequently found with them, and in consequence of which they are shot down. So far as my experience goes they do not injure newly planted young trees in the same way that Blackgame do, as they will not go to a plantation where there are no trees they can roost upon; they will not pick out the tops while standing on the ground, and it is not till the trees in a plantation are somewhat grown that the Capercaillies settle in it, and then, as they are heavy birds, it is only the side shoots they can get at, as the top shoot is not strong enough to carry them. I am of opinion that it is no fault of the Capercaillies that the plantations of Scotch fir are found not to do well, but that a very bad sort of that tree is now sold out of the nurseries that will never become trees; plants that do not make a leader like the true Scotch fir, but, on the contrary, have no stem, and abound in branches, both above and below. This sort of Scotch fir is an importation from the Continent, now of some years' standing, and young plants are now sold as 'true natives' that are seedlings taken from trees originally grown from this imported seed. When these are not found to be doing well the Capercaillie is blamed; but I think it is the seedsman who is in fault, and more care should be taken to see that the young Scotch-fir plants are of the right sort, when the plantation will be found to do well enough, though there are a good many Capercaillies in it.'"

From my own experience I can say nothing as to whether the Capercaillie ever attacks the small plants of the Scotch fir, but I have seen and carefully examined the manner in which the trees, between five and ten feet in height, have had their leaders cut or broken and the uppermost branches and twigs bent down, torn to pieces, and trampled on, while large flocks of these birds have been either feeding or resting and basking in the rays of the sun.

While exploring various parts of the Northern Highlands in the spring of 1878, I obtained permission from Mr. Duncan, who rented the Kinnaird shootings near Dunkeld, in Perthshire, from the Duke of Athol, to obtain some specimens of Capercaillie. Leaving Inverness on the 17th of April, Dunkeld was reached the same evening; but for several days the weather was most unpropitious, blusterous squalls of wind, rain, and sleet followed one another in rapid succession. On the 20th, though dull and foggy, there was a slight improvement, so a start was made and I drove over to Logierait, where Mr. Duncan's men, together with the keepers and foresters from several of the adjoining shootings and a number of beaters, were found waiting to drive the woods for the Capercaillie. It was, of course, almost hopeless that one gun could obtain a shot at birds when driven in these large woods, where about fourteen guns are usually required to hold all the passes. Stalking quietly through the dense cover would have been my best chance of success, and I had only anticipated being met by two or three keepers[*]. As so many beaters had, however, been brought together, I gave in and submitted to the usual routine. During the day, which turned out somewhat unsuitable, the air being thick with mist,

---

[*] I did not ascertain at the time that all the keepers and foresters, when first assembled to ... my arrival, were carrying guns with the intention of assisting to procure the specimens required. It appears that Mr. Menzies of Foneonie, who was factor for his brother, Mr. Menzies of

three or four drives were made, with the result that might naturally have been expected, and only a few hens passed within sight of my stations, not a single cock bird coming in view while I remained on the hill. On the return of the beaters, I ascertained that they had discovered a couple of old males fighting desperately in an open space in the densest part of the forest, and had run in and attempted to capture them. If these thoughtless individuals had only watched the conflict and sent one of their number off to give information, both birds might have been procured, as I was not more than a quarter of a mile away, and their battles frequently last a considerable time. I learned in Dunkeld that two fine old cocks had been caught by some labourers on the highroad, where they were picked up almost entirely disabled, having fought till both combatants were incapable of making an effort to escape. The same men were awaiting my arrival on the 22nd, and we agreed, after one or two drives, that I should try to obtain a shot by going quietly through some parts of the woods not yet disturbed. The weather was now fine and clear, and at the first drive about fifty birds passed over, one third of the number being cocks; not one of the latter, however, came within range. Just at the conclusion of the second drive, which was also a failure, I happened to catch a glimpse, through an opening in the forest, of an old cock alighting in one of the largest larches in the forest. Here he remained perfectly motionless drawn close up to the massive stem, and although one of the beaters passed below and actually struck the tree with his stick, the bird took not the slightest notice. As he seemed likely to stop some time, I called all the men together just within sight of him, giving directions for them to keep moving about and getting their lunch ready so as to draw his attention. I then started off, picking my way carefully down one gully and stalking with the utmost caution up another, which led right below the tree he had selected, and having taken the bearings correctly there was no necessity to look up till well within range. As I expected, he was now intently regarding the actions of the group of beaters, and the first intimation of my approach that he received was a charge of No. 1 shot, which brought him as dead as a stone to the roots of the tree. On examination he proved to be a fine old bird, slightly cut about the head by fighting, but by no means damaged as a specimen. Capercaillies are stated to be remarkably tough and strong, requiring a severe wound to disable them; and this I can readily believe, as a fine old male I fired at while posted for a drive on the summit of a ridge of rocks at least three hundred feet in height, fell as if struck lifeless to the foot of the cliffs among large blocks of stone, and still retained sufficient vitality to flutter away and escape when one of the beaters descended to bring him back*. I should have imagined that the force of the fall alone would have been sufficient to break every bone in his body, as he pitched down apparently killed by the effects of the charge of shot. On the following day, the 23rd, our number of beaters was considerably reduced, and while proceeding along the ridge of the hill at the summit of Logierait I was enabled to ascertain the damage caused by the large flocks of Capercaillie. On over half a mile of the forest the whole of the young shoots of the Scotch firs were eaten off and destroyed, the trees being apparently utterly ruined. I learned from the keepers that in winter, when the ground was covered with snow, these birds occasionally collect into immense bodies in this locality, and that it was at this time the greatest amount of mischief was done to the young trees. Just as we reached the end of the ridge a single female Capercaillie was put up by one of the beaters and passed overhead at a considerable height; not wishing, however, to lose a chance, I fired a shot, and the bird was seen to turn over and fall headlong over the precipice into the large fir-wood on the slope of the hill towards the north-east. That we should find her seemed extremely doubtful, as a long circuit had to be taken to reach the spot on which she was supposed to have dropped and the ground was littered by broken limbs of trees and thick undergrowth. On reaching the spot we had marked where the bird disappeared from sight, a careful search was commenced and almost immediately she was discovered lying spread out on a bare patch where only the dead spines of the pine trees covered the soil. As this completed the pair of Capercaillie, our work was now at an end, and, after calling the whole of our men together, we rested for a time in a sheltered gully on the hill-side, and after lunch I made my way back to Dunkeld, well satisfied with the result of the three days spent on the slopes of the hill of Logierait and also with the attention I had met with from the keepers, foresters, and beaters of the district.

# BLACK GROUSE.

## TETRAO TETRIX.

In England I have met with these fine birds only in one or two of the Sussex forests; they are, however, still to be found in several counties from north to south. To observe Black Grouse in their true home one must cross the Tweed and visit the rocky glens of the Highlands.

Though Black-Game shooting does not commence till the 20th of August, a few cheepers now and then fall to the lot of inexperienced sportsmen before that date, no little practice being needed to distinguish at the first glance the immature of this species from Grouse. The young birds are in most instances exceedingly disinclined to get on wing, and frequently rising one or two at a time, offer the easiest possible shots; unless in outlying districts, it is injudicious to tax the juveniles heavily at this season, as during the latter end of autumn and winter Black Game may be depended upon to give excellent sport to those who are not afraid of hard work; to kill them down in their infancy can only be compared to farmyard slaughter. A short and condensed extract from my game-book for 1867 will show how rapidly a bag of young birds, even when strong and well-grown, may be made in early autumn. Being anxious on one occasion during the last week in August to obtain some game by a certain hour in the day to forward to friends, I determined, as there was little spare time, to try some small corries near the back of a stunted wood of birch and alder where both Grouse and Black Game were frequently found. On emerging from the cover and facing a steep brae, Masco and Minnie (a brace of steady setters) were loosed, I then climbed to the top of a low ridge to keep the dogs in view, the course we were following being for some three or four hundred yards exceedingly rough, owing to the inequalities in the ground and the straggling patches of rank heather intermixed with coarse grass and rushes. One of the setters having followed the line I took, crossed the ridge into the next gully, and on reaching some open ground free from rocks and stones, where heather, juniper, and other plants grew thickly, he immediately came to a dead stop. The next moment a wave of the hand from the keeper in the hollow I had left indicated that Minnie, though out of sight in the dense cover, had also settled to a point. To this call I was unable to give immediate attention, so, followed by a gillie with a second gun, I scrambled down the bank and made my way towards the spot where the infallible Masco, standing rigid as a statue, was evidently close upon his birds. The instant the low ground was reached a full-grown and vigorous young bird rose at our feet, and in due course paid the penalty; having succeeded in inserting a fresh cartridge, the old Greyhen and another youngster fluttered out at a fair range and were immediately disposed of. Another brace next made off in company, and just sufficient time having elapsed to exchange guns with the loader, suffered in consequence, both being struck by the first barrel, one dropping dead as a stone, and the other skimming off with extended pinions and needing the charge of the second barrel in order to avoid the loss of time incurred by watching and marking a distant fall. A momentary check ensued; then the setter drawing cautiously forward, it was evident that game was still ahead, and a few yards farther on a single bird, rapidly followed by another, sprang almost below the old dog's nose.

offering the easiest chances imaginable. While picking our way in haste from the gully to the next hollow, the sound of wings was again heard, and turning rapidly I was just in time to drop the last of the brood, disturbed by one of the pony-men coming to gather up the slain. On reaching the spot where the keeper had last been seen I found him standing over and doing his best to cheer up poor Minnie, who having been held back so long was anxious to be drawing on; after moving forward, the little bitch speedily came upon the birds, which again proved to be Black Game. Springing from among the cover in much the same manner as the first brood, eight were stopped; the ninth, however, twisted so sharply to the right that, owing to the steepness of the ground, I was unable to swing round sufficiently to obtain a shot. After leaving the sloping hill-side up which we had just made our way, another pack of Black Game, evidently consisting of two broods intermixed, was found in the first patch of heather on the open moor; the cover, however, being scanty, and affording little shelter, the birds, with the exception of a few that had strayed from the main body, rose all together and three brace only were obtained. In order to make up the number required, I now turned further out on the open moors for Grouse, being of opinion that Black Game had suffered sufficiently. It was soon ascertained that there was no necessity to proceed beyond the lower flats, as several packs were met with in rapid succession, the birds in almost every instance being extremely loath to rise. Twenty brace (the number required) having been obtained, we turned homewards, and taking merely what chances came in the way, the bag was increased by six and a half brace. At the moment I much regretted that we had not taken the hill better prepared; with but one brace of dogs and little over a hundred cartridges no great result could possibly be anticipated. Never during the autumns spent on the moors have I met with birds lying so well, and a heavy bag might undoubtedly have been made had the whole day been devoted to the object. A start for the hill-side had not been made till 10 A.M., the early hours of the morning having been passed in searching out some downy young of the Land-Rail for specimens, in a hayfield on the low ground near the river. As the lodge was reached before 2 o'clock after leaving the moors, the twenty-six and a half brace (together with two hares and three rabbits that had also been turned over—fifty-eight head in all) must have been obtained in little over a couple of hours' shooting. Though so regardless of their own safety early in the season, by November Black Game have gained both strength and experience, and on most moors hard work will be needed to make a bag in open weather. Without a thorough knowledge of the ground and the usual course followed by the birds when on wing, driving is of little avail; by stalking the old cocks on the commanding positions they so frequently pick out on the hill-side but few shots will be obtained during the course of a day's work, so careful is the watch kept by these wary birds. Severe weather, however, affects them considerably; during heavy snow-storms I have on more than one occasion seen them so cut up by exposure to the cold that they would sit in the birch trees with their plumage puffed out till they resembled balls of feathers, paying little or no attention even when approached within the distance of twenty or thirty yards. While returning home one wintry day in December 1866, from shooting on the marshy ground near the banks of the Lyon, I observed a couple of Grey-hens swaying backwards and forwards in the branches of a waving birch. A blinding squall of snow which drifted as it fell was passing over at the time, and we arrived almost below the tree before the slightest signs of alarm were exhibited, a shout being needed to put them on wing. Further in the plantation, where more shelter could be obtained, several others were seen, seven or eight being perched among the branches of a single tree. In all probability they were collected in still greater numbers in other parts of the wood, as the packs appeared to have been entirely driven from the higher slopes along the hill-sides to which they usually resorted.

In fine weather during winter and early spring the oldest birds collect at daybreak on some open spot and go through the most extraordinary manœuvres; at times these performances appear to be indulged in simply for amusement; as spring advances, however, the animosity of the birds increases. In December 1867, having frequently watched these gatherings from a distance without a chance of closely inspecting the whole of the proceedings, I carefully marked the place (a bare spot on a heather-clad slope of the hill-side facing towards the south) where the birds had collected for several mornings in succession, and determined to make an attempt to witness their antics at close quarters. The ground having been previously looked over and a good hiding-place decided upon, we arrived on the spot an hour before daybreak, and creeping into a regular nest of rugs and plaids which the keepers had arranged, I was covered well over with dry heather and brakes, and finally sprinkled with snow. The men were then sent away, and I quietly awaited the course of events. Shortly after the first streak of light had appeared in the east a rush of wings was heard, and a magnificent old Blackcock passing within a few feet of my head settled on the open space some twenty yards in front. For fully ten minutes there were no other arrivals, and I began to fear some other spot had been chosen for the day's amusements; suddenly three or four more old cocks appeared on the scene, having probably alighted quietly on the other side of the bank. For a few moments they remained silently watching one another, apparently waiting for a signal from the leader. I next caught sight of two or three small parties flying high in the air direct from the hills on the opposite side of a steep burn. After circling once round the spot they alighted lower down on the hill, and some of them, principally Greyhens, remained where they settled, while the males gradually ascended the rising ground, picking their way with the greatest care, carrying their tails high over their backs, either to show themselves to the greatest advantage or to avoid contact with the snow. These were speedily followed by others, and they kept on gathering till between thirty and forty more were collected in a kind of irregular circle. The old cock who had first appeared, and who was evidently looked upon as the master of the ceremonies, now advanced into the centre of the arena; his comb was elevated, his wings drooped, his tail curled over his back, and every feather, even down to his toes, spread out to its fullest extent. After bowing all round, and apparently being satisfied that no one wished to dispute his title to be considered the greatest swell present, he proceeded to execute a kind of *pas seul*, which seemed to consist of a kind of double shuffle, hop, skip, and a jump, and was concluded by an almost complete somersault; others with ruffled plumage then made their way towards the open ground, strutting jauntily forward as if eager for the fray. Though the demeanour of the combatants was certainly threatening, their encounters appeared almost perfectly harmless. After a short interval a dozen or more engaged in a general scrimmage or tournament [*], which resulted in little or no damage to any of the performers beyond the loss of a few feathers. The greater number of those that had assembled then took their departure, rising on wing after uttering a few low notes and betaking themselves to their respective haunts, the last stragglers eventually dispersing over the adjacent hill-side. There had been little or no real fighting; but this may be accounted for, as the fiercest battles are known to take place in early spring. Towards the end of March a few years back, while passing silently in a punt along the shores of Loch Shin just after daylight, I came unexpectedly upon a small party of five or six Blackcocks with a few Greyhens on an open patch in a straggling birch-plantation that stretched down to the water-side. Two of the cocks were indulging in the most savagely contested fight I ever witnessed; tumbling over one another, either up or down, they hit and flapped with the greatest fury, till rolling over a slope on the bank they were lost to view. Some of the Greyhens who were spectators had perched themselves on the boughs of the trees and appeared to regard the combat with the utmost attention.

On a ridge on the hill-side below some spreading beeches within view of the lodge at Innerwick, in Glenlyon, a few birds used often to gather on fine still evenings in spring. During May I repeatedly watched an old cock running round and round in circles with raised and outspread tail, evidently showing himself off to the admiration of a group of females who surrounded him; more than a single male being seldom observed

[*] To accurately describe the whole of the evolutions gone through is utterly impossible.

at these meetings, this was in all probability the spot to which he resorted to divert himself in the society of the lights of his harem. In the first week in June 1877, while crossing the hills in one of the northern counties to inspect the haunts of some Golden Eagles, I met with an opportunity for observing a most singular assemblage, and remarked the comical and demure manner in which these strange birds comport themselves at their meetings at this season. Having learned from one of the keepers that Black Game frequently congregated on the moors a short distance on the right below the gully up which we were then making our way, I cautiously ascended the steep bank, and having reached the summit was enabled to overlook a ridge of the hill sloping down towards the south-east. Though the ground was clothed with a luxuriant crop of grass, almost free from heather, with the exception of a few stunted roots, an oblong space of some thirty or forty yards in length could clearly be discerned where the herbage was much worn and trampled down. Around this bare spot some thirty or forty Blackcocks were drawn up; though two or three Greyhens could be distinguished, it was plain that they were not present in any numbers. Not the slightest order could be observed in the manner in which the party had arranged themselves; three or four might be in close proximity, next a single bird or two, and then an interval of several yards, the company being on the whole evenly distributed round the arena. Few, if any, showed the least signs of animation, the majority, indeed, exhibiting attitudes of repose or indifference; the whole, however, without an exception faced towards the open space, and I particularly remarked that the front line was most admirably kept. After waiting some time in hopes of observing a general movement, I withdrew without causing the slightest alarm, and on returning an hour or so later discovered that little or no alteration in the general aspect of affairs had taken place, though a few birds had strayed away and scattered over the rough moorland stretching down the mountain-side. For the best part of an hour I delayed our return journey; at length, as there appeared little chance that any animation would now be infused into the inanimate group assembled, and daylight had already commenced to fade, I turned down hill, the sound of wings a few minutes later indicating the dissolution of the meeting. From the worn appearance of the turf it was evident that this was a regular and well-frequented place of resort; that the spirit did not move those who had collected to more doughty deeds on this occasion may be accounted for by the season of the year. It was a somewhat singular fact that within half a mile or so of this spot there was a favourite resting-place of the Golden Eagle; that these birds also hunted for prey over the adjacent ground I had many opportunities for observing *.

During the summer of 1868 I detected by chance the nest of a Greyhen containing three fresh eggs on a flat stretch of open moorland at least a mile and a half from the nearest cover; and, strange to say, it was within a few feet of the cradle of a Hen-Harrier in which the eggs were then on the point of hatching. As a rule these birds, according to my own experience, appear to prefer a spot in the vicinity of some shelter on which to rear their young. In several of the northern counties of the Highlands I have come across their nests within a short distance of either the stunted birch or pine woods, or among the outlying bushes that grow here and there in patches on the moors; in Perthshire I repeatedly found them in the groves of beech near the banks of the Lyon. Where more cover is not to be obtained a rough and sloping bank rather than a stretch of flat moor is for the most part selected.

Black Game evince a great partiality for grain; at times they settle in large numbers on the stooks, causing no small amount of damage when, as is often the case in the more remote glens, it is well on into winter before the pieces of cultivated land are cleared of the crop. Though I have never witnessed this method of poaching, I learned from residents in more than one locality that numbers of birds are at times secured by snares set on the stooks; this is doubtless an exceedingly easy means of capture unless an efficient watch is kept. Some years back, while shooting in the west of Perthshire, I heard an amusing account of the manner

---

* This haunt of the Eagles is described in the last paragraph on page 3 of the Golden Eagle.

in which an old woman had been in the habit of catching Black Game in the Rannoch district. For the truth of this story I do not hold myself responsible, it is merely given as related by the keepers and gillies on the hill-side. Shortly before their accustomed feeding-time the "guid wife" used to secrete herself carefully in a stook on some part of the field to which the Black Game had previously been seen to resort. As soon as a bird alighted on her place of concealment and commenced feeding on the oats, it was seized by the legs and immediately drawn out of sight. This plan was declared to have been carried on for some time with remarkable success, till at last a keeper who happened to be passing, having noticed the extraordinary manner in which an old cock had disappeared, made his way to the spot and discovered the old hag with a couple of brace she had already secured.

# RED GROUSE.

## *LAGOPUS SCOTICUS.*

---

The moors furnishing the best bags, and the counties in which this species may be looked for, are so well known to the majority of sportsmen and naturalists that it is unnecessary in these pages to enter into particulars concerning the distribution of this popular game bird throughout the British Islands.

With regard to the disease which has completely puzzled the most scientific authorities, as well as those who have passed their lives on the hill-sides, one fact alone is certain, viz., that we are as far off as ever from discovering either the cause or a remedy for the scourge, which seems to make periodical ravages over the moors, attacking the birds with as much severity on ranges where only a few scattered packs are to be found as on the most prolific beats. Grouse, I am convinced, would retain their health longer and better if the moors were more evenly shot over. In many parts, and frequently where the birds are most abundant, the slaughter is merely carried on for a few days at the commencement of the season, whilst the ground could well stand two or three guns shooting judiciously over the beats from the 12th of August till the 10th of December. It has frequently been declared that the killing down of vermin destroys the balance of Nature and is prejudicial to the well-being of game. I do not deny that this may be the case where a too heavy stock of game is kept up; but on ordinary moors, where the ground is properly shot over, the vermin must be kept down, or the very balance of Nature, which so delights the theorist to talk about, would soon be lost.

My own experience concerning the management of Grouse-shootings has only been acquired on moors where the rental was small, the more extensive and well-known ranges being entirely beyond my reach. Some years back I hired a moor in Perthshire where the vermin had been allowed to multiply almost unchecked, and but few precautions taken to ensure the welfare of the Grouse. At the commencement of the season of 1865 the two best bags for a couple of guns were merely 17 and 16 brace of Grouse. In 1867 one gun was enabled to average above 40 brace a day for the first ten days' shooting, without counting two or three hundred head of other game, the two best bags being 62 and 50 brace. In conjunction with vermin-trapping, I consider the improvement was mainly due to securing the assistance of the shepherds and inducing them to aid in raising the stock of game; the killing down of the single old cock Grouse that invariably drove and harassed the breeding pairs proved also exceedingly beneficial. For a couple of years I treated these quarrelsome old birds as vermin, and shot them down for a month or two after the close of the season. In early morning shortly after sunrise they will be found strutting and crowing on the slabs of rock or stones by the hill-tracts as well as by the roadside; in order to obtain shots, a dog-cart or a pony may be used with great success, if the animals employed are thoroughly broken to the work. While driving up the hill road leading from Glenlyon to Killin early one frosty morning in December 1866, engaged in picking off these pests, I was much astonished at the unaccountable behaviour of an old and trusted retriever, often referred to in these pages; the mistake, for which I can offer not the slightest explanation, was, however, never repeated. Having knocked down a noisy old cock as he rose from a high crag of rock on to a piece of swampy ground, with pools of partially frozen water, I left the cart in charge of the groom and proceeded to search for the bird myself. Nell, who was as usual located in the back compartment, looked wistfully after me and gave vent to audible signs of grief on being left behind; as she happened, however, to be suffering from an injured foot, I would not run the risk of working her over the hard ground unless her services were absolutely necessary. Having reached the spot where the bird had been marked, he was found at once on a bare patch of peat; and on returning to the conveyance, I pitched him on to the floor of the compartment, remarking—"Nell, here's a nice hot Grouse for your breakfast," never, of course, imagining that she would take me at my word. A quarter of a mile or more was then passed over before another shot was obtained; again I alighted to retrieve the bird, and on returning was much surprised to discover that the first had entirely vanished, with the exception of the gall and a few other portions of the intestines usually rejected by predatory animals. Nell appeared by no means disconcerted in consequence of her depravity, and her tail was heard beating loudly against the sideboard, giving evidence of her satisfaction at my approach. In order to ascertain the manner in which she would conduct herself for the remainder of the drive, I took not the slightest notice of the disappearance of the bird; and though four or five brace more were killed before returning to the lodge, the whole were found intact at the end of our journey. So fearless do the old cock Grouse become if unmolested, that shortly after daybreak I have repeatedly seen one or two alight and crow on the thatched roof of a summer-house in the garden adjoining the lodge of Innerwick in Glenlyon, also on the walls surrounding the buildings, and on two or three occasions on the top of a barrel that formed the kennel of a Tweedside retriever, taking not the slightest notice of, and utterly disregarded by, the lawful occupant.

Care and attention is always necessary when placing out traps on the moors, or much injury may be inflicted on the flocks: neglect to take proper precautions invariably causes ill feeling in the district, and no amount of watching can make up for or avert the spite of a shepherd who fancies himself aggrieved. During the years I was killing down the vermin on the Innerwick moors in the west of Perthshire, where the hills were entirely under sheep, none were taken in the traps, sites for the baits being invariably chosen on mossy spits or tiny islets in the springs as well as on the summits of the "false men" or cairns of stone built up as landmarks on conspicuous ridges of the hills. While endeavouring to obtain specimens of Eagles in the Northern Highlands and also among the Western Islands, at least ten or twelve ewes and lambs must have come to grief; the land on which the traps were set being for the most part deer-forests, the spots were less carefully chosen, and the sheep suffered in consequence. It was ascertained, however, in every instance that they either belonged to the crofters who owned small patches on the low ground, or were those that had strayed from large farms many miles across the hills, neither of which were to be looked for in that part of the country. As a rule, little or no injury had been inflicted on the captives, and when released they at once made tracks with most vigorous bounds towards their native haunts. A piteous spectacle, however, was observed one morning in the Island of Lewis on visiting a trap set several miles from where sheep were supposed to feed. A shaggy-coated Highland ewe was lying dead, suffocated in the spongy moss into which she had fallen in her efforts to escape, while her lamb, apparently utterly regardless of the fate that had befallen its dam, was sleeping peacefully curled up on her back. Highland sheep are much addicted to stray long distances, and while in quest of fresh grass, when food is scarce, frequently make their way to apparently inaccessible spots in the face of the cliffs, from which they are utterly unable to return. Many also follow the ebb of the salt water along the shores of the loch-side to nibble at the seaweed, and wholly oblivious of the fact that safety can only be obtained by returning the same way as they came, stolidly face the rising swell of the flowing tide till swept away and drowned. While crossing Loch Shell on the day following that on which the dead ewe and lamb were discovered, I met with three

# RED GROUSE.

... little difficulty was experienced in effecting ... to bear in mind that his own interests ... more particularly with the shepherds. When it ... the ... ground much more frequently than even the most energetic of gamekeepers, and if so inclined can report anything going wrong, the advantage of making allies of them will be easily recognized. I found it a good plan to give to each shepherd one penny a head for every Grouse bagged on his beat; he was then certain to do his utmost to preserve the nests and young birds and promote sport. Unless these men have an interest in increasing the stock of game, they can scarcely be expected to exercise much care in looking after their dogs, and there is certainly no worse poacher than a Highland collie when left unrestrained and allowed to procure his own living; old birds are frequently caught on their nests, and the eggs or the helpless downy mites are swallowed whole. It is an easy matter for any one who takes the trouble to look at the droppings of a collie to ascertain if he has been living on eggs or young birds. While driving near Lairg in Sutherland I detected a couple of collies in the act of snapping up a brood of Black Game in one of the fir-woods by the roadside; the young birds were just able to top the heather, but the dogs sprang up and seized them while on wing, clearing off the whole number in a few minutes; the old Greyhen fought well for her offspring, but little or no attention was paid to her attacks. On another occasion while watching for some Red-necked Phalaropes that frequented the shores of Loch Craggie, a few miles to the north of Loch Shin, a collie came in view working backwards and forwards in the most deliberate manner on the sloping hill-side. A few minutes later it was ascertained that the dog was slowly but steadily driving a blue hare down to the sandy shores of the loch; and having at last forced it on to a bank of fine gravel that stretched some distance into the water, he immediately rushed on and seized his victim, apparently paralyzed with fear and utterly at a loss which way to turn for safety. In a marvellously short time, three or four minutes at the most, that unfortunate hare entirely disappeared, the skull and bones having been crunched up with the flesh, and the flock finally bolted. Probably the gall, which is usually rejected by foxes, dogs, and several of the birds of prey, was left, though our glasses were not sufficiently powerful to detect the slightest morsel on the spot where the feast had been held. From the skilful manner in which the collie manœuvred his intended victim and dashed in as soon as the spit of sand was reached, it was obvious that this was not the first time the performance had been enacted. I have often heard shepherds in different parts of the Highlands complain of the way in which they had been treated by the shooting-tenants; when this is the case it is no wonder that the sport is not so good as might be expected. For my own part I invariably found them the most obliging and hard-working set of men, thankful for the smallest trifles that were offered, and always anxious to hear that a good bag had been made on their beats. It is always advisable to secure the assistance of three or four shepherds with their collies when undertaking a hare-drive in winter on the hill-tops; working at any distance, if within sight of their masters, these clever and tractable animals are of far more service than fifty beaters.

On a few of the wild rocky islands off the shores of the Western Highlands, where only small patches of one or two up to perhaps half a dozen acres of coarse heather are to be seen, I have occasionally noticed a few pairs of Grouse, as well as now and then a single old cock or two; whether the birds were residents on these inhospitable shores or had merely paid a flying visit, it was impossible to form an opinion. No broods were ever observed, though my visits frequently occurred in summer, the presence of Grey Crows and Ravens harbouring about the cliffs or nesting on the ledges precluding all chance of an increase in their numbers. A few of the larger Gulls occasionally resorting to the shores, and at times rearing their young on the grassy slopes, would also have proved by no means agreeable neighbours on such a confined space. Shags, Black Guillemots, and Rock-Pigeons, with a few pairs of Rock-Pipits, were, with the exception of those already named, the sole occupants of these desolate quarters.

So many writers have stated their convictions that the stock of winged game on our moors has been diminished and the health of the survivors impaired by the killing down of birds and beasts of prey, that a few lines with reference to the subject may not be out of place. My own experiences with regard to the habits of those that are by some condemned as the worst offenders (placed erroneously, in many instances, on the vermin list) are also given. Golden Eagles, I am of opinion, cause little damage to Grouse, where hares, rabbits, and lambs (dead or alive) may be readily obtained; now and then I have observed one make a swoop at a wounded bird, but never witnessed those that were uninjured selected for attack. The Sea-Eagle, having now been banished from the majority of its inland breeding-haunts, passes the greater part of its time in the neighbourhood of the coast, and feeding principally on lambs, stranded fish, and other offal may be held perfectly blameless with regard to the Grouse, not the signs of a feather or even a bleached skeleton having ever been detected near their nests; the immature birds that a few years back used to winter on the open moors about Glenlyon, Rannoch, and several of the more northern straths were, when roused from the hill-side, invariably found to be feeding on dead and putrid sheep or other carrion. It is not to be denied that Peregrines destroy large numbers of Grouse, frequently striking down birds for the mere love of slaughter. Though it is certainly advisable that their numbers should be restricted, I should be sorry to see this bold and dashing robber banished from our hills. Kites, though formerly abundant, are now seldom to be met with, unless in a few of the deer-forests, where fir-woods cover the hill-sides. Beneath a single tree to which a pair resorted I counted over a score of carcasses of Grouse, many almost fresh and the remainder weather-beaten skeletons; the greater number, however, I fully believe, had either suffered from disease or fallen from the stroke of the relentless Peregrine. I am well aware that Kites will stray to long distances from their breeding-quarters, but have seldom observed them hunting over the open treeless moors that form the favourite feeding-grounds of the Grouse. Against either the Hen-Harrier or Merlin, both of which breed out on the open moors, I can bring no charges based on personal observations; the fact that a Greyhen, on one occasion, selected a spot for rearing her young within six or eight feet of the nest in which the eggs of a Harrier were on the point of hatching, must be regarded as evidence in favour of the latter species. The thievish propensities of the Sparrow-Hawk have been dinted on by endless writers; my own observations, however, taken during several years' wanderings in the Highlands, scarcely assist in confirming the bad character usually ascribed to this handsome bird. He is doubtless a dashing robber, but I have yet to learn that game in the north suffers to any great extent from his attacks. A few Ring-Ouzels with now and then a Lark and a constant supply of Pipits formed the greater portion of the food discovered on the nests examined. A male and female I secured as specimens, and whose brood is figured in 'Rough Notes,' were each shot within a few minutes of one another, with a Meadow-Pipit in their talons, while attempting to reach their young before it was fairly light. The pairs whose operations I watched were for the most part residents in plantations situated on wide-stretching moorlands, where both Grouse and Snipe were plentiful; still no signs of their misdeeds could be ascertained. Exceedingly suspicious of danger and easily allured by a bait, Buzzards are rapidly disappearing throughout the northern counties of the Highlands. I remarked in almost every instance, where their breeding-quarters were inspected, that the adjacent ledges, as well as the grassy mounds and slopes in the vicinity, were strewn with castings or the remains of their food, the fleck of blue hares or rabbits plainly indicating the nature of their prey. No feathers or bones of birds having been detected, I am unable to bring forward any evidence to prove that the presence of these interesting birds is undesirable on the moors. Though the Kestrel has been declared in several instances to carry off the downy young

I repeatedly remarked that, while breeding on ... consisted ... the most part of rats and mice. Not a single member of the Crow ... to ... Grey Crow being without doubt the most mischievous of ... troublesome crew. Ravens usually hunt at higher elevations on the hills than the rest of the family, and Ptarmigan suffer considerably, their nests being frequently sought out and plundered by these sturdy rascals. Jackdaws are well known as inveterate thieves; I noticed the empty shells of hundreds of Grouse eggs scattered over the ledges of rock on which a colony were breeding in the face of a cliff in the west of Perthshire. In dry weather, when food is scarce, Rooks are especially addicted to hunting over the lower portions of the hill-sides, and may frequently be seen with an egg in their beaks. Both the Greater and Lesser Black-backed Gulls breed on the moors in several counties, and levy a heavy tax on their less powerful neighbours, any eggs or young falling in their way being gulped down with the utmost avidity. I once detected a Common Gull in the act of devouring a downy nestling of the Golden Plover; it is, however, doubtless on small fish, captured in the shallows of the rivers, that this species chiefly subsists. Judging by the castings observed scattered over the moss-grown mounds on the flat moors of Caithness from which parties of Arctic Skuas had been seen to rise, it is possible that they possess a taste for eggs. It is, however, but fair to state that I never met with an opportunity of watching them in the act of committing a robbery of this description; and there is of course a chance that Hooded Crows might have been the real culprits, none of the specimens of *S. parasiticus* I shot on the moors, near their breeding-quarters, containing any other food than smolts. An inspection of the supply of prey collected in the larder of a mountain-fox will at once reveal the fact that game of all descriptions must suffer to a large extent from the rapacity of these marauders. On returning to my shooting-quarters in Glenlyon in May 1866, I learned from the head keeper that the foxhunter* had recently been over the greater part of the ground with his dogs, but had utterly failed in detecting signs of the object of his search. Being well aware that the vixen not unfrequently conveys her cubs long distances on signs of danger, removing them to some den among the rocks, which is unknown or inaccessible to her pursuers, and again transporting them from place to place, I was anxious to ascertain if it was possible that the whole of the old badger- and fox-cairns on our beats had been deserted. In order to make a thorough exploration of the earths near the summit of a low range of hills to the south of the Lyon, an early start was decided upon, and after driving some miles on our way the conveyance was left before the rays of the sun had struck down into the glen. An ascent of but a few hundred yards had been made, when feathers scattered about among the heather attracted attention, and on examining the spot it was at once apparent that a hen Grouse had been seized on her nest. The track over which the bird had been dragged was by no means difficult to follow, and after taking the line for a couple of hundred yards I was convinced that it led to the upper cairn, and accordingly made straight for the hill-top. From the widely spread traces of feathers and down scattered ... the roots of the ... the bird had probably been carried off alive, the down and feathers having ... flap. On reaching ... was at once evident from ... by our small pack ... at ... at home. ... to ... down towards the ... we desisted, and set to work to construct ... await the arrival of the vixen at dusk, at ... she ...

killed prey. I then mounted the hill-pony that carried the panniers, and rode rapidly homewards, despatching on my arrival a supply of necessaries to enable the watchers to remain throughout the night on the spot. At daybreak the following morning, as the men had not returned, I again started for the hill and learned that a fox had been seen at dusk; a drifting squall of sleet passing over at the time, the dim light had probably interfered with the aim, and the charge fired appeared to have taken little effect. A thick coating of snow to the depth of several inches had fallen during the night, and the shelters put up as well as the wraps provided had proved most acceptable to those on the watch. As it was quite possible that the cubs might be deserted owing to the alarm given, we determined to dig them out at once; after setting the men to work, I proceeded with a couple of terriers to make a cast round the lower part of the hill, in order to ascertain if by chance any fatal injury had been inflicted by the shot. At length, after nearly an hour's search, I came upon a fine old dog-fox lying dead and stiff in a dry gully about half a mile from the cairn. On returning up hill it was evident from the excitement shown by a couple of the dogs that had been left, and their reluctance to advance any distance into the den, that the vixen had succeeded in escaping observation during the darkness and had made her way into the earth. After several hours' labour the family, with the exception of the vixen, whom I was forced to shoot, and one cub torn by the terriers, were safely secured in hampers and brought down to the lodge. On carefully examining the contents of their larder, we discovered the remains of four hen Grouse and two Greyhens all fresh; the fragments that were left also gave evidence that over a score of blue hares as well as a few rabbits had been lately brought in and partially consumed. On putting the terriers into another cairn, half a mile further along the ridge of the hill, they dragged out two more Grouse partly eaten, and in all probability the cubs had only lately been removed from this den; the dogs exhibiting little excitement while exploring the innermost recesses, we did not waste time to dig down and investigate the amount of prey collected. The whole of the birds discovered having proved to be hens engaged in sitting, ample proof is afforded of the numbers of broods of Grouse that must be destroyed to supply the requirements of a single litter of cubs. Though condemned by some who have claims to be considered authorities on the subject, I can bring no charges based on personal observation against the badger, whose numbers have greatly diminished of late years. As my knowledge concerning the habits of these animals was exceedingly limited, I made inquiries of Donald McKerchar, the head keeper at Innerwick in Glenlyon, and he furnished the following information:—"With regard to badgers destroying Grouse, I cannot say that I have ever seen them doing harm; they feed for the most part on dead sheep or other carrion found decomposing on the hills; I believe, however, that they will occasionally take eggs. Nothing in the shape of food is to be seen about their dens[*], whatever they carry to their young is first swallowed and afterwards disgorged. They are also very fond of wild honey: when living with my father near the head of the glen, I have often seen where they had been engaged in digging out the comb; by some means or other they were enabled to kill the bees, which were to be seen lying dead round about the place." Wild cats are now so scarce, banished, in fact, in almost every district to the deer-forests or the remotest ranges of the hills, that the injury they inflict on the interests of the Grouse-shooters must be exceedingly small. The domestic pussy, when weary of basking before the fire in the shealing or shooting-lodge, rarely strays to any distance up the hill-side unless to take up its quarters in a rabbit-warren. As far as I was able to ascertain in the Highlands, we seldom suffered from the depredations of these marauders, unless a few young rabbits were carried off; a good look-out, however, had to be kept that the door of the larder was in perfect order, or an entrance would be effected and any game hanging within reach torn down and carried off. Rats also are seldom met

[*] This fact I noticed on more than one occasion, but do not assert that it is invariably the case, having only examined three or four of the dens or cairns to which badgers resorted in the Highlands.

... the stacks about the farms or the outbuildings round the shooting-lodges. ... pests, the Innerwick keeper wrote to me as follows: "I do not remember to ... our Grouse-moors, they do not go so high. Last spring we found a dead rat ... on one of our hills; but that is no proof it was obtained on the moors, as it is most ... down and captured his prey about some of the steadings." I ascertained by personal ... that martens will carry off the young of game birds. In the Highlands their range appears limited to the beech- and pine-woods, and I have seldom seen their tracks at any distance from the timber when snow was on the ground. Several trapped by gamekeepers and foresters have been examined; but all, I believe, were captured in the plantations, where there could have been little chance that Grouse had suffered from their predatory habits. Stoats and weasels, considering their size, are the most merciless and bloodthirsty little wretches it is possible to imagine; none who have watched their performances while in pursuit of prey can doubt that they exercise a peculiar fascination over their victims. I have repeatedly come across hen Grouse lying dead on the moors, evidently dragged from their nests and killed by these destructive creatures, the wounds on their necks and the marks of the blood that had been sucked plainly indicating the cause of death. After satisfying their appetite in the first instance, it is obvious that they return at times and in some manner convey the dead carcasses to their dens, the immense quantities of bones collected in the cairns to which they resort affording conclusive evidence as to their misdeeds. Some years back, while crossing the hills to the north of the Lyon in Perthshire, the keepers pointed out a large cavity among some blocks of stone to which stoats had frequently resorted. Although the men stated that during the past season the place had been deserted, owing to the destruction of its former occupants, I felt inclined to make an investigation of the old quarters. As both picks and spades were on the ponies (we were on a trapping-expedition at the time), it took but a few minutes to excavate sufficiently to allow the removal of the largest slab of rock behind which the animals had made their way. The stone proved of considerable weight, but at last gave way before the efforts of half a dozen sturdy Highlanders. The fall of earth from above that accompanied its displacement unfortunately obliterated all signs of the markings; the remains, however, of the bones of birds (many evidently belonging to Grouse, both old and young), as well as those of rabbits, that were dug out would probably have filled a bushel measure. I now and then come across smaller collections in the cairns or rabbit-burrows on the steep hill-sides, but never met with an opportunity for examining one of their breeding-places in England.

In addition to the other dangers to which they are exposed, Grouse suffer considerably, in many districts, from the effects of striking while on flight against iron fences and the lines of telegraph-wires stretched across the moors. While exploring the upper ranges of the Crossfell in Cumberland, early in June 1876, I noticed several clots of blood and feathers adhering to a wire fence, of about three feet in height, that formed the boundary between some sheep-farms. Though not a bird was to be seen, it is probable that the shepherds by keeping a sharp look-out secured a constant supply. At various points where the Highland railway runs through the desolate region lying between the Straths of Tay and Spey, I obtained evidence that numbers of Grouse were killed by the telegraph-wires; and again further north, in Sutherland, there was little difficulty in ascertaining the heavy losses sustained by this species from the same causes.

The enormous bags of Grouse recorded during the last few years appear to have stirred up the animosity of certain writers; and many of them have indulged in unlimited abuse of those whose names headed the lists. The most venomous attack on a sportsman that has come under my notice is, however, contained in MacGillivray's 'British Birds,' vol. i. p. 183, and is so quaintly bitter that I offer no apology for quoting a portion:—"The diversion which 'grouse-shooting' affords is well known, few persons residing in districts where the Brown Ptarmigan abounds not having to some extent engaged in it, in despite of game laws and other impediments. In my opinion, it is a pitiful and barbarous sport, as pursued by a regularly equipped and legally qualified slaughterer, who, even without the labour of charging his gun, still less of carrying home the produce of his idle industry, destroys as much game in one day as might serve for a dozen." As this outburst of indignation was penned some fifty years ago, when the heaviest bags were small compared with those of the present day, it is hard to imagine what would have followed had the observant naturalist perused the account of the 220 brace of Grouse killed by the Maharajah Duleep Singh over dogs in Perthshire on the 12th of August 1871, and the 121 brace of driven birds obtained by Lord Walsingham in Yorkshire on the 28th of August 1872.

With the exception of one season in Ross-shire and a few weeks in other northern counties, the whole of my observations on the breeding and general habits of Grouse, as well as on the preservation of the birds and management of the ground, were made in the west of Perthshire. The most prolific of the moors in Glenlyon were at a high elevation on the hills; the deep and sheltered corries and the mountain-sides being steep and frequently rocky, hard work was necessary in order to procure a bag. It was seldom that Grouse would lie to dogs in this locality after the beginning of September, the month almost invariably commencing with rain and blusterous weather; a fine day with a light favourable breeze, however, occasionally proved an exception. 20 brace having been twice bagged during the first week of that month in 1867 by one gun. For the remainder of the season it was only when birds were taken by surprise in some gully or hollow shut in by rocky surroundings that a few shots could be obtained. On the approach of winter the Grouse usually joined in immense packs; and after having noted their accustomed line of flight round the hill-tops, I was occasionally enabled to secure a few brace by driving. Though the nature of the country differed considerably from that in which this style of sport is usually carried on, several shots were occasionally obtained; concealed among the slabs of stone on a stretch of rough ground, I was now and then enabled, by using a couple of guns, to stop three or four brace while the pack in straggling parties continued to sweep past. The whole of the Grouse on the hillside appeared at this time of year to gather into one large body; the magnitude of these flocks varied according to the severity of the winter, consisting, as far as one was able to judge, of from five or six hundred to a thousand birds. During protracted storms of frost and snow Grouse are occasionally to be seen in immense flocks on the higher and more exposed moors; in many instances the birds have been observed by the keepers to gradually draw off towards the low-lying straths and flats where food and shelter is more readily obtained. It is seldom, if ever, that any stragglers return when once driven from their native haunts by stress of weather. Under date of March 1866 I find the following in one of my old game-books:—" During the whole of the month it was exceedingly stormy, with much snow. The Grouse at the commencement of the severe weather collected into packs of several thousands on the roughest portions of Rchleon and Kerromore hills; in such numbers did they gather that the ground for acres was black with birds, many of which must have come down the glen from Argyleshire. Fortunately the weather broke up before any general movement had taken place, and saved the majority from leaving that part of the country." Even after the termination of winter Grouse frequently suffer from a late fall of snow, which destroys the greater part, if not the whole, of the eggs. I witnessed a terrible storm in Strath Spey in May 1869, when widespread destruction took place; a keeper in Glenlyon also lately informed me that for the first ten days in May 1884 the hills were deeply covered with snow, and the whole of the earlier nests deserted.

Many probable and still more improbable causes for the Grouse-disease have been brought forward and thoroughly discussed without any beneficial result being obtained. That the disease will ever be successfully grappled with appears hopeless; should the landed proprietors as well as the tenants of even the whole of a county combine and carry out under competent supervision all the measures that are supposed to be conducive to the well-being of the species, and succeed in keeping their birds in health for a time (which I believe is possible), there are certain contingencies that no human foresight can avert. On many portions of the hill-sides frosts and the cutting east winds of early spring will occasionally blight the young heather-shoots that form the chief nourishment of the birds, and rendering their food indigestible lay the foundation of a disease which, though at first only attacking those exposed to the same influences (i. e. typhoid in character), eventually becomes epidemic and spreads far and wide. A keeper, who had acquired his experience during many years' service in the west of Perthshire, informed me that he had noticed the disease was most deadly on the moors facing towards the south, and consequently more exposed to the rays of the sun than on the shaded ground on the northern slopes. Judging from personal observation, I was led to believe that the old cocks were the earliest sufferers, their dead bodies being the first seen on two occasions when the disease made its appearance. Thirst is doubtless one of the symptoms of the malady; I met with both weather-beaten skeletons and decomposing carcases lying thickly round the loch-sides, and also by the burns running through the flat moors of Sutherland and Caithness, in the summer of 1869. Various opinions as to the origin of disease have from time to time appeared in print: a too liberal diet of corn obtained from the stooks in autumn has been supposed prejudicial; the wash applied to sheep as well as worms from the animals themselves have been considered to affect the internal organs; and the infatuated birds are, moreover, declared to have attempted to emulate the powers of the Ostrich and subsist on the unlimited stores of shot scattered over the moors. It has frequently been remarked that a careless and irregular system of burning the heather, carried out regardless of consequences, with an insufficient staff of keepers and shepherds to conduct the operations and guard against the undue spread of the flames, deprives the birds of the most tender and wholesome portion of their food as well as the adjacent shelter necessary for their safety, rendering them more liable to disease and exposed to the attacks of vermin. Though overfeeding on grain is by no means conducive to health, disease often proves most virulent in localities where it is utterly impossible for the birds to have made their way to cornfields; I have seen them lying dead in scores on the moors around the shores of Loch Slatel, on the borders of Sutherland and Caithness. Its ravages may also be traced in glens where only small patches of land adjoining the river-sides are fit for cultivation, and to which the birds seldom if ever descend to feed on the grain either when in stook or scattered over the fields. In a recently published work on 'Grouse Disease' the following quotation appears:—"My opinion is that corn is a very unwholesome food for Grouse. Let any person examine the droppings of Grouse when fed on corn, and they will find them similar to tar, but rather browner in colour." It is doubtless a fact that corn is not so suitable as their natural food; the droppings, however, referred to (which are of a reddish-brown tint and slimy in texture) are by no means uncommon on the moors and cannot be relied upon as a proof that the birds have been feeding on corn.

In September 1867, while excavating for the foundation of an underground shealing * on the summit of Baloloan, a hill some 3000 feet in height, lying between Glenlyon and Rannoch, a Grouse egg, apparently petrified, was discovered at the depth of seven or eight feet below the surface; its colouring was most brilliant and perfect, and the weight nearly, if not quite, double that of an ordinary egg. Unfortunately on leaving the lodge at the close of the season this curiosity was forgotten and in all probability thrown away at the time of the annual cleaning.

* This shelter, constructed for purposes of observation, was built in the face of a steep and rocky ridge just below the mountain-top, with an entrance by means of a long underground passage from the back of the hill. A dead horse, sheep, or some other carrion having been placed on an open stretch of green turf well within view and shot from the interior, and a fresh carcase laid down when necessary, there was always an attraction to the spot for birds of prey. Through the window, formed by a gap in the rocks, their movements and contortions while consuming or struggling over their unsavoury banquet could be easily watched and noted down, any rarities also, if needed as specimens, being well within range. The door to the passage (carefully concealed by heather and stones) being out of sight of the bait, an entrance could at any time be effected without giving the slightest warning to any bird or beast feasting on the offal.

While awaiting the commencement of a drive for Black Game on the hill of Kerromore, to the south of the Lyon, in December 1867, I narrowly escaped a collision with an old cock Grouse which might possibly have been attended with serious results. My station was on an elevated ledge of rock overlooking the open moor, and having crawled to the edge of the precipice, I was in the act of stretching over to ascertain the position of the beaters, when, with a sudden rush of wind, a bird dashed past with incredible speed; having suffered merely from a slight derangement of my stalking-cap (evidently brushed by the pinion-feathers of a wing), I turned in time to discern a Grouse disappearing on the sky-line over an adjacent brae.

Though I have never witnessed Grouse perching on trees or shrubs, it is a well-known fact that they occasionally do so. I was informed by my artist, Mr. Neale, that while staying in North Galloway during the latter half of December 1859, the weather being exceedingly severe at the time, he frequently observed Grouse feeding in large packs, sometimes numbering over a hundred, on the stubbles. Occasionally a few were noticed to fly up and settle on the stunted whitethorn bushes and commence feeding on the hips and haws; while so engaged he succeeded in shooting six or seven brace.

While shooting on the moors in the west of Perthshire during winter I have often killed old cocks exhibiting a larger number of white feathers about the breast and belly than I have noticed in other parts of the Highlands. The adult male figured on the Plate represents a fine specimen obtained in Glenlyon in December 1866; this bird was, however, by no means so strongly marked with white as many others seen and shot in the same locality.

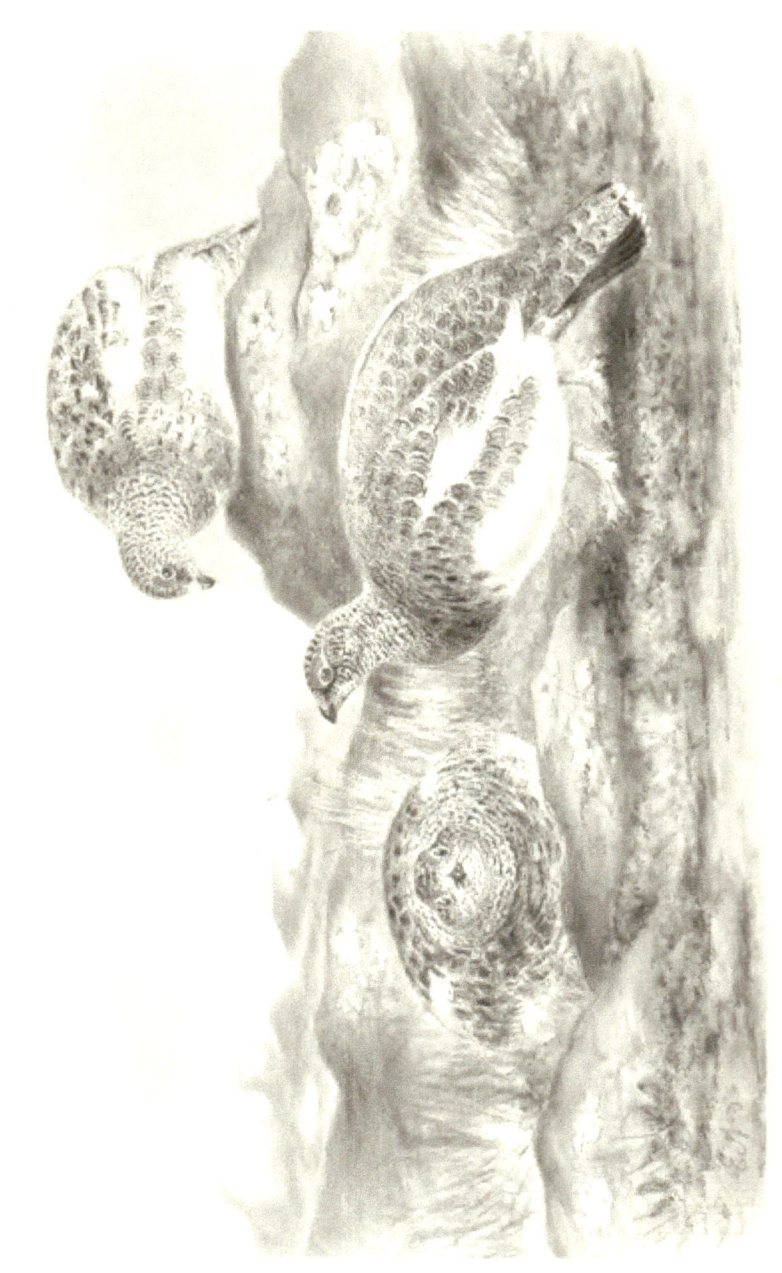

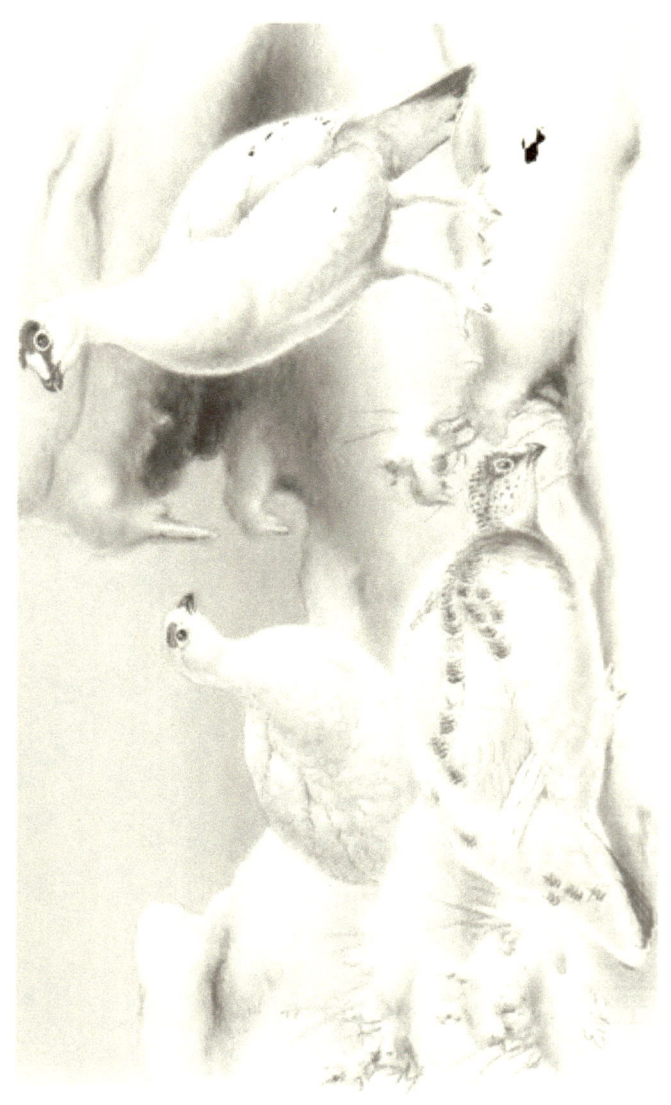

# PTARMIGAN.

## *LAGOPUS MUTUS.*

------

         of          of

well as the rough nature of the ground itself, render                                           The uncertainty attending the whereabouts of the packs                   flights, at times            hill-top to another, tend also to increase the work *.                                        not aware of any beats where heavy bags may              For                       more intent on           an insight into their habits and watching        movements when                I never attempted to procure any number—a few hence, perhaps five or six, from which to select specimens, being the utmost ever killed, under even the most favourable circumstances. The changes to which this hardy species is subject are remarkable; spring, summer, autumn, and winter each find the Ptarmigan arrayed in a different dress. Although birds exhibiting many various stages may occasionally be met with, the Plates show the usual plumage at the seasons stated, and render a lengthened description of the changes unnecessary.

As previously stated, Ptarmigan-shooting, from the commencement to the end of the season, is, at best, uncertain sport. The birds are almost invariably unsuspicious of danger during fine and still weather; wind and wet, however, usually render them unsettled, and, even under circumstances utterly inconceivable, I have found them as unapproachable as the wildest Grouse. Should their haunts be visited on a still day in August or the beginning of September, the packs, if the ground is carefully scanned, will be detected creeping over the stunted herbage or running quietly among the adjoining grey and weather-beaten slabs of rock, squatting occasionally if approached, but taking little more notice of the intruder than barn-door fowls; even a shot within the distance of a few yards will frequently have no greater effect than causing them to lie closer. To make a heavy bag under such circumstances could scarcely be considered satisfactory by sportsmen. The call of the Ptarmigan is a low croak; unless the attention is attracted by the note, packs may often be overlooked, so exactly does their plumage assimilate with the surrounding tints.

Ptarmigan probably have as strong a scent as Grouse, though owing to the stony nature of the ground, or possibly some unknown cause, I remarked on one or two occasions that even the steadiest dogs in my kennel were of but little service on the hill-top †. When the summits are covered with snow any animal but a retriever is, of course, useless. Considering the length of time the poor beast may be exposed to the effects

------

* Where but one or two packs resort to a hill-top long flights are far more frequent. The birds, on being disturbed, appear to seek for company, dropping almost instantly should a few scattered individuals be passed over, but continuing at times on wing till the summit of some adjoining mountain is gained.

† Blue hares, of course, were common; but being also abundant on the Grouse-moors, they were utterly ignored by the beater of setters referred to

of the wintery blasts and driving storms, as well as the dangers of the frozen sheets of ice, which any high-couraged dog will attempt to cross if despatched in search of a dead bird, I always prefer to leave my faithful followers at home when in pursuit of winter Ptarmigan.

Although I have visited at different times during my wanderings in the north several Ptarmigan-ranges in the counties of Inverness, Ross, and Sutherland, in each of which the nature of the country varies considerably, the whole of the specimens I collected were obtained in the north-west of Perthshire. Between 1865 and 1866 I had many opportunities, at all seasons, for making observations. My notes contain repeated accounts of sport on the hill-tops during autumn; but as one day's work much resembles that of another, it will be useless to make any lengthened extracts. The greatest drawback to the sport in this part of the country is the steep and dangerous nature of the hill-side over which it is necessary to follow the packs. There is no little difficulty and risk in making a successful shot at a bird rising unexpectedly while picking one's way across loose and slippery flakes of stone, overhanging perhaps a precipice of some hundred feet in height, or climbing a steep mountain-slope among huge blocks of rock and granite. Though Ptarmigan, when driven up from their accustomed feeding-grounds in the vicinity of the short green herbage and stunted vegetation that alone flourish on the hill-tops, often seek refuge in the rough and stony gullies, such localities are by no means their favourite haunts; unless previously disturbed or constantly harassed, they are seldom found harbouring in such inhospitable quarters.

A short extract from my notes for 1865 will give some slight idea of the difficult nature of the ground in the west of Perthshire. When shooting in this part dogs were seldom employed: forming five or six keepers and guides in line, some ten or a dozen yards apart, I usually took one of the higher stations, and in this manner we made our way over the rough ground.

"September 6. Light breeze from the north-west; weather favourable in every respect. Tried the top of Benderg for Ptarmigan. The first time of going round the hill a large pack rose among the broken stones on the east side. Though scattered, the whole number sprung within twenty yards, the ground, however, was so dangerous as to preclude all chance of a shot. A few moments later a single bird, which had remained behind, was detected running in front of the line, and in fifteen minutes was eventually bagged. A couple of hundred yards further on the pack was found again, and a second time escaped from the same cause, the whole of this face of the hill being almost impassable. The old cock on this occasion separated from the rest of the pack, and marking the ledge on which he pitched, I managed to scramble up, and succeeded in obtaining a shot. A thick mist now came suddenly on, with a cold breeze, and it became exceedingly dark. During a slight break in the clouds a low croak was heard, and a couple of young birds were discovered squatting on a knoll within the distance of five and twenty yards. As they rose I fired, but on reaching the spot, not even so much as a feather could be found. After hunting about for some time with no further results, it appeared that both birds must have escaped. As it was now too dark to proceed, and the drizzle had increased to a shower, a halt was made and lunch brought out. In less than half an hour the mist and rain cleared off and the sun again broke through. A setter which had been kept up all the morning, owing to the rough and stony ground across which we had been working, was now tried. On being loosed he did not move above half a dozen paces before he stood, then drew on a few yards and stood again; and on looking just in front of him the two birds were discovered close together, one unable to fly and the other retaining sufficient strength to flutter downhill. The latter, being shot, rolled to the foot of the rocks and caused some delay before it was retrieved. Having now as many birds as were needed and a long tramp before us, we turned homewards. On reaching the flat ground on the summit of the hill a single old bird persisted in running just in front of us, jerking his tail in such an insulting manner that I could not resist shooting him when he rose."

Many more extracts concerning the shooting of autumn birds during the seasons of 1865, '66, and '67 might be given; but they are almost repetitions of the facts related above. The birds at these seasons were, for the most part, as tame as chickens, though occasionally unapproachable, and at times crossing the valleys to the neighbouring hill-tops. It appears a common occurrence for one or possibly two birds to be left behind when the pack take wing; these, if unmolested, will continue running and turning from time to time, with but slight signs of alarm, to watch the intruders on their haunts.

On the approach of winter, Ptarmigan show a considerable addition to the white on the plumage, though it is only the oldest birds that assume the pure white dress so early as the end of the shooting-season. The young occasionally retain several grey feathers in their plumage a month or even six weeks later; and, judging by my own experience, it is probable that some of the more backward birds do not become thoroughly white till their second winter. This change is not a moult; the white appears first at the point of the feathers, and then gradually spreads down to the root or quill. I have now and then killed Ptarmigan which, at the first glance, appeared perfectly white, but on being more closely examined showed several stains or lightly marked blotches on their plumage; on turning back the feathers it was obvious that a few were still half grey; and their darker side showing dimly through the pure white covering of the adjoining or overlapping feathers, imparted the stained appearance to their otherwise spotless plumage.

Ptarmigan-shooting in December is a very different sport to the slaughter of the innocents in August. The hills have now put on their winter covering of snow and ice, and a good bag of white Grouse is seldom ................... It is a matter of small importance to be lost all night on a Ptarmigan-hill .................... on a winter's evening, with a snow-storm coming on, might ......................... In order to avoid such mishaps, I found it the safest plan, ............... leave the lodge by 3 or 4 o'clock in the morning, and so ................. as it was possible to commence shooting), I was ....... or ........................... daylight for the roughest part of the ....................... the dark, it was discovered, on arriving at the ................. of the summits were enveloped in cloud and ........ circumstances, ........ of ................ the question, it only remained to beat ...................................................... be seen by an extract from ..............

It was well on towards mid-day before we reached the top of the hill, and on approaching ............... was evident that all the surrounding ranges were enveloped in mist, which was gradually advancing from the north-east. An immediate start in search of birds was consequently made, in hopes of obtaining a brace or two before the mist compelled us to desist. Forming at once in line (two keepers, two gillies, and myself), so as just to keep one another in sight, we made the best of our way round the face of the hill. The surface of the snow being hard and frozen, we were able to advance at some speed, though of course walking on the slopes was risky. On reaching a large patch of broken stones on the north side of the hill, perhaps a wee bit over the march (but the mist was so thick it was impossible to tell our whereabouts with any certainty), the croak of a Ptarmigan was heard; and on stopping the line and looking round, I soon made out a white head over some large blocks of stone. Almost immediately it was detected the bird dashed downhill, though just too late to escape, and, falling dead, rolled to the foot of the rocks. On being recovered it proved to be a young cock, the plumage still exhibiting a large amount of grey among the white feathers. After passing two or three ugly spots, where the line was forced to open right and left, we started several birds, which were lost sight of in the mist before there was an opportunity of firing a shot. At length, during a slight break in the clouds, as the mist was somewhat less dense, a drive was attempted. Taking my station on a ridge on the east side of the hill, the men were despatched right round. One bird only could I clearly discern, though several others passed in the haze. Being uncertain whether the shot had taken effect, we searched the direction which the bird had followed, and found him, at once, perfectly dead, with the wings spread out, on an open patch of ground from which the snow had drifted. While again going round the hill, some birds were heard croaking a hundred yards or so in front of the line. On making towards the sound, intently examining the outline of the snow to obtain an early view of the pack, a large sheet of ice was overlooked, and, my feet slipping, away I went downhill. Luckily there was a drift of newly fallen snow (soft as a feather-bed) about twenty feet below, and into this I pitched quite easily, none the worse, not even a shake. Had it not been for the snow, I must have gone over one hundred feet to the bottom of a steep gully. The birds were started by a couple of the men descending the slope to ascertain if any damage had resulted from the fall. One of the pack, however, a fine old cock, settled again directly, and I was able to crawl within range before he rose. This bird and the last were adult males in the most perfect winter plumage.

"It was now nearly dark, and time to be leaving the hill, so the keeper called the men together. As two of them were not forthcoming and had not been seen for over an hour, I fired several shots, without, however, the slightest result. The three of us that were left then turned back and went round the hill, but though firing again and calling repeatedly, could gain no tidings of them. While going round this time I killed one more bird, a female that had half assumed the winter dress. When the circuit of the hill-top had been accomplished, darkness had set in, and it appeared probable that the two men, having missed us, had left the hill and proceeded homewards in advance. As a last resource I fired a few more shots, and we then started downhill, finding no little difficulty in picking our way, owing to the uncertain light and extent of the tracts of frozen snow. Luckily our pace was slow, as after proceeding about a couple of hundred yards, a faint cry some distance to the north was audible during one of our halts. After answering and waiting a few minutes, the men came up. Both were nearly beat; but a pull at the "Doctor"* and a few mouthfuls of food soon revived them. We learned that, while holding the two lower stations on the line, the poor fellows had been going round the east side of the hill, cutting their way as best they could through a frozen snow-drift, till at last it was discovered impossible to proceed further; and on turning back they found, to their dismay, that some fresh snow had fallen over the tracks previously cut; consequently, owing to the mist and gloom, they were in a decidedly critical position. However, after about an hour's careful work they had succeeded in cutting their way to the top of the drift, and on reaching the hard ground on the highest part of the hill had wandered about, searching for the remainder of the party, till, losing nerve, they were utterly at a loss which direction to take. It was lucky the shouts were heard, as, weary and benumbed by cold, they were utterly incapable of reaching shelter, even if aware of the line to be followed. A heavy fall of snow commencing as we at last took leave of the mountain-top, it is unlikely that any tidings would have been learned concerning their fate till the snows had melted from the hills in the following summer."

In 1866, though frequently shooting on the hill-tops, I did not attempt to obtain specimens of white Ptarmigan, a few brace only being bagged during hare-beats. The observations recorded in my notes for this season may be passed over without reference, as they contain no facts concerning their habits or actions that can throw further light on the history of these interesting birds.

A somewhat ludicrous mistake, which occurred one night in November 1866, was brought about by the preparations occasionally necessary when large numbers of beaters are employed. A few lines from my notes may prove a warning to the tourists of shootings-lodges in remote districts:—

"Having decided on a horse-beat and Ptarmigan-drive for the following day, I turned in early, intending to be up and off betimes. My night's rest was not long disturbed; but shortly before 1 a.m. I woke up with the conviction that something was wrong. The fire burned low in the grate; but the light falling on the face of my ... looked to the back of a chair, the heavier ... audible ... I was ... the value of ... to ... inconvenience of being forced ... in perfect working-order, in case ... speedily asleep. Troubled ... The dying embers of the ... hour had elapsed since my ... footsteps it was evident that the ... was the spot ... packing their plunder. At once a horrible ... sleepy ... off the guns, what should we do ... idea caused ... and in less than a minute I was up and ... Armed ... first minutely inspected, ... that invariably creaked having been successfully avoided. ... light gleamed through ... It was ... after my expectations of ... the ... to be confronted ... of taking scones! ... sudden intrusion, ... learned that ... to be prepared ... of ... to make ... than ... to ...

In 1857 I made ... during December to the Ptarmigan ground ... procured as many ... One short ... from my notes will give an ...

... with a direct precipice down to the river, some ... a breeze sprung up, and had greatly increased an ... On ... was overcast, and it was impossible to ascertain whether the tops were free from mist. In some parts the peat-track we followed for the first mile or two up the mountain-side was simply a sheet of ice. At length an old shealing was reached where a part of our provisions were left, in order to lighten the load and insure a supply on the homeward journey. On leaving the track and making for the top, our chief difficulty consisted in keeping the whole of the gillies together while climbing over the rough ground; owing to the darkness, a man was invisible at the distance of four or five yards, while the howling of the wind prevented a call being audible.

"The first streak of light appeared in the east while halting to rest in a small hollow, about half a

\* A hill on the north side of Glenlyon.

mile from the summit. Here we were forced to wait some time for daylight before crossing into the next corrie, where the birds would probably be found if the spot was sufficiently sheltered. When day fairly broke, all the tops were enveloped in mist, and on crossing into the gully it was obviously useless to search that part for birds, as the wind blew with irresistible force and the snow drifted in every direction. We were first saluted with a regular whirlwind of frozen snow and small particles of ice, which completely blinded us for some time, and while in that unpleasant predicament, were nearly swept off our legs by a furious gust that came roaring round the hill, carrying a flock of unfortunate Snow-Buntings nearly into our faces. We next turned further east to try if it was possible to find some shelter in that direction. While crossing the intervening space (a mass of snow, with here and there a patch of broken and exposed rocks) a brace or two of birds were started; these being all excessively backward were allowed to escape. Immediately on gaining a sheltered corrie, three birds, as white as the snow they rose from, got up close by; but struggling in a drift of newly fallen snow, I was unable to fire. We watched them for some time till they were lost in the mist, which had nearly descended to the line we were following. In a few moments they again came in view through a break in the clouds, and were marked down in a patch of broken moss. I had not gone fifty yards in their direction, before two more birds were detected feeding among some stones where the ground was almost bare. Not the slightest notice was taken of our approach till we were within half a dozen yards of them; and being able to examine their plumage closely, I satisfied myself that, as specimens, they were of no use. On arriving at the spot where the three birds had pitched, they were nowhere to be seen; but hearing loud croaking close at hand, I kept following the sound, when a dozen birds at least sprung within ten yards at the very moment the coating of snow and ice covering a small gully gave way and let me down to the bottom, a distance of ten or twelve feet. Fortunately the snow was soft and dry, and on being extricated by the gillies, I followed in the line taken by the pack, coming suddenly on six or seven birds feeding, without the slightest suspicion of danger, among some fine gravel and plants from which they had scraped the snow. A male and female, both perfectly white, were among them; but all drawing together as they rose (though two fell) to the first barrel, and one to the second), the female only was secured, the two others killed being exceedingly backward.

"Blinding squalls now followed one another in rapid succession, and the snow commencing to drift in a most dangerous manner, we decided that it was the safest plan to leave the high ground as speedily as possible. Though having worked hard, with merely a nip of mountain-dew by way of refreshment, for several hours, no halt was made till the shealing was reached. Here, after lunching, we remained for some time in hopes of the weather improving; the longer, however, we waited the worse grew the storm. At last, as the daylight began to fade, we started homewards; and only just in time, as on reaching the low ground we found the newly fallen snow a foot deep and drifting fast."

Though repeatedly passing severe winters in the north, I never met with Ptarmigan at a low elevation on the moors or mountain-slopes. The tops and higher ranges are at times almost entirely deserted when the snow is frozen to the consistency of ice. The packs under such circumstances frequent hill-sides, where at other seasons they are seldom or never observed. White Grouse evidently cling with true Highland pertinacity to their native mountain homes. But one solitary instance of these birds appearing on the low grounds has come to my knowledge. A keeper in the west of Perthshire informed me that his father, a small farmer in the upper part of Glenlyon, many years ago, during an exceedingly cold and protracted winter, discovered a pack of seven or eight birds in his barn-yard: the old man, I learned, always spoke of it as a remarkable occurrence and a proof of the extraordinary severity of the weather.

The nest of the Ptarmigan is invariably found near the summits of the highest hills. Here, among the mists and clouds, and not unfrequent snow-squalls, without a neighbour save the Dotterel, Snow-Bunting, or blue hare, they hardly dare pass the summer, till driven by the storms to seek shelter from the wintry blasts a lower elevation. [...] would doubtless increase were it not for the [...] A bird or two may occasionally fall victims [...] by the king of the air have, according to my own observations, [...] their numbers. The nest and eggs are by no means easily discovered; though frequently searched for, I never had the luck to meet with a nest except by accident. At last, after many unsuccessful attempts, three nests were found within a few hundred yards of one another on the hills above Glenlyon, in the north-west of Perthshire. A few extracts from my notes for June 1867, while engaged in procuring specimens in summer plumage, will describe the retiring and artful habits of the female and the noisy and demonstrative actions of the male at that season:—

"Having repeatedly gone over the ground within eight or ten miles of the lodge without success, I at length determined to search the land belonging to some adjoining shootings, over which I had liberty to hunt for any specimens required. Accompanied by one keeper and a gillie leading a pony with provisions and plaids in case we did not get back that night, an early start was effected, the lodge being left at daybreak. By midday several of the rough hills lying between Loch Rannoch and the Lyon had been closely examined without success. Having started but a single female after about ten hours' work, we came to the conclusion, as heavy thunder was rumbling away among the hills to the west, and there appeared every indication of an approaching tempest, that it would be the wisest plan to return home and renew our search in more favourable weather. While resting for a short time after lunch on the top of the hill before turning back, we were surprised by a shot, and on looking with the glasses far below us, three men with about a dozen dogs were discerned attempting to bolt a fox from a rough cairn of stones. We afterwards learned that although the foxes had been there very lately, as was clearly indicated by the remains of some fresh Grouse and hares which the terriers dragged from the earth, none of the family were then at home. The shot had been fired at a young Raven, hatched in the rocks above the fox-cairn. The old birds were very noisy, circling round and round in the air above their nest, but being too good judges of distance to venture within shot, unfortunately escaped. Almost at the same moment a fine cock Ptarmigan appeared on a large rock close by; here he stationed himself for some time, croaking loudly, and going through various amusing antics, puffing out his feathers, spreading his tail, and showing himself off to the greatest advantage. As he resolutely refused to leave the spot, running only a yard or two in advance when approached, we searched every inch of the ground, which was almost a mass of large stones, without putting up the female; it was, however, evident from the actions of the male that she was close at hand. I also tried a brace of steady setters, brought uphill by way of an experiment*, though I had not much faith that they would be of any service. On returning to the lunching-place we discovered the three men (who were soon recognized as two keepers and a shepherd) coming in our direction. While making their way uphill, the rain which had been threatening some time came down in torrents, and the thunder becoming more distant, the afternoon turned cold, a dense mist drifting up with the wind.

"The keepers were agreeably surprised on ascertaining the identity of the intruders on their beat, especially as they carried neither meat nor drink, and needed but little pressing to commence operations on what we were able to provide them with. When their hunger was appeased, finding they were desirous of the assistance of an additional gun whilst trying another large cairn where they expected to find the cubs missed down the hill, I agreed to finish the day with them. As the top of the hill was nothing but rocks and stones piled on the top of one another, we were forced to leave the pony where we had lunched. Our course was now kept north, as the earth we were going to was on the Rannoch side of the hill. One hollow we passed through seemed alive with Ptarmigan, the rocks were flying and croaking in all directions; but as no hens were started

---

* I was anxious to learn whether there is any truth in the statement that a sitting bird has no scent. As the rough ground and heat had already affected the dogs, it is uncertain whether the female would have escaped them had they been in working order.

and the weather had turned thick and dark, we resolved to leave our search for nests till a finer day. On arriving at the fox-cairn and putting in the terriers, we found it bore no signs of having been used this season. As it was now too late to try further, the dogs were coupled and we turned back. Not more than a hundred yards had been passed over, when hearing a scuffle behind, we turned round and saw a hen Ptarmigan struggling in the mouth of one of the terriers; on shouting to the dog the bird flew away, none the worse excepting the loss of a few tail-feathers. It was evident the terrier had seized her on the nest, which contained seven eggs. He had luckily only succeeded in catching her tail, as the dog to which he was coupled was tugging in the opposite direction, and had most probably so saved the life of the bird. As I required the female in summer plumage, we retired to the shelter of a large rock about a couple of hundred yards distant to await the return of the bird to her nest. I then sent off one of the men to the pony for what was left of our eatables and drinkables, and we made ourselves as comfortable in the heavy downpour as circumstances would permit. The head keeper who had joined us remarked he had observed our pony from the lower cairn, and thinking we were from the Rannoch side of the hill had come up to order us off the ground, entertaining a great antipathy to the people who marched with him in that direction, as they frequently came on his side of the hill and shot his hares and Ptarmigans. On the last occasion, he stated, they were encountered about half a mile over the march, and after informing them that he had no desire to afford another day's shooting, had sternly walked away, refusing all manner of tempting liquors which had been pressed upon him. Poor old Sandy is gone, and I should be sorry to throw doubt on any of his statements; but still I can scarcely credit the latter part of his story, as Sandy dearly loved his native mountain-dew!

"We had been rather more than an hour sitting under the shelter of the rock with all the dogs gathered round, when a collie, which had been lying within a yard of my feet, got up, shook the ⸺ ⸺ ⸺ ⸺, and again laid down, this time changing his position by about a foot. He now chose the brown ⸺ ⸺ ⸺ ⸺ female Ptarmigan to recline upon, which, causing a great flutter, startled the dog as ⸺ ⸺ ⸺ ⸺. On her flying off it was discovered she had been sitting on eight eggs. The ⸺ ⸺ ⸺ ⸺ ⸺ of the spot where we had sat for more than an hour, and it was a wonder ⸺ ⸺ ⸺ ⸺ ⸺ some of them had not stumbled on her sooner. As this bird had lost ⸺ ⸺ ⸺ ⸺ ⸺ instead of the one which had been caught by the terrier. It was now getting late, ⸺ ⸺ ⸺ ⸺ fox-hunters left us and proceeded home, the head keeper kindly giving ⸺ ⸺ ⸺ ⸺ many Ptarmigan (although, of course, out of season) as I required. His generosity was not so surprising when it was afterwards ascertained that we were at least half a mile on the ground of his Rannoch friend, to whom I am indebted for my specimens of Ptarmigan with nest and eggs! It had now become so thick and dark that it was scarcely possible to see a gunshot ahead. In order to give the female a chance to return to her nest, I left the spot and went in search of a male. Though several were croaking in all directions, it was some time before I could get a shot. At last a chance presented itself at a bird flying past; but as he went on out of sight, though evidently hard hit, I was just looking out for another, when Donald, the keeper, who was some distance behind, shouted out that he had the bird. On retracing my steps I found it had fallen dead within a few feet of the spot where he stood. Then cautiously approaching the last nest, we discovered that the female had returned. She sat very close, and it was not till the keeper put down his hand and lifted her up, that she could be induced to fly. We next took ⸺ ⸺ ⸺ ⸺, and after securely packing the whole of the specimens, made our way back to the spot where ⸺ ⸺ ⸺ ⸺. On our arrival the gillie pointed out the nest we were in search of after lunch. ⸺ ⸺ ⸺ ⸺ ground on which the pony stood, and here the female had sat unmoved till ⸺ ⸺ ⸺ ⸺ one of the pannier-straps falling on her back while the lunch was being repacked.

"We had now over twelve or fourteen miles of rough travelling to get over before reaching the lodge. As the mist was so dense that it was impossible to see half a dozen yards before us, I was of opinion that it would be the safest plan to follow a dry gully down to a burn which we knew fell into Glenlyon. Although a few miles out of our road, this track would be sure to bring us home at last. The keeper, however, was so exceedingly confident that he could find his way back across the hill, that I at last gave way, though entertaining great doubts on the subject. After leaving the rocky ground we made good progress for about an hour and a half, when I noticed that Donald's cheerful countenance began to wear a troubled look, and he at length proposed that we should make casts for a large rock, which ought (supposing we were in the right line) to be at no great distance. For half an hour we searched diligently, but without meeting a single mark that would serve to guide us on our way. At length we found it useless to proceed any further in the direction we were going, and on retracing our steps soon got so confused, that even the trusty Donald was forced to confess that he was at a loss to know which way to turn. After wandering about all night we found ourselves, when the mist cleared off at daybreak, within a short distance of Loch Rannoch, being then just a mile or two further from the lodge than when we started for home the previous evening. Twice during the night the unfortunate pony had been bogged, and it was only after an hour's hard work that we had succeeded in extricating her on the second occasion. I fully expected the poor beast would need to be shot in order to save her from suffocation. The continuous rain of the last twelve hours had completely blackened the water in the springs and burns; and, although somewhat fatigued, thirst was the only inconvenience from which we suffered, our extra supplies of liquor having been cleared out by the unexpected meeting on the hill. I was in great doubt as to whether we should succeed in getting the dogs home. In order to assist them along they had been fastened by a line to the pony, and every time a halt was made, if only for a moment, the worn-out animals stretched themselves on the ground to sleep, and it was necessary to lift them up before they could be induced to proceed."

A few days later, being anxious to know where we had first missed our way, I went over the same ground, and was enabled to discover, by the tracks of the pony, that after proceeding about a couple of hundred yards we had in some unaccountable manner turned round and taken a nearly opposite course.

On passing the nest of the Ptarmigan on which the bird had been caught by the terrier, I found she was sitting on only three eggs, the others having been without doubt carried off by the Ravens. While collecting the tail-feathers, which had most probably drawn their attention to the nest, I heard a harsh croak, and on looking up the Raven was circling round above my head, only, unfortunately, out of shot. As the day was clear, I was enabled to thoroughly examine the plumage of the male Ptarmigan with the glasses, and obtained a much finer specimen than the one previously shot. No females were seen, with the exception of the one whose nest I visited, though several miles of rough ground were passed over. From the numbers of males observed either strutting about on some commanding ridge or perched on the summit of a large stone, it was obvious that many pairs must resort to this range of hills; in every direction they were calling and croaking defiantly, disporting themselves with drooping wings and elevated and expanded tails*. The cocks in the finest plumage I remarked were by far the most ostentatious in their behaviour. There appears to be a great diversity in the colouring of the males; several were noticed exhibiting but a few dark feathers on the breast; these were probably young and backward birds of the previous season.

* The feathers of the tail are raised and spread out like a fan, giving a most comical appearance to the bird.

# COMMON PARTRIDGE.

## PERDIX CINEREA.

Our old English Partridge, which stands high in the estimation of all sportsmen from north to south in the British Islands, is to be found in almost every part of the country where cultivation is carried on—most plentiful, of course, where the farmers are proficient agriculturists, though a few coveys are not unfrequently met with in the remotest Highland glens. In these wild districts the birds are forced to put up with such accommodation as is to be obtained; this usually consists of scattered patches of land devoted to growing grain, and a few swampy hay-fields on the low ground along the course of the river or loch or adjoining the burn-side. During my wanderings in the Outer Islands of the Hebrides I did not fall in with this species, though it is asserted on good authority that they are established in several localities where protection is offered and the situation is suitable to their requirements.

In former days the old-fashioned sportsman, armed with his antiquated flint and steel, and attended by a well-broken pointer, was content with a very moderate bag, twenty or thirty brace being considered a grand day's work and well worthy of mention. By driving, and even over dogs, immense bags have been obtained since those days, 390 brace of hand-reared and 157 brace of wild birds being recorded as secured in two days' shooting by an enterprising individual a few years back. As is still the fashion, several writers in days gone by vented their irritation by having a fling at those "slaughterers" who took a pleasure in "destroying" inordinate quantities of game, as they were pleased to term such bags of Partridges. "Unreasonable sportsmen," we are informed by these sarcastic reporters, "killed twenty and sometimes thirty brace in a day." In the time of William Macgillivray, author of the well-known 'History of British Birds,' though the supply in the market must have been exceedingly limited compared with what it is at the present day, the price was decidedly low, that thrifty Highlander remarking, with regard to this species, "as an article of food, they are not beyond the reach of the middle classes of society, the average price of a pair being half-a-crown."

The years I devoted to shooting and collecting having been mostly passed either on the Scotch hill-sides and firths or the Snipe-marshes adjoining the Norfolk broads, or in the fens of Cambridge, as well as on the open seas surrounding our shores, I have never come across any really first-class stretch of ground adapted for Partridge-shooting. There was, however, little difficulty in ascertaining that closely killing down the vermin, and keeping a constant watch to check all poaching, in addition to remaining on good terms with one's workmen and shepherds, were the main points to be considered in order to raise a fair stock of birds in any locality where the nature of the country was suitable to their requirements. Stray cats, Crows, weasels, and stoats should be exterminated if possible, and last, but not least, the prowling roadside gunner, who makes his raids either on foot or mounted in a light cart with a fast-trotting pony in the shafts, requires careful watching before he can be captured. Those who sweep the country at night with drag-nets, if well up in their business, are bound to cause much loss, unless the fields are well protected with bushes, and the depredators kept in constant fear of interruption. I ascertained from some of the worthies who make a living by bird-catching and dragging at night for Larks (which occupation of course includes the capture of every feathered creature coming within their clutches), that the bushes in the fields give considerable trouble, the land on which they are placed needing to be carefully examined by day and a wide berth allowed to the obstacles when at work. Barley-stubbles are reckoned the most attractive roosting-places for Partridges, though, of course, wind, weather, and other circumstances only learned by experience have to be considered. The present system of close-cutting, which has now been carried on for over the last twenty years, finds little favour in the eyes of these men, as their prey is more easily sprung on the approach of danger. A new lay of clover, intended for the next year's feeding, and also rape are likewise favourite resorts for the birds, and require extra guarding, as the poachers are well aware of the fact. Eleven brace obtained in one night is the highest take I have heard of, my informant also stating that he had now and then secured eight or nine, and once a dozen Partridges at one drop of the net. Early in the season the majority of the young birds are small and weak, and a few even succeed in effecting their escape, though towards the close of winter, when they have gained strength, some occasionally go right through the net, should it happen to be old and worn. Hares are now and then taken, if rolled up and entangled, but more often they force their way through the nets and tear away a portion.

The following letter which appeared in 'The Field' of September 3, 1881, gives such an excellent and amusing account of the attempts made by the writer, a well-known sportsman, to find a means to check this kind of poaching, that I offer no apology for inserting it in 'Rough Notes':—

"*Partridge Nets.*

"SIR,—The partridge-season is at hand, and the poachers will be running their nets. I got hold of a poacher's net, and I have been running it over the fields in daylight, to try and find out the best means of stopping it. The net is 35 yards long and 12 yards deep, made of very fine string, with a large mesh; it will roll up into a ball about the size of a hat-box. Sometimes the nets are made of silk, seventy or eighty yards long; but they are very expensive, £9 or £10. A common partridge-net, such as I was using, can be got at any net factory for 25s. or 30s.

"The most usual appliances employed for the prevention of netting are gorse bushes, branches, brambles, thorns, and stakes. I tried the net over the whole of these. First we tried a gorse bush, with a green head standing firmly about two feet out of the ground; the bush yielded, and the net passed over like a tablecloth—nothing to catch it. When the gorse bush was stuck lightly in the ground the net took it away, and the gorse bush acted; it gave two or three somersaults, and wisped up the net; but when the gorse bush was placed so lightly in the ground that it would go away with the net, it would also go away with the first breeze. Verdict, gorse bush not effectual. We next tried brambles. When lying on the ground they are very low, and only caught the tail or drag of the net; we felt them strike and dragged on to see what they would do (they were lying loose); by the time we got to the end of the field they were merely hanging in the net where they had first struck. We pegged out the net, and they were pulled out quite easily. Verdict, brambles won't do. We then tried branches, stuck in pretty firm, 3 ft. or 4 ft. out of the ground. Green pliable branches were of no use, they yielded, and the net travelled over; stag-headed, stiff, half-dead branches were pulled out and rolled over and over, and made a rare mess; wild roses did the same thing, only better, if they went away with the net. Half-dead larch branches are good, the little nobbly warts and cones catch the net. Old gorse that has been clean burnt leaving a long stag-headed stump we found good to lay down loose, it won't blow and tumbles well. The higher the net is caught the better, but we found nothing so effectual a stopper as a good honest stout stake driven or sunk with a ▓▓▓▓▓ ▓▓▓▓ ▓▓▓▓▓ into the ▓▓▓▓▓▓▓ ▓▓▓ ▓▓▓▓▓▓ ▓▓ a couple of feet; when the net came on this we ▓▓▓ ▓▓ ▓▓▓ ▓▓▓▓ ▓▓ to ▓▓▓▓▓▓▓▓▓ ▓▓▓▓ ▓▓ ▓▓▓ ▓▓▓ about it. Many men and keepers have a ▓▓▓▓▓▓ ▓▓▓▓ ▓▓▓▓ ▓▓▓▓▓ ▓▓▓▓ ▓▓ net or render ▓▓ ▓▓ ▓▓▓▓ anything catching a net high up will ▓▓▓▓▓▓▓▓ ▓▓ ▓▓▓▓▓▓▓ ▓▓, but ▓▓▓▓▓▓▓ catching the tail does no great harm, except it is firm or likely to ▓▓▓▓ ▓▓ ▓▓▓▓▓▓▓▓. We dragged a lot of thistles in the tail of the net, stretched the net, pegged it out and took ▓▓▓▓ out easily. A thorn bush catching high up and going away with the net is nasty; a thorn in the tail of the net is not much, it won't stop it or wisp it up. Birds don't lie very close to the fence, but generally about the centre of the field, all the field won't require pegs. A good peg for every acre will protect any field—for twenty acres say twenty pegs. The net takes in about half an acre (70 yards square is about an acre); the net won't go twice its own length before being pulled up; the finer and longer the nets the fewer pegs required. Poachers sometimes run a large square net with laths or bamboos along the sides to stretch it; it requires four men, one at each corner; it is carried clear of the ground, and there are droppers from it to start the birds—when they hear them, they drop the whole concern. It is a troublesome net to rig up in the dark and to conceal, and is not often used except the country is all bushed. There is always a bit of a sag in the middle, and longer stakes like sheep flakes will reach it and stop it. Poachers take good stock of the ground before they run a net; if there are some old harrows with the teeth uppermost lying about the fields, and if they are occasionally shifted, a poacher won't care about the chance of being maimed. A tumble over a harrow in the dark is no joke. Of course, harrows can't be left in a hunting country; but in a non-hunting country an honest man has no more chance of being off the road in a dark night than he has of being on the spikes of your area railings. Poachers don't like a rainy night, or even if the grass is very wet, it spoils and clogs the net; nor a very windy night, the net beats them. A dark dry night, with a slight breeze, just enough to carry the net when going against it, suits them best.—J. D. B."

Some years back, after a conversation with a friend whose land was occasionally visited by one or two parties of lawless individuals in possession of drag-nets, I drew a plan for an artificial metal thistle, which was most skilfully turned out according to my orders by an ironmonger in the Strand. These imitations could be placed either in a socket, in a stump of wood driven into the ground, or merely fixed by being pressed down sufficiently deep into the soil. Shortly after, it was stated that my invention had the desired effect, though strong stumps armed with crooked nails or hooks were more easily procured and replaced if removed. A year or two later I learned that the ground, as far as could be ascertained, was left entirely unmolested, and this style of poaching was no longer carried on in the district. The sharp points of one of the thistles was said to have inflicted some ugly wounds on a well-known offender, and this probably intimidated the rest of the gang. When carefully turned out and coloured these thistles were very difficult to detect in a field at any distance, and no amount of watching from the roadside by those intending a raid would reveal the whereabouts of the whole that were planted out. Of course such means of putting a stop to poaching can only be efficiently carried out where a staff of well-trained keepers and watchers are employed and all loafers kept constantly in view while in the neighbourhood. The first pattern sent for my approval, which I showed to an old hand whose delight it had been "on a shiny night," &c., greatly astonished this wary individual, and after closely examining its construction, and expressing an opinion that it must inevitably cut its way through any net, he concluded by remarking, "And how about one's blessed shins if he came across a thing like this in the dark?"

Pheasants' eggs always fetch a good price in the market; but there is not the same demand for those of the Partridge, and consequently this species does not suffer to such an extent from the depredations of the rascals that prowl about the hedgerows and tracks through the forests and woodlands under various pretexts in the spring. Domestic pussies, when once they have taken to stray and deserted the fireside, soon become the most destructive of four-footed robbers; and so energetic was one of my father's keepers in years gone by, in his attempts to free his charges from the attacks of the feline species, that he roused the animosity of all the old wives in the village. It was seldom that this indefatigable game-preserver deserted his post and left the ground he guarded; but happening on one occasion while on his rounds to meet the parson and receive a lecture for his non-attendance at divine service, he declared it would be impossible for him to put in an appearance, as the whole of the women whose anger was aroused would seize the opportunity to rant and rage at him for the losses they had suffered. Stoats and weasels destroy large numbers of eggs, and also succeed in pinning sitting hens by the neck and sucking their blood as well as in carrying off young birds. Traps carefully set may clear off a few, though an experienced keeper, who always carries his gun when looking over the ground, is sure to meet with many chances for a shot. While shooting or crossing the country, making notes, or while in pursuit of specimens, I exist at various times have killed several hundreds of these tiny marauders, of which no account was kept on my vermin lists. Only a few months back, in the course of a drive across the South Downs, a couple of stoats were stopped just in time to prevent mischief: the first was rolled over while in pursuit of a rabbit down the Dyke Hill, near Saddlescombe, and an hour later the second was knocked off the roof of the house at the turnpike-gate at Pyecombe, where the cunning little thief had succeeded in making his way in order to reach a fine old cock Chaffinch hanging in a cage against the wall.

In many country districts stoats and weasels are confused, and exceedingly curious titles are bestowed on them. In the east of Sussex a weasel is known among the country people as a "kine," and in the Broad district in the east of Norfolk both species are termed "lobsters." It may not be generally known that stoats make their way to almost the summits of many of the higher mountains in the Highlands. I frequently placed traps baited with hares on the cairns or "false men" *, and several of these animals were taken at an elevation of nearly three thousand feet. In marshy districts it is easy to learn if stoats are plentiful. Though these destructive creatures will prowl to the dampest parts, they appear to have a dislike to swimming the water-dykes, and invariably make use of the planks thrown across for footways. I remarked that they speedily defile any fresh-cut pieces of wood that are put down, their droppings being left most conspicuously on the plank. This fact I noticed in the portions of Pevensey Level adjoining the uplands, and also repeatedly in the Broad districts in the east of Norfolk. Small wandering parties of from six or eight up to a dozen stoats have often come under my notice; on one occasion in East Lothian my attention was attracted by the loud screams and growls of a white terrier that accompanied me, and on hastening to the spot I discovered him fighting for his life, surrounded by a pack of from twenty to thirty stoats. Having gripped one of his small antagonists successfully, I distinctly saw him shake his head, when three or four which had fastened round his jaws were flung off. Luckily we were within call of one of the men, who was instantly despatched for my gun left against a tree some hundred yards distant. In the mean time a heavy hedge-stake was my only weapon, and with this I managed to disable three or four. On the arrival of the breech-loader, the animals, which had hitherto exhibited a disposition to attack (hissing loudly and rising up on their hind quarters), were rapidly put to flight. A dozen or fifteen were accounted for in addition to the wounded that escaped, the dog having settled about half the number, and the last four or five falling to the gun. Though highly elated at his victory, poor Bob, a white bull-terrier, presented a pitiful spectacle. His damaged "mug" commenced at once to swell, and the blood from the cuts had deeply stained his head, neck, and throat. A careful sponging with warm water soon

* This is the name given by the natives to the piles of rough stones of from five to six feet in height, probably built up for landmarks, on the tops of the hills.

........ his death the marks of the
........ weasels, as these tiny
........ I have often seen them turned out
numbers ........ of ........ dragged ........ of the
ricks where ........ attracted them to the spot.
I particularly noticed that the farm-labourers, though ........ pursue and kill other vermin,
always ceased their efforts when the "kine," as they termed the weasel, was dislodged from beneath the
sheaves and put to flight, evidently making due allowance for the assistance given in exterminating the
thievish rats.

In the pits at some of the sporting "cribs" five-and-twenty or thirty years ago, I have now and
then seen well-contested battles between a weasel and a rat. The most desperate fight, however, I ever
watched, terminating in the death of both combatants, was witnessed between two wild animals in the
garden at Ferrygate, in East Lothian. An immense rat was first detected in the act of creeping quietly
beneath a small heap of rubbish collected on an open space for burning; a few moments later a weasel
came in view, sniffing slowly and carefully over the newly turned mould across which the rat had made
his way. On perceiving his actions were observed, he drew up at once, but made not the slightest
attempt to retreat. As matters seemed at a standstill, I directed a man who was working close at hand
to turn over the litter below which the rat had concealed himself. Though by far the most powerful in
point of size and weight, the rat evidently had but little heart for the encounter; when driven from his
hiding-place, he made slowly off some ten or a dozen yards, and was then tackled by his former pursuer,
who had quietly awaited his opportunity. Though unwilling to come to the scratch while hopes of escape
remained, the rat when attacked fought well and pluckily, and for the first few minutes had by far the
best of the struggle. Almost twice as bulky as his active antagonist, he appeared to bear him down each
time they rose; but, small and wiry, the weasel gradually obtained an irresistible grip on the neck of his
victim. At last the blood began to flow, and the combatants grew rapidly weaker; still, each retaining
its hold, they rolled over and over, till suddenly relaxing the grasp they had obtained, they staggered
back a few paces, and rising up fell dead at the same moment. This battle, lasting several minutes, was
fought utterly regardless of the spectators who had closed round within the distance of a few feet.

The eggs of Partridges and Pheasants are without doubt more frequently destroyed by stoats than
we generally imagine; not even the nests of our familiar friends the barn-door fowls escape the attentions
of those bloodthirsty and merciless little thieves. While stopping at a farm-house in the marshes at
Potter Heigham, in the east of Norfolk, in the summer of 1885, I ascertained the truth of a statement
concerning these animals, which I previously considered impossible, viz., that they were constantly in the
habit of robbing the nests of the hens and carrying off the eggs. An immense number of fowls were
kept at this farm, and though many laid in the baskets prepared for their accommodation in the hen-
houses, and also in the mangers in the stables and cattle-yards, several resorted to the plantations round
the gardens, as well as to the adjoining hedgerows. There was a nest near the house from which
ten or a dozen eggs, the produce of as many industrious and noisy old hens, were removed every
afternoon; and having remarked on one occasion, about mid-day, that it contained eight, nearly the
full complement, I was standing on the front-doorstep a few hours later, when on looking up the
garden, a stoat caught my eye trotting down the path, and finally springing jauntily over the box-edging
that bordered the patch of Portugal laurel under which the nest was situated. Though considerably less
than half a minute was spent in snatching up a gun, I arrived on the scene too late, as not a glimpse

of the marauder could be obtained, and on proceeding to search further, I discovered that every egg had already disappeared from the nest. It was a fact that in this, as in every instance where stoats were believed to have been the culprits, not even a single hen ever returned to lay in the same nest, and even the surrounding shelter in the immediate neighbourhood was entirely deserted. How a stoat conveys an egg is a question I should much like to see solved; the means also by which he breaks it and extracts the contents appears also a mystery. These eggs had in all probability been transported to a large heap of rotten stumps and roots of trees, stacked in a ditch overgrown with nettles and brambles, about thirty or forty yards distant from the nest, as some broken shells were detected in the cavities among the rubbish by one of the farm-labourers, who endeavoured to find traces of where they had been taken. As I intended leaving the district in a day or two, there was not sufficient time to obtain the assistance of any one who possessed ferrets, and to make a thorough clearance of the litter, in order to reach the quarters of these freebooters, which were doubtless situated in the innermost recesses of this large pile of decayed timber[*].

It is a curious fact that Partridges, if driven over water or towns, appear to get bewildered, and losing all powers of flight, drop down and suffer themselves to be picked up rather than rise again. There is a mistaken idea that a land-bird is unable to rise from water; I have, however, repeatedly seen several of the waders that have fallen wounded get up from both salt and fresh water when an attempt was made to effect a capture. The present species is without doubt one of the most reluctant to make an effort to escape, though they will occasionally do so. The first year that the Easter Volunteer Review was held on the Downs in the neighbourhood of Brighton the wind was blowing strong from the north, and during the sham fight great numbers of Partridges were disturbed by the crowds of spectators and the noise of the firing, and becoming confused flew out to sea, where they fell into the water. Several boats which happened to be under the cliffs profited by their misfortunes, one alone getting between twenty and thirty birds. Next year over a score of boats were on the spot, awaiting the coming of the unfortunate Partridges; the wind, however, was luckily from the south, and carried the affrighted birds inland, not one going out to sea. Early one morning in December 1862, I was going towards the central station at St. Leonards, when a covey of ten or a dozen Partridges caught my attention as they were in the act of settling in a small open square in the back part of the town. On being chased by some boys and a few snapping small dogs, they never attempted to use their wings, but rushing rapidly before their pursuers, sought shelter in the open doors, or fluttered helplessly down the areas.

Telegraph-wires often cause heavy losses to Partridges; the lines that stretch across the Rep's Marshes near Heigham bridge, in the east of Norfolk, have brought down at one time or another many birds of various kinds, and the present species has repeatedly been picked up near this spot. In the winter of 1867, I was watching a covey flying west over the downs near Rottingdean, in Sussex, when three birds fell after contact with the wires, the head of one unfortunate being cut off as clean as with a knife. It does not follow that a bird that has suffered from a broken wing and made its escape never recovers from its injuries. Some years back I killed a brace from a covey in the marshes near Ludham, in the east of Norfolk, all of which appeared strong on wing; the bones, however, that I kept plainly indicate that a fracture had previously taken place in the first joint of the wing of one, which by some means had become set, and joined again in a most satisfactory manner.

I was not aware that Partridges were accustomed to be on the alert or move about by moonlight, till, while proceeding in search of winter Ptarmigan, and commencing to make an ascent of one of the lower slopes of Cairngorm, a hill to the north of the river Lyon in Perthshire, about 3 A.M. one morning

---

[*] A change of tenants at the farm and a sale were about to take place; and much as I wished to excavate the retreat of our enemies and examine their haunts, I was forced to desist.

in December 1867, I happened to turn round and detected some dark objects slowly making their way over a stubble on the low ground below us, on which was a thin coating of snow. After a few minutes' watching, a steady view through the glasses convinced the keeper and myself that they must be a covey of Partridges engaged in searching for food; the fact that we were well aware a brood had been hatched near at hand, and still resorted to that part of the ground, also strengthened the idea. As we were only a hundred yards or so up the hill-side, and there was sufficient time for reaching the higher flats of the mountains before daybreak, we turned back to obtain a closer inspection and ascertain what could have induced the birds to be on the move at such an hour. On crossing the road at the foot of the hill which runs up the glen, I directed the keeper to take my second gun, and if the birds rose within range to do his best to fill the bag. There was no difficulty in ascertaining the whereabouts of this covey, as they were all clearly in view, and it was now evident that we had not made a mistake as to their identity. Before we arrived within five-and-twenty yards, the small party ran together, instantly rising on wing, when four out of the five were accounted for. The survivor returned, circling round and finally pitching in some rough cover over a wall near at hand; but though calling loudly there was not sufficient light to make another attempt for a shot, so we left the poor bird to its own resources and at once made tracks for the hill-tops. On our return in the afternoon, after a most satisfactory day's sport, we reached the same spot as the day was closing in, and just as the children from the few scattered shealings, termed a village, were leaving the school. Remarking that the youngsters were in pursuit of some small object uttering shrill cries, we hastened to ascertain what had attracted their attention, when, on arriving within a short distance, the bird that had escaped us in the early morning rose from the middle of the road and passed over our heads, offering a chance for a shot that was not thrown away. A few years back, when writing to the keeper, Donald MacKerchar, I referred to this fact of the birds being on the move before daybreak, stating I had never since that time met with a similar occurrence, and received the following lines in reply:—" You are quite right about the Partridges we saw feeding before dawn. I remember it very well, and about the winged bird that was piping after the children as they were going from school." Some of the circumstances had, however, slipped the memory of this very observant keeper, as he referred to the Partridge that escaped in the morning as being winged; though the curious shrill notes the bird uttered, which he described as "piping," and were certainly the most singular sounds I ever heard proceed from the throat of this species, were evidently still impressed on his mind.

During the years I rented the shootings of Innerwick, in Glenlyon, in Perthshire, I found the ground adapted for Partridges was limited to the narrow and winding stretch of land under cultivation adjoining the river-banks, and the lower slopes of the hills, where brakes and long coarse grass took the place of the heather. Barley and oats were the only scanty crops of grain that were grown, and I have often seen these in stock on the fields by the river-side so late as November. There were a few green parks that provided good feeding for cattle and horses, to which the Partridges now and then made their way, and some extensive grass-marshes with swamps and slades, where rushes and other rank plants flourished in profusion; the small patches of potatoes were also one of the favourite resorts of these birds. I soon discovered that the stock of Partridges on my land, which extended for about five miles along the course of the river, amounted to only six or seven coveys. The first season I was there the Grouse and Wildfowl, together with fishing and the work of setting traps for vermin, occupied nearly the whole of my time, and only three or four brace of Partridges were bagged. The next year, owing to the numbers left, I anticipated that many more coveys would be seen; this, however, was soon discovered to be a mistaken idea, as only seven or eight broods could be found, and one or two of these kept so closely to the "marsh," that there was no telling on which side they might be met with. As sparing the birds appeared of no avail in increasing our stock, I determined to kill down all that fell in our way, and ascertain the following season if any diminution in the number would be noticed, when if there was a great falling-off some hand-reared birds might be turned down. Early in September the hay-field to which the two best coveys resorted was not cut; but the old farmer, who would always assist in promoting sport, sent word that if I wanted a shot at the birds I was not to stop on that account. As they were, however, merely cheepers no larger than Blackbirds, it was advisable to give them another month's law, and in the end they afforded capital sport on two or three occasions. One afternoon early in December, just as I had returned from the hill-side, Duncan, the fisherman *, to whom I had given the right of rabbit-killing on the condition of his supplying the lodge, informed me that on his way home he had marked a Woodcock in a beech-plantation near the river. As there was still sufficient light to reach the spot before dark, we started at once to try our luck and ascertain if it could be found again. But few minutes were spent in the search, as the bird fluttered off like an Owl, offering the easiest shot imaginable, within half a dozen yards of where it had been lost sight of. By the time we had reached the outskirts of the plantation, which was in this direction surrounded by a wall, the light had commenced to fade rapidly. Just as I was on the point of mounting this dry stone dyke, old Duncan quietly drew my attention, and whispering "Partridges, Partridges!" pointed towards the left, where a number of dark shadows were to be seen scattered about on the barley-stubble below us, within the distance of between twenty-five and thirty yards. Pausing for a moment, I comprehended what the man had intended, and saw at once there was a chance to ascertain the truth of a statement that I had never credited, viz., that these birds will not stir when shot at in the gloaming, if only the flash of the gun is visible. Keeping low down and well out of sight, I was enabled to cover the birds through a small gap, where some blocks of stone had fallen from the dyke, and setting rapidly to work, the whole covey, nine in number, were turned over in less than a minute. The fluttering of the wings of a wounded bird, which attempted to make off and was instantly stopped by a lucky shot, removed all doubts as to whether large stones and clods of earth had not been mistaken in the uncertain light for Partridges. At the close of this season but a small stock of birds remained for breeding-purposes, nearly thirty brace having been bagged, still there were, as near as could be judged, at least two or three more coveys the following year. It appeared, from the experience I gained during the seasons passed in the glen, that should our small stock be entirely spared or nearly all shot down the number of coveys would be much the same the next season.

While staying at Tain for the punt-gunning on the firths and lochs in the east of Ross-shire and the adjoining counties, during the autumn of 1868 and the following year, I hired from my landlord, at a small rent, the shooting over a stretch of land he farmed in a flat district, termed the "Fendom." The greater part was cultivated, and the rest a tract of rough marsh, with a few sandy pools and slakes which still remained unreclaimed. Having heard from the owner that the potatoes were sure to hold many additional coveys of Partridges beyond their usual complement of residents when the adjoining farms had been shot over, I resolved to keep a sharp look-out. This was by no means a difficult undertaking, as we were generally up and down the firth some part of the day, and it only required to run the punt ashore and take a view of the surrounding country from the summit of the sand-banks, as my ground bordered the shore for about a mile inland from Tain to the farthest point of the "Fendom." We had not long to wait, as on a fine morning early in September, after having made our way quietly along the

* The fisherman is a necessary attendant at most shooting-lodges in the Highlands, as during the absence of the tenant and his friends while out on the hill-side it is his duty to supply the house with salmon and trout from the lochs and rivers. By this time of year the fishing-season was over, and having put aside his rod, Duncan passed his time either as a gillie, if required, or in ferreting or shooting rabbits, as stated above, on

firth towards the bar, without meeting any signs of fowl or seal, it was decided to put the boats ashore, and having left one man in charge, we proceeded inland. After passing the flats above the tideway and reaching the sand-hills, a view was obtained of the farm and the surrounding country, and several shots were heard further south, two or three guns shortly after being observed obtaining good sport on the other side of our boundary. In the course of half an hour, during which we watched their proceedings from the cover of the bent-grass on the hills, three or four coveys were seen to drop on our ground. As the party drew off and were working away out of sight, an individual carrying a gun and followed by a dog, who seemed somewhat doubtful as to the direction he should take, was observed to leave the farm and slowly make his way towards the potato-fields, though keeping under the shelter of a ridge of hilly ground thickly covered with furze. His appearance on the scene added interest to the proceedings, as the Highlander from whom I hired the shootings had dropped a gentle hint that his younger brother, who lived with his mother at the farm, was, in his estimation, a "ne'er-do-well," who, if he could get possession of powder and shot, might prove a nuisance if we did not keep a constant watch. His own occupation as factor to one of the largest sheep-farmers in the Highlands kept him almost constantly employed, but he nevertheless promised to do his best to have the delinquent kept in order. It was soon evident that this character had by some means ascertained our presence, as he speedily disappeared from sight among the furze bushes; after waiting a short time we started to walk over the ground, much regretting that the setters had been left at home. On reaching the cultivated land at the foot of the sand-hills, a covey of a dozen or more rose at once, and three birds fell, luckily without a kicker amongst them, the heavy ten-bore I carried having, as usual, done its work effectively. On starting again after collecting the slain, I discovered we had been joined by a liver-coloured pointer, that made her way towards us from the furze when the shots were fired. It was soon evident that she was but half broken; still on our moving on she commenced to hunt round on her own account, without receiving a word, and in rapid succession she pointed three or four coveys, all of which were satisfactorily accounted for. A brace of birds wounded by the shooting-party that had made their way to our grounds were also picked up when we went over the cover on which they had been marked down, next a hare she made an attempt to chase was rolled over before she had gone many yards in pursuit; and just as we had finished the potatoes and were considering towards which point we should next make our way, a second hare was started, and away went the new comer in chase regardless of rating. There happened to be a small gap in the turf wall thrown up round the piece, and for this I saw the hare was making, and as she sprang through the aperture over the fallen blocks of earth, I fired, being anxious to avoid any injury to the pointer, though it was evident from the sudden turn she made that some of the charge must have taken effect. On arriving at the spot the hare lay stretched out as dead as a stone, and the poacher's assistant was still in view going her best pace, holding a straight course for the farm, having doubtless received a reminder that might possibly teach her better manners, if it did not make her gun-shy. Shortly after, while on our way towards the boats, we again fell in with the young farmer who had been so fortunately checked in his attempts to make a raid on our birds; he was now without the gun, which had doubtless been hidden away in the furze, and as no remarks were made as to what had been observed, all went well, and he showed no reluctance to join us at lunch in the punts on the shore. On future occasions he usually accompanied us on our rounds, and pointed out some of the best parts of the marshes for Snipe, as well as for fowl at flight-time, and, as far as I could see, the Partridges and hares remained entirely unmolested.

Partridge-shooting with a punt-gun is a sport seldom indulged in; accidentally, however, I met with a couple of chances for shots, both of which proved successful beyond expectation. Before daybreak one morning early in the winter of 1868, the weather at the time being fine and calm, without a breath of air to ruffle the surface of the water, I had put off from my boat-house on the Tain Sands in the double punt, and was intending to proceed down the firth. As no fowl were seen or heard, I determined to ascertain if the slades in the marshes in the "Peudoms" were frozen over or sufficiently open to harbour Snipe. With a view to discover the state of affairs, our craft was worked as near the shore as possible, and the puntsman despatched to make an examination of the nearest pools of fresh water. As fowl were occasionally found about these moist parts of the ground, he took one of the ten-bore cripple-stoppers, and had only been gone a few minutes when a shot was heard, and immediately after a rush of wings breaking the stillness of the morning air caught my ear, and a flock of birds I failed at the first glance to identify swept round, and were then seen to alight on the edge of a sand-bank, where small scattered patches of rank grass struggled for existence in the dry unfruitful soil. The pack, which I soon came to the conclusion were a covey of Partridges, were drawn up together in a dense mass, so dropping the barrel of the big gun over them, I pulled the lanyard, and two only were observed to flutter off. On searching round the spot to which the charge had been directed, six and a half brace of Partridges were discovered, all dead with the exception of a brace, which attempted to make off, but were soon secured with little exertion, owing to the scanty cover, as John, the puntsman, speedily returned with a Mallard he had knocked down and assisted in their capture. A week or so later the same season I was gunning further up the firth, near Invershin, and just as the day was closing in we happened to be sculling towards some diving fowl in the pool near the railway bridge. Suddenly, while we had eased for a few moments as the ducks were out of sight below the surface, and the direction in which they would appear was uncertain, I detected a covey of ten Partridges flying at a tremendous pace across the water, from the south towards the opposite shore. It was evident that they would pass within range; and as the gun was ready for use at the moment, I had merely to fire, holding about six or eight feet ahead, to allow for the sixty or seventy yards' distance at which I judged the birds to be; the dim light, however, rendered it somewhat difficult to form a correct estimation. Three brace dropped to the shot, and the seventh bird pitched headlong against a slab of rock by the shore just below the steep wooded bank, over which the remainder of the covey held their course.

The breeding-habits of this species are so well known, and have been described so often, that any remarks I could make concerning them would be superfluous, and a short reference to a couple of nests discovered in the south of Scotland will be sufficient. In the summer of 1864 I detected a Partridge sitting on fourteen eggs in a hole scratched in the thatch of a wheat-stack, about five-and-twenty feet from the ground, at Ferrygate, a large farm near North Berwick, in East Lothian, where I studied agriculture for a couple of years. To the best of my belief, the old bird brought off her brood safely, though we failed to ascertain the manner in which they reached the ground. Within a quarter of a mile of the stack-yard, and only a fortnight later in the same season, another nest was found by one of my dogs, in a thick plantation of young trees and low stunted bushes, containing a number of eggs, seven or eight being those of the Partridge and the remainder Pheasant's. To which species the care of this nest was finally committed there was no chance of ascertaining, as I was obliged to leave the district for the south a few days later, and remained away for several weeks.

# RED-LEGGED PARTRIDGE.

## *PERDIX RUFA.*

---

This brightly coloured bird is not held in such general estimation as our English Partridge, the disposition to make more use of its legs than wings having stirred up the animosity of sportsmen, and its inferiority in flavour rendering it far less desirable for the table in the opinion of epicures. In some parts Red-legged Partridges have been killed down in every possible manner, and an attempt has been made to exterminate them entirely; still they hold their own, and when their habits are better understood and driving is resorted to by those who have watched their movements and learned the course they are accustomed to take, there is no reason why they should not find more favour in the eyes of those who would have brought about their destruction. For my own part I can see no reason why this species is so little called for, as I have rather a preference for them myself. During the present month (September 1886) I have passed my time in Brighton, and discovered that the majority of the Common Partridges at the poulterers' shops were by no means fit for killing, being exceedingly small—in fact hardly half-grown. The Red-legged Partridges were for the most part fine plump heavy birds, and I had my pick of the lot. Strange to say, our Common Partridges were seven shillings the brace, and the Red-legged birds only four shillings the brace, and nearly double the weight of these expensive morsels. This species being more hardy had been better able to stand the severity of the weather during the breeding-season than our Common Partridge.

I have only met with this species in Sussex, Norfolk, and Cambridge; in parts of the two first counties these birds appear particularly abundant, and several coveys were met with in the fens about Bottisham, Qui, and Swaffham, when I shot in those districts during the terms spent at the University about five-and-twenty years ago. Many residents and naturalists who have made observations on the habits and movements of the Red-legged Partridges on the Norfolk coast are of opinion that they arrive on their shores early in spring, during March and April, from the Continent, after having made the passage across the North Sea. There is no contradicting the fact that these birds are frequently seen on the beach bewildered and exhausted; many are also captured weary and worn out by prolonged flights and possibly by want of food. While hard pressed they often alight in towns and villages near the coast, where they are speedily hunted down, appearing to have lost all sense of self-preservation. Having often at this season watched the Red-legged Partridges that are met with in considerable numbers flying round one or two of the larger broads in the east of Norfolk, and occasionally falling into the water, I ascertained that the birds remaining inland are also affected by a desire to make a move in spring. One morning early in March 1873, I picked up several floating dead on the surface of the water, or attempting to conceal themselves in the beds of reeds, on the swampy islets on Heigham Sounds, and a few that were crossing and recrossing from one side of the pool to the other were shot. I believe it to be an utter impossibility for a Red-legged or any other Partridge to cross the North Sea from the Continent to the Norfolk coast; and as a proof of this assertion it may be stated that there is no mention made in any work of the presence of this species, till foreigners were imported and turned down on our shores. That the birds are restless and excited in spring, and make occasionally vain attempts to change their quarters, is by no means unlikely, and this is doubtless the cause of the additional numbers seen near the coast and round the broads. If we were annually visited by these wanderers from foreign countries in the spring, some would certainly take their departure again in the autumn. I can, however, find no reference to any having been seen while gathering in the vicinity of the coast at that time of year, nor have they been observed on the passage by the men on the light-ships or the crews of the fishing-boats I have conversed with.

It is stated by several writers that Red-legged Partridges often settle on trees or on hedges and walls; it is, however, but seldom I have seen them in such elevated positions. A few years back one was noticed perched on the point of the shaft of a farm-roller which was tilted up in a field near Brighton; a week later as I drove along the road a bird was again calmly surveying the scene from the same spot. In September 1864, while in pursuit of a mixed bag over the flat country between Cambridge and Newmarket, I noticed three or four clustered on a stack of peats in Qui fen; two or three also at different times have attracted my attention on gates or the adjoining posts and rails.

I was not aware that the marten was found in Sussex, or even in the south of England, till early in the summer a few years back, while passing through one of those long straggling beech-woods that spread along the slopes of the South Downs facing the north, I caught sight of what at first appeared an immense stoat descending the trunk of a large beech tree. The animal came down slowly, deliberately placing one foot below the other, and proceeding with the greatest ease, though how it held on to the smooth bark was a mystery. On reaching an extending root it dropped to the ground at once, and disappeared in the dense undergrowth, before I had time to pick up my gun, which had been laid down, and ascertain with certainty its identity. A further view of the stranger had just raised a doubt as to whether it was not a beech-marten; and this I now believe to have been the case. Though a thorough search was shortly after made through the grove with the assistance of a keeper and his dog who had arrived on the scene, no signs of the robber could be discovered. The fresh-killed remains of a newly hatched young Red-legged Partridge had first attracted my attention, lying on the bank at the side of a rough cart-track through the wood, and an examination of the surrounding stunted bushes and long coarse grass revealed the nest also on the top of the bank, from which the juvenile must have but lately made its way. Ten egg-shells were laying around, and it is probable that the youngster had been seized and killed while the brood were making their way for the first time from their cradle. By the nature of the wound in the throat from which the blood had been sucked, it was evident that one or other of the stoat tribe had committed the murder, and doubtless my approach had prevented the marauder from bearing off his victim to the spot where his larder was stored up. Before leaving, the keeper pointed out the nest, with the egg-shells still remaining, in which a Common Partridge had hatched off a brood of sixteen, on the top of the bank on the opposite side of the road, and within the distance of four or five yards of the spot the Red-legged bird had selected for her nursery. An hour or so earlier, and immediately after the marten had descended from the tree, I had sat down on the twisted roots of a large beech to watch quietly for a few minutes in case this peculiar-looking creature might again be observed within shot. Suddenly a sound as though small twigs among the branches were being cut, followed by a sharp crack or click, as if a bullet had buried itself in the bark of the tree above, caught my ear, and there was little doubt that a ball from a rifle had struck the stem of the beech tree. The day was fine and with scarcely a breath of wind, still no report had been heard; and wondering where the weapon could have been fired, I looked carefully round in all directions with the glasses, but detected no signs of any one, with the exception of the gamekeeper with a gun over his shoulder, and followed by a retriever, slowly making his way down the steep side of the hills from the high downs to the south of the wood. The deep brown glossy velveteen in which he was attired at once drew my attention; although this material may be most appropriate for keepers while attending to a shooting-party, when it is necessary that their whereabouts should be well known to all the sportsmen while they are employed in enforcing order among the beaters, or working a pack of beagles in the large beds of furze, it must be a great drawback to success when on the watch for prowling egg-stealers in the spring, or waiting for the loafing ruffians from the lowest quarters of the nearest towns, who now and then work over the furze-clad downs with ferrets and nets. The various shades of grey and brown homespun shepherds' plaids, generally made use of by the Highland foresters and keepers, render the wearers almost invisible at a short distance, and would doubtless prove far more suitable than such a conspicuous material for the southern guardians of our preserves while engaged in protecting the game committed to their charge from the attacks of the poaching fraternity. The keeper who, as previously stated, assisted in searching for the marten said he had never seen any animal of that family, with the exception of stoats and weasels, either on the downs or in the woods on the low grounds; and he imagined that if one was to be met with in the locality it must have escaped from confinement, as he had heard of one or two being brought into the district from Scotland by some sportsmen who had moors in the Northern Highlands. With regard to stoats and weasels, this relentless destroyer of vermin asserted that these merciless and bloodthirsty little tyrants defied all his attempts to exterminate them, the large extent of rough cover and broken ground on the sloping sides of the downs in which they sought refuge affording them ample protection. On further inquiry I ascertained that he was of opinion that the bullet in the beech tree had been fired by a volunteer, after practising at a range a few miles off towards the north-east, the direction from which the missile evidently came. Some of those who occasionally shot there, he declared, were in the habit of firing at Rooks, Crows, or any large birds that came in view while on their way homewards by the cross-country roads, utterly regardless of all consequences.

It is somewhat strange that while this article, composed a year or two ago and forwarded recently to London, has been in my hands (returned by the printers for revision), I have had a chance of examining a Little Grebe, an adult in most perfect plumage, obtained by a shot from the rifle of a volunteer within a few miles of Brighton. While passing along the banks of a small mill-stream, he noticed the bird rapidly making its way at the depth of about a foot, and having discharged his rifle, it rose to the surface quite helpless and soon succumbed to the effects of the shot. There were no signs of a wound, and I am of opinion it must have been the shock, caused by the force with which the bullet struck the water, that killed the bird.

# QUAIL.
## COTURNIX VULGARIS.

---

With the exception of a straggler or two observed in Norfolk, I have only met with the Quail in the counties of Cambridge and Sussex: according to my own experience, the numbers of this curious bird have greatly decreased of late years.

The bevies hatched on the fenlands between Newmarket and Cambridge (especially about Bottisham, Quy, and Swaffham) afforded, some five and twenty years ago, fair sport at the commencement of the season. What bags were made on the strictly preserved lands I had no means of ascertaining; seven brace, killed by a couple of guns in half a day's shooting on the poor lands or free fens, was the largest number that came to my knowledge. In November 1860, and again in 1861, I visited repeatedly all the likely ground in this district, but never, on any occasion, succeeded in obtaining above a brace or two, even after a long day's tramp. The birds were commonly found on oat-stubbles; mustard, however, appeared the cover for which they exhibited an especial preference. Occasionally they were met with in the rough grass and coarse herbage round the outskirts of the fens, though seldom penetrating far on to the moist portions of the land.

Quail, according to my own experience, lie for the most part exceedingly close, rarely springing till approached within the distance of three or four yards. When once on wing they make way with considerable speed, offering, however, a remarkably easy shot, their line of flight being usually straight and, as a rule, at no greater elevation than two or three feet from the ground. It is seldom this species flies far, though on alighting again, even if carefully marked, they generally prove exceedingly difficult to find. A cunning old lemon-and-white setter, my constant companion on the fens, was thoroughly up to the work, and rarely in the end did a bird succeed in escaping. Instead of following at once a single Quail marked down into the scanty cover of the open fen, a good half-hour was usually allowed to pass before approaching the spot. Though water-dykes frequently surrounded the piece of ground and prevented all chance of running, it was by no means certain that the setter would immediately hit off the scent.

Quails bred in considerable numbers in this locality during the seasons of 1861 and 1862, a nest or two being discovered without difficulty whenever sought for. The morning and evening call of the male having been previously noted by the observant natives of the fens, they were usually well informed as to the spot near which the female was sitting. The nests I examined were placed             scratchings or natural hollows in hay or rough grass, generally at no great distance from some          or other commanding elevation, on which in the twilight the male might be seen

In Norfolk I never met with this species in spring or summer;                    within at the moment both barrels of my gun had been discharged at came under my observation in this apparently very suitable locality. middle of October 1871, in a patch of stunted rushes on a grass-marsh in of the coast.

Until within the last fifteen or twenty years, Quails were abundant during summer in the immediate vicinity of Brighton*. Numbers bred within a few hundred yards of the town, and their nests were frequently mown out when the seeds and clover were cut. Any fine still evening in May and June the well-known "whit-whit" of the male might be heard on various parts of the Downs, the race-hill being an especially favoured spot. In the spring of 1872 I also recognized the note on the chalky hill-sides, a few miles inland up the valley of the Adur, between Shoreham and Beeding. As few, if any, were obtained during the shooting-season, it must be supposed that the birds were merely migrants to the south coast; the times of their arrival and departure, whence they came and whither they went, were, however, unknown. The cause of their gradual falling off in numbers and ultimate disappearance† also remains a mystery, the nature of the surrounding country having undergone little or no alteration.

In the east of Sussex a few brace were killed early in September 1856 by my father's keeper on a stubble adjoining the Pevensey marshes; the birds, even at that date, were extremely scarce in the district.

The Quail feeds on a variety of small seeds, and doubtless also on diminutive insects, together with their eggs and larvæ. The improvements lately carried out with regard to the land may account for the decrease of the birds in the neighbourhood of the fens; no changes have, however, taken place in Sussex that could possibly have affected the supplies of food needed to meet the humble requirements of this retiring species.

* I am well aware that my statements, which are the result of personal observation, do not agree with those of A. E. Knox, who, in the third edition of 'Ornithological Rambles in Sussex,' published in 1855, remarks:—" The Quail is only an occasional migratory visitor to Sussex."

† I have not heard their note during the last ten years.

# STONE-CURLEW.

## ŒDICNEMUS CREPITANS.

So many different names are given to this species by writers on British ornithology that it is somewhat difficult to decide on the most appropriate title to bestow upon it. As the Stone-Curlew, it is referred to by Yarrell, Seebohm, Dresser, and Stevenson, while Hancock, Morris, Gray, Knox, Thompson, and the inimitable Bewick call it the Great Plover. In Gould's magnificently illustrated work on the 'Birds of Great Britain' it is described with a more imposing appellation as the Thick-kneed Bustard, and the persevering Highlander, William Macgillivray, writes of it under the heading of the Stone Thick-knee. Several of these naturalists add the name of Norfolk Plover, and C. J. and James Paget, in their 'Sketch of the Natural History of Yarmouth and its Neighbourhood,' published in 1834, make the following observation concerning this species:—"Œdicnemus crepitans, *common thick-knee, Norfolk plover*—rarely met with here." The Rev. Richard Lubbock, in his 'Observations on the Fauna of Norfolk,' issued in 1848, gives a short account that appears to have escaped the notice of all other writers, and may consequently prove interesting to the readers of 'Rough Notes:'—"I should have mentioned a bird immediately after I spoke of the Bustard, which is very local in its habits, and being as plentiful in parts of our county as anywhere in England, has obtained the name of NORFOLK PLOVER,—the general term is STONE CURLEW (*Charadrius œdicnemus*). In comparison with the numbers of these birds which are seen congregated in autumn, they appear very scarce throughout the summer. The open heaths and very large fields adjoining are their favourite haunts. The young follow their parents when full grown, and the strongest attachment seems to subsist between them. One was shot this last summer in an open field near my house, and being only slightly wounded in the pinion, was run down with some difficulty, brought home alive, and turned into a walled garden. Next morning at sunrise, according to habit, the prisoner was very clamorous, uttering its peculiar cry repeatedly for about an hour. When the servants rose, a young bird was observed in the courtyard, within a few yards of the house, pacing backwards and forwards under the garden wall, which must have come either through an open doorway or through a thick clipped fence; for, though nearly full grown, its powers of flight seemed imperfectly developed. Repeated attempts were made for hours to take it, which it eluded by swiftness of foot, and hid itself among the shrubs, returning again to the wall as soon as disturbance ceased. At last, by careful watching, it was driven into a corner and secured. Being turned into the garden, it seemed delighted to rejoin the parent, whose cry must have brought it nearly half a mile. The most singular part of the affair was, that, as the day advanced, the Plover in the garden was totally silent; but this had no effect in causing its young one to leave the place; having once discovered the place of captivity, it seemed determined to share the prison at all hazards. Mr. Paget, as his catalogue has reference to the vicinity of Yarmouth, justly notes this bird as rare; but towards Thetford and Swaffham, where the country is open, it is abundant. It may be observed in parties of from 80 to 100 before its migration. The greatest allurement to them is an extensive new plantation made in the open country, and on the improved plan of double trenching the soil. The loosened ground affords better means of obtaining worms and beetles, their usual food; and the birds appear particularly to delight in the partial concealment which the young trees afford in the first year or two. As soon as the trees attain any size, all attraction ceases. This bird, with us, is, I believe, reckoned worthless for the table, being very hard and dry; in India, where it is called the Goggle-eyed Florican, it is in great repute. It stays very late before it migrates,—in mild seasons to the very end of November, and even into December." When referring to the remains of Falconry in Norfolk the same author also states "Occasionally the Norfolk Plover (*Œdicnemus crepitans*) was pursued, and gave very good flights. The Carrion Crow also, and the Magpie, were in turn objects of sport."

The headquarters of this species in the British Islands are, as one of its names, the Norfolk Plover, denotes, in the eastern counties. About the large warrens in the neighbourhood of Thetford and other parts of Norfolk it is reported to breed abundantly; in this locality I never explored their haunts, and only observed a few of these birds about the Broad districts in Norfolk, where they were merely accidental visitors usually seen late in autumn or early spring. On the South Downs in Sussex, from above Worthing to Newhaven, these fine Plovers * are by no means scarce, being perhaps most plentiful on the range of hills between Brighton and Lewes. Here numbers of pairs are to be met with in spring and summer, but, unless searched for by those who understand their habits, the whole would in most cases escape observation. I never came across this species during winter, though they are said to be occasionally flushed from turnip-fields late in autumn; and it is most probable that the majority leave the country on the approach of cold weather for a warmer climate. A specimen shot near a pool of brackish water on the coast near Bexhill in Sussex was brought into a bird-stuffer's shop in St. Leonards-on-Sea during the hard winter of 1860, about the latter end of December, and doubtless a few remain every winter, though they generally escape notice owing to their retiring habits. A few years back I was informed by a shepherd who tended his flock on the Downs near Falmer, halfway between Brighton and Lewes, that he had seen five flying together in January 1876. The man was well acquainted with this species, which he spoke of as the Hill-Curlew, and had pointed out to me several nests on this part of the Downs during the previous spring.

Some years back I reared two or three broods of these birds taken on the Downs near St. Mary's Farm, a mile north of Falmer; it was, however, discovered after a few weeks that the Herring-Gulls with which they were confined could not be trusted. At last I caught them in the very act of murdering one with which they had lived in peace and quietness for five or six weeks; looking over into their enclosure I detected a couple holding down the unfortunate bird, while the third rascal was hammering in its skull with repeated strokes from his powerful beak; the whole party immediately retreated on my appearance, but the crime was already accomplished. At this misfortune I separated the survivors from their persecutors; but having little or nothing to learn concerning the habits of this species by retaining them in captivity, their wings were eventually permitted to grow and they took their departure when inclined to make a move; for some weeks after leaving they were heard calling at night, indicating that a flying visit had been paid to the neighbourhood of their old quarters. Each of these birds devoured about half a pound of chopped meat or the same quantity of worms every day; they were, however, always timid, retreating to shelter when inspected, and it appeared improbable they would ever become confiding and tame like Gulls, Ducks, 

The specimens obtained for my collection were procured on the open Downs and also on the slopes hollows of the Hillocks devoted to the feeding of sheep, rabbits and game where no attempt at cultivation had been made. The workmen employed in a farm near Falmer drew my attention to a couple of eggs on a field of young corn; I failed, however, to 

* Here they are generally known as Norfolk Plovers.

Black Crows carried off the eggs. A short and condensed extract from my notes, taken while collecting in Sussex in 1872, may possibly give an insight into the habits of this species and also draw attention to a peculiarity in the formation of the beak of the adult male that has previously escaped the notice of all writers:—

"May 10. Drove from Brighton on to the Downs near Falmer, following the hill-road to Plumpton Bostle to the spot where a shepherd had found the nest of a Stone-Curlew with two eggs. On carefully approaching, the birds rose before we came in view and did not return for some hours; at dusk I was again on the spot, and the male and female a second time got on wing before we were within a hundred yards.—May 11. Again tried my luck at the same pair of birds; soon after daybreak I crawled near the nest while a man walked boldly from the opposite direction to the spot where it was situated. The birds, however, succeeded in getting away without being observed, as on handling the eggs they were found to be hot, and it was impossible they could have been left many minutes. Three hours later another attempt was made, and I now crept flat down in among the rough grass up to about forty yards from the nest, while the man came openly from the opposite direction. This time the male bird came running close up to me before detecting danger; so low did he crouch down that he appeared no higher than a rabbit while gliding stealthily through the short heather and grass. After obtaining this specimen, we constructed a shelter of dead branches, furze, and heather, and I was then concealed and watched the place for the return of the female; a couple of hours later she circled round once or twice, and then settled about two hundred yards lower down the hill, but on crawling silently to the mark I had taken when she alighted, no signs of her could be discovered. Shortly before dusk she again flew past, calling loudly, and after remaining in view for a few minutes took a course away towards the east and was not seen again. As the darkness commenced, very heavy clouds gathered suddenly all round from the north and east and a terrible hailstorm broke over all the country within view. After five minutes the whole expanse of the Downs was covered thick with immense drops of hail and ice, the hills appearing as white as if a fall of snow had taken place. The following morning no signs of the bird could be detected, and the eggs, having evidently been deserted, were taken. The male bird I had procured had two small fleshy protuberances on the base of his beak, somewhat resembling those of a Pigeon, but rather larger; the female, I remarked, did not show any elevation of this description on her upper mandible. On the 15th I learned from the shepherds that three of the Curlews had been seen in company near the spot where the nest had been taken on Sunday, but to-day none were to be met with."

Another nest or, rather, clutch of eggs, as there is only a scratch in the soil to do service for a cradle, was heard of at St. Mary's Farm near Falmer, and on the 17th of the month I drove over to secure the female, if possible, as one was still needed as a specimen. She had selected her quarters in a field of young oats, on very open ground, and the first two attempts to get within range were failures, as she left her eggs while we were more than a hundred yards distant. On the third occasion I risked a long shot; but, though evidently hard hit, the poor bird flapped on out of sight over the brow of the hill, and, as far as I was able to ascertain, never returned to her eggs, having perished from the effects of the wounds received from the charge. Only one bird was seen by the men employed at the farm to resort to that part of the ground for the remainder of the season, and the eggs, I ascertained on a subsequent visit, were sucked by the Crows.

Again over to St. Mary's Farm on the 23rd, as I had been informed that another pair of "Norfolk Plovers"[*] had been observed by the gamekeepers frequenting some ground about a mile and a half further west than the last nest. While proceeding with two or three attendants along the hill-side to

---
[*] This is the name the keepers gave them.

take up a position and examine the surrounding slopes of the Downs through the glasses, I came unexpectedly on the female Curlew, who got up within the distance of half a dozen paces and made off, running rapidly for twenty or thirty yards before spreading her wings. Having a few minutes previously handed my gun to a keeper, so as to make use of the binoculars, I lost an easy chance of procuring the bird. There was little doubt she had risen from her eggs, which were soon discovered, and I then looked about for the nearest cover to afford concealment and from which to watch her return. At the distance of about sixty yards a stunted thorn-bush offered a capital hiding-place, but it was clear that a closer approach must be made in order to obtain an effective shot. From the bush to the spot where the eggs were deposited the ground sloped upwards, and was a bare open hill-side with very short grass and a few small tufts of heather and furze. After taking up my position the male came in sight, flying slowly round and finally alighting near the nest; he was once within shot, but the female only was required to complete the pair. The small protuberance on the beak was distinctly visible through the glasses as the bird stood upright with outstretched neck near the eggs; a few minutes later the female came in sight and at once settled down higher up the hill. The male then rose and flew straight away up the valley between the Downs, and the female commenced descending the hill towards the nest. She was apparently somewhat restless or alarmed, and moved very slowly, pausing from time to time, stretching out her neck to its fullest extent and gazing intently around with her large yellow eyes. About a quarter of an hour was passed before she dropped on her eggs, and then she sat turning her head from side to side, the great length of her neck affording a good chance for observation. I could see no chance to approach within range, unless it was possible to creep up behind a small bush of wild raspberries and brambles, about a couple of feet in height, that grew within twenty yards of the nest. It was impossible to proceed straight to this small raspberry-plant from the thorn bush without attracting the attention of the bird, so I carefully crawled backwards down hill till she was lost sight of. Then moving under the brow till the cover I was making for was brought in line with the spot where the bird was sitting, I commenced the ascent. It was slow work, forcing the gun along in front and creeping flat down over the surface of the ground, as the shelter afforded by the plants and weeds was so small. After making my way about fifty yards, a glimpse of the bird was caught through the upper twigs of the raspberry-bush; the last few yards up to the plant occupied some time, but at length it was reached, and a rest was now needed before making an attempt to shoot. The Curlew still kept her neck stretched out and continued turning her head in all directions; on rising suddenly up the poor bird fluttered off, offering an easy chance for a shot, and fell dead to a charge of No. 3 at about thirty yards' distance. I remarked that all the breeding-places of this species met with and examined on the South Downs were on the slopes of the hills facing the south or west; there is never any appearance of a nest, only a slight depression in the ground, in which the eggs are deposited. After taking the eggs, I had them placed at once under a hen at St. Mary's Farm in hopes that the young might be produced in due time. On referring to a couple of our best-reputed authorities on British Birds, I learned that one asserted that this species sat for sixteen, and the other for sixteen or seventeen days; the man who had undertaken to look after them was accordingly directed to remove the eggs if not hatched out in twenty days. As no sign of a change was seen at that time, he took them away, but accidentally breaking one discovered that the young were just on the point of hatching. I saw the downy mites shortly after death, and it appeared that they would shortly have broken the shell; as such was the case, twenty-one or twenty-two days must be the period of incubation of this species.

The Plate gives a life-sized representation of the heads of the male and female of this species, and is taken from the birds, previously referred to, shot on the Downs between Falmer and Lewes, in Sussex, on the 11th and 23rd of May, 1872. The small knobs or protuberances on the base of the upper mandible of the male are shown as they are seen in life; being only soft and fleshy they disappear in a day or two after the death of the bird. This fact sadly puzzled many of the ornithological wiseacres some years back, and they hunted out the dried specimens in several museums to discover if the birds had signs of these marks, as they had never heard before that the males exhibited this peculiarity. Possibly it is only very old birds that show it: the two adult males, however, that I closely examined while alive on the Downs had those knobs well developed on the base of their beaks, though, if I am not mistaken, all signs of them vanished in a couple of days from the specimen I shot.

# GOLDEN PLOVER.
## CHARADRIUS PLUVIALIS.

GOLDEN Plovers breed in considerable numbers on the Grouse-moors of many of the northern counties of the Highlands; I have come across their haunts repeatedly in Perthshire, Ross-shire, Sutherland, and Caithness, as well as in the Western Islands.

A late snow-storm in the spring appears occasionally to put an almost entire stop to their nesting operations and to drive most of these birds from the country. While living in Glenlyon, in Perthshire, where I rented the Innerwick shootings, I noticed there were hundreds of pairs of this species on the moors in 1866; but the weather being exceedingly hot, I deferred procuring any of the downy young for specimens, as it was utterly impossible that they could make the journey to the taxidermist at Brighton without decomposition setting in. I then determined to bring, next season, a naturalist to the glen, who could attend to them the day they were obtained. On reaching Innerwick the following year in June, I learned from the keepers that the Golden Plovers had arrived at the usual time and in their accustomed numbers; a heavy fall of snow, however, had driven nearly the whole of them away, and but very few had returned to breed on the hills; I do not think there were above eight or ten pairs engaged in nesting operations over the whole stretch of ground. After a week's hard work, we succeeded in finding three broods and one nest of eggs; in no single instance did the family consist of more than two juveniles, and this fact tended to prove the effects of the cold and the hardships to which the newly hatched youngsters had been exposed. We found it almost impossible to watch the old birds settle to their young, as they always kept at some distance from the spot where their treasures were concealed; and it was eventually discovered that not until after the parent birds had been shot could the whereabouts of the juveniles be detected. While the old birds are flying round, the young remain perfectly quiet; in a few minutes, however, after they are killed the tiny mites commence calling. The note is very low, and when the cry seems to be uttered at a distance of about twenty or thirty yards the small bird is generally at your feet. After procuring all the little Plovers needed, we were preparing to turn down hill towards the lodge, when a pair of old birds and a couple of downy juveniles came in view, making their way across a large patch of frozen snow in a deep gully in the side of the hill. The family were allowed to depart unmolested, their actions being carefully watched till they disappeared from sight in the black peat-moss beyond the snow-drift—and a very pretty sight it was. There is little doubt that in this season nearly the whole, with the exception of the most backward, of the birds must have laid before the snow fell, and the greater part, if not all, of their eggs have been destroyed.

To obtain specimens of the old birds in their greatest beauty, they must be shot some time before they commence their nesting operations; the glossy black feathers then rapidly become speckled with white, and the general brightness of the plumage fades and disappears as soon as the cares of a family are undertaken

I have also repeatedly observed Golden Plovers very tame, resting in the fields and paying little or no regard to my conveyance, while driving along the road between Brighton and Shoreham in Sussex during winter after severe storms of wind and snow. These poor wearied birds occasionally suffered for this misplaced confidence, and several plump and in very good condition were occasionally obtained, as scarcely any traffic that resented my shots was met with along the roads on such occasions.

These birds must leave their breeding-quarters on the Highland mountains, and the slopes of the lower hills occasionally, at an early date, as there is an entry in my notes for July the 8th, 1868, stating that great numbers were seen along the shores of the Dornoch Firth on that day. I well remember discharging both the punt and two or three shoulder-guns on my way along the coast from the Meikle Ferry to Tain, close in upon the sandy shore off Morangie and the mudflats stretching up towards the old-fashioned town that goes by the name of Tain*. There was only one complaint to be entered against these excellent birds—viz. that they had been living too sumptuously and were rather more coated with fat in several parts than is necessary to improve their very delicate and delicious flavour. We did not, however, spare them on this account, but continued to follow the flocks for several days, giving them a turn whenever a chance occurred, as long as they remained in the district. On the 29th of August, 1872, I found a very tame flock of Golden Plovers on the sandy flats between Yarmouth and the mouth of the harbour, where the fishermen used to dry their nets stretched out on the links just to the south of the Nelson monument. Several were stopped with two or three doubles of my shoulder-gun just at dusk, as they circled round before taking their departure.

It is some years since I made a good bag of this species; but so late as December the 8th, 1883, there is an entry in my notes recording the fact that "Snow-Buntings, Golden Plover, and Peewits were very tame along the upper road between Shoreham and Brighton. I could only obtain one shot at the Plover, which stopped about three couple, as a number of carts passed and the birds rose and moved further into the open field, where it was impossible to drive within range."

Many years ago, during the hard winter of December 1863, when residing at Ferrygate, near North Berwick, in East Lothian, I met with a capital and most singular evening's sport at this species, and the result has by no means faded from my memory after nearly five-and-twenty years. Wishing to procure a Mallard or two for our dinner the following day, I started for the ridge of rocks in a wild unfrequented bay on the shores of the Firth of Forth, immediately below our very comfortable quarters where I was then supposed to be rapidly picking up a knowledge of farming. The pursuit of the various species of wild birds was even then the object I had in view, and intended, if possible, to carry out †. The moon was shining brightly when the rocks in the bay were reached, and making my way in among the shelter of some of the large slabs, I awaited the course of events. One Mallard came over, a fine old drake, and was dropped almost on to my head, and then I noticed a number of smaller birds rising on wing, but alighting again immediately on the damp and glistening sand below the light of the moon, which was shining brightly. Crawling quietly among the very abundant shelter afforded by the slabs of rock, I soon came to the conclusion that the unknown were some kind of Plover, though the species I could not ascertain, as they uttered no sounds while running over the sands in pursuit of food, and dark rolling clouds occasionally obscured the moon, rendering my glasses useless. Both barrels of my ten-bore breech-loader discharged into the thickest part of them revealed the fact that they were Golden Plover, and almost before I had collected the slain, the remainder of the flocks, for there were two or three lots about, were again circling round, anxious to be back on their feeding-ground and searching for food. About half a dozen double shots from the heavy ten-bore were fired into the densest parts of the flocks, and the

---

* The natives of the locality always used to call this place the "toon of Tain."

† Revising this article the last week in 1886 I find I have been able to carry out the object of my aspiration; and as all the risks incurred during its pursuit were successfully overcome, I am sure I have good cause to be thankful.

slain collected amounted to about from a dozen to half that number at each discharge. A squall shortly after blew over and the moon disappeared, and then my sport was at an end. The next night I again visited the spot, but unfortunately it was discovered that the majority of the Plovers had moved off, and not a hundred birds put in an appearance at the same hours when thousands had been distributed over the sandy bay the previous evening. The result of three or four shots was about a dozen brought to bag, and then I made my way homewards, following the course of the eel-barn for the chance of a shot. A large-winged stranger that flapped up, and which ought to have been recognized immediately in spite of the darkness, was knocked down, and proved to be an immature Heron. I was in hopes it would turn out to be a Bittern or some strange wanderer of the Heron tribe from the northern parts of Europe across the North Sea.

# DOTTEREL.

## CHARADRIUS MORINELLUS.

This interesting species is a summer visitor to the British Islands, arriving on our south coasts in April or early in May, and after rearing its young on the lonely mountain-tops of several of the highest ranges in the northern counties, taking its departure from our shores before cold weather has set in. The Dotterel has of late years either greatly decreased in numbers or totally disappeared in many localities where it was formerly abundant; there are, however, still a few remote districts to which the birds annually resort on the approach of summer. The nest is by no means difficult to find\*, and the small parties of old birds on their first arrival evince such an utter disregard of their natural enemies, that there is little wonder that this species, which invariably attracts attention when met with, has been gradually almost exterminated. Were it not that the remaining haunts are situated near the hilltops (in most instances in wild and lonely districts, where their presence is unknown to all, except some wandering keeper or shepherd), it is probable that the few survivors would long ago have been swept from the British Islands.

On their first arrival from across the Channel, Dotterel in former days invariably passed some time on the South Downs, within a few miles of the coast, before resuming their journey towards the north. Certain open spots along the range of hills (free from furze bushes or other cover) possessed peculiar attractions, and here at the accustomed date the birds might be looked for to the day, though the downs for miles on either side were but seldom visited. Since 1867 I have heard of but one or two small parties ("trips," I believe, is the correct name) being noticed in this locality, though up till that date they not unfrequently rested for a few days during spring on the ranges of the South Downs.

The last flock of Dotterel that came under my observation was seen passing over the downs near Brighton early in September 1880, the birds were flying west, following a course taken by Golden Plover, Whimbrel, and other Waders at the season of migration. In the Highlands I never noticed Dotterel later than the end of the first week in September; about the beginning of August they were usually met in small parties consisting of from eight or ten individuals to double that number.

On no occasion did I ever recognize this species at a low elevation on the hills, the quarters they frequent appearing to lie far above the range of the Golden Plover. Their nearest feathered neighbours are doubtless the Ptarmigan, though these birds for the most part during summer resort to the more rocky portion of the hill-side. While making their way from one mountain-top to another, I remarked that this species invariably held a course at a considerable elevation across the intervening glens. Flocks of Golden Plover, if pursued in stormy weather, often swept down into the mosses in some sheltered corrie, though the Dotterel, when alarmed, after flying round for a time, would at last strike boldly out for

---

\* In making this assertion I am aware that my experience differs from that of the majority of observers. I have only on two occasions sought for nests containing eggs, and both, after waiting and watching for an hour or two, were discovered, patience and a slight knowledge of the habits of the birds being all that is needed to insure success.

one of the adjacent summits. During windy weather in autumn I occasionally found the flocks somewhat difficult to approach within range; with a little driving, however, it was generally possible to procure a few couple. The young birds commonly retain the down about the head and back of the neck long after they are strong on wing. A few days before the 12th of August, 1867, six or seven couple were bagged by two guns, while hare- and Plover-shooting* on the hills in the west of Perthshire; and with one or two exceptions a quantity of down still showed round their heads.

A short account extracted from my notes of 1866 concerning the capture of the specimens figured on the Plate may possibly be of service in giving some information about the nesting-habits of this species.

Having failed on two occasions, owing to a strong wind and mist, to meet with the birds on the hills lying between Loch Rannoch and the river Lyon during the middle of June, a third attempt was made on the 26th, when the weather proved all that could be desired. In order to avoid the necessity of climbing the steepest part of the hill during the midday heat, an early start from the lodge was effected, and the high ground reached before the rays of the sun caused the slightest inconvenience. While making our way slowly up the winding peat-track an immature White-tailed Eagle came in view, circling over a portion of one of the neighbouring hills where gents had recently been cast; at last he settled on a ridge, and turning his head from side to side calmly surveyed the scene. Unwilling to waste the time that must necessarily have been spent in stalking the bird, we proceeded on our journey, though I had little doubt, owing to the direction of the wind and the rugged nature of the ground, that this specimen might have been obtained. For an hour longer, while he still remained in view, not the slightest change from the position first taken was observed; doubtless some dead sheep or other prey had been detected near at hand, and would prove an attraction to the spot till all signs of danger had vanished. On leaving the track and striking out into the open moor, a flat was shortly reached where Golden Plover were breeding about the swampy ground on each side of a small burn that trickled slowly down the mountainside. In many instances the birds would barely rise on our approach, running a few yards and turning again and again to face us with a low plaintive cry, their young being evidently concealed in the bright yellow moss that extended some distance over the flat. A few cock Grouse were seen in the patches of heather round the outskirts of the mossy ground; but no further signs of bird-life were encountered till a wide expanse of broken ground on which I had met with two or three broods of Dotterel during the previous autumn was entered upon, and a pair of Meadow-Pipits were detected creeping quietly through the scanty herbage. A haze that had hung in early morning over the low ground near the river-side had now cleared off, and from our present position, at an elevation of considerably over 2500 feet, a magnificent stretch of scenery was in view. Not a cloud or a vestige of mist obscured the mountain-tops, and even the most distant hills stood out well defined in the clear morning air. To the north the whole outline of Ben Nevis could be discerned, as usual exhibiting a considerable amount of snow in the higher gullies; the rifts and chasms in the rugged mountains about Glen Coe looked dark and gloomy as ever; while at our feet the whole surface of Loch Rannoch was spread out, resembling in the bright sunlight a sheet of molten silver. To the south the course of the Lyon could be traced for twelve or fourteen miles, winding through the glen, with the higher slopes of Ben Lawers rising up stern and majestic immediately beyond the lower ridges that look down upon the river; to the east and west Schiehallion and Ben More, with many another craggy peak, broke up the sky-line and added to the wildness of the scene. Having now reached a sufficient height to commence our search, the pony with the lunch-hampers was made fast, while with the keeper and two gillies we formed in line and made our way slowly over the ground in order to raise the birds. Scarcely one hundred yards had been passed over when a low whistle from the

* In order to keep on good terms with the farmers, it used to be the custom some years back on many of the shootings in this district to kill down a number of blue hares before the opening of the Grouse-season.

station attracted my attention, and proceeding a short distance uphill a Dotterel ... round in circles, its actions at once leading us to suppose that eggs or young were close ... carefully examined every hole and inequality in the ground without success, ... sat ... to rest and watch; whilst we were in motion the bird continued sweeping round, ... low whistle, but as soon as a halt was made it settled on an adjoining knoll within ... of thirty yards. A few minutes later a downy nestling was seen to rise from a bare patch of ground, and make off uphill at a pace that, considering its size, was most remarkable. The colouring and markings on the down corresponded so closely with the general tints of the moss and herbage that this tiny creature had escaped observation, though the spot on which it squatted had been passed over repeatedly. A second shortly after attempted to escape uphill, in answer probably to the low call of the old bird, and the third an hour later was detected in the same manner. On the few occasions on which I had met with the nest of this species the eggs never exceeded three in number; and judging that the entire brood had now been taken, the old bird was next easily procured. It was not till well on in the afternoon, between four and five o'clock, that its mate came in view and proved far more wary, flying round in wide circles and resolutely refusing to approach within the distance of sixty or seventy yards. At last it was knocked down, but falling winged over a brae in a patch of broken ground where blue hares had scratched numberless holes in the turf, it succeeded in evading capture, and no dog having been brought uphill in consequence of the distance and heat of the weather, we were forced at length to relinquish our search.

Having noted the direction from which this bird came in view, I ascended the neighbouring hill, Cairngorm, a few days later, and soon fell in with three small trips, consisting each of three or four individuals. A specimen was at once procured, and for several hours the actions of the survivors were watched. All the time we remained on the high ridge the birds gave no signs of separating, and paid but little regard to our presence. The specimen obtained on this occasion proved to be a female, while the bird shot with the brood turned out, contrary to my expectation, a male. The brightness of the colouring on the feathers of all the birds composing the small parties on Cairngorm would lead one to believe that these were females, the care of the juveniles appearing to devolve on the males, who at this season exhibit more worn and far less showy plumage.

The adult male and female figured in the Plate with the brood are the pair whose capture is described above. As the plumage of both specimens was considerably worn, these birds, to be seen in full beauty, should probably be procured before the nesting-operations have been commenced. I also repeatedly remarked this fact in connection with Golden Plover.

# RINGED PLOVER.

## *CHARADRIUS HIATICULA.*

---

The Ringed Plover, or Dotterel, as this species is sometimes called, is a resident on our shores, being found in greater or smaller numbers on all parts of the coast-line of the British Islands that are suited to its habits. To the marshes surrounding the freshwater broads of the east of Norfolk it is a frequent visitor, though not a summer resident; on the warrens further inland several pairs of these birds may be seen to take up their quarters early in the spring and rear their young. In many parts of the Highlands Ringed Plovers resort to the shores of the lochs and the stony banks adjoining the course of the rivers, taking up their quarters within a short distance of the water-side and departing with their broods for the sea-coast early in the autumn.

The eggs of the Ringed Plover are usually laid on sand, fine gravel, or shingle near the sea-shore, the river-banks, or the localities where the birds have taken up their quarters. The nest, if it may be so termed, is occasionally merely a natural hollow or depression in the surface; at times it is evidently scratched out and a lining of small stones carefully added. In May 1866, while staying at Rye in Sussex, I discovered a most elaborately constructed cradle on a grass-marsh, only a couple of years reclaimed by a mud wall from the saltwater flats of the Nook. Here in the fresh green turf the birds had scraped out a well-formed circular nest, in which they had arranged a copious lining of small flat white shells*. Considerable labour and time had evidently been expended in the collection of this attractive lining, as the whole must have been transported from the beach or shingle-banks, between a quarter and half a mile distant.

At the commencement of the Preservation Act, when freed from the general persecution to which they had been exposed, the whole of the smaller Waders became at once exceedingly unsuspicious of danger. While on Breydon mudflats on the morning of the 8th of May, 1873, I remarked that the large flocks of Dunlins and Ringed Plovers drawn up alongside the channel paid but little attention to the gunning-punt, even when approaching to within the distance of three or four yards, affording excellent chances for watching their actions as well as detecting any rarities in their ranks. Hundreds that were resting on one leg, with the head turned over on the back, only hopped a yard or two further on to the mud.

Ringed Plover vary considerably in size and colouring; those that remain along our southern coast-line during winter and take up their breeding-quarters in early spring on the extensive shingle-banks of Kent and Sussex are a far larger race or form than those that reach these islands from across the Channel in flocks early in May. The residents, in addition to being considerably larger and consequently of greater weight, differ much in the colouring of the plumage of the back, which is of a far lighter tint of greyish brown; the legs are also more fleshy and of a paler hue, the colour being a yellow flesh-tint, while those of the smaller race are always of a bright and often of a deep orange-yellow. These small forms do not make their appearance on our shores till after the larger are well on with their nesting-operations. The following extracts taken from my journals will show the dates at which the smaller were passing over our coasts, and the time when the larger forms were observed while engaged with their eggs or young:—

"May 5, 1880. Over at Shoreham. Wind north-east, very cold. Several flocks of the small Ringed Plover lately landed were feeding on the muds in the harbour at low water and resorting to the shingle-banks when the tide flowed. Eggs of the larger form were seen on the shingle-banks, several pairs being met with between the Shoreham Coastguard Station and the west end of the wide water opposite Lancing."

"May 21, 1881. Wind west. Brood of four young of the Ringed Plover (larger form) seen running after the old birds on the mud in the harbour near the ferry at Shoreham. Many of the small variety in flocks flying up and down the tide-way in the river at low water." I never met with a chance of examining a nest of the small form of the Ringed Plover, and believe that the whole of this diminutive race proceed further north to rear their young.

So late in the season as August 23rd, in 1879, I noticed a downy brood of this species near the Coastguard Station at Shoreham; these must have been a second brood, unless the birds had suffered from repeated losses of their former eggs or young. Large flocks of both Dunlins and Ringed Plovers in immature plumage were at the same time driven into the harbour by a heavy gale accompanied by drifting squalls of rain.

The colours of the soft parts of an immature bird shot at Shoreham on the 16th of September, 1882, were as follows:—Bill black, with the exception of a dingy yellow-ochre tinge at the base; legs and feet pale livid greenish yellow; soles of feet yellow.

# KENTISH PLOVER.
## CHARADRIUS CANTIANUS.

This diminutive Plover was first discovered in Kent at the close of the last century, and derives its scientific appellation from the county in which it was obtained; in Sussex it is almost equally plentiful, and a few have regularly come under my observation while shooting in spring and autumn on Breydon mudflats in Norfolk. In no other part of the country have I met with this neat and attractive bird, though its similarity to the Ringed Plover may reasonably be supposed to account for a straggler having been occasionally overlooked.

Along the flat line of coast lying between Rye Harbour and Dungeness this species was formerly very abundant; during the last twenty years, however, they have greatly decreased in numbers, their nests having been plundered to supply the demands of collectors, and the birds themselves shot down for the same purpose. The first arrivals not unfrequently put in an appearance about the middle or latter end of April, but May had usually set in before any numbers were observed. The nest in this locality is invariably placed in the sand or fine gravel a little above high-water mark; I never observed one on the grass-marshes a quarter of a mile or so inland, which are often resorted to by the Ringed Plover. By the close of summer the young birds are seen in small parties on the sands to the east of Rye Harbour, betaking themselves, as the tide rises, to the mudflats in the Nook and the slades and watercourses adjoining the beach in Romney Marsh. In September 1869 I noticed for several days an immense gathering of immature Waders on the sands between Camber Coastguard Station and the harbour mouth; the birds composing this flock covered at least a square half-mile of ground when spread out to feed at the small pools on the flats, the various species keeping for the most part to themselves, though occasionally intermixing while changing their quarters. Sanderlings proved to be the most numerous, though at least a hundred Curlew Sandpipers were present, and there were also several small parties of a score or so of Kentish Plovers, which, when alarmed and rising on wing, struck out a course for themselves without joining any of the larger flights. Dunlins, Ringed Plovers, and a few Knots were also scattered about, while Gulls and Terns in hundreds hovered over the tide-way or flapped slowly up and down the course of the winding channel towards the harbour, the immense concourse of Waders and Sea-fowl making up a most animated scene.

After the first week in October I never met with this species, neither have I heard of a specimen having been obtained or seen by either the fishermen or coast-gunners, who are perpetually on the look-out for any varieties.

On Breydon mudflats, where a few Kentish Plovers stop for a day or two during spring and autumn while on their passage to and from the north, these birds are known as Alexandra Plovers among the professional punt-gunners.

# GREY PLOVER.

## SQUATAROLA HELVETICA.

As far as I have been able to ascertain, this species has never been known to remain and breed on our shores; and it is only within the last few years that its eggs have been properly authenticated, owing to a discovery made by Mr. Henry Seebohm and Mr. Harvie-Brown in 1875, when they "took ten nests between the 22nd of June and the 12th of July in the valley of the Petchora, in lat. 65°." This information is extracted from Mr. Seebohm's work on British Birds, and the author also states, "It is not known that any authentic eggs of this interesting bird have been taken during the last ten years." As Mr. Seebohm's account of finding the nests and eggs of this species is exceeding amusing, I offer no apology for making an extract of one portion and inserting it in 'Rough Notes.' The remarks concerning his repeated unsuccessful shots at the birds, eventually secured, show how carefully he records the whole of his proceedings, utterly regardless of drawing attention to his failures and mishaps.

"We had not walked more than a couple of miles inland before we came upon a small party of Plovers. They were very wild, and we found it impossible to get within shot of them; but a distant view through our binoculars almost convinced us that we had met with the Grey Plover at last. We had not walked very far before other Plovers rose; and we determined to commence a diligent search for the nest, and offered half a rouble to any of our men who should find one. Our interpreter laughed at us, and marched away into the tundra with a 'C'est impossible, Monsieur.' We appealed to our Samoyede, who stroked his beardless chin, and cautiously replied 'mózhno.' (possible). The other men wandered aimlessly up and down; but the Samoyede tramped the ground systematically, and after more than an hour's search found a nest on one of the dry tussocky ridges intersecting the bog, containing four eggs about the size and shape of those of the Golden Plover, but more like those of the Lapwing in colour. The nest was hollow, evidently scratched, perfectly round, somewhat deep, and containing a handful of broken slender twigs and reindeer-moss. Harvie-Brown concealed himself as well as he could behind a ridge to lie in wait for the bird returning to the nest, and after half an hour's watching shot a veritable Grey Plover. Soon afterwards another of our men found a second nest, also containing four eggs, in exactly a similar situation. Harvie-Brown took this nest also in hand, and in about an hour succeeded in shooting the female. The third nest was found by the Samoyede. This time I lay down behind a ridge some thirty yards from the nest, and after waiting a quarter of an hour caught sight of the bird on the top of a distant tussock. Presently she ran nearer to another ridge, looked round, and then ran on to the next, until she finally came within fifty yards of where I was lying. I had just made up my mind to risk a shot when she must have seen me, and flew right away. In a quarter of an hour I caught sight of her again, approaching by short stages as before, but from an opposite direction. I must have been in full sight of her. When she had approached within fifty yards of me, as near as I could guess, I fired at her with no. 4 shot and missed. I remained reclining where I was, with little hope that she would make a third attempt to approach the nest, and whiled away the time with watching a Buffon's Skua through my glass as it cautiously approached in my direction. Turning my head round suddenly I caught sight of the Grey Plover running towards the nest within fifty yards of me. I lifted my gun and fired again, but was so nervous that I missed her a second time. I was so vexed that I got up and walked towards the Skua, which still remained *in statu quo*. I missed a shot at it too, spent some time in a vain search for its nest, and returned to my old quarters. In ten minutes I saw the Grey Plover flying up. It wheeled round in my direction, coming almost within shot, and evidently took stock of me, and satisfied itself that I was a harmless animal practising with blank cartridge, having no evil design upon its eggs. It alighted about fifty yards beyond the nest, and approached less timidly than before. When it came within fifty yards of me I fired, this time with no. 6 shot, and laid the poor bird upon its back. As we returned to our boat Harvie-Brown found a fourth nest, and, after watching as before, secured the bird. We accidentally broke two of the eggs belonging to the third nest, but reached Alexievka at midnight with fourteen identified Grey Plover's eggs. Two sittings were quite fresh, and made us an excellent omelette for breakfast the next morning. The other two were very slightly incubated." It is only on the mud-flats and the salt-water shingle-banks that this species is found, and there are few, but punt-gunners, who could give an account of its habits. In all my wanderings I never met with one of these birds on Highland lochs, Norfolk broads, or any inland water. Though a few scattered flocks are occasionally seen in winter, it is, as a rule, only in spring and autumn, while on their way to and from their breeding-haunts in the desolate regions of the far north, that the Grey Plovers pay flying visits to our shores.

Under the date of January 1st, 1882 (wind south-west and moderate), I find it entered in my notes that, while shooting in the punt off Shoreham, we met with large flocks of Curlew and Grey Plover, and both species remained for some weeks along the shingle-banks between the coast-guard station and Shoreham pier. The waves rolling on the shore were generally too heavy to work the gunning-punt sufficiently close for a successful shot, but ten or a dozen were now and then stopped, and once or twice over a score. The Plover I remarked were very heavy at this season, so it was evident they fared sumptuously on some of the flats near at hand, probably in the harbour, when all was still and quiet at night.

I find the following entries in my notes concerning this species when observed on the south coast along the shores of the Channel :—

"September 18th, 1882. Shot half a dozen young Grey Plovers at Shoreham, while flying along the coast, the birds being in remarkably good condition and exceedingly heavy. The colouring of the upper mandibles was dark horn, lower mandibles near the base warm red flesh; legs and toes a grey slate tint, nails darker. It had been too rough for us to get out to sea, and we had walked along the shore to Worthing and back from Shoreham."

"October 24, 1882. Wind south in the morning and towards the afternoon south-west. A terrible gale with awful squalls of wind and rain in the early morning. Grey Plovers, in immense numbers, were found about the flats, in the harbour at Shoreham, and at different parts of the long stretch of brackish water that had collected where the soil had been taken out to make an embankment, to break the force of the tide on towards Lancing, and two or three parties were seen along the course of the marsh-dyke in front of the village. The birds appeared worn out and tired by the continued buffeting of the storm, and were easily approached. Some of the Plovers were intermixed with large flocks of Gulls, and were sheltering from the storm under the ridges of the shingle-banks on the beach. Many other sea-fowl were affected by the gale; I heard, after my return to Brighton, when it was too late, that several Skuas had been riding out the storm on the smooth water on the lee side of the new pier."

These birds are often heard at night hovering round towns in squally weather, probably attracted by the lights. On the night of the 3rd of September, 1872, there were numbers of Curlew, Redshanks, and Grey Plovers flying over Yarmouth, setting locally, and at daybreak, on the 4th we met with several flocks on the Breydon muds at low water. As the tide rose, these left the water, and but a few scattered birds were seen during the remainder of the day; I, however, fell in with both Kentish Plover and Temminck's Stints, and succeeded in obtaining specimens of each species.

The first arrival of black-breasted birds in full summer plumage is usually about the 10th or 12th of May. I see by notes taken while shooting on Breydon, in the spring of 1871, that the earliest Grey Plovers were observed that season on the 12th, and several with other waders and a handsome Curlew Sandpiper were shot during the course of the day. These birds continued to arrive on the flats daily for nearly a fortnight, large numbers being seen on three or four occasions.

On the 24th of May, 1871, there were several flocks of Grey Plovers gathered together here and there on the flats at Breydon, and I obtained as many specimens in perfect plumage as were required for my collection, and for the future refrained from molesting them in that state. Repeated shots with both punt- and shoulder-guns at Bar-tailed Godwits, Curlew Sandpipers, and Little Stints, which secured several specimens of each species in their full summer dress, also kept us so continually occupied, that it was not till we had been a considerable time on the water that we had a chance to partake of any refreshments.

My notes contain the following remarks on the subject:—"About mid-day we were able to get our breakfasts, and having been over ten hours at work on the water, we were not inclined to find fault with the slight flavour of mud that some of our joints and other eatables had contracted by being stowed away in the unclean and close quarters in the bows of our boats three or four times on the appearance of birds, just as we were on the point of commencing to satisfy our hunger."

# PEEWIT.

## *VANELLUS VULGARIS.*

---

The most numerous perhaps of all the denizens of our marshes and mudflats, the Peewit may be met with at one season or another in almost every suitable locality on the mainland from north to south; it occurs also on several of the surrounding islands where uncultivated lowlands, bogs, or extensive tracts of sand exist.

In many of the northern counties of the Highlands there are marshes along the course of the rivers winding through the straths and glens where a few pairs of Peewits take up their summer quarters. Now and then I have come across a nest or two in some damp spot among the heather, but it is seldom these birds breed at any elevation on the hills. The country surrounding the sandy links of Gullane in East Lothian was, in former days, a great resort, and immense numbers of eggs were gathered in the locality. On much of the unreclaimed ground in the neighbourhood, as well as on the rabbit-warrens stretching further east and bordering on the shores of the Firth, many hundreds of pairs might be seen collecting in the vicinity of their haunts as early as the middle of March. How thickly the birds nested over certain parts of the ground may be judged from the fact that in the spring of 1864 I took 275 eggs from a piece of ploughed land between three and four acres in extent. A field of ten or twelve acres was divided by a farm-road leading to the shore, and for some cause, utterly incomprehensible, the birds resorted in numbers to the smaller portion (only lately reclaimed) while the remainder was left almost untenanted. By searching over the ground on a few occasions, during April and early in May, the above-mentioned number of fresh eggs were secured.

According to my own experience, the Peewit commences its nesting-operations at least ten days or a fortnight earlier in that portion of East Lothian bordering the shores of the Forth than in either the east of Norfolk or the marshes and levels of Sussex. On the flat stretch of sandy soil to the east of Tain in Ross-shire, known in the district as the "Fendom," I also remarked, during the seasons of 1868 and 1869, that the Peewits which nested in large numbers on the barren and uncultivated portion of the ground were fully a week earlier than those in the southern and eastern counties of England.

Immense bodies gather towards the end of autumn on the mudflats of many of the Scotch firths, a gunner on the upper waters of the Forth, some years ago, bagging 2400 of these birds alone in a couple of months.

On the marshes in the vicinity of the broads of the east of Norfolk this species is to be seen during early winter in large flocks. When gunning in that locality, I have frequently watched a mixed multitude of Peewits, Golden Plovers, and Starlings settled on the lolls near the water. If alarmed, the Plovers and Starlings wheel round with rapid flight, each in a compact and separate flock, while the Lapwings, true to their name, flap slowly with open ranks to some neighbouring part of the marsh, or mounting gradually in the air, make off in a straggling body to other quarters. During the first rime-frosts of the season I have often shortly after daybreak, seen these birds huddled together so closely on some point of land extending into the broad, that from one to a couple of hundred might have been stopped by the discharge of the punt gun. As winter advances, the numbers gradually fall off, and but few are to be seen till shortly before the breeding-season. The Redshank is usually the earliest of the Waders to appear about the marshes surrounding the broads, followed, after an interval of some days, by small parties of Peewits. By the middle or latter end of April the majority have laid; a succession of cold winds, however, frequently throws them back a week or two. Though large numbers breed on the rush-marshes, a spot is almost invariably selected where the ground is bare with the exception of the short turf. By the end of July the young may be seen in large flocks. Immense numbers collect on the hills * round the broads in autumn, and remain shifting their quarters from one part of the marshes to another during open weather. Severe frost and snow, however, usually drives them to the sea-coast or the mudflats on tidal rivers or harbours.

Five and twenty years ago the Peewit was to be found breeding in considerable numbers in Pevensey level, but latterly they have deserted the district almost entirely, constant persecution undoubtedly being the cause. In the west of Sussex, between Shoreham and Lancing, several pairs used to nest annually on the fields and marshes near the coast; these birds, during the past two seasons, have for the most part changed their quarters, and now resort to the shingle-banks just above high-water mark. The nests are merely slight hollows scratched among the fine beach-stones, with now and then a strand or two of dead grass, the only signs of vegetation in their vicinity consisting of a few tufts of rank grass, a plant or two of the sea-campion (*Silene maritima*, more generally known as the catchfly), and that pretty little red flower so common in most country lanes, *Geranium robertianum*.

Few birds exhibit greater anxiety when their breeding-haunts are approached than the Peewit. In almost every district their wailing cry will be heard long before their quarters are invaded. In many parts of Norfolk and usually in the more northern counties the Redshank and Peewit breed in company, the two species frequently uniting in their endeavours to draw the intruder from the spot where their offspring are concealed. On one occasion, while watching the movements of a newly hatched brood of downy young of this species on a small piece of marshy ground in Edenbyre, in Perthshire, I noticed the parent birds in their excitement repeatedly flying at and buffeting a pair or two of unoffending Redshanks breeding in the same locality. No other instance of Peewits conducting themselves so strangely has come under my observation.

While out on Hickling Broad early on the morning of the 10th of March 1873, my attention was attracted by the curious antics of a Peewit on one of the adjoining hills. Lying flat on his breast with his beak almost level with the ground, the bird was apparently engaged in watching out a site for a nest, turning round from time to time as if on a pivot. It is probable, however, from the manner in which he kept jerking his tail and spreading out his feathers, that it was simply the male bird showing himself off for the admiration of the female, who was quietly looking on at a short distance. For the following week I watched the same performance repeatedly by several males, and on examining the spots closely could find not the slightest signs of nests.

While on the North Sea during October, I remarked large bodies of Peewits for two or three seasons making their way straight for the shores of Norfolk or Suffolk. The birds usually fly slowly and steadily at some elevation, moving forward in three or four lines, each individual keeping its station with the utmost regularity. Flocks numbering from three to five hundred would pass out of sight with hardly a change in their formation during the time they remained in view. As Peewits on passage, however, only came under my observation in still weather or light favouring breezes, it is impossible to state whether the same order could be preserved in their ranks when exposed to a gale of strong wind.

In severe frosts during the depth of winter I have met with Peewits in Norfolk and Sussex following

* Hills must of course, be taken in the Norfolk acceptation of the term—simply a marsh.

the coast-line and pursuing a course from north to south in the former county, and from east to west in the latter. At times numbers were passed at sea in the Channel working their way towards the west. I cannot, however, advance any evidence to show that our native birds or the migrants from the north of Europe move to more southerly countries to pass the remainder of the winter. I did not meet with this species while on the return journey in the spring to its northern quarters, or receive any information from the light-ships off the east coast relating to the subject.

Though Peewits have greatly decreased in many parts of England during the past five and twenty years, there are still many extensive breeding-grounds in the Highlands, on which few, if any, eggs are collected. This unfortunate bird suffers much persecution; not only are its eggs carried off for weeks in the spring, but as soon as the large flocks make their appearance on the mudflats, the punt-gunners deal death and destruction in their ranks. At times hundreds and thousands may be seen exposed in the markets, where they fetch but a low price. For the table the Peewit cannot compare with its relative the Golden Plover, lacking at all times the delicate flavour of the latter, and in open winters when loaded with fat possessing a strong and almost disagreeable odour.

The Peewit, as a rule, lays four eggs, though towards the end of the season, after having been repeatedly robbed, I have more than once noticed a bird sitting on three and even two. On one occasion only have I met with five eggs; these were taken in April 1864, on the ground adjoining the curling-pond on Gullane Links in East Lothian, the whole proving perfectly fresh.

With the exception of "Pawype," by which title the Peewit is most commonly known by the marsh-men in the east of Norfolk, I have heard no local names applied to this species.

# TURNSTONE.

## STREPSILAS *INTERPRES*.

---

At one season or another this species is scattered over every suitable portion of our coast-line with which I am acquainted; for the most part it resorts to mudbanks and sandy flats as well as low-lying reefs of weed-grown rocks; occasionally, however, I have met with a few birds about the grassy hills round the Norfolk broads and at other inland waters.

Though Turnstones are not generally allowed to nest in the British Islands, many of these birds pass the summer along our northeast coast, being especially numerous on the shores of the Firth of Forth between Canty Bay and Dunbar; a few also may be seen at this season on the Fern Islands. In order to examine the state of their plumage, I have on two or three occasions shot a few of these late-staying birds, and invariably discovered that although in what might be styled full summer dress they were never so perfect in colour as those that pass along the coast in May when on their way to the remote breeding-grounds in the far north. Flocks of many of the various species of Waders that frequent our coasts, marshes, and mudflats may also be met with all through the summer; these, I am of opinion, are juveniles that have not yet attained the age at which they pair and nest. Judging from observations made in many parts of the country, I consider it is improbable that birds of this species breed before the third or fourth year.

The Turnstones that arrive in spring usually appear in small parties of from six or eight up to double that number; it is seldom that flocks consisting of above thirty or forty are met with at any season, though a few instances where these birds were densely packed have come under my notice. In May 1873 at least a couple of hundred, in the very finest plumage, settled on the "lumps" towards the east end of Breydon mudflats, where, driven together by the flowing tide, they offered a chance for the punt-gun that must, if taken, have resulted in the death of almost the whole body. Not needing specimens, I watched their actions for some time while crawling still closer, at the distance of only forty or fifty yards, greatly to the disgust of my punt-man, who was anxious to see the effect of a shot. The largest gathering I ever observed was at the Little Ferry near Golspie in Sutherland, where, in March 1869, at least five hundred swept round the punt and settled on one of the mussel-scaups near the main channel. The whole of these birds exhibited the dingy plumage of the immature state, with dull yellow legs and feet; being able to examine their ranks carefully, I did not need to molest them, this species being utterly useless as an article of food. Throughout June and July 1867 at least fifty or sixty of these birds remained in company on the rocks on which the beacon stands in front of Seacliff on the Firth of Forth. Since that date, when visiting this part of the coast, I usually met with small parties of ten or a dozen, though never again observing them in such numbers; here they occasionally associate with the Purple Sandpipers resorting to the same ledges of rock.

When undisturbed, this species for the most part permits a near approach till constant persecution has aroused suspicion; the young on first reaching our shores in autumn are utterly regardless of danger. Turnstones occasionally suffer severely from the buffetings of long-continued gales; several with puffed-out plumage were noticed moping round the pools of rain-water on the drive at Yarmouth during the storms in November 1872; the poor birds, which were in company with a few Purple Sandpipers, appeared to retain scarcely sufficient strength to avoid the traffic along the road.

Though Turnstones must be constantly passing over the North Sea during spring and autumn, I received information of but a single bird (a female taken on board the 'Inner Dowsing' early in July 1873) striking the light-ships during the seasons I was in correspondence with the vessels off the east coast.

The adults probably moult during August and the following month; an old male shot on the 28th of August 1879 at Shoreham still retained a sufficient quantity of bright feathers on the head and back to indicate his age and sex, while the remainder of his plumage was mottled and much resembled that of the immature birds, with which probably the dress of the adults corresponds in winter. The legs and feet were also a dirty yellow, having completely lost the bright orange, though the strength of the limbs and black claws also pointed to the age of the specimen.

# SANDERLING.

## *CALIDRIS ARENARIA.*

---

The home of the Sanderling in this country is, as its name would seem to indicate, along the sandy shores of the open sea; I can find no entry in my notes referring to the fact that this bird has been met with at any distance from salt water. I well remember, however, during the severe weather in December 1871, when Hickling Broad was entirely laid with ice, with the exception of the wakes in the channel kept open by the keepers for the Swans and Coots, that a Sanderling, in company with a couple of Dunlins, swept round the open water and finally settled on the ice. This species, according to my own observation, may be met with during every month in the year on various parts of the shores of the British Islands. So late as the 10th of June in 1869 a large flock of these birds in the finest breeding-plumage were seen on the sands of the Dornoch Firth, half a mile or so inside the bar; these or others were also observed on two occasions during the following week near the same spot. In July and August I have noticed small parties of birds in apparently an intermediate stage of plumage; these might possibly have been non-breeders or those weakened by wounds or other causes, and not possessing sufficient strength to make a lengthened journey. The last week in August or early in September is usually the date of arrival of large flocks of immature birds on the flats along the coasts of Kent and Sussex. For the first fortnight in September 1869 an immense flock of small Waders, numbering at least five or six hundred, frequented at low water the wide stretches of sand on each side of the outlet of the river flowing through Rye Harbour. Sanderlings in the juvenile plumage formed about three fourths of the gathering, the remainder being composed of immature Curlew Sandpipers and Kentish Plovers, about equally divided. If adults of any of the three species were present I failed to detect them, though the whole body were exceedingly unsuspicious of danger before the few I needed as specimens were obtained, and it is very unlikely that they could have escaped notice.

The greater part of the month of October in 1869 was exceedingly fine on the north-east coast of Scotland, and during the second week both Wildfowl and the smaller Waders were met with in swarms on the Tain Sands of the Dornoch Firth. The men working my boats having requested that some of the latter might be procured, I fired one barrel of a double 10-bore into the first three flocks (one of which proved to be composed entirely of this species, and the others of Dunlins) that flew past the punt, and on the slain being collected they amounted to exactly one hundred and twenty birds, forty-two of which were Sanderlings, and the remainder Dunlins, thirty-eight and forty falling to the next two charges, and the whole being secured, the shallow water into which they dropped offering little chance of escape for the wounded. On the 9th of October, 1882, wind south and fine, I remarked that both immature and adults in autumn plumage were passing along the Sussex coast off Shoreham, flying west in numberless flocks for several hours during the day; Terns also of various species were following the same course. In the pale grey and white dress of winter the Sanderling is abundant between

Dungeness and Rye Harbour, and, again, along the flats as far as Winchelsea; about Shoreham and Lancing and on towards Goring they are also not unfrequently met with. During stormy weather in December and the two following months they may be seen running actively just above the reach of the surf on the exposed banks at low water, their colouring corresponding with the foam blown off from the breakers and drifted along the sands by the force of the cutting blasts of wind. If any of the small Waders may be considered fit for table, the Sanderling, in my opinion, stands first on the list, as it does not possess the fish-taint that renders the Dunlin and others of the family so unpalatable.

# OYSTER-CATCHER.

## HÆMATOPUS OSTRALEGUS.

This conspicuous and attractive bird is only an occasional visitor to any of the southern or eastern counties of England with which I am acquainted; on the Fern Islands, off the coast of Northumberland, and throughout the Highlands it is a resident, breeding along the sea-shore as well as by inland waters, and remaining during the winter on the mudbanks of the saltwater firths or the rock-bound coasts in the vicinity of its summer-haunts. On the extensive mussel-banks of several of the firths in the Northern Highlands these birds collect into immense flocks, thousands at times being observed in company. The mudflats at the Little Ferry, near Golspie, in Sutherland, and the sands on each side of the harbour-mouth were most attractive feeding-grounds for this species, and here I have found them in far greater numbers than on any other part of our coast-line. When unmolested they become exceedingly confiding: having invariably refrained from causing them unnecessary alarm, I often passed within a few yards of their ranks when working up the channel through the flats towards fowl or to procure specimens of any species I required. If alarmed, their shrill cries at once arouse every flock within hearing, and all chance of success is lost. Being of little use for culinary purposes, I never attempted to discharge the big gun at them, though, if so inclined, I might easily have bagged from one hundred and fifty to two hundred at a shot.

The Oyster-Catcher chooses a variety of situations for breeding-purposes, making but slight preparations for the accommodation of its expected brood. At the Fern Islands it lays its eggs in a mere scratch in the shingle or sand at a short distance above high-water mark. Along the course of several of the Scotch rivers, such as the Spey or the Tay, it forms its humble cradle among the rough stones by the water-side, and is not unfrequently deprived of its eggs or newly hatched brood by the floods that are caused by storms among the hills. In many parts of the Highlands they rear their young in a potato or oat-field, the female sitting plainly in view until the crops get up sufficiently to afford concealment. While travelling by the Highland railway from Dunkeld towards Aberfeldy or Blair Athol, I often watched several birds sitting on their eggs in the fields near the line. The last time I passed through this glen in spring Oyster-Catchers were by no means so numerous as in former days, though a few were noticed near the station at Ballinluig. I have also seen the eggs lying openly on the summit of some of the large detached blocks of rock that are found along the shore off the west coasts of Ross and Sutherland.

In Sussex and Kent I have heard this species spoken of by the local gunners as the Sea-Pie or the Olive; in my opinion the Scotch name of Mussel-Pecker is far more appropriate than that of Oyster-Catcher. The hard and powerful beak of this singular bird enables it to detach a limpet from the rock as well as to crush a mussel with ease. The broken shells scattered about where a meal has been made bear evidence to the strength of its beak; the succulent morsel inclosed in the impenetrable shell of the oyster must, however, be entirely beyond its reach.

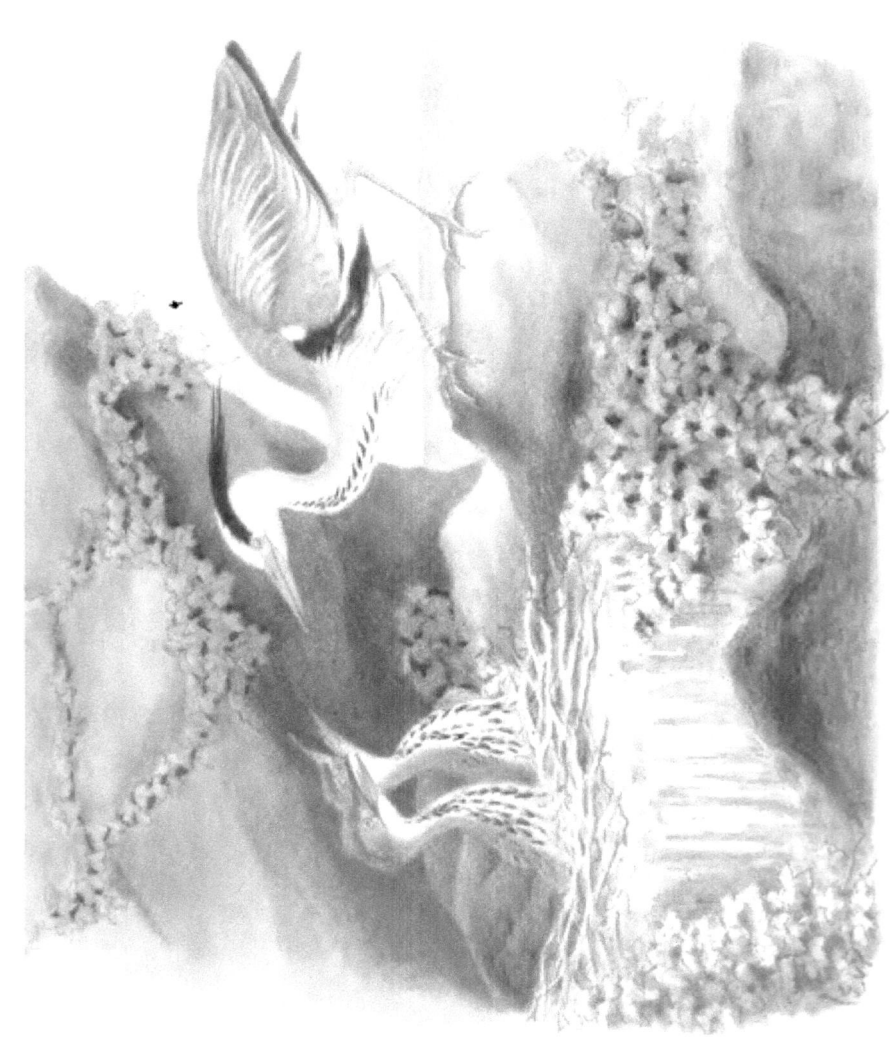

# HERON.

## ARDEA CINEREA.

FORMERLY the head of the game list, the Heron, since the decline of Hawking, has fallen from its proud estate, and at the present day is but little esteemed by any, save plumassiers. Anglers, as well as keepers in charge of lakes and rivers that abound with fish, are but little impressed by the beauty of these handsome birds, and not unfrequently view with intense disgust their arrival to prey on the scaly denizens of their well-stocked waters. Occasionally these birds are shot down as vermin in consequence of their depredations, and, considering the result of observations taken in many parts of the country, I am by no means surprised at the reception they meet with.

From north to south the Heron is distributed in larger or smaller numbers over most of the English and Scotch counties I have visited—more abundant in well-preserved districts where their ancient haunts are carefully looked after, though breeding also in parties of from a score or two down to even single pairs in several of the forests in the Northern Highlands. During the years I was collecting in Ross-shire I also met with ——— ——— ——— rearing their young in the dwarfed and weather-beaten pines or stunted bushes ——— ——— ——— ——— ——— ——— ——— ——— of this species in the rocks overlooking the open sea to the north of the entrance to the ——— ——— ——— portion of the range of cliffs known as the Cairn Hnui their nests, at the ——— ——— ——— ——— spot in May 1869, were placed thickly in the vigorous plants of ivy that here creep up the ——— ——— ——— on some of the bare ledges of rock. A colony of Jackdaws had also established themselves ——— ivy, and many of their domiciles were in close proximity and in some instances joined to those of the Herons, the occupants appearing to agree in a marvellous manner, considering the bad character usually attributed to the Daws. I spent many hours in watching the animated scene to be viewed from the summit, and on one occasion, while carefully examining with the glasses the birds flying round, I detected a fine old male making straight for the ledges on which the nests were placed, and requiring a good specimen at the time I fired in hopes of securing him. Though evidently hard hit he turned and flew out to sea; after flapping with difficulty a couple of hundred yards or so, he circled round and again made for the cliffs, finally doubling up and pitching headlong among the large blocks of stone on the shore at the foot of the rocks. A shepherd who had watched the effect of the shot at once volunteered to fetch the bird, and after proceeding a short distance along the edge descended by a track that I should have imagined utterly impracticable for any human being without the aid of a rope. An hour or so later he returned, having failed to discover the object of his search, which we came to the conclusion must have fallen on to the water and been swept away by the tide before he reached the spot. Later in the day, however, when we had reached the shore by a longer, though far safer, path down the cliffs near Shandwick, and were obtaining a few specimens of Rock-Doves from the caves, we detected our lost prize stretched out on the top of a high crag; not a leg or wing extended beyond the edge of the rock, and it was only a gust of wind ruffling the long drooping feathers on the neck that revealed its position. The assistance of the shepherd, who had accompanied us to point out the best caves for the Doves, was again necessary, or the bird would probably have remained where he had fallen. After some little difficulty the Highlander succeeded, with the aid of what assistance we were able to render, in scaling the face of the crag and dislodging the bird, which turned out to be a magnificent specimen. The shepherd proved himself even more sure-footed than the mountain goats* that still frequent the ledges near the summit of this range of cliffs. After watching a small party of about half a dozen that were gazing down from a grassy slope at the intruders on their domain we proceeded further south towards some caves near the Suitors †, and discovered three magnificent white-fleeced animals with grand heads lying dead at the foot of the cliffs. As often befalls the Highland sheep, these poor beasties had in all probability made their way while in search of food to some small patch of bright green grass from which it was impossible to return, and had at last, in a vain attempt to escape, perished from the effect of the fall. So early as the 9th of June in 1860, while examining the nests of the Herons in view from the top of the rocks, I was unable to detect a single young bird, all having evidently taken their departure from this portion of the rocks. There were, however, in all probability a few late stayers on other parts of the range, as many old birds were still flying round their quarters. In the Western Highlands I repeatedly observed the juveniles still in their cradles a month and even six weeks later than this date.

During the summer of 1877, while making observations on birds and fishing in the west of Sutherland, I explored the islands on Loch Beannoch, an inland piece of water about seven miles from Loch Inver, and on two of the larger found many pairs of Herons breeding in stunted and weather-beaten trees, most of which (if I remember right) were birches, destroyed in many instances by the weight of the nests and the droppings of the birds. On inspecting the inmates of the nests on the 8th of June, I ascertained that the majority were ready to fly, though several clutches were still in the down; these were probably the offspring of birds robbed of their eggs early in the season. Ten days later (the 18th) I was again on the loch, and made sketches of some of the young which the gillies brought down from their nests, and after they had sat for their portraits they were restored to the parental care. The newly hatched were most hideous little objects; the body nearly naked, the wrinkled flesh a livid greenish neutral tint; legs and toes greenish grey, back of legs and soles of feet yellow. The soft parts of a pair of juveniles just ready to leave the nest and secured as specimens were as follows:—Eye pale bright yellow; upper mandible dark horn and scurfy, lower mandible yellow. Legs dark horn, with large scales, exhibiting a thin covering that resembled a white powder. The call-note of the juveniles while piteously crying for food after the old birds had been driven from their quarters on the islands and prevented from attending to their wants by our presence on the loch was one of the most monotonous and discordant sounds I have ever listened to, particularly irritating when dinned into one's ears in the stillness pervading this lonely and desolate loch; it appeared to resemble the clamour that might be produced by beating the inside of a tin can or pail with an iron rod or a hard-wood stick. That Loch Beannoch is not to be despised by the trout-fisher, may be judged from the following abridged extracts taken from my notes made in the west of Sutherland during the summer of 1877 :—"June 8. At Loch Beannoch, wind west, morning fine, several squalls of drifting rain during afternoon. Trout rising well; 6 dozen and 2 taken in a few hours."—"June 11. At Loch Beannoch, wind west, showery all day. Took 13 dozen trout, the majority of the usual size, five or six to the pound, one, however, turned the scales at 3 lbs. According to the record kept by the gillies and keepers this was the heaviest trout ever taken on the loch, the largest up to that time having only weighed 1¼ lb."—"June 18th. At Loch Beannoch, wind variable, blowing lightly at times from all quarters. Far too bright during the day for fish to rise, though they took well towards 8 o'clock in

*
†

the evening. Taking a few casts occasionally and landing now and then on the islands to rest and make notes on the manners and customs of the young Herons, we had by 7.30 P.M. only 6 dozen small trout. After a short pause for refreshments a sudden change took place, and during the last hour and a half that we remained on the water 10 dozen were taken by two rods from the same boat. The 16 dozen obtained during the day weighed exactly 30 lbs." I mention these facts and draw attention to the small size of the trout in a loch so favourable for the production of this species in order to suggest that it was simply owing to the tax that the unfortunate fish are compelled to pay to the rapacious Herons. Doubtless these birds are ever on the alert, and in early morning soon after daylight as well as towards dusk, when the fishermen and their gillies are absent, they alight in full force in the shallows and on the limbs of the dead trees overhanging the water, and deal death and destruction on all the finny tribe within reach of their powerful bills. The Black-throated Divers also that frequent the loch in summer, paying little or no regard to any strangers in the boat, are doubtless also detrimental to the interests of the angler; and if the quantity of fish they consumed was only known to those who look after the water, it would certainly prove astonishing.

In 1868, when inspecting the feathered residents on Fing Island, situated near the centre of Loch Shin, in Sutherland, I found Herons breeding in small bushes and low trees of not more than ten or twelve feet in height, the spots selected being almost precisely similar to those on Loch Benevesh. In a remote inland district in the same county, where juniper, heather, and rough grass alone appeared to flourish, a small colony of these birds took up their quarters some years back and put up with such accommodation as the country afforded, constructing their nests with dried stalks of dead ling on the open hill-side.

I often remarked that this species is somewhat nocturnal in its habits; while afloat on the Norfolk broads after dark, I repeatedly noticed these birds flying round and finally dropping into the plantations adjoining the water so late as 10 or 11 P.M. At every season of the year, while in pursuit of fowl or specimens, I have detected their harsh cries when disturbed on the marshes or mudbanks at all hours of the night.

On the 30th of May, 1883, while fishing on Hickling Broad in the east of Norfolk, I happened to be watching a Heron which had attracted my attention as it rose from the side of a dyke and made its way inland towards the marshes. Having flown about a hundred yards, the bird slackened speed and became unsteady, then after circling round for a few seconds it appeared to lose all power and fell straight down into the rush-marsh behind the bank that encircles the broad. In all probability the unfortunate bird had been choked or strangled by some prey recently seized—possibly an eel or a fish so strong or bulky that it was utterly beyond its ability to swallow. Cases where the Heron has suffered in this manner have been recorded by various writers in shooting-publications as well as in several works on natural history.

During my visits to the flat country in the east of Norfolk, I was often much puzzled to account for the presence of eels on the marsh-wall* round Hickling Broad. This bank was a favourite resting-place for the Herons, and here numbers were occasionally seen as we made our way on foot towards the broad, the birds flying off to distant parts of the marshes as we came in view. It was seldom while passing over the portion of the bank from which they rose that several eels were not detected lying on the path or the adjoining patches of grass; these fish were invariably small, usually about a quarter of a pound in weight, and all exhibiting wounds. The scars consisted, in most instances, of a couple of stabs in close proximity going clean through the fish; now and then there were additional perforations, all evidently inflicted by some sharp-pointed instrument. The beak of a Heron might easily have caused such wounds, and the marshmen who accompanied me were strongly impressed with the idea that the eels after being captured and swallowed by the birds had eventually succeeded, in some extraordinary manner, in effecting their escape. My opinion was that the Herons had previously been feeding along the edges of the dykes, and having fared far too sumptuously would naturally need repose, which

---

* A bank thrown up to keep back the water of the broads from flowing over the surrounding country is in this district always termed a "marsh-wall."

they sought on the commanding position offered by the bank. When alarmed by our approach they would naturally throw up some of their prey in order to lighten themselves before taking wing. Such tactics are often employed by the larger Gulls; and being well aware of the fact when making notes on these birds, I now and then fired a bullet or two into the flocks resting on the rocks on the shores of the Firth of Forth in order to cause confusion in their ranks as they made off, and in hopes of ascertaining whether they had been feeding inland or at sea along the coast *.

* This fact is referred to under the heading of the Herring-Gull, page 1.

# BITTERN.

## BOTAURUS STELLARIS.

I have but little information, gathered from personal observations, to give concerning the Bittern, only a single bird having been met with at close quarters, and a few seen and heard while passing over the Norfolk Broads. From the Hickling keeper, now over 70 years of age, I learned that in his remembrance this species nested regularly in the marshes and on the hills round Hickling and several of the other Broads. He remarked that the last brood reared in the locality succeeded in taking their departure without having been molested. This, I believe, is a fact, as one of his sons recollected the occurrence, and it was not many years ago, though they could not remember the exact date.

In the fourth edition of Yarrell it is stated that "the latest recorded instance is of a nest found on a small Broad at Upton, on the 3rd of March, 1868, containing two eggs, now in the possession of Mr. H. M. Upcher, of Feltwell; and on the 25th of that month a young bird was caught alive in the same locality."

The following extract from my notes refers to the specimen depicted in the Plate, and gives nearly all I know concerning this species:—

"December 5th, 1871. A cold breeze from the north-east. Hickling Broad entirely laid * with ice, but we succeeded in making our way across to see the keeper. On our return, as we were passing Pleasure Hills, I caught sight of a Bittern flying over Swimcoats towards the east; the bird continued till over Whitesica, when it circled round twice and then alighted on Rush Hill hover †. We were a long time making our way to the spot, as the ice was very strong to break through; on reaching the dyke through the hill the bird was sighted on the ice in the thick cover of sedge and rushes. It did not rise till the boat was within a yard, when it flapped slowly off and offered an easy shot. Our prize proved to be a very handsome old female in perfect plumage."

Another extract refers to a glimpse caught of three Bitterns on wing:—

"June 13th, 1873. Wind from all points during the day, blowing from the east and south and finally west. Three Bitterns having been seen and heard by several marshmen and keepers who had sent to inform me, I was on Hickling Broad in the evening, and taking up a position in the bush where they had been observed that morning, a couple of hours were passed in awaiting their appearance. I was on the point of returning, as darkness was setting in, at about half-past nine, when we heard them calling, and the three birds, flying together, passed at a distance of about eighty or ninety yards, just out of range; they were holding a course straight for Heigham Sounds.

"14th. Wind again from all quarters, and a heavy thunderstorm in the early morning. I was on the Broad an hour before daybreak on the look-out for the Bitterns. The Cuckoo and the Nightjar were calling loudly in the plantations, and the Warblers and frogs were having such a concert in the reed-bushes that it was almost impossible to hear anything else. After waiting till the sun was well up, and having seen nothing of the Bitterns, we searched all the likely spots on Hickling Broad and Heigham Sounds, but without success. Towards evening I was again on the water, and shortly before dusk observed (as on the previous night) half a dozen Herons fly singly into one of the plantations where they were in the habit of roosting. Nothing was heard with the exception of the notes of the Nightjars, Warblers, Redshanks, Peewits, Snipes, and frogs\*, and the occasional slushing of a large pike on the look-out for his supper. Snipe were drumming till long after dark; I never remarked them so late before, though, likely enough, they may have been often heard. Just as I was leaving the water, a man who had been eel-picking † at a short distance from where I was brought up informed me that about half an hour before he had seen a bird, which he believed to be a "Bottle" ‡, alight in a slade close at hand. It was now quite dark; but as the sky was clear towards the north-east and reflected a light on the Broad, I thought the bird might possibly be dropped if it flew over the water. Unfortunately before I could get near enough for a shot, the unknown was put up by the Peewits coming dashing down, calling loudly. From the glimpse I obtained of the bird, it was impossible to state whether it was a Bittern or a Heron. Herons, as a rule, retire to rest about dusk; but I have occasionally disturbed one which has apparently been taking a late supper in some quiet pool in the middle of the night.

\* The natives she ore call these noisy croaking reptiles toads.
† Capturing eels with a dart driven deep into the mud.
‡ "Bottle" is the name by which the Norfolk marshmen speak of this bird.

# WHITE STORK.
## *CICONIA ALBA.*

The White Stork is a scarce and accidental visitor to the British Islands; its striking appearance invariably attracting attention, the unfortunate wanderer seldom escapes the fate of all rare or conspicuous strangers that approach our shores.

The information derived from personal observation that I am enabled to give concerning this species is exceedingly slight, as on two occasions only have I met with opportunities of watching these interesting birds in a wild state within the limits of this country. While gunning in the east of Norfolk, in June 1873, I fell in with a Stork in the Potter-Heigham marshes round Hickling Broad, and not having obtained one previously, this individual was secured as a specimen. Though others were heard of, none came under my notice again till, early one morning in May 1883, we saw a pair, in very glossy plumage, on some marshy ground within a mile or two of the spot where I had shot one ten years previously. Having no wish to obtain more specimens, I withdrew the punt a short distance in order to watch their actions; and both birds appearing more in need of rest than food, I gained but little information after patiently waiting for over an hour. I was unable to learn whether the strangers had been noticed in the district; and it is probable that the large extent of marsh near which they were found had drawn their attention while flying over at some considerable height. Intending, if possible, to renew my acquaintance again, I visited the spot later in the day, when it was discovered that both birds had taken their departure and no further tidings concerning their movements could be learned: on landing and examining the soft mud on which they had settled I ascertained that they had been busily engaged in searching for food before quitting the spot, having evidently stalked over a large extent of ground. The keepers informed me that a pair made their appearance in this locality in the summer of 1882; after remaining some hours on the marsh they rose on wing to a considerable height, flying in large circles, and then headed straight for the coast.

Two other unrecorded instances of the presence of White Storks on the southern and eastern coasts may also be mentioned. On the 24th of May, 1871, a single bird pitched on Breydon mudflats, soon after sunrise, within about eighty yards of one of my puntmen who was stationed near the "humps." I happened to be some distance further west at the time, and though the man did his best to attract our attention, the glare of the rising sun and its reflection on the wet mud rendered his signals unintelligible. After remaining about half an hour on the flats and feeding up to within fifty or sixty yards of his punt, the bird was alarmed by a shot, and at once made off, flying due east; as far as I was able to ascertain, this Stork was not noticed again in the same district. Early in the spring of 1875 I received word from a "looker" *

---

* A person who engages to look after the cattle on the marshes is termed a "looker" in this part of Sussex. Having much time at his disposal, he usually turns his attention to egging in the spring and shooting in the winter, and many of these men become well acquainted with the habits of the birds frequenting their own particular district.

## WHITE STORK.

in Pevensey Level that a strange white bird, with black wings and red beak and legs, had taken up its quarters near the coast, having repeatedly been seen in the neighbourhood of the "polls"*. Having little doubt that the unknown must be a White Stork, and not being in need of a specimen, I despatched a servant who was acquainted with the species to gain information before starting myself. While on his way across the marshes, the man clearly identified the bird winging its way towards the Channel, and turned back at once to report the result of his journey. I made no attempt to secure this specimen, and, to the best of my knowledge, it was not seen again on that part of the coast.

The specimen in my collection had been, I believe, noticed for some days in Suffolk before he made his appearance in Norfolk. I first received word of his arrival from a carrier, who, while on the road from Yarmouth to Hickling, observed the bird fly in from the sea and pitch in the marshes near the coast; here he was speedily discovered by some Rooks and Peewits and, after continued buffetings, driven further inland. On searching the ground on the following day I met with no success, and it was not till a few days later I learned he had been seen in the neighbourhood of Hickling. On reaching the broad and examining the shores with the glasses, I could find no signs of the bird, and the hill to which I considered it most likely he would make his way was tenanted by some hundreds of Rooks quietly resting on the bushes or feeding on the marsh. These birds seldom allow a conspicuous stranger to alight in their immediate vicinity without at once making a noisy attack; and while watching in order to ascertain if any of their number exhibited signs of excitement, I remarked a Heron that was flying across the hill wheel round and attempt to settle in a thick bed of sedge. Before he had time to alight, the Stork rose on wing, and making a most savage attack on the Heron, forced him with loud screams to alter his course. After driving off the intruder, the Stork took up his position on the banks of a dyke; then drawing up within range of the punt-gun, we stopped the boat and waited quietly to watch his movements. At last he flapped some twenty yards out to a shallow pool of water on "Rush Hills," where he remained for an hour at least, stalking and peeking on the mud; as the direction in which he moved was taking him out of range of the shoulder-gun, and the punt-gun was useless on account of the narrow dyke up which we had worked, I was forced to make sure of him, and he fell, shot through the neck, to a charge of No. 3. On examination the bird proved to be a male in full plumage; although he had been (as I afterwards learned) for a couple of days in a country abounding with frogs and other suitable food, there was nothing except a few large spiders in his stomach.

The Hickling keeper, John Nudd, who had shot one about thirty years previously on "Breydons marshes," near Horsey Mere, informed me that it had been feeding voraciously on young pike of five or six inches in length, captured on some flooded ground. He stated that when he shook the bird to dry its plumage a score at least of these small fish dropped from its beak.

* The pools of brackish water put inside the sea-beach are usually known among the natives living along the east coast of Sussex by this name.

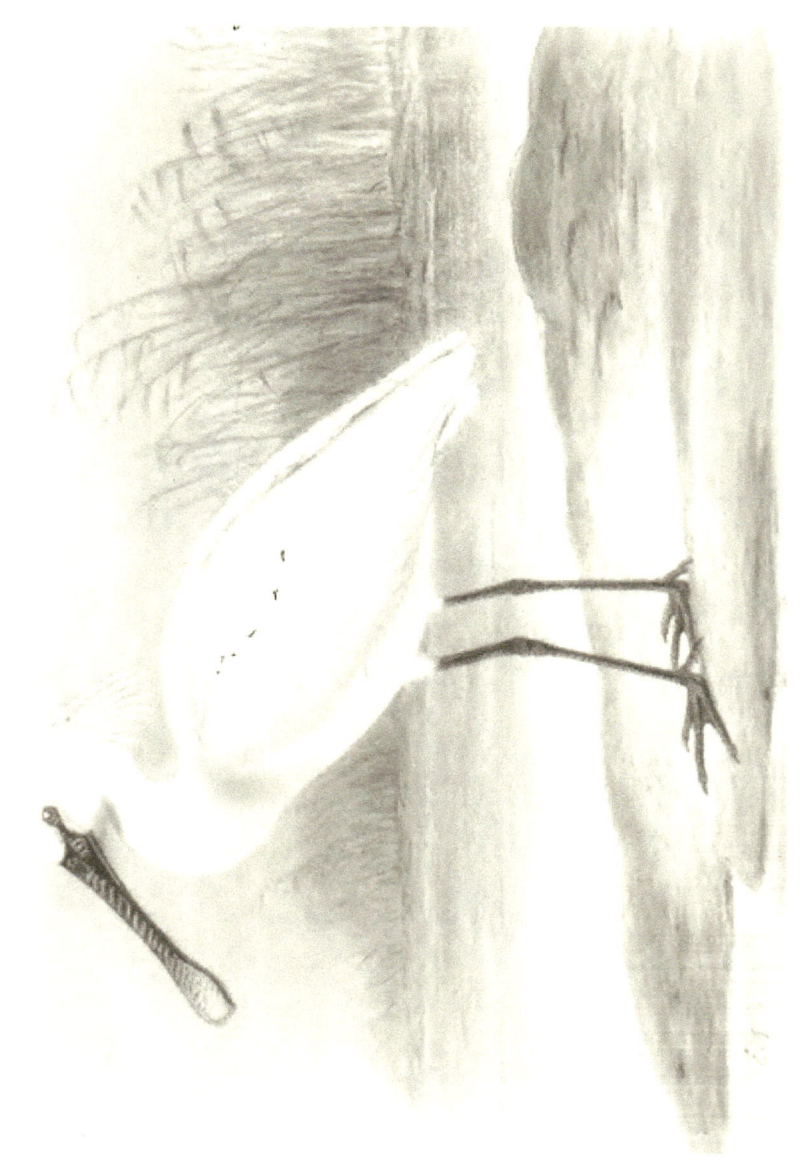

# SPOONBILL.

## PLATALEA LEUCORODIA.

Many old gunners can remember the time when flocks of these birds were far from uncommon during spring on the marshes and mud-banks round our coasts; in decreasing numbers they still, however, make their appearance nearly every season about the middle of May along the flat country between the mouths of the Humber and the Thames. Their visits to the southern counties are less frequent, though I have seen both adults and immature procured in Sussex; during the past ten years several young birds, minus the crest and the black and white markings on the bills, were shot in the months of September and October in the neighbourhood of Shoreham Harbour and Pevensey Level. The marshes in the vicinity of the south coast appear more in the line of the autumnal migration of this species than the flat shores of the eastern counties.

A Spoonbill, when settled upon a mud-bank where food is plentiful, may generally be approached within gunshot. On the 20th of May, 1871, shortly after daybreak, I watched one feeding on the muds on Breydon for two or three hours; though the sun was shining, a thick fog at the time hung over the flats, rendering objects at any distance indistinct and hazy. The punt being concealed in one of the drains\*, the bird had not the slightest suspicion of danger and continued searching the grass and weeds in the shallow pools for food. At times I remarked the bill was worked sideways, and its actions strongly resembled those of a Duck stirring up the mud round the edge of a puddle. I could gain no further insight into its manner of feeding, as it did not approach within fifty yards, and the mist prevented the movements of the head and bill being clearly discerned. As the tide rose the bird made its way to the edge of the main channel, and the fog gradually clearing off, the sun broke through, when two or three noisy Gulls were attracted by the appearance of the stranger. There was little chance that any further observations could now be made, so I secured the specimen, which proved to be a female in fair plumage, by a charge from the punt-gun.

On several occasions I noticed the Black-headed Gulls greatly excited by the sight of a Spoonbill, numbers flying screaming round and seldom allowing the unfortunate bird a moment's peace. A male I shot near Yarmouth, in May 1873, had frequented the north and south marshes within a few miles of the town for ten days or a fortnight; and evidently entertaining a strong desire to reach the attractive muds † of Breydon, the bird at every opportunity attempted to alight on the flats. So persistently however, was the persecution carried out by these noisy birds, that to settle for any length of time was utterly impossible; in a few minutes after his appearance the watchful Gulls collected, and the wanderer was compelled to quit the spot and seek the solitude of the marshes. It was only by waiting near his accustomed feeding-ground at daybreak, before the Gulls had arrived on the scene, that I was enabled to obtain a shot. The proceedings of several of the Laridæ were decidedly eccentric; about half a dozen Black-headed as well as two or three Common Gulls appeared to be fascinated in some strange manner by the sight of the conspicuous visitor to their haunts. If after sweeping around, screaming loudly, their outcry failed to put the object of their solicitude on wing, they would pitch down on the mud a few yards distant and remain for a time intently gazing, evidently either amazed or awe-struck by the large white bird. A Rook or two would occasionally join in the general commotion, though the Black-headed Gulls were by far the most vociferous among the disturbers of the peace. Spoonbills being at that date frequently seen on Breydon mudflats, the behaviour of these noisy and meddlesome Gulls was somewhat unaccountable. As they also "mob"* the Ospreys which appear over the flats at the same time of year, their conduct is, however, not so remarkable, any large and conspicuous stranger in all probability attracting attention and raising their anger when intruding on their accustomed haunts.

The male Spoonbill figured on the Plate was shot on Breydon mudflats on the 14th of May, 1873; and a few words taken from my notes with reference to this handsome stranger may not be out of place. I was informed that the bird had first made his appearance on the flats near the main channel soon after midday on the 12th, and several gunners had immediately started after him, but without success. I had left the harbour early in the afternoon in a steamboat, to make observations on the flocks of Waders passing along the coast outside the sands, and we had failed to notice the signals of one or two men with whom we were acquainted, who had attempted to draw our attention while passing out to sea between the piers. On the 13th (wind north-east, cold and strong) we were up the water by 3 A.M.; the bird, which had already left the flats for the marshes, had been seen by one of my puntmen, but there was not sufficient light for him to discern where it had settled; although we remained on the watch till dusk, no signs of our visitor could be detected. Just before daybreak on the 14th, the weather at the time being rough with frequent squalls of cold wind and rain from the north-east, we arrived at "Bessies drain" just before daybreak, and as soon as the light was sufficiently strong we detected the Spoonbill flying over in a line from the south marshes. He first attempted to alight on the upper part of the flats; but the Gulls gave him no peace, both large and small combining to drive off the stranger into the north marshes. After a short interval, however, he returned and pitched with some Herons near the centre of the flats. He was now within fifty yards of where I had shot a Spoonbill two years before, and there was every chance of making a successful shot; but before we were within range he was disturbed by a small Gull which kept swooping down and hovering over with loud cries. He next pitched near the centre of the lower flats; although well mobbed by the Gulls, he utterly disregarded their noisy attacks, and we were enabled to work up to within about eighty yards before he rose and was knocked down as dead as a stone by a flying shot from the punt-gun. This bird proved to be a fine male, weighing 4 lbs. 1 oz., with a good crest, but not quite so darkly marked with orange as some specimens I have examined; the tawny colour, however, fades soon after death, and a stuffed bird gives but a faint idea of the richness of the tints exhibited during life. The larger Gulls appeared to fly at this bird more from curiosity than anger, as after hovering over him for a while they usually settled down and commenced feeding close at hand; the smaller Gulls, Common and Black-headed, were by far the most active of his persecutors. We afterwards ascertained that the bird had first been seen on the 10th, when a punt-gunner, who kept the information to himself, had attempted three times to approach within range; but the numbers of Gulls collected about the muds would not allow the bird to rest sufficiently long, and at length drove him right off the flats.

* An old woman, a drunken man, or a bird causing a disturbance, and doing what is esteemed to answer for bad language, is always referred

# CURLEW.

## NUMENIUS ARQUATA.

---

There are few Waders or shore-birds so well known all round our coasts as the Curlew; from north to south and from east to west it is numerous—a resident during summer on many inland moors and hill-sides, and a visitor, either constant or occasional, to almost every mudflat or harbour of any extent.

Though there are, as we learn from the pages of the various writers on British birds, several breeding-stations of this species in both the southern, midland, and northern counties of England, it is only in the Highlands that I have, up to the present, met with a chance of closely observing their habits during the summer months. In almost every glen I have explored to the north of the Tay the Curlew may be found nesting in larger or smaller numbers. In certain localities, such as the sloping hill-sides between the Tay and Loch Rannoch, and again in the flat country to the north of Loch Shin in Sutherland, as well as in other districts too numerous to mention, these birds frequent the open moorlands. They are, however, but little less plentiful in many parts of the valley of the Spey, where the ground is either well timbered or still littered and strewn by the jagged and broken stems of the rapidly decaying pines uprooted by the terrible gales that some years back swept over this part of the Highlands [*]. Many of the spots in Strath Spey, where these birds resort during summer, are simply clearings of a few acres in the forests; and it is no uncommon occurrence to observe one or both of the pair when startled from the vicinity of their nest, after flying screaming round for several minutes, settle at last on the bare and weather-beaten limbs of some old and rotten stump, or even at times on the waving boughs of a young and vigorous sapling.

When its quarters are seldom invaded and the flocks have been for a time allowed to rest in peace, the Curlew is by no means the wary and restless bird that so often, on the mudflats of the southern and eastern coasts, gives warning of the approaching gunner to all the surrounding fowl. Some years ago I moved a punt to a muddy salt-water estuary in the north where the shooting had been strictly preserved for years. I had not the slightest wish for useless slaughter, and while sculling quietly among the unsuspecting Waders and Wildfowl, was enabled in three or four days to gain a greater insight into their habits and actions than could possibly have been acquired by any amount of indiscriminate shooting. The Curlews were perfectly unsuspicious of danger, and but one or two would occasionally halt and quietly regard the punt for a few moments as, dropping silently past on the tide or grounded on the flats, I closely scanned their ranks with the glasses.

These birds are apparently far less sociable than many of the Wader family. Though Duck, Wigeon, and Gulls were not unfrequently carried by the tide, or even occasionally settled down in close proximity to the

---

[*] The sudden fury of one of the hurricanes that brought about this destruction may be judged from the account I received from an old native of the district. My informant stated that he passed through the wood at the commencement of the storm, and within twenty minutes after reaching the shelter of his cottage, which was then situated at the edge of the forest, there was scarcely a tree standing on the last half-mile across which he had just succeeded in making his way.

main body, the "Whaups" (as my Highland puntsman termed them), in some instances at least, drew off as the strangers advanced. Godwits, Plovers, Knots, and even the diminutive Dunlins, when driven from their quarters by the bare-legged lads and lassies who now and then invaded the flats in quest of shell-fish, would at times alight on the same bank, and rapidly spreading out, join in company with their larger relatives. The slightest alarm, however, would at once dissolve the partnership. The Godwits and Plovers, together with their small followers, would invariably (though in separate flocks) make for some well-known feeding-ground, while the Curlews, when all was again quiet, would be seen drawn up by themselves on a distant mudbank or mussel-scaup.

While brought up for a few minutes late one evening, intently examining an immense flock collected by the flood-tide on a rapidly contracting space (mentally computing whether a bag of eighty or one hundred would be nearest the mark if the trigger were pulled), an unaccountable fluttering of wings suddenly caught my ear; and on looking up, a Cormorant was seen hovering with extended pinions and drooping feet within a yard of our heads, evidently about to settle on some part of the punt. On perceiving his mistake he sheered off in desperate haste, though without in the slightest degree arousing the suspicions of the usually watchful Curlew.

The regularity with which this species will make its way to the mudbanks on salt-water estuaries or along the open coast-line as soon as the tide has fallen sufficiently to expose its food, is well known to all who have watched the habits of these wary birds. Though the spots to which they retire are often situated some distance inland, it is seldom that their accustomed quarters can be explored for any length of time before the flock are seen approaching. The banks near Goring, in the west of Sussex, are generally resorted to at low water by from fifty to one hundred Curlews. It is a strange fact that instead of making their way inland, these birds invariably betake themselves as the tide flows to the shingle-banks near Shoreham Harbour. Their usual station is on the ridge of the bank just above high-water mark. At times they will spread over the wide expanse of shingle-flats, but a few are always left to guard against a surprise by way of the sea. During the night some of their number at times appear on the mudflats in Shoreham Harbour; but their daily routine all the year round consists of half their time on the flats at Goring and the remainder on the shingle-banks. If disturbed, they make their way out to sea, and occasionally fly some distance along the coast, though in less than half an hour they are again seeking to alight on some portion of their accustomed haunts. All through the summer months I have for many years watched these birds in the same locality; there is occasionally in winter a slight increase in their numbers.

Curlews while on flight are commonly mistaken for Geese or Ducks by those unacquainted with their habits. At times they proceed in a long string in single file, and occasionally for a short distance in the V form similar to wild Geese; while not unfrequently they may be seen passing along the line one without the slightest attempt at order, every bird in the ranks from time to time shifting its position. It is seldom that a flock is in view for many minutes without some changes in the formation being noticed. Though not usually seen flying in company with other species, occasionally it happens that at a short distance Grey Plovers, or other small Waders may be discerned on the lines during their passage to some feeding-ground in one line. Every wild-fowl shooter must have constantly observed the small size of some of the passing flock, though a powerful glass and a clear sky are necessary to demonstrate the identity of the stragglers with any degree of certainty.

This species is by no means so frequent a visitor as might be expected to the inland counties in the eastern counties. But I am disposed to say others have come under my notice in this district though at times when but little of their usual pastures to be seen. But more frequently I watch flying over. I repeatedly remarked that their observations while during autumn and early winter were here few, and speaking of why their low Curlews are making their appearance, and compared to the mudflats or coasts by birds on the coast of Norfolk.

These birds are exceedingly jealous of any strangers, featured or otherwise, appearing near their quarters

While passing over the moors on a low-lying portion of Strath Glass during the last week in May 1878, the loud and angry cries of a Curlew were heard, and the next moment the bird came in view, following and buffeting with the utmost fury a large female Kestrel, which happened in the most inoffensive manner to be crossing the flats on which the nest of the Wader was situated. The Hawk appeared but little disconcerted by the attack, and kept steadily on its way across a loch from which scores of Black-headed Gulls turned out and joined in the clamour.

If their proceedings are carefully watched it will be seen that these birds extract immense quantities of marine worms and other insects from the mudflats. Though they may at times obtain a small amount of sustenance, such as soft crabs and other crustacea, off the sandbanks and rocks, it is, I believe, principally by boring in the ooze of the mudflats that their food is obtained. In the south of Scotland (East Lothian) I have repeatedly noticed large flocks frequenting the grass-parks as well as the arable lands during the autumn. At this time they are more fit for table than at any other season.

Curlews, during severe frosts, are occasionally to be seen exposed for sale in numbers in the markets, and are not unfrequently hawked about the streets as Sea-Woodcocks. Under some circumstances they may possibly afford a passable dish, though I am decidedly of opinion that any person purchasing one with the expectation that it will compare with a Golden Plover or a Woodcock will meet with disappointment. For my own part, not considering these Waders worth a charge of powder and shot when required for the table, I have but seldom of late years molested them\*, especially as it is the best policy to remain at peace with the large flocks that occasionally fall in the way of the punt-gunner. After a few shots they are usually unapproachable, and the noise they make when alarmed is as well understood by all wildfowl as the warning cry of the Oyster-catcher or Redshank. Though exceedingly tempting chances were repeatedly passed over, I have occasionally, when anxious to blow a charge from the antiquated muzzle-loaders on the coasts of the Scotch friths or on the Norfolk flats, stopped as many as a dozen or a score with the discharge of the old gun. But one fair shot at these birds is recorded in my notes. On this occasion forty-two Curlews and six Wigeon were gathered to the boats. As is almost invariably the case, a mishap (in this instance the accidental grounding of the punt on a detached and partially submerged piece of mud) occurred and considerably interfered with the results.

The plumage of the Curlew during the breeding-season has been, in the case of the few individuals I have closely examined, far richer in tint than in the winter months. The markings on the breast are also more clearly defined and extended, the feathers on the underparts being but slightly streaked and almost white in winter. I particularly noticed that in the only pair I ever procured as specimens during the summer the beaks were decidedly smaller than in those killed in winter. I am also of opinion that these Waders attain a greater weight throughout the latter part of autumn and winter than during the summer. The young, I have repeatedly remarked, when shot on the south coast shortly after their first arrival from the north, appear both larger and heavier than the adults obtained at their breeding-haunts.

The black and brown markings on the down of the nestlings are not unlike those on young wild Ducks; the colours, however, are more intermixed, the black patches being of smaller extent. The beak for some weeks is short, and resembles in shape that of the Golden Plover, though slightly longer and thicker. The young birds run as soon as hatched, and are almost as large as the adults before they can get on wing. In parts of the ............... the moors, the juveniles may be watched stalking about in the heather ............... and by no means alarmed by a passing conveyance. If approached, ............... and clumsy attempt at escape, squat down in some thick cover, and on ............... up, ...... a low and plaintive whistle, which frequently summons the old bird from some

---

\* I am not aware whether my own experience in such matters is singular; it is, however, a fact, that after shooting any quantities of wild-fowl or Plover, I have for a time entertained the greatest aversion to even the smell of their cooking.

commanding bine: wheeling round the spot and screaming loudly it alights at a short distance and attempts to attract attention.

The eggs are large and usually pear-shaped, their colour and the markings resembling to a certain extent those of the well-known Peewit. The scanty nest is commonly placed in some slight hollow, either sheltered by a heather bush or in the midst of a tuft of coarse herbage.

The young for the most part take their departure from the hills on which they are bred shortly after attaining sufficient power of wing to undertake an extended flight. Before the end of August considerable flocks of immature birds may often be seen on Breydon mudflats in Norfolk; and on two or three successive seasons I shot them in the Nook at Rye in Sussex as early as the last week in July.

Owing to the numbers that are to be seen on many parts of the coast during summer, I am of opinion that the Curlew does not pair and nest before the age of two or, more probably, three years.

Every fowler is well acquainted with the note of this species. A very faint idea, however, of anything approaching the wild and far-resounding cry can be conveyed by words to those who have not listened to the birds themselves. Large flocks often fly mute by day, while the smaller bodies proclaim their presence by an exceedingly noisy demonstration. During the night, in rough and stormy weather, Curlews may frequently be heard screaming loudly as if separated from their companions. At such times, especially during autumn, when large bodies of Waders of various species are passing over, I have repeatedly remarked that the cries of the Redshanks would almost drown the voices of the other denizens of the mudflats. The note is by no means difficult to imitate; but although a single wandering bird can usually be decoyed within range, it is seldom that any large number are to be imposed upon; their line of flight may possibly be slightly changed and the whistle occasionally responded to, but they almost invariably continue on their course.

Late in autumn large flocks of Curlew have, on two or three occasions, come under my notice in the North Sea some miles from land; in every instance they were heading southerly. Whether these birds were migrants from the north of Europe, or merely on the passage from one part of our coasts to another, I can offer no opinion. During the years I was in communication with the light-ships off the east coast, but little could be learned concerning their movements in this quarter, none being taken on any of the vessels. A few years ago, however, nine were secured one stormy night on the "Owers" light-ship, stationed in the Channel a few miles west from Bognor.

# WHIMBREL.

## NUMENIUS PHÆOPUS.

On almost every  of the English and Scotch coasts with which I am acquainted this species has  For three or four successive seasons from May 1859, I  resorting to the mudflats  appeared to harbour  a week  most instances I was  their places from day to day.  showing themselves as early  till early  was held about this time, was eagerly anticipated by the old gunners of this remote part, the  district) being supposed to arrive in full force  The Bar-tailed Godwits, which also passed along the shore at this season, were  the majority of these gunners. Occasionally I heard both species termed  Whimbrel and Godwit will often settle in company on the flats when either resting or feeding, on flight it is seldom that they are intermixed during the spring. As a rule, Whimbrel reach the Sussex coast shortly in advance of the main body of the Godwits. The alterations that have taken place in this locality, owing to the reclaiming of the mudflats, have gradually lessened the haunts of all the Wader family, and the numbers that now make any halt in the neighbourhood of their old quarters are small indeed.

Whimbrel still pass along the coast of Sussex at the same dates as formerly, though of late years the flocks that have come under my notice seldom consisted of above twenty or thirty individuals; I observed the same decrease on the east coast in spring. It is no uncommon occurrence for one or two, probably nonbreeding birds of the previous season, to be noticed in these localities in June or July. During autumn I have seldom, either in Sussex, Norfolk, or the adjoining counties, remarked any large bodies in company, though the birds are constantly seen while on the return journey from their breeding-quarters in the north. Late stragglers not uncommonly delay their departure till the end of autumn; but I have never met with this species in winter, though wildfowl-shooters on the south coast assert that they have occasionally seen them at that season.

On more than one occasion during the autumn I have come across specimens of the Whimbrel so exceedingly diminutive that they might with good reason almost be supposed to belong to some other species. I much regret that every individual of this small race that came into my possession has been lost sight of, consequently there are none to refer to for measurement. Under date of September 12, 1872, while gunning on Breydon mudflats, I find the following entry in my notes:—" Wind still blowing strong from the north.

---

\* This, I am well aware, is contrary to the statements usually seen concerning the local names of these Waders. Many of the old gunners, however, in those days, did not appear to distinguish between the two species.

Shot the smallest Whimbrel I ever met with. It was impossible to form an opinion as to the species till the bird was in the boat, even after a close inspection with the glasses while it fed alongside of the dinai at a distance of only twenty-five or thirty yards. The beak was remarkably short, and exhibited but the slightest signs of the curve. No other Whimbrel, or even a Wader larger than the Dotterel or Dunlin, were seen all day." Two gunners, well acquainted with every member of the Wader family frequenting the Sussex mudflats, stated that during a severe winter some twenty years ago they noticed a couple of strangers in the flock of Curlew which habitually resort to this district; and the birds happening to pass within range, the pair were obtained. According to their description, these two birds belonged to the small race or variety of the Whimbrel *. The very accurate manner in which every peculiarity of this small form was described was sufficient to satisfy any one who had previously met with them. Whether these pygmies are simply the young (which is my own conclusion) or a smaller form of the Whimbrel, I must leave to scientific naturalists to decide.

After the manner of all the family, the Whimbrel is frequently heard at night, especially in stormy weather. The following lines are extracted from my notes of 1873, while shooting at Croydon:—

"August 25. Wind south, weather dull. During the latter part of the afternoon and evening the sky had worn a most threatening appearance, and shortly before dark it commenced to rain and blow, and a thunderstorm of great severity passed over the town (Yarmouth). During the whole of the tempest immense numbers of Waders were attracted by the lights, and remained for several hours flying over the houses. The cries of Whimbrel, Curlew, Godwits, Plovers, Knots, Redshanks, and several other birds could plainly be distinguished. It was afterwards mentioned in some of the sporting papers that large flocks of Waders had been heard calling over London during the storm of the same date."

Along the west coast of Ross-shire and also in the Hebrides the note of this species was recognized repeatedly during spring, even if the birds themselves escaped notice. In Sutherland and Caithness they appear at the same season, though I have remarked but few in autumn. On the east coast I met with small parties along the shores of the Firth of Forth, the sands at Aberlady and the rocks between Canty Bay and Dunbar being favourite feeding-grounds.

I can give but little information derived from my own experience concerning the breeding of the Whimbrel in the British Islands. Though searching with the greatest care and patience over miles of moorland in the north of Caithness, where I learned, on good authority, that these birds were in the habit of nesting, there was not a single specimen to be observed at the time of my visit in June 1869. Particular attention was given to the country in the vicinity of Huna and Duncansby Head; I was, however, at length reluctantly forced to come to the conclusion that the birds must have entirely deserted their former quarters.

But two or three pairs of Whimbrel which might reasonably be judged to be engaged in nesting-operations were fallen in with during the two seasons (1868 and 1869) in which I devoted particular attention to examining the reputed haunts of these birds. While off the west coast of Ross-shire early in June 1868, in a small fishing-craft during a fresh breeze of wind, a pair of Whimbrels flew up from one of the rocky islets lying outside Loch Ewe, and continued for some time hovering over the boat, calling loudly and evidently greatly distressed by their lonely abode being threatened with a visit. These noisy birds were shortly joined by two or three others which came from some of the adjacent islands. Though several attempts were made, the surf was breaking so heavily round the rocks that there was not the slightest chance of effecting a landing. There did not appear above a quarter or at most half an acre of coarse heather and grass on the summit of this wild and rugged mass of red rocks, that rose but twenty or thirty feet at the highest point above the water, which were constantly breaking around with terrific force. On the following day the attempt to search the spot was renewed, though unfortunately without success. The same birds were again seen, and from

* Curlew whelps * for the nam

their actions I was convinced there could be little doubt they were nesting. A continuation of stormy weather, which set in with still greater fury, put an end to all hopes of exploring this terribly exposed coast before I left the district.

To give an accurate description of the food or eggs of the Whimbrel is well nigh impossible. The note, however, is one of the easiest to imitate, and in most instances readily respond and frequently approach without hesitation.

The food of this species is probably much the same as that of the Curlew. As a rule, however, the localities it frequents are more exposed to the influence of salt water than fresh, marine worms and insects doubtless forming their chief means of sustenance.

# SPOTTED REDSHANK.

## TOTANUS FUSCUS.

I can say but little, derived from personal observation, concerning the distribution of the Spotted Redshank over the British Islands, having only met with this species in Norfolk and Sussex. In the former county these birds frequently resort to Breydon mudflats, and a few occasionally are either seen or heard flying over the marshes around Hickling Broad. It is many years since I met with these Redshanks in Sussex, though early in the autumn of 1859, and again in 1861 and 1862, single birds and now and then small flocks were observed about the muddy edges of the backwaters in the marshes near Rye and Winchelsea. The pools inside the shingle-banks opposite Lancing and the muds in Shoreham Harbour also attracted a bird or two, though their visits were seldom of long duration, the numbers of prowling gunners that have always infested that locality speedily driving them to more retired spots.

These birds appear to be by no means abundant in any part of the country I have explored, a small flock of ten or twelve being the most I have ever met with in company. This juvenile party, all exhibiting the immature plumage of the first autumn, took up their quarters on the mudflats in the Nook at Rye Harbour for three or four days after the 16th of September, 1859; though repeated attempts to get within range were made, only a single specimen was obtained, the first shot having put them on the alert and rendered a near approach an impossibility. During that week an immense number of Waders were scattered over the saltwater flats, as well as around the backwaters and dykes on the reclaimed ground; the pools also in the ballast-holes * in the marshes proved most tempting feeding-grounds. On referring to my notes, I find that specimens of the following species were obtained on the 16th of September :— Spotted Redshank 1, Green Sandpiper 3, Wood Sandpiper 17, Black-tailed Godwit 3, Snipe 1, Curlew Sandpiper 17, Little Stint 10, Little Grebe 1.

On a single occasion only have I observed above one or two in company on Breydon: at daybreak on the morning of the 20th of August, 1873, after a heavy thunderstorm in the night, when thousands of Waders attracted by the lights of the town had been heard calling over Yarmouth, a dozen at least, all young of the year, were detected scattered here and there in the ranks of an immense gathering of the commoner species. On first reaching our shores in autumn the immature birds are exceedingly fearless and while circling over the flats readily respond to the call-note and, flying towards the punt, offer the easiest shots imaginable. The call of this bird is most difficult to imitate correctly, and I have met with but one or two gunners who could successfully accomplish it; the attainment, however, appears to be of little service, as the bird is attracted quite as easily by the note of the Common Redshank or the call of the Grey Plover. Though this species is occasionally met with in winter, I have never fallen in with even a single bird

---

* Wherever the shingle had been transported from the banks for the formation of the railway, the rain-water collected in pools in the excavations, and as reeds and rank grass increased, and shelter was afforded, these spots (which were termed ballast-holes by the natives) proved exceedingly attractive to Waders and Wildfowl.

at that season. A pair of Spotted Redshanks, however, in the full adult black dress that is assumed during the breeding-season have come under my observation; these were seen about halfway up the flats on the east side of Breydon just as day was breaking on the 13th of May, 1871, and a shot would doubtless have been obtained had not the train from Norwich, due at Yarmouth at 3.20 A.M., put them on wing just as the punt was coming within range. After circling round for a time, uttering their singular and unmistakable cry, they sheered off towards the "lumps," where they alighted for a few moments and eventually, disturbed by a shot on the upper part of the water, went off towards the sea-coast, holding a due north-east course.

When a large flock of Waders, in which both Redshanks are represented, is fairly within view through the glasses, it is easy to distinguish the two species at a glance; in addition to the extra length of leg, the dull grey colouring of the breast and belly of *T. fuscus* differs greatly from the pure white plumage so conspicuous on the under parts of *T. calidris*, and at once attracts attention. Though I failed to ascertain that these birds were known to the shore-gunners in either the east or west of Sussex, the majority of the Breydon puntmen were well aware of the difference in the size and colouring, and a few could imitate the note with great accuracy. On several parts of the east coast I remarked that the gunners invariably termed this species the "Shank," while the Common Redshank was spoken of as the "Redleg."

# REDSHANK.
## *TOTANUS CALIDRIS.*

―――――

The Redshank is a summer resident ................................. autumn to ......................................................................... met ......................................................................... I cannot ............................................................. there are doubtless many ................ to which ................................. In .......... the species is abundant in ........ of the ........................... and ....................... or glen in the .............................................. two where a few pairs or even a colony take up their summer quarters.

Early in autumn immense flights make their appearance on the flats along the sea-shore. The birds evidently prefer localities where an extensive stretch of mud, sand, or low reef of rocks allows them to rest unmolested after feeding. Near Morangie, on the Dornoch Firth, I have frequently noticed large flocks of from two to four hundred, and occasionally double that number, alighting on the floating seaweed; at times a patch of weed from fifty to one hundred yards in length would be completely covered by the living mass; a strange and striking sight is then presented by the long line of Waders as they rise and fall with the undulating motion of the waves. I have often watched the Redlegs * betake themselves to such stations when they were flooded off the sands just before high tide. Passing them occasionally in the gunning-punt, at a distance of forty or fifty yards, they would take but little notice, one or two rising from time to time, and a few spreading their wings to steady themselves as a wave broke up and ruffled the surface of the water. On their first arrival on the coast, Redlegs are remarkably fearless, though if constantly harassed they soon become wild, when few birds cause more annoyance to the gunners, their warning cry putting all Wildfowl and Waders on the alert. The note of this species may be heard at all hours of the night, a solitary whistle from the mudflats occasionally breaking the silence, and a general outcry bursting forth as a flock takes wing, either flooded off their standing-ground by the tide, or alarmed by the passing craft of a gunner or fisherman.

Redshanks usually return to their breeding-haunts on the Norfolk marshes early in March: the 3rd is the earliest date on which I have noted a pair or two showing themselves in the vicinity of their summer quarters. The marshmen usually look upon the return of the Redleg as one of the first signs of spring. In several of the Highland glens I remarked the birds were seldom seen till a month or five weeks later, but when once they make their appearance, nesting-operations are speedily commenced. The date at which eggs are laid varies with the season. In the broad-district in the east of Norfolk, I noticed in 1883 that the majority of the birds had their full complement of eggs by about the 22nd of April; the weather at the time was cold with cutting east winds, and it is probable they were a few days later than usual. The Redleg

\* Among the gunners on the east coast, this species is usually known as the Redleg.

commonly selects the centre of a tuft of rushes* about sixteen or twenty inches in height in which to scrape out the small circular depression that forms its cradle: either a few blades of soft dead grass are added, or the weaker strands are broken down and thus supply a scanty lining. The long rank marsh-grass that grows about the roots of the surrounding rushes frequently meets over the eggs and forms a covering that effectually conceals them in the absence of the parent bird. Unless carefully examined, it is difficult to ascertain where the bird enters or leaves the nest, so closely do the strands of waving grass entwine above the space; at times a track may be detected among the grass and herbage; but doubtless the bird is able to force its way through the unresisting covering without leaving the slightest trace. Though apparently concealed so as to defy detection, scarcely a nest escapes the practised eye of the marshman, who has learned his trade by working every spring to supply the market.

In the neighbourhood of the broads the young seldom remain long on the dry portions of the marshes on which the nests were placed. When newly hatched, the old birds lead them to the slades, where the shelter of the reeds and sedge and the boggy nature of the soil afford security from their numerous persecutors. The over-anxiety of their parents, however, invariably betrays their place of concealment. Where Peewits and Redlegs breed in company, both species generally unite in mobbing the intruder on their domain. A passing Crow is invariably assailed, and the visit of the Moor-Buzzard to their haunts at once attracts every bird in the neighbourhood. On the 17th and 18th of May, 1883, I watched an immature Marsh-Harrier that was hovering about the marshes near Hickling Broad, followed for at least twenty minutes on each occasion by a noisy swarm of from fifty to sixty Peewits and Redlegs. As they swept screaming round, the Hawk at times was almost hidden by the wings of the excited throng; he appeared, however, to pay not the slightest attention to the clamour: two or three times he alighted for a moment among the reeds, but I was unable to ascertain if any prey was secured.

The usual call-note of the Redshank is too well known to need description; though the birds are most clamorous in the breeding-season, their warning cries may be heard at all times of the year on the mud-flats and along the shore. I have hitherto seen no mention of a singular habit in which this species indulges during the breeding-season after the young are hatched: occasionally the whole body resorting to one part of the marshes will simultaneously give vent to a succession of loud and prolonged calls, the combined notes forming a most singular chime, which is continued for a minute or more at a time.

Early in June 1881 my attention was attracted by a particularly dark-plumaged Redshank, whose loud notes were heard on every occasion when I passed a thick patch of reeds on Pleasure Hills†, a small island on Hickling Broad. The position the bird took up was strange—invariably perching, on the approach of the boat, on a point just level with the top of the highest reeds. Considering it impossible that one of the stems of *Phragmites communis* could sustain his weight, I landed and discovered that a thorn bush had been driven by ice or floods on the hill, and one small twig stretching upwards formed the observatory from which he gave warning to his brood of approaching danger; while returning to the boat, the downy young, a day or two out of the shell, were detected attempting to escape among the roots of the sedge. A week later I discovered that the old bird (easily recognized by his conspicuous colouring) had shifted his quarters, and with his brood was domiciled on Rush Hills, a marsh on the Heigham side of the broad, one hundred and fifty to two hundred yards from the nearest point of Pleasure Hills. I was at first under the impression

Woodcock; but on ............................................................................ he stated that ........................................ of young
............................................................................................................ to this means of progression. On
............................................................................................ four Waders feeding on the mud at
.............................................................................. startled by a dog, they got on wing,
............................................................................ in the water exactly opposite where I was
concealed, .................. once ............ a distance of five or six yards; their heads were bobbed up and
down .................................................................. the Moorhen. A couple which I shot, in order that there
.................................................................................. in winter plumage and a young bird of the

These Waders, at their summer haunts, may frequently be seen taking up a commanding position, and resting for a time or calling loudly on stakes, rails, boat-houses, stacks of rushes, and occasionally on shrubs and bushes. I have watched one now and then endeavouring to steady itself on a waving twig of willow, spreading its wings from time to time as its perch swayed to and fro with the breeze.

During storms of thunder, towards the close of summer or early autumn, large flights of this species, together with other Waders, are frequently attracted at night by the lights of towns in the neighbourhood of their haunts, and may be heard flying over, calling loudly, for hours at a time. Immense flocks are usually to be found collected on the mudbanks at daylight on the morning following their aerial demonstrations. This was particularly the case on Breydon Flats on the morning of September 5th, 1872, and again on August 26th the following year. On the latter date the movements of Waders appear to have been general all over the southern and eastern parts of the country. The cries of Whimbrel, Curlew, Redshanks, and other mud-birds could be distinguished over Yarmouth for hours, and the fact of large flocks of Waders having passed over London during the same storm was recorded in more than one publication. On this occasion, for a few hours after daylight, Redshanks were collected in the largest numbers that ever came under my observation; there were within view on the flats three or four flocks, each numbering over a thousand. There was not another gunner on the water (a rare occurrence on Breydon), and the birds being unsuspicious of danger, I was able to examine the whole of the flocks at short distances with the glasses. A few hundred Knots, a score or two of Greenshanks, and about a dozen immature Spotted Redshanks were the only strangers to be detected in their ranks. At last after waiting for several hours, as no rarities were forthcoming, and the early morning had been exceedingly blusterous with squalls of driving mist and rain, I was anxious to fire the charge from the big gun and load afresh. Selecting as my mark a long-legged Wader that appeared conspicuous in a dense mass of Redshanks, I pulled the trigger and proceeded to collect the slain. Owing to a heavy shower, this bird had not been inspected through the glasses, and I was somewhat surprised to find that the specimen mistaken for an immature Spotted Redshank was simply a young bird of the common species. Numbers of Rodges, both old and young, laid around, and five or six immature Greenshanks had also fallen to the shot, but not a sign of a Spotted Redshank could be seen. On carefully examining the bird, it proved to be in the usual immature plumage of the Common Redshank, and presented not the slightest difference in the colouring of beak or legs; the legs, however, when measured from the thigh downwards, were precisely 1½ inch longer than those of any of the others, either old or young, killed by the same discharge. This extra length of limb and consequent height must have caused the mistake, which a glance through the glasses would have rendered impossible, as the colouring of the breasts and underparts of the immature birds of the two species differs considerably[*].

Redshanks, probably non-breeding birds, are to be seen occasionally frequenting Breydon mudflats all

[*] This specimen, having been unfortunately overlooked and forgotten at the close of the day's work, was not preserved.

through May. Under date of May 17th, 1873, I find in my notes that several parties of Redlegs appeared in company with a few Greenshanks. The young birds usually arrive on the south coast at an early date. A small flock was seen on the muds at Shoreham Harbour the last week in July 1883.

It is uncertain at what time the summer plumage is assumed or at what age the young put off the immature dress. The birds that gather at their haunts in the Norfolk marshes about the middle of March are all, as far as I was able to judge, in full breeding-plumage; in order to be certain, a couple were shot (March 26th, 1873), which proved to be in that state. On March 28th, 1883, I killed on the coast of Sussex, with one barrel, an adult in full winter and a young one in immature plumage[*]. On May 4th, 1859, two birds were shot in Rye Nook, in Sussex, showing full adult winter plumage. That this species does not assume the full plumage at the age of one year appears evident. Whether they pair and nest before the age of three years is, I consider, doubtful.

The eggs of the Redshank are sent in large numbers to the local markets from the marshes of the east of Norfolk. For the table they can scarcely compare with those of the Peewit, from which they may readily be distinguished by the warmer tints of the ground and blotches as well as the gloss on the shell; in size they are also slightly smaller. I have more than once come across eight eggs in the nest of a Redshank; but on every occasion it was evident that two birds had laid in the same nest, each set of eggs differing materially in the tone of colouring.

The young shortly after breaking the shell are covered with a light yellowish-brown down, paler about the throat, breast, and belly. A few conspicuous black or dark brown markings appear on the back, the head being mottled with dark brown. On the upper portions of the body the down is of a more tawny hue. The legs and beak are of a pale brown or dirty flesh tint, the ridge of the upper mandible being somewhat darker.

[*] The latter exhibited little or no change in plumage or colour of beak and legs from immature specimens obtained in autumn.

# GREEN SANDPIPER.

## TOTANUS OCHROPUS.

---

I can give no fresh information regarding the distribution of this species over the British Islands; during the years spent shooting and collecting in the Highlands, and also in the south of Scotland in East Lothian, I never caught a glimpse of a Green Sandpiper. Gullane Links and the glens of several of the larger rivers (such as the Tay, the Spey, and the Beauly with their tributaries) were haunts that might have been imagined attractive at one season or another; still these conspicuous birds escaped observation.

The furthest north that I met with this Sandpiper was in the valley of the Esk, a few miles inland from Whitby in Yorkshire; parts of the wild glen through which the river flows towards the North Sea were densely wooded, and these proved to be favourite resorts of the birds. When alarmed they frequently appeared to fly out from the upper branches of some of the larger trees, being, however, at that time unacquainted with the breeding-habits of this species, I made no attempts to search for any nests in which their eggs or young might be concealed. These observations were taken early in June 1862, the time of year at which the birds might naturally be supposed to be engaged in breeding-operations. It is also recorded in the fourth edition of Yarrell that the Green Sandpiper was several times shot, in all cases during the month of June, in the neighbourhood of Hummanby near Scarborough, the locality being only a few miles to the south of where I met with the birds. In addition to these remarks the following statement occurs:—" The keeper there says they breed in old Crows' nests; he has seen them come off from the nests." As I repeatedly watched them myself in a wooded district at no great distance, and the keeper referred to seems to have been acquainted with their habits, there can, I am of opinion, be little doubt the birds have now and then bred in this country. There are also statements in the third edition of Knox's 'Ornithological Rambles in Sussex' that would lead one to believe that this species had occasionally remained through the summer near Midhurst in Sussex, though for what purpose it would be hazardous to express an opinion.

The only Green Sandpiper exhibiting the perfect mature summer plumage that I obtained was shot as he rose from the marsh-dyke surrounding the south side of Hickling Broad on the 25th of May, 1873. During the latter part of June and throughout July adults may be seen singly or in pairs scattered over parts of the Suffolk marshes near Yarmouth; these are probably birds lately returned to this country from their breeding-haunts in the far north of Europe. While collecting specimens on two or three occasions in 1871, I put up as many as four or five pairs and a few single birds along the dykes or in the damp slades in these marshes; the feathers of all procured for examination at this time were much frayed and worn, and the gloss on the plumage, so striking in summer, had entirely disappeared. A few young birds are occasionally noticed about Breydon mudflats, this species, however, appears to prefer a grass-marsh or the banks of a water-dyke for a feeding-ground. On the 28th of August, 1871, I shot a very small one, evidently a bird of the year, as it flew past the punt over the roads on the north side of Breydon; this specimen was in very dingy plumage and in poor condition, giving evidence of having met with rough usage, which might possibly have been encountered on its passage to our shores, the weather having been exceedingly stormy for some days past. Immature birds are also frequently met with during autumn about the mudbanks on some of the Sussex rivers, and they also visit the pools of brackish water inside the shingle-banks along several parts of the coast-line. The winding course of the river Adur, from Shoreham Harbour to Bramber, is still a favourite resort for immature birds every autumn, and further east the flats between Rye and Winchelsea were formerly always frequented at this season.

The first entry in my notes concerning this species occurs under the date of the 16th of September, 1859, when three young birds were shot at a large pool of brackish water near the centre of the wide-stretching shingle-banks near the Nook at Rye*. An extraordinary number of Waders were then scattered over the mudflats and along the course of the broad dyke that led from the backwater near Winchelsea guardhouse to the tideway in the harbour. A great change has now taken place over this once famous resort for Fowl and Waders; the whole stretch of mudflats covered at every tide have, after several failures, been at length drained and turned into grass-marshes, and the chance for observing rare species formerly to be obtained must no longer be expected.

* The birds obtained on that day are referred to under the heading of the Spotted Redshank on page 1.

# WOOD-SANDPIPER.

## TOTANUS GLAREOLA.

Why the name of Wood-Sandpiper was bestowed on this handsome graceful species appears a mystery; to the Green Sandpiper, often approaching nearly our hedge-sides, or even perching on that wary bird, it is well known from the early Norse times that nest-holes in trees, or in clefts on the branches, squirrels' dredges, or even deserted Pigeons-nests, mossy bowers, or any other hollows are suitable in the greenwood trees.

The first occurrence of the Wood-Sandpiper in this country in the spring is recorded in my notes under the date of May 10th, 1882, when a remarkably fine adult male in full summer plumage was shot in a marsh-dyke near Sidlesham Harbour, in West Sussex. While shooting, fishing, and collecting in the flat country in the east of Norfolk, I repeatedly remarked during the summer months that a sudden change of weather, or an unaccustomed rise or fall of the water, would immediately bring these birds in larger or smaller numbers to the hills round the broads. On the 18th of May, 1883, the wind blowing strong from the north, with frequent squalls, a flock of about thirty Wood-Sandpipers were in company with as many Reeves on the hills round Hickling Broad; after getting on wing the two species separated at once, but joined again on alighting, after flying over the water for a time. I was unable to obtain a sufficiently close view to ascertain the state of plumage exhibited by these birds; in all probability, however, they were immature, as adults at this season are usually to be seen singly, in pairs, or in small parties.

The water on Hickling Broad, which had been gradually falling for a week or so, was lower on the 9th of June, 1870, than any of the natives had previously witnessed, and the tide did not commence to flow up the river for several days. During the interval, two or three flocks of Little Stints and several pairs of Wood-Sandpipers in perfect plumage were seen, some of both species being obtained as specimens. All these Waders were busily engaged in searching for food among the weeds exposed by the fall of the water, and proved exceedingly fearless when approached by the punt, allowing a very close inspection to be made.

Early in August 1859 I ascertained that a pool of water, collected in an excavation where the shingle had been carried away from the wide-spreading banks for the formation of a line of railway near Rye, in East Sussex, was a very favourite resort for these birds. A flock, varying from twenty to twice that number, usually frequented this spot every season for several weeks during the years I visited the district. The birds proved to be all immature, and were generally found feeding in the long grass and among the rank vegetation round the pool; now and then I noticed one or two perched on a line of posts and rails that crossed this large piece of shallow water.

This species is to be seen all through the summer in the broad country in the east of Norfolk; I find the following in my notes for 1873 under the date of June 30th:—" Heavy rain had fallen during the night, with squalls of wind from the north-east; soon after daybreak there were many flocks of Waders on the marshes round the broad. At least a score of immature Ruffs and Reeves and as many

Wood-Sandpipers, also juveniles, were on Rush Hills, and several Curlews and Dunlins appeared on wing as soon as I fired a shot, which dropped a couple of this species, in order to ascertain their state of plumage with certainty. In the afternoon the Ruffs and Reeves had taken their departure and the Wood-Sandpipers were scattered in small parties of two or three over the slades on the different hills." I remarked that Wood-Sandpipers in immature plumage remained in the vicinity of Hickling Broad during the whole of that summer; on the 24th of July a large flock of thirty or forty were observed, and seven were stopped by a shot as they sprung on wing while feeding on one of the slades. Five only were secured, owing to the dangerous nature of the moving bog on which they fell; all, however, exhibited the state of plumage assumed by the non-breeding birds remaining in this country during the summer months.

The difference in the plumage of the adult and immature is apparent at a glance, and may often be detected through the glasses while the birds are moving about feeding. On the former the colouring of the back is a dark blackish brown with clear white spots, while on the latter the feathers on the back are of a dull brown-green tint, and the spots a dirty pale yellow; the old birds also are generally larger and far more weighty.

But a single instance where the nest of this species has been discovered in the British Islands appears to be recorded in any work on ornithology; it is, however, possible, from the accounts given by one or two writers, that this species has bred in the same locality in former years. In this case the nest was found on Prestwick Car (now drained), in Northumberland, by Mr. John Hancock, on the 3rd of June, 1853.

Early in June 1867 I fell in with a pair evidently nesting on Gullane Links in East Lothian; the birds had taken up their quarters on the lower portion of the sandy flats towards the west, where there were large patches of green rushes and long coarse grass. My attention was first attracted by one of the birds darting through the air and going through much the same performance as the Common Snipe, though the sounds emitted were not so loud; these extraordinary antics were carried on for some time, and finally both birds were lost sight of during a prolonged flight towards the east. All would, without doubt, have gone well, and the nest been discovered, had not a Snipe appeared on the scene, and continued hovering round over the same spot, where it was shortly joined by another. Half an hour later one of the Wood-Sandpipers was again soaring over, dashing down in the same manner as previously witnessed, in a few minutes the Snipes were also circling round. As the number of birds on wing was somewhat perplexing when an attempt was made, at a distance, to follow the movements of the Sandpipers through the glasses, I determined to shoot one or, if possible, both of the Snipes, and leave the place clear for the inspection of the Sandpipers. An opportunity soon occurred, as one of the Snipes dashed round; but, unluckily, at the moment the trigger was pulled one of the Sandpipers happened to be crossing the line of flight without attracting my attention, and both birds dropped to the shot. The Sandpiper, when examined, proved to be the female, and consequently all watching was at an end, as the male would without doubt now desert the spot. Though there were but slight hopes of success after this unfortunate mishap, a long and careful search was made; the nest, however, in the end remained undiscovered. That the birds nested here in days gone by I have little doubt, as, while a temporary resident in this part of the country, studying farming at Ferrygate near North Berwick, in 1863 and the following year, I noticed these birds in spring on two occasions and imagined them to be Snipes, not having had access to any of the works that describe their habits during the breeding-season. The last time I went to inspect this favourite haunt of Waders and Wildfowl, a few years back, a change had taken place in the aspect of its surroundings, and it was evident that the former denizens of the slades and swamps had been compelled to seek other quarters.

# COMMON SANDPIPER.

## *TOTANUS HYPOLEUCUS.*

The Common Sandpiper is a spring and autumn migrant, arriving on our southern coasts about the end of the second week in April, and, after rearing its young in many parts of the country, leaving our inhospitable shores to seek a warmer climate before the frosts of autumn and early winter have set in.

In Sussex these birds may be observed (in spring for the most part singly) about the pools of brackish water in the vicinity of the sea-beach. After a few days' halt they gradually make their way inland, usually following the course of the rivers, and so on through the country to their summer-haunts. Stragglers and late arrivals may be seen for a month or five weeks later, but no instance of the species remaining to nest in the county has come under my notice. I am aware that the fact of this Sandpiper having bred in Sussex is recorded on what ought to be good authority. The banks of the rivers and streams in this part of the country are scarcely suitable to the requirements of the species, and possibly (as I judge from eggs that have been shown as undoubted specimens) mistakes, in some instances at least, may have occurred. In Norfolk this attractive bird makes its appearance at much the same date as in the southern counties, frequenting during its short stay in the district the sides and moist portions of the hills round the broads, or the edges of the drains that run through the saltwater mudflats.

By the lakes in Cumberland and the winding streams of some of the adjoining counties I have seen this Sandpiper in June; and it is probable that it passes the summer there, though, not needing specimens of eggs or young, no search was made for the nests. Along the shores of the Tay these birds usually take up their quarters early in May, and from this point to the extreme north of Sutherland and Caithness I met with them in almost every suitable locality.

On one occasion four young birds in the down, evidently but lately hatched, were detected a few yards above high-water mark on the shores of a sandy creek in Gairloch, on the west coast of Ross-shire. The spot was flat and open, similar in every respect to the usual haunts of the Ringed Plover, several of which species were breeding close at hand. That the Sandpiper should have chosen a situation for nesting so devoid of cover is most improbable, and I conclude that the tiny mites, notwithstanding their apparent want of strength, had succeeded in making their way down the course of a rocky burn from the adjoining moorland. Where Sandpipers take up their summer-quarters in wooded localities they may frequently be seen sitting (at times at a considerable height) in the surrounding timber. Numbers are to be met with in various parts along the canal between Inverness and Dochfour, near the bend of Loch Ness. When put up from their feeding-grounds, I repeatedly watched them alight on the limbs of Scotch firs or other large forest trees and run rapidly along the branches jerking their tails.

I was informed by the keepers at Pitmacree and other shootings along Strath Tay (where these Sandpipers are especially numerous during the breeding-season) that great difficulty was experienced in keeping open the traps set for Crows about the pools near the river-side. The unfortunate birds were continually falling victims, flies or other insects that settled on the baits probably attracting them to the spot. A man who looked over a part of the ground declared that at least a dozen Sandpipers had been destroyed on his beat in less than a week.

The Common Sandpiper swims well, and is an excellent diver when wounded. I have watched many an inexperienced sportsman greatly excited by his frantic and unavailing efforts to secure a winged bird which had fallen close to his boat. Each time he stretched over to grasp the active swimmer it would plunge under, with the ease and rapidity of a Guillemot, and, ducking from one side of the craft to the other, would frequently succeed in evading capture. Unless winged, I have only on one or two occasions noticed an adult taking to the water, though now and then they might be seen in the act of paddling across some small pool or creek along the river-side by which they fed. While fishing on the Lyon, in Perthshire, in June 1867, a Merlin made a sudden dash at a Sandpiper skimming across the river within twenty yards of where I stood. Instantly the bird dived below the surface, and did not emerge again till the shelter of some stunted willow bushes (whose branches overhung the water) had been reached. Forcing my way an hour later through the thick cover to reach a pool lower down the river, I disturbed, in an open space, some living creature that appeared, as it rapidly threaded its way among the shrubs and plants, to be either a rat or a rabbit. On searching closely I came upon the nest of a Sandpiper with four eggs, and doubtless it was the parent bird that had attracted my attention. A collector of eggs who happened to be present was anxious to secure the clutch as specimens, and immediate steps were taken to ensure the safety of his treasures till our return from fishing. A stoat or two had shown themselves in a stone dyke near the river-bank, and, in order to guard against an attack by these destructive animals, a covering of coarse grass was first laid across the nest, and next a heap of sand and small stones was cautiously spread over to the depth of several inches. Late in the evening, on making our way to remove the eggs we were much astonished on discovering that the bird had returned to its nest and, in no manner disconcerted by the change effected, had scraped off the sand and grass and was again sitting.

The young swim as soon as they leave the nest and are capable of running along the banks of the streams and rivers. I have watched the downy brood washing and sporting in the pools, and the anxiety displayed by the old birds has frequently drawn my attention to the small family secreting themselves in the water beneath the roots of trees or some overhanging slab of rock to which they had made their way, by diving or swimming, on the first signs of danger.

On its arrival in the spring the Common Sandpiper is an extremely neat and handsome bird. The greenish-brown tint of the feathers on the back is suffused with a pinkish gloss, and contrasts admirably with the pure white of the breast. The black markings on the back (somewhat resembling broad-pointed arrow-heads) are clearly defined, and the whole appearance differs greatly from the worn and faded state of plumage exhibited by the end of summer. The young in the immature dress are deficient in the strong markings on the back, the feathers being edged with delicate black lines. The colouring of the throat and breast, as well as the back of the head, is also more clouded. Shortly after breaking the shell the nestlings are covered on the upper parts with a greenish-grey down, variegated with occasional lighter tints, speckled and streaked with dark brown. The throat, breast, and belly are white, slightly stained at times by the action of the water.

# GREENSHANK.

## TOTANUS CANESCENS.

---

In spring and again in autumn, in still greater numbers, this species is to be seen in the southern and eastern counties of England while on the passage to and from its breeding-grounds in the far north. Though the majority cross the sea, a considerable number rear their young in the more remote districts of several counties in the Highlands as well as on some of the Western Islands. Those that came under my observation during summer in the south were in every instance in immature plumage, plainly indicating that the perfect adult dress is not assumed till after the second or third year.

Though it appears there is indisputable evidence that the nest of this species has been repeatedly found close to the edge of a Highland loch, those I met with were invariably placed on the driest portions of the moors; and although small pools of rain-water might possibly have collected in the adjacent peat-holes, the nests were always at a considerable distance from either loch or river, never, to the best of my recollection, nearer than a quarter of a mile. I remarked at a nest in the west of Ross-shire that both birds regularly left the moors in company and came down to the sea-shore to feed, frequenting both the sandy bays and pools of salt water among the weed-grown slabs of rock. Throughout the inland districts, such as the central portions of Sutherland and Caithness, they were usually found searching for food in the vicinity of the lochs, along the river-sides, or by the pools, either on the floes or the open moorlands. Though four is doubtless the full complement of eggs laid by the Greenshank, the first nest I met with contained eight; these were arranged with the centre egg balanced upright on the smaller end and the others surrounding it, the shape of the shells and the depth of the cradle allowing the formation of a perfect circle. The old bird sat exceedingly close and might have been captured on the nest, as she allowed her back to be stroked over two or three times before rising on wing and making off. In many other instances where the nests were frequently passed, the female took not the slightest notice of intruders when inspected at the distance of a few yards. The nest with eight eggs previously referred to was found in the west of Ross-shire in May 1868, and a month or so later I heard of another being seen with the same number; the following year seven eggs and one downy youngster just released from the shell were observed by a keeper, with whom I was well acquainted, on the moors between the Crask and Altnaharra in Sutherland. In each of these cases a couple of birds must have laid in the same nest. In the shaded domicile of the Redshank, of which a far greater number have come under my notice, I only once found so many eggs, while five is the most detected in the humble cradle provided by the Peewit for the accommodation of its brood.

Large numbers of Greenshanks intermixed with Redlegs and Shanks* were swarming on the Breydon muds on the morning of the 26th of August, 1872, and a shot with the big gun aimed at one of the latter unfortunately caused more slaughter than was anticipated, as, in addition to the specimen required, at least a dozen of this species were stopped by the discharge. I remarked that the adults were in almost full summer plumage and nearly double the size of the immature birds; the legs and feet of both old and young were of a dirty greenish-yellow tinge. While shooting on Breydon in May 1873, we noticed that a few Greenshanks, in company with Redshanks, came daily to the flats as the tide fell, betaking themselves at high water to the slades in the marshes; these were doubtless the young of the previous year, the feathers on the head and neck being exceedingly light and totally different to the state of plumage exhibited by the adults during the breeding season.

During stormy nights these birds are often attracted by the lights, and may be heard in company with other Waders screaming over towns; I repeatedly detected their shrill outcries among the varied notes of several large and noisy flocks that passed and circled over Yarmouth on the night of the 4th of September, 1872, and again on the 25th of August the following year. Even when undisturbed by sudden atmospheric changes, Greenshanks may be heard while on wing during the hours of darkness; half an hour after midnight on the 22nd of July, 1873, while quanting quietly up one of the rivers running through the flat country in the east of Norfolk, we listened for some minutes to their unmistakable notes as a pair winged their way overhead, apparently holding a course pointing due north-east.

A stiff breeze of wind not unfrequently brings flocks of these and other Waders to the hills and marshes around the Norfolk broads at any season of the year. On the 28th of April, 1883, the wind blowing strongly from the east-south-east and exceedingly cold, a number of Black and Common Terns as well as Waders were driven for shelter to the flooded marshes and sheltered portions of Hickling Broad. Chance visitors, such as Curlew, Whimbrel, Greenshanks, and Dunlins, were in swarms, while the Peewits, Redshanks, and Ruffs and Reeves had greatly increased in numbers, their ranks having been recruited by birds on passage to more northern quarters.

I have met with this species only on a single occasion in winter, and then its presence at that time of year was evidently compulsory. On the 14th of December, 1882, an adult bird in light-tinted plumage, with the breast streaked with black, was shot at a brackish pool just inside the shingle-banks between Shoreham and Lancing. On rising from the water's edge, I remarked that its flight appeared to be much impeded by wounds or weakness, and on further examination it was discovered that the wing had been either imperfectly pinioned or cut by a shot. It may not be out of place to state that the points of both upper and lower mandibles were of a dark horn tint, an olive-greenish brown showing at the base, the legs and feet exhibiting a dull olive-green tinge.

While shooting round the islands near the head of the Cromarty Firth in the early autumn of 1868, I found several small parties of Greenshanks, evidently hatched out on the moors in the neighbourhood, feeding among the weeds that grow profusely on the moist soil of the mudflats. A few of the younger birds that were killed by the punt-gun while in pursuit of fowl or other Waders proved by no means unpalatable, though excessively fat, when properly dressed. As Snipes, however, were abundant and easily obtained, I did not molest these interesting juveniles to any extent.

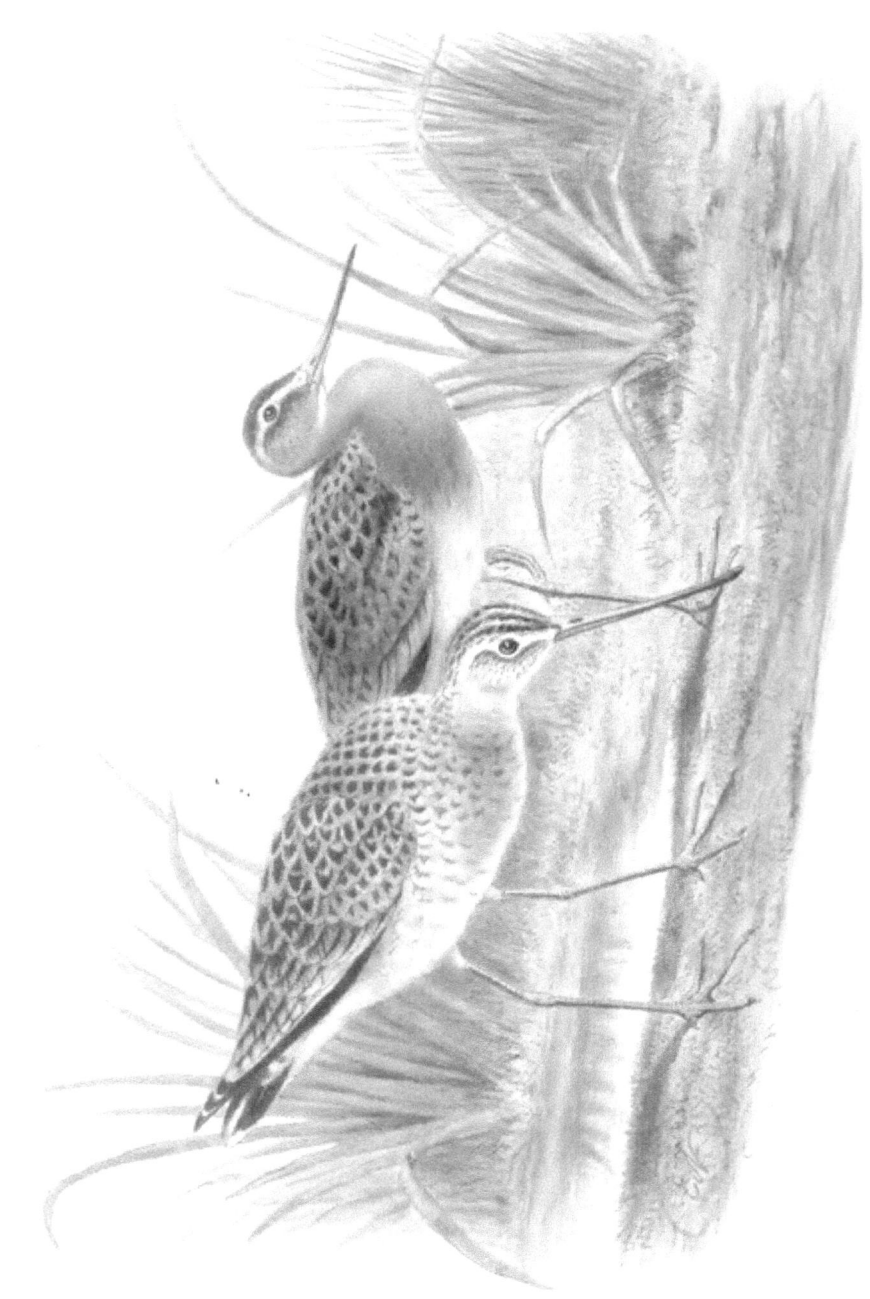

# BLACK-TAILED GODWIT.

## *LIMOSA MELANURA.*

---

From the information I was enabled to gather while shooting and collecting in the marshlands of the east of Norfolk, this species appears to have been scarce in the earlier days of even the oldest fenmen. Though these birds have long ceased to breed in this locality, I seldom passed the spring on Breydon mudflats, or the broads about Hickling, without meeting with one or two specimens, stragglers evidently still continuing to pass over and occasionally to alight for a short time about their old haunts at the season of migration.

On referring to my notes for 1871, I find that small parties of Black-tailed Godwits were seen regularly for two or three days on the hills of some of the Potter-Heigham marshes during the first week in May; the whole of these birds proved exceedingly wary, and in the end escaped without offering a chance of a shot. Their shrill cries were sure to attract attention, little difficulty being experienced in ascertaining if they were in the vicinity when once on wing. The flight of this species will readily be recognised by those who have previously met with opportunities for observing their actions; while circling over the marshes they usually keep at a considerable elevation, the movements of the wings appearing slow and regular. I have, however, watched them on more than one occasion dash down and swoop to the ground with almost the same actions as the Snipe. A few days later (on the 11th of the month), when shooting on Breydon, an exceedingly deeply coloured bird (evidently in full breeding-plumage) settled on the open flats at a safe distance from any of the drains, and after remaining feeding for an hour or two, well out of range of even the heaviest punt-gun, eventually took its departure unmolested, flying towards the north-east.

A remarkably large and light-coloured individual (probably a female) was noticed for a day or two from the 16th of May, 1883, on the hills near Hickling, my attention being first drawn to the bird by its loud note, uttered at a great height while flying over the broad.

From the entries in my journals it appears that the number of Black-tailed Godwits passing in autumn along the flats of the south coast have greatly decreased during the last five-and-twenty years. The small muddy pools in the marshes near the Nook at Rye were commonly in those days visited about the middle of September by a few small parties of immature birds; at this season they were usually confiding, but little difficulty being experienced in procuring any specimens required. On the 16th and 17th of September, 1859, these birds, as well as many other Waders, were especially numerous about the pools near the Winchelsea Watch-house, and several (all in immature plumage) were obtained. I remarked that this species resorted to the more brackish parts of the marshes, and were seldom seen, in this locality, on the salt-water mud-banks frequented by the Bar-tailed Godwits. I have repeatedly observed them, in company with Greenshanks, Redshanks, Dunlins, and Sandpipers, about the pools near Rye, and with Green and Wood-Sandpipers, as well as all the previously mentioned species, in the Norfolk marshes; though resting and feeding amicably together, the partnership invariably dissolved when rising on wing. During the autumn of 1871 and the following year several in immature plumage made their appearance on Breydon, the specimens from which the figures in the Plates were taken being shot on the 31st of August, 1872.

The last Black-tailed Godwits that came under my notice during the autumn migration were a couple of immature birds seen on the 15th of August, 1881, on a rush-grown marsh within a few miles of the sea-coast, and seldom of late years have I met with a chance of closely inspecting such a mixed party of Waders and Wildfowl. Owing to the heavy rain which had fallen incessantly for several days, much water was out on many of the marshes, the land in some instances being entirely submerged with the exception of the banks thrown up along the dykes. Expecting that the floods, as was commonly the case at this season, would have attracted a few fowl, I made my way cautiously in a punt to a spot near which a small party of Teal had been previously observed to settle. After working the bows of the craft carefully into a thick patch of rushes, I crawled forward, and with the help of a powerful pair of glasses at once discovered that my approach had been made without raising the slightest alarm in the assembled multitude. Though a couple of Common Sandpipers rose within three feet of the bows of the boat, they alighted again immediately on a heap of old timber, used to form a bridge when cattle were driven from one marsh to another. A few yards further a flock of Garganey, that must have consisted of at least a couple of broods, were swimming round about the sedges or trampling on the broken rushes where a footing could be obtained, apparently engaged in searching for food. The adjoining patch of flags afforded shelter to some eight or ten Shovellers, squatting lazily among the roots of the plants till roused and put on the alert by the arrival of a "coil" of Common Teal, which swept rapidly round for a couple of turns and then dropped out on the open water. On examining the short grass by the dyke side more closely a Snipe or two and several Dunlins were detected; while on a patch of mud and weed that rose up slightly above the surface of the flood two Black-tailed Godwits, resting contentedly with necks contracted and their heads drawn back, showed up most conspicuously above a swarm of smaller Waders that I was unable at the moment to identify, owing to the spots of drifting rain collecting on the glasses. After watching this animated scene for over an hour, scarcely a bird, with the exception of Snipes, Ring-Dotterel, and a few stray Prewits and Redshanks, having risen on wing or shifted their positions, the assemblage was suddenly broken up with no little uproar by a shot fired at some distance on the uplands. For a few moments the whole marsh appeared alive with wings as one after another the various parties of Wildfowl and Waders rose up, some only to settle again, and others after wheeling in the air for a time to make rapidly off for other quarters. The Black-tailed Godwits surrounded by a swarm of Wood-Sandpipers (identified at last) sprang up and, mute, as usual * at this season, flew steadily off in a line for the coast, the Sandpipers circling round the marshes and drawing up a few Dunlins in pursuit for a time, but eventually rising high in the air and following a course of their own. In the midst of the general outcry the well-known note of the Whimbrel was heard, as three or four couple that had escaped notice among the thick cover on some of the rush-grown banks sprang up and made off direct for the shore; a small party of Reeves as well as two separate pairs of Green Sandpipers were also unobserved till after clearing the reeds and willows. After a few minutes' absence the Wood-Sandpipers, shortly followed by the Reeves, were again circling over the spot from which they rose, darting down with rapid flight, and after hovering for a moment on fluttering and extended wings disappearing into the long grass. The Common Teal and Shovellers had long ago settled on some outlying slades, while the Garganey, having paid not the slightest attention to the uproar, were still slushing in the shallows. Invariably suspicious of danger, and jealous of the slightest intrusion on their haunts, the Green Sandpipers refused to alight for a time, but eventually dropped on a rotten bog in an adjoining marsh.

# BAR-TAILED GODWIT.

## LIMOSA RUFA.

With the exception of the height of summer, when but few stragglers remain in Great Britain, the Bar-tailed Godwit is to be found at all seasons in more or less abundance wherever mudflats or an open coast-line afford a sufficient stretch of uninterrupted feeding-ground. At various times I have met with this species in large numbers on the shores of several of the Scotch firths from Dornoch to Dunbar, again in a few instances on the muds and rocky islands off the coast of Northumberland and on numberless spots on the flat shores of the southern and eastern counties of England. So far as my own experience goes, this Wader is far from common on the coast of the Western Highlands. On one occasion I noticed two or three small parties flying over the Minch in the beginning of May, and a flock numbering from fifteen to twenty on the shores of Loch Broom.

If all the yarns of the old Breydon fowlers are to be credited, these birds must in days gone by have visited the mudflats in that district in countless thousands. An immense body stretching, when alighted, in a long line on the south shores over the space between three of the stakes marking the course of the navigable channel, was a favourite theme of conversation among these worthies. At the present day their numbers have sadly fallen off. I have often spent the whole of May, from daylight almost till dark, on the water without seeing more than two or three hundred pass during the month. Along the shingle-banks of Kent and Sussex, as well as on the Norfolk flats, the arrival of the Godwit was formerly eagerly looked forward to by all the shore-gunners of the locality. The sands stretching from Rye to Lydd, with the well-known Nook and the creeks in Romney Marsh, were the spots on which they usually settled in the largest numbers. Further west the flats of Shoreham, Goring Banks, Pagham Harbour*, and the extensive muds about Bosham, Emsworth, and Chichester were visited in favourable seasons both in spring and autumn.

Though numbers of Godwits remain during winter in Great Britain and are to be met with occasionally in all suitable situations from north to south, the spring flights of birds that have passed the cold weather in a warmer climate commence to arrive on the south coast shortly after the beginning of May. A few days later the flats of the eastern counties are thickly tenanted, should the wind continue easterly. A change of weather and a gale from the west or south-west, however, puts a sudden stop for a time to the migration. With cold cutting breezes from the east or north-east, I have of late years repeatedly seen large flocks of Godwits passing along the Sussex coast near Shoreham, from half to a quarter of a mile at sea. The birds now appear to prefer drawing in beneath the shelter of the shore and continuing their journey further east to settling for a time on the muds they formerly frequented. The flight-time on Breydon usually commences about the 8th or 9th of May, the 12th to the 15th being considered the best days. As on the south coast, light easterly breezes with a slight inclination from either north or south appear the most favourable quarters. With a strong wind from west or south-west during the third week in May I have seen large flocks of Waders flying in rapid succession direct in the face of the gale for several hours; these were probably birds which had previously passed over Breydon flats, and made considerable progress on the passage when the change set in, their line of flight being straight from the open sea. With a continuation of wind from south or west few, if any, of this species will make their appearance along the east coast, the course followed under such circumstances being some miles off the land, the greater portion of the migrants missing our shores entirely*. I have on two or three occasions observed large flocks passing twenty or thirty miles from land; and fishermen, who were old gunners, assured me that they have met with all the various species of Waders in immense flights for several consecutive days outside the Dogger Bank, the quarters usually frequented by these Waders on the east-coast sandbanks being at such times almost completely deserted until a change of wind. On the return journey in the autumn the majority of our visitors are young of the year. Though these birds are occasionally seen at this season in large flocks, the numbers that have come under my observation can by no means compare with the dense masses of Knots repeatedly met with on the shores of the Scotch firths.

At the Little Ferry near Golspie, in Sutherland, I met with immense numbers of Godwits in full winter plumage in March 1869. A short extract from my notes may possibly give some idea of the aspect of the sands at the harbour-mouth on the evening of the 10th of March. It may be as well to state that I had during the day been shooting on the upper waters of this muddy estuary, and consequently driven many Waders and Wildfowl towards the coast. "On reaching the harbour, as there was still another hour of daylight, we dropped down to the bar, and on rounding the point came at once within view of the largest gathering of the feathered tribe I ever witnessed. Several acres of sand and mud as well as the intersecting pools to the west of the channel were densely packed with birds, while above the busy throng hundreds and thousands of Waders in flocks both large and small flew hither and thither, turning and twisting with their well-known velocity, seeking an open space on which to alight. Oyster-Catchers were present in the largest numbers, especially conspicuous owing to their attractive colouring. At no great distance (though each species kept for the most part separate) flocks of Curlew were eagerly exploring the ooze. Godwits, Knots, Grey and Golden Plover, together with countless Dunlins, spread out in all directions over the flats. Gulls by hundreds hovered over the channel or settled on the pools, while Cormorants in small parties were ranged by the water-side. Brent Geese to the number of at least a couple of hundred, with several bunches of Mallard and Wigeon, had dropped in the vicinity of the wash of the tide and plumed their feathers regardless of the noisy multitude. In the centre of the channel a flock of some forty or fifty Long-tailed Ducks, many exhibiting the finest stages of plumage, floated quietly, paddling slowly against the flowing tide. Having sat down for a moment, the punt was worked silently into a small creek, and the movements of the incessantly shifting birds partly watched in hopes some strangers might be detected. At last the gradually increasing gloom of a dull wintry night gave warning that a move must be made, especially as a landing would need to be effected at a point with which we were but little acquainted. On reaching the shore, however, there was not the slightest cause for anxiety. On the punt being sighted through the dusk, here, now dotting inland from the sea, the fishing population of the neighbouring shealings—wives, boys, and lasses—rushed down in a body to the waterside, and seizing hold of the craft dragged it at once out of reach of the swell. The punt with its occupants, as well as the big gun, was next lifted by means of ropes laid on spars, and carried straight off to a shed prepared for our accommodation. A small gratuity handed over the previous evening to such of the natives as had rendered assistance had

Before leaving this locality, as some Fowl and Waders were required to distribute among the people, I availed myself of a few of the chances offered, without, however, meeting with any great success. At the first discharge an excellent opportunity for heavy slaughter was lost, fifty-two Godwits only and a couple of Knots being obtained. The combined flocks were sweeping rapidly down the flats, following the course of a winding channel in which the punt was stationed, and on approaching within the distance of eighty yards the whole body in an instant turned off to the right and swept across the mudbanks, a small portion only of the immense flight being exposed to a hasty cross shot. On another occasion twenty-four Godwits and seventy Knots were gathered: this was a second failure, the tide rising so rapidly that large numbers of cripples were swept from the shore by the rush of water before those nearest at hand were collected.*

In addition to the Godwits met with at the Little Ferry, I have also seen this species in winter on the shores of the Firth of Forth between Gullane Bay and North Berwick. A few small parties were noticed in the marshes in the neighbourhood of Salthouse and Cley in Norfolk, in January 1872. Breydon flats would doubtless be resorted to all through the season, were the birds allowed but a short cessation of hostilities. All round the south coast Godwits appear annually during severe weather on the mudflats and occasionally on the marshes. It is seldom this species is met with on grass-lands; the frosts and snows of January 1867, however, brought several scattered parties to Pevensey Level. I noticed these Waders eagerly searching for food among the patches of green rushes in a marsh where the ground was free from snow.

To give all the extracts from my notes referring to the presence of the Bar-tailed Godwit during spring and autumn is useless. At such seasons this species, as previously stated, is by no means uncommon on all suitable parts of the southern and eastern counties. The flocks migrating towards their breeding-haunts appear, according to my own experience, for the most part to strike across the North Sea before reaching the Scotch coast. A few stragglers at times remain on our shores in summer; these birds, however, at this season seldom show the perfect breeding-plumage. I noticed a small party in company with Knots on the sands in Edderton Bay, in the Dornoch Firth, at the end of June and beginning of July 1868.

The young on their first arrival in autumn are exceedingly fearless. Like the majority of the Fowl and Waders reared in the deserted regions of the far north, these birds appear, unfortunately for their own safety, to be totally unacquainted with the destructive propensities of human nature.

Though I am unable to speak from personal experience, the edible qualities of the Godwit are evidently held in but slight estimation. On the counter of the game-dealer this species is seldom, if ever, seen, though hundreds recently killed are now and then exhibited on the stalls in the markets. During severe weather they are also hawked about the streets by itinerant traders, who bestow various high-sounding titles on their wares in order to tempt unsuspecting customers.

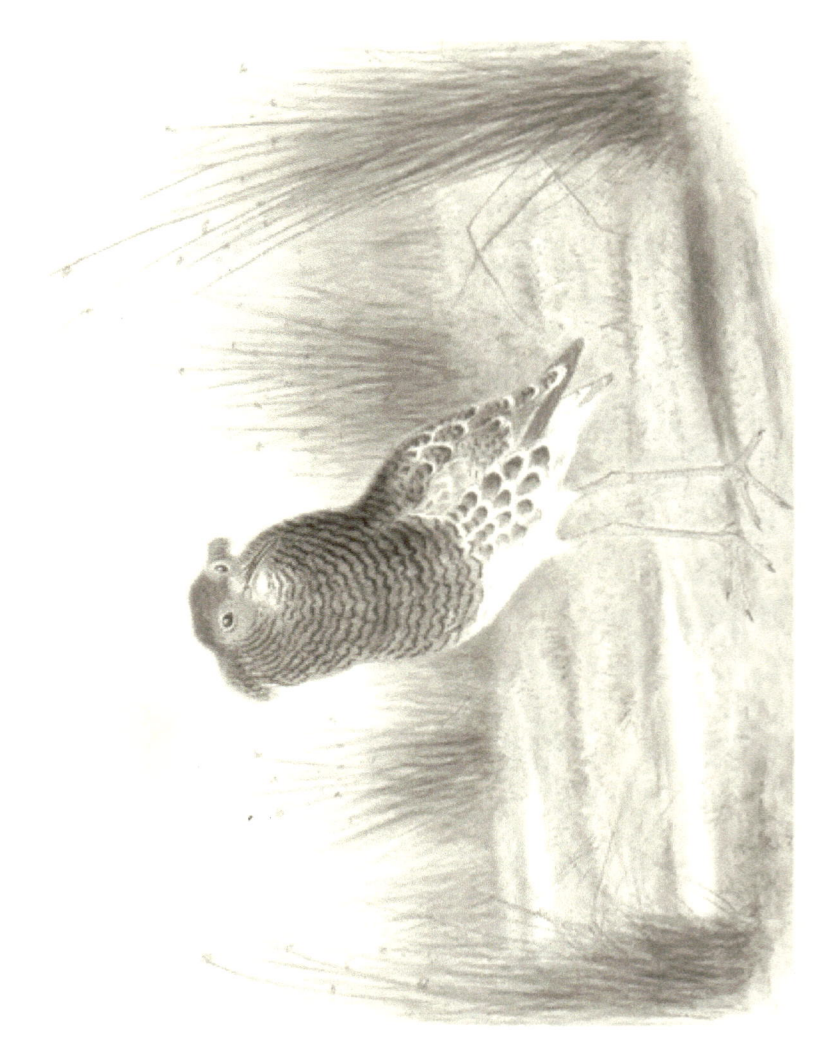

# RUFF.

## *MACHETES PUGNAX.*

---

There is no denying the fact that it was at first a difficulty to decide as to the scientific name of this species; having, however, considered the observations taken while watching their habits for several years, I quite agree with the remarks in the first paragraph in the fourth edition of Yarrell, which is as follows:—" The Ruff differs in so many points from the species included in the genera *Totanus*, *Scolopax*, and *Tringa*, that the generic division and term *Machetes*\*, in reference to its pugnacious habits, proposed for it by Cuvier, has been admitted by the majority of systematic writers."

During the last thirty years this singular bird has greatly decreased in numbers throughout the British Islands; though several make their appearance every spring in the eastern counties, there are at the present time but two or three localities where they remain to rear their young, if they are not molested. The swamps and marshes formerly frequented by them having been so reduced by the improved system of drainage, few spots suitable to their requirements are left; added to which the demand for their eggs and the general persecution to which they are exposed have rendered it almost impossible for the residents to resort to their old haunts during spring and summer. When I first visited Hickling Broad, on the east of Norfolk, in May 1870, there were several Ruffs and Reeves on the hills; the Redshanks and Peewits, however, by dashing down and screaming, disturbed them whenever an attempt was made to get within range.

On the 2nd of June we started in the boats from Heigham Bridge an hour before midnight, in order to reach the Broad by daybreak; unfortunately, however, the Ruffs and Reeves were put on the alert by the same two species. These noisy pests (too numerous to be shot down) continued flying round, giving notice of our approach, when the whole flock of birds we were in quest of were either fighting or feeding on a low part of the marsh, and quite unable to discern the punt, from the height of the bank and the patches of reeds and rushes surrounding the hill.

To pass the time while making our way I, rolled up in a couple of warm rugs and pushing my head into some soft cushions just under the fore deck, dropped off to sleep. While quanting slowly over the deep water in the channel over Heigham Sounds, after having left the river, the man who was working my punt roused me up quietly and drew my attention to one of those curious lights known in some parts as "Jack-o'-Lanterns," and in others as "Will-o'-the-Wisps" †. This luminous mystery was first observed on the small island called Mid-Sound Bush, and continued flickering about among the reeds and water-plants for a minute or two. It next hovered further into the dense cover extending towards the Heigham marshes, and was finally lost sight of among the high reeds that flourish here, the light becoming gradually more indistinct. Perhaps this singular illusion remained in view a little over five minutes; the night, however, being dark, I could not take the time by my watch. These lights are not now so often seen in this part of the country as in days gone by, the reclaiming of the marshes having rendered the ground too dry. At one time they were said to hover

\* Pugnator. † Ignis fatuus.

about in the ditches round the churchyard at Potter Heigham and the adjoining marshes, where stagnant pools were to be found. Under the name of "Jack-o'-Lanterns," these extraordinary visions were reported to be still common in many parts of the low-lying flats of Kent and Sussex, where reeds and rushes have flourished for many years. The decomposition of the roots and stalks of the water-plants is supposed to account for the fantastic vapour that flitters about and often puzzles the natives of marshy districts.

Many years ago I remember the gamekeepers and lookers over the marshes in Pevensey Level, to which our shooting extended when living at Catsfield in the east of Sussex, relating wonderful stories about these mysterious vapours. "The Jack-o'-Lanterns," as they were called in this district, were reported to be frequently seen about some of the slades and shallow pools in soft parts of the marshes in the Level, and also at two or three of the pells* near the river and adjoining the shingle-banks.

A few of these flickering lights were also stated to have been recognized hovering around the moist spots and the pools near the banks of a nice little trout-stream that bordered a large stretch of land covered with furze bushes, known as the "horthy" field, and affording cover for immense numbers of rabbits. This wild and uncultivated extent of useless ground has now undergone a great transformation. I also ascertained that a bright, luminous, flickering light was exhibited by fresh-caught whiting, when cut up for feeding our captive Gannets and Guillemots; this we learned at a small village in Canty Bay, while providing for the young birds brought from the Bass Rock and reared in the boat-sheds; when our charges were visited after dark, their stock of provisions attracted attention as soon as the door of the shed was opened. The rays of the glittering shine that casts such a lustre around the herrings used as bait for the traps that protect the nests and eggs we wish to preserve from the depredations of any predacious vermin are very attractive.

On the 20th of June four very handsome glossy eggs were taken off Rush Hills, and these are the clutch depicted in the Plate. The eggs of another nest were removed a week later from the same piece of ground, as there was but little doubt they would have been taken on such an exposed spot. These I placed in the nest of a Partridge well concealed in long grass, on a marsh in a quiet part that was seldom visited, in hopes the young birds might be hatched. The old bird performed her duties well, sitting closely, and the downy juveniles would soon have been out, when a donkey, turned out to pick up his living on the marsh, trampled on the nest and broke most of the eggs. The Reeve belonging to the last-mentioned nest was shot and sent to be preserved, as I imagined it was too late in the season to expect her to lay again.

There is an entry in my notes for 1871, while again at Potter Heigham and watching Hickling Broad, that the first arrival occurred on the 14th of April. On the 17th, the weather cold and stormy, I was out on the Broad in the punt, and while carefully inspecting the most likely parts of Selsmouth, in order to ascertain if any Ruffs were about, a flock of nearly one hundred came rapidly in sight, making straight towards the hill, on which they alighted after sweeping round two or three times. Ruffs and Reeves were in about equal numbers, and sending the punt up under the shelter of the bank, I had a capital chance of examining them through the glasses, as they were not fifty yards from where my punt was brought up. There were Ruffs of all colours, but none had above half assumed the full plumage; and as I only expect to find a perfect plumage, I thought that it left no doubt that they would remain on these hills round the Broad and increase in numbers in appearance. This I discovered to be a mistake, as all but the large flocks only stopped a few days while on their way to more northern breeding-stations, and then took their departure. The few that remained in the district with the Reeves were not seen till later on in the season, and came singly or in very small parties of two or three. On the 12th of April I found the Ruffs on Rush Hills, and there under a were congregated by about a score that were passing over, which, being disturbed by the noise on the hill, darted down and settled close at hand. There was one Ruff with a white neck and black tail that looked very peculiar, and this bird I intended to shoot, but unfortunately he got into the midst of the others, and I was not able to fire at it on him again.

* The Sussex name for the small pools to which a little salt water penetrates.

Down at Hickling Broad before daylight on the 27th, and a man at work on the north side of the water informed us that two Ruffs and a Reeve had just pitched on Rush Hills. We sculled all round the hill, but were unable to catch sight of them; then turning the punt we prepared to cross to Swimcoots, when a Ruff passed and alighted near the point of Rush Hills which we had just left. It would have been easy to get within twenty yards, as he had dropped down among some small patches of rushes, but three Swans swimming ahead of our boat alarmed him, and rising on wing he flew about a hundred yards farther along the side of the hill. As he did not, however, seem to be out of range from the water, we made another attempt, and sculling in as close as possible, I stood up and cautiously inspected the ground beyond the bank. The bird was standing quietly on the look-out at ... of about fifty yards, and as he sprung from the ground I fired, when his wing was broken, and ... to the ... of thick cover on this part of the hill. ... the ruff being of a dark red tint ... the ... of a cock Pheasant. As this ... handsomest specimen I ... in one of the ...

... Ruff that was feeding on the side of the ... the following ... a ... shot in Bessie's drain. ... out, and a ... Reeve settled down ... and a ... they took their departure. ... were ... bird, ... the neck and breast.

... ice *. Nud (the Hickling ... but was of opinion that this species is only to be observed in this ... I am aware it is unusual to find them during winter; they do, ... in an appearance, as when shooting on Pevensey Level in December, 1859, two were obtained a ... the end of the month. Immense numbers of Wildfowl were then in that district, and in most instances fell easy victims, being weakened and worn out by exposure to the long-continued severity of the weather.

While working at our boat-house in the Heigham corner of Hickling Broad on the 18th of October, 1881, I noticed a Ruff and a couple of Peewits circle round and settle down on the south point of Swimcoots: the big gun was not on board, so the large punt worked easily and I sculled rapidly across; luckily the birds proved utterly unsuspicious of danger, and the three were turned over by the two barrels of my 10-bore breechloader. The Ruff weighed 8 oz., and exhibited the usual brown mottled plumage of autumn: the upper mandible was almost black, the lower a flesh tint near the base and pale horn at the point, the legs a light olive-brown, with a yellow tinge about the joints and on the toes. For the next few days there were numbers of Ruffs and Reeves about Rush Hills, and several were obtained, all being easily approached when feeding on the slades within reach of the water, where the punt could be worked. This species usually holds a great reputation for the table, and these proved quite equal, if not superior, to Snipes and Plovers.

While shooting on Breydon on the 28th of August, 1872, I noticed a Ruff feeding on the flats near the Lower Drain with a flock of Dunlins. They proved restless, and would not allow the punt within distance; later in the day, however, they flew past within thirty yards, when the Ruff fell to the shoulder-gun together with over a score of his small companions. He turned out to be an exceedingly large specimen, of course now in his autumn plumage.

On the 3rd of September, after the dummies had been put out on the Lumps, a Reeve was attracted and

* The natives of the east of Norfolk thus speak of the Broad when it is frozen over.

settled down; after remaining some time she was easily approached and obtained. Shortly after a Ruff that had joined a large flock of Knots was killed by a shot from the punt-gun, as they were on the point of alighting to the dummies. The unfortunate Knots suffered considerably, as over thirty were picked up, having fallen among the decoys. The last Ruff that I observed this season was a single bird with a flock of about a dozen Golden Plover on the 6th of September. Attracted by the dummies, they flew across the bows of the punt at a reasonable distance, and the big gun was discharged; eight of the Plovers dropped at once, but the Ruff continued his course as if uninjured, though he seemed to flinch when the shot was fired. While proceeding to pick up the slain, I heard one of the men exclaim "He's down." On producing the glasses a speck was seen on the water, and one of the punts being despatched towards the spot, the bird was discovered and brought back.

There was a great falling-off this year in the numbers of Ruffs and Reeves; I did not observe above a dozen all through August and September. The season before, hundreds frequented the flats early in September, and they continued to arrive till the 25th of the month, when I fell in with and shot the last straggler. Over a hundred and fifty were obtained with the assistance of the punt- and shoulder-guns; the greater number, however, were killed while firing at other Waders.

I have ascertained, by examining my notes, that on the 30th of June, heavy rain having fallen during the night, and squalls of wind continued from the north and east, there were in the morning numerous flocks of Waders on the marshes round Hickling Broad. About twenty Ruffs and Reeves and as many Wood-Sandpipers were on Rush Hills, and several Curlew and flocks of Dunlins appeared on wing as soon as I fired a shot. A dozen Reeves and two Wood-Sandpipers were picked up, several that were wounded escaping into the thick cover about the swamps, where it was impossible to follow them over the waving bogs. After this the birds became remarkably wild: in the afternoon the Ruffs had disappeared, and the Wood-Sandpipers were scattered in small parties of two or three, or perhaps double that number, over the slades on the different hills and marshes.

There is no further reference to Ruffs in my notes till after ten years, when I again happened to be at Potter Heigham in April 1883. On reaching the Broad at daybreak on the 26th, the wind blowing strong from the south-east, I put up two Ruffs on Rush Hills, but unfortunately they rose out of range and made off at once towards the east; there were also eight Wigeon, a pair of Garganey, and a single Teal on the various slades on the hill. The wind was still from the same quarter the following morning, and two Ruffs and a Reeve were moving about and feeding on the centre of Rush Hills; one of the males showed a brown frill, and the other was sandy-coloured, but neither was quite perfect. It was impossible to get within shot of either punt- or shoulder-gun, so in order to put them up, in hopes they might pass at a moderate distance, we despatched one of the boats to go round and attempt to drive them in a line for the position we had taken up. A Ruff, entirely black, which had escaped notice behind a patch of rushes, was the first to start, and he instantly joined the others when they rose on wing. After circling round for a few minutes, they all made off, head to wind, and were not seen again that day.

On Saturday the 28th, the wind had veered more to the east; on our way down to the Broad, the Grasshopper-Warbler was heard for the first time that season. The party of Ruffs seen the previous day were now on Swimcoats, but proved exceedingly wild, and there was not a chance to get within range for a shot. They were evidently only on their way to "lands ayont the sea"*, as they were gone the next day. Rain fell

---

\* In 'The Moor and the Loch' (by J. Colquhoun, 1840) we find :—

"Dk does't that blooms on foreign fell
Wad mind me o' the heather-bell;
Ilk little streamlet's jouk and turn
Wad mind me o' Glenautrek burn;
Lands may be fair ayont the sea,
But Blackwood hills and lochs for me!"

on Monday the 30th, with wind from the north-east. There were five Ruffs and three Reeves on Rush Hills, but all wild and keeping a good look-out in case of an approach, and rising on wing on the first signs of danger. I watched them through the glasses running at one another and jumping up, but no real fighting could be seen; the females were standing together at a short distance, looking on quietly. There was one solitary female standing on another part of the hill, that had a nest among some low tufts of grass. On the following day, May 1st, I only saw one Ruff, and he was probably in attendance on the female with the nest. Other Ruffs, which were evidently on the passage to the north, were seen on the 4th, but only two resident on the 5th, and on the 9th he was again sighted. After this the nest was robbed, and then the birds took their departure. On the 18th a flock of fifteen Reeves was seen on Rush Hills, and they remained in the district till the 21st, when I observed them for the last time, feeding on Swimcoats.

While staying in Norfolk, I frequently remarked that on the first arrival of these birds, about the second week in April, the long feathers forming the frill round the neck of the male had scarcely attained half their length. In those days they were to be seen in flocks of from ten or twenty to five or six times that number. On two or three occasions, on the hills around the Broads, I have been enabled to watch these large gatherings at close quarters, and have met with good opportunities for observing their actions while fighting and feeding. Their battles, however, appear to be soon over; a couple of Ruffs square up to one another for a moment or two, and then separate to feed or again go through the same performance with their nearest neighbour. Though occasionally jumping and striking after the manner of a gamecock, I never noticed any of the combatants receive the slightest injury. A large flock of Ruffs and Reeves is a most curious sight, the various-coloured plumages of the males, as they run here and there, giving a strange appearance to the whole assemblage.

# WOODCOCK.
## *SCOLOPAX RUSTICULA.*

From personal observation I am enabled to state that so far back as 1850 Woodcocks nested plentifully in the east of Sussex; in my birds'-nesting days they were frequently met with during spring in the neighbourhood of Catsfield and Ashburnham. Though the eggs, as a rule, were respected, several clutches came into my possession owing to the nests having been placed in coverts or shaws *, in which the undergrowth was then being cut down in the regular course for hop-poles. In consequence of the continued interruption, the birds were invariably driven from the spot on the approach of the woodmen; four clutches of eggs, I well remember, were detected in one covert as the ground was gradually cleared.

From north to south Woodcocks commence to breed at an early date; I have noticed young birds full-fledged, both in Sussex and Perthshire, by the end of May. In some localities it is probable that a second brood is reared: the eggs figured in the Plate were taken, when fresh, on the 9th of June, 1869, in the east of Ross-shire, and the following year a female was seen sitting on the 12th of August near Dingwall. Many writers have spoken of the nest of the Woodcock; I have, however, failed to detect, in any single instance, more than a slight depression among the dead leaves on which the eggs were laid.

It is doubtless a mistaken idea that only of late years have Woodcocks nested in Great Britain in any numbers: the larger area devoted to plantation has doubtless induced them to extend their range during summer; but from all I have been able to learn, while discussing the subject with keepers and foresters in various parts of the country, the birds were simply overlooked—it was supposed they left the country, and there was no disputing the general opinion. In many parts of England Woodcocks were regularly shot at flight-time during the evening twilight in early spring; wherever this senseless destruction was permitted it is probable the breeding-stock was much reduced.

The first or second week in October is considered to be the usual date for the earlier flights of Cocks to make their appearance along our north-eastern coasts; in the more southern counties it is, as a rule, some weeks later before any number are met with. The question as to what becomes of the home-bred birds appears to have puzzled sportsmen in many parts of the country; early in September I have remarked, in several localities, that not a single Cock could be flushed in the coverts where numerous broods had been reared during the summer months. Though nearly a month in advance of the usual time of arrival, there was undoubted evidence in 1869 that a flight had reached the shores of Ross and Cromarty during the third week in September, several being noticed shortly after daybreak in the vicinity of the coast, apparently fatigued by a protracted flight.

While conversing with the crews of the light-ships off the east coast with reference to the number of Woodcocks striking the lights, I learned that the quantities falling on board the vessels varied considerably. Not a single bird, however, was obtained during the winter of 1872 and the following spring at any of

* A long narrow plantation is usually known in East Sussex by this name.

the stations with which I was in correspondence. Woodcocks, I ascertained, were considered by the men particularly swift-flying birds, being frequently picked up on deck much cut and injured by striking against the lamps or rigging. The real cause of such mishaps must, I should imagine, be attributed to the weighty condition of the birds at the time of the accident. I am aware that there are statements to the effect that Woodcocks usually arrive singly or in small parties; flocks have, however, been recorded as seen approaching the land. While steaming out through the Cockle gat towards the open sea one cold November morning in 1870, just as day was breaking, a flock of at least forty hovered for a few moments round the vessel, and then heading towards the land disappeared in the gloom; unfortunately the guns were covered at the time, in order to avoid the effects of salt air and damp, or several couple might have been obtained.

It is seldom that this species or Snipe recover sufficiently from the effects of a shot to rise on wing after having been once knocked down; a somewhat singular instance, however, of a Woodcock flying off after falling apparently dead occurred some years back at Catsfield, in East Sussex. The beaters had almost completed a drive through a portion of a large covert when a Cock, flushed near the boundary, attempted to cross an open stubble, on which I had been posted, towards another angle of the wood\*. The bird presented the easiest possible shot, and dropped, apparently as dead as a stone, on the open ground at the distance of about five and thirty yards; while opening the breech to insert another cartridge, my attention was attracted by an exclamation from an attendant, and on looking up the Cock was again on wing and little the worse for the mishap, continuing the course previously held towards the wood. A second time the bird was fairly hit and, several feathers being left floating downward in the air, pitched headlong into a thorn bush at the edge of the covert. Before entirely disappearing from view it again (as far as we were able to judge) recovered, and after a momentary scuffle among the twigs and brambles twisted off through an opening between the branches of two large oaks and was speedily lost to sight. As the beat was just concluded, both shots had been distinctly seen by a couple of keepers, who the entire up remarking they had never witnessed the like before. Perfectly convinced that the Cock had evidently escaped, or proceeded at once to take up stations for the next drive, when on passing the bush into which the second descent had been made, a slight movement among some dead ferns was observed, and on the spot being examined the bird was discovered in the last gasp in a dense tangle of brambles and rank herbage. There could not be the slightest doubt from the actions of the Cock flushed at this spot that it had been struck by the falling bird the moment after rising from the ground, causing the singular fluster observed, and leading to the belief that our old friend was perfectly invulnerable and had again succeeded in making off.

As the notes in these pages relate simply to my own observations, I am unable to record any bags of Woodcocks that can compare with the long lists mentioned by various writers. A few lines, however, extracted from my journals concerning the sport obtained on two occasions may not be out of place, as certain facts relating to the birds are briefly referred to; though the lists of slain are exceedingly short, the most captious critic could scarcely complain of waste of ammunition.

During the continuation of the severe snow-storm in January 1867, I bagged in Pevensey Level, in a couple of hours' shooting (the train had been snowed up and caused a delay in reaching the ground), two couple of Cocks, four couple of Snipe, two brace of Partridges, and four hares: twenty cartridges expended. The whole of the marshes were deeply covered with snow and the travelling exceedingly heavy; the first couple of Cocks were flushed from the railway-hedge while crossing the line, and the second from a patch of rushes which grew on the open level a mile further inland. Just before dark I marked a flock of six or seven alight near a few stunted thorn bushes; but having to make a considerable circuit in order to avoid a dyke, darkness would have set in before the spot could possibly have been reached. Though the snow was deep and drifted in patches, the frost was not excessively severe, and a few spots being still open in the slades

---

\* A grass field surrounded on three sides by the wood, my station being near one of the corners.

and about ............... the 15th of September, 1869, during ............... of the ............... swarming in the ............... within a short distance of the firth.

An impression formerly existed that Woodcocks transported their unfledged young from one spot to another by lifting them in their beaks; this idea has long since been proved a fallacy, and of late years several writers, whose descriptions, however, differ considerably, have given their observations concerning this singular operation. So many sportsmen and naturalists have recorded their opinions on this subject with such assurance, that it is some slight consolation to learn that I am not the first observer who has failed to thoroughly comprehend this remarkable performance. The following occurs in Thompson's 'Natural History of Ireland,' "Birds," vol. ii. p. 253; after giving a considerable amount of information gained from the keeper at Tollymore Park, county Down, the author proceeds to state, with reference to this man :—" The keeper believed himself, to have witnessed the old hen carrying off her young when suddenly disturbed. Under the impression of his having been deceived in this matter, he several times followed hens apparently thus burthened to where they alighted, and saw them run off without any young birds being there. It is, he says, 'the body behind the wings, the tail, legs, and feathers of the belly, that she droops down in a peculiar manner, that gives the appearance of a young bird being clutched up.' He has several times been quite near to birds presenting the appearance here described." My own experience on one occasion in Ross-shire, in June 1869, was almost identical. A Woodcock, whose singular flight attracted attention, leading to the belief that she carried a young one, was marked down, and on reaching the spot a few moments later no signs of the juvenile could be discovered; well knowing it was quite possible that a young Woodcock might escape detection by human eyes, a retriever accustomed to search out downy nestlings was worked over the ground, but without success.

In Sussex, Perthshire, and Ross-shire I have had many opportunities of watching the curious evening flight of the old birds; in the two latter counties also the fact that the young were lifted and borne off on wing appeared on several occasions unquestionable. Being forced, however, to confess that I am unable to speak with certainty as to the manner in which the juvenile is grasped, the result of my observations (considering the time and labour expended) is far from satisfactory.

In a wooded ravine on the hill of Tarlogie, near Tain, a Woodcock (as far as I was able to judge) was twice seen in the act of conveying its young. The following extracts from my notes of June 1869 may afford some explanation as to the difficulty of ascertaining accurately the manner in which the young one is carried or (as some observers are inclined to believe) whether the whole idea does not arise from misapprehension caused by the excited actions of the bird while endeavouring to draw the attention of intruders from its brood.

While descending the hill towards the coast late one evening, after a hot and sultry day, our course lay through a thicket of birch, fir, and alder; though the timber was by no means lofty, the cover was dense, a deep shade being thrown into the gully. This sloping hill-side was admirably adapted for affording concealment to young birds—tufts of coarse grass sprung up on all sides, while here and there dead leaves were blown together in masses among the twining plants and brambles; a few patches of green moss also showed conspicuously in the course of a tiny streamlet, down which moisture drained from above. Having paused for a few moments to listen to the jarring of the countless Night-Hawks just commencing their evening concert, a retriever, hitherto following closely at heel, drew slowly ahead, and, watching her actions, I became aware that game of some sort was before us. The ground immediately in front dropped abruptly for ten or twelve feet—so steep, in fact, was the fall, that it was necessary to make a circuit to avoid the declivity. From below this rough and overhanging bank a Woodcock, apparently retarded by the weight of its offspring, rose on wing, displaying at first an unsteady and wavering flight, but gaining increased speed after a few flaps, was soon lost sight of behind the foliage of a spreading birch. The light was far from good and the view obtained, looking down on the bird from above, much against forming an accurate opinion as to the manner in which a young one, of which a mere glimpse could be caught, was conveyed. In order to ascertain if other juveniles were in the vicinity, the retriever was hunted over the ground and at once picked up a downy and querulous youngster, bearing a strong resemblance to a newly hatched Curlew, which she presented with the greatest care. No further captures were effected, and shortly after an old bird appeared on the scene flapping round for several minutes and eventually settling at a short distance. The youngster was then placed on an open spot where his cries might be heard, and retiring into the cover, I watched for some time, in the hopes of seeing him carried off. Though several Woodcocks were observed on wing, none approached or alighted near at hand, and the darkness increasing I was at length forced to make my way homewards. Being anxious to gain further information on the subject, I again visited the wood towards evening a few days after in company with a couple of keepers. The whole of the ground on which the birds were previously met with was explored without success; then, as a last resource, having taken up a position on a lower slope, the men were despatched to beat crossways through a portion of the wood and work gradually down the hill. At last, when within a couple of hundred yards of my station, a shout gave warning that a Cock was astir; a moment later the bird skimmed past an opening in the cover, flying low and apparently bearing a youngster pressed closely to the underparts.

The manner in which the young one was carried seemed to differ considerably on these two occasions; light and the shadows thrown by the foliage as well as the directions taken by the birds, however, combined to frustrate all attempts to obtain a satisfactory insight into the proceedings. Were I to express an opinion as to the manner in which this singular operation is performed (judging from the observations recorded above) it would be that the young one is grasped on rising by the feet of the old bird, which necessarily droop in the first instance; when well on wing the tarsi are raised, bringing the weight nearer to the body and enabling the bearer to hold a steadier course.

A keeper who had been many years at Achany, near Lairg, in Sutherland, assured me that in the woods between Loch Shin and the Kyle he had, on more than one occasion, distinctly seen a Woodcock hover over her young one, and after clutching it between the legs rise on wing and make off for other quarters, his description corresponding in every respect with some of the latest published accounts. Other evidence tending to prove this habit has been received from various quarters in the north; I have, however, met with two or three sportsmen, natives of the Highlands, and careful observers of nature, who utterly discredit the idea, contending that the singular appearance of the female while rising from the ground is merely caused by the movements of the tail and legs, the feathers also at the same time being puffed out through fear or anger.

The arguments advanced by some writers, in order to prove the necessity of this habit of transporting the young, scarcely hold good; it has been stated that the brood are commonly hatched in "dry heathery woods," where they would inevitably perish unless carried to more favourable feeding-ground. The driest of coverts in which this species nests, as far as I have been able to ascertain, contain spots where, in ordinary seasons, ample food might be obtained for the juveniles within the distance of a few hundred yards. It is undoubtedly during the hours of night and early dawn, when the dew is on the ground, that the Woodcock proceeds in quest of prey; worms and insects invisible by day are then obtainable in profusion.

In the summer of 1868 the weather in June and July was exceedingly hot in the north of Scotland, and in more than one locality I learned that broods of young Woodcocks had been found dead, owing (in the opinion of the keepers) to the long-continued drought. In two or three instances I examined the unfortunates, but decomposition having set in, the cause of death remained undiscovered; there could be little doubt, however, that the want of rain and the tropical heat of the midday sun had dried up all their haunts. During the whole of that season I was engaged in making observations on the habits of this species, and on one occasion, while discussing the matter with a forester who had met with many opportunities for watching the birds, the man remarked, "If the Cocks can move their young, as you declare, why do they allow them to die in the woods when the flats on the low ground are still moist?"

The plumage of the Woodcock differs considerably with the seasons, the colouring being more varied in summer, a warm red-brown intermixed here and there with a cream tint taking the place of the dull brown and grey exhibited in winter. A lengthened description of the plumage, however, is needless, as the figures in the Plates were taken from specimens procured at each season.

In Plate I. a female shot on the 9th of June 1869, near Tain, is represented with her three eggs. The male was closely examined both on wing and when motionless at a few yards distance, and his plumage having been ascertained to resemble that of his mate in every particular, further slaughter was unnecessary. The female proved exceedingly tame—several times I had passed her within a few yards, and when at last approaching in order to obtain a shot, it was not till a keeper had placed his hand below her that she could be induced to rise on wing. From notes taken on several occasions, I am inclined to believe that the second laying rarely consists of more than three eggs.

A couple of Woodcocks obtained in Glenlyon, in the west of Perthshire, in November 1867, are depicted in Plate II. Having frequently examined fresh-killed specimens at this season, I am of opinion that there is little difference in the plumage of males and females.

# SNIPE.

## *SCOLOPAX GALLINAGO.*

---

THE Snipe is a resident in Great Britain, breeding wherever suitable localities are met with from north to south. Its numbers are also considerably increased in autumn by arrivals from across the North Sea.

In the Highlands these birds nest out on the moist portions of the open moors, as well as on the swamps round the lochs or along the river-sides. Occasionally I have seen the young in low-lying hay-fields\*, and in the east of Ross-shire several pairs resorted to the neighbourhood of the pools on the flat sandy waste near Tain, known as the "Fendom." The patches of rough grass and the dense cover about the fens and broads of the eastern counties afford in most instances a secure retreat; the birds, however, that attempt to rear their young on the more exposed marshlands on which the Peewit and Redshank annually take up their quarters are not unfrequently robbed of their eggs. A few Snipe still breed on the bogs adjoining the springs or streams in some of the large Sussex forests of beech and birch; in the same county a nest or two are also occasionally to be found in the water-meadows bordering the course of the sluggish rivers making their way towards the shores of the Channel.

It is probable that in some districts, if unmolested, two broods are reared during the season. On the Fendom, near Tain, I have seen young birds, apparently five or six days old, as early as the 10th of April, and a brood was hatched out the same year (1869) on the 9th of July on the marshy ground to the east of Loch Doula, near Lairg; it was unlikely that, in such a remote locality, the birds had suffered from interference. In the south of Scotland, Norfolk, or Sussex it is seldom, according to my own experience, that Snipe commence to lay before the second week in April; as a rule, I should think that but one brood is brought out in these parts, the late nests occasionally met with having resulted from the first set of eggs being taken †.

The very unpleasant, not to say dangerous, nature of the ground over which the sport has to be followed in many districts is a great drawback to the enjoyment of Snipe-shooting. The uncertain footing and the possibility that the next step may precipitate one up to the neck into some rotten hole is by no means conducive to steadiness of aim ‡. Considerable experience is needed to step with safety and ………………………… bog or floating hovers to be met with about many of the Norfolk ……… a few seconds on the green roots of the water-plants that alone sustain

---

\* It frequently happens in the remote Highland glens that no attempt is made to cut the hay till the first or second week in September; ample time is consequently afforded for the latest birds to get strong on wing before their haunts are invaded.

† On the 20th of July, 1871, I put a Snipe from eggs on a marsh in the east of Norfolk; the ground, however, had been repeatedly scratched over by egg-stealers, as well as hunted by Buzzards (Marsh-Harriers).

‡ On one of the very last roots of the reeds round Heigham Sounds, in Norfolk, there were several holes from which a strong …………………

one's weight will invariably lead to the thin covering above the swamp giving way. If held fast at each footstep in the soft clinging soil, such as is commonly found on a marsh where cattle and horses have fed during summer, almost every shot will be lost unless the bird flies straight or veers towards the left, a sharp twist to the right usually resulting in a clean miss, unless the sportsman is capable of firing with equal precision from either shoulder. Many a doleful tale might the conscientious gunner (if so inclined) unfold concerning his first exploits on such ground, the attempt to swing one's self round towards the right not unfrequently being followed by a sprawl in the marsh, with one of the long boots left firmly fixed in the mud.

I have met with few localities where Snipe-shooting with a fair chance of success could be followed with such ease and comfort as in the fens of Bottisham, Qui, and Swaffham, situated some eight or nine miles from Cambridge. Doubtless many changes have taken place in the nature of this flat and dreary country, my acquaintance with the district having terminated on leaving the University. On certain portions of the ground termed poor-lands the natives exercised the right of cutting turf for firing. The way in which this operation was carried out differed somewhat from the manner in which the Highlander casts his peats: the turf was dug out from numbers of small oblong cuttings and afterwards dried and stacked by the side of the gap from which it was taken; towards autumn the moisture drained into the cutting (leaving the fen dry and firm for walking) and a pool of black peaty water was formed. Here Snipe were to be found as soon as flights arrived in the district, the birds for the most part lying well. The stacks of peat scattered over the fen proved also a most convenient means of concealment when stalking the small bunches of Mallard or Teal frequently dropping about the pools or dykes on the approach of winter. Though this had been, according to the yarns of the old fenmen, a great locality for Snipe in days gone by, the bags were now exceedingly light, seven couple being the heaviest I ever secured. A hare or two of Partridges, now and then a hare, a couple of Mallard or Teal, together with the three or four couple of Snipe usually obtained afforded, however, in my humble estimation, a fair day's sport; the chance of falling in with, and occasionally bagging, a Quail was also a never-failing attraction to the spot. To Wicken Fen, near Ely, formerly a well-known resort for Snipe as well as many rarities, I made several excursions during summer, autumn, and winter: though the ground had lately undergone much alteration, there still remained a considerable stretch of marshland with waving bogs and large reed-beds, somewhat resembling the country surrounding the Norfolk broads. A strong jumping-pole armed with a round clog of wood near the foot, to guard against sticking too firmly in the mud, was always a necessity in these fens, in order to cross the broad water-dykes intersecting the ground in every direction.

To an undergraduate with a strong predilection for the gun, the proximity of the various fens and rough marshlands was a temptation scarcely to be resisted. The pursuit of the longbills, however, for several consecutive days in the week during term-time, and consequent absence from lectures, coupled with a "scratch" for more than one examination, raised at length the long-cherished wrath of the authorities. It became obvious at length, in order to avoid unpleasantness, that a change of scene was necessary, and my departure from the classic shades of Alma Mater was regarded with equal satisfaction by all parties concerned. "Before ten years have passed you will repent the time wasted while up at the University." These were the parting words of my College tutor, uttered in his most solemn and impressive tones. In one sense, though certainly not in the one intended by the worthy man, his words have been fulfilled. More than twice ten years have passed rapidly away, and my sole regret at the present moment is, that the whole and not three fourths of my time had not been spent in the fens. After quitting the University I speedily discovered that the study of agriculture in East Lothian was far more to my taste than reading for a degree. As "a mud"* in the south of

---

* Those who visited the district in order to gain an insight into the knowledge of agriculture were known among the natives as "mud students" or more euphoniously "muds."

so aged. I spent..... with excellent chances of making further observations in the ground of a numerous ........ species of Widgeon and Scaup ........ A large party of Snipe tended to feed on liedge overhung by the low green cover growing thickly on the ...... ly portion of the ........ Numbers ..... occasionally flushed about the open burns and pools among the sand-banks, the small ...... of water that escaped from the curling-pond and trickled slowly down towards the Firth proving an especial attraction in severe weather; on this part of the links an excellent chance of a heavy bag was lost owing to a deficiency of ammunition, the Snipes, as usual, having been fallen in with when least expected. As the birds exhibited an unaccustomed disregard of danger, though by no means pressed by long-continued frost, a short account extracted from my notes may not be out of place.

Having awaited the break of day in the wooden house erected at the curling-pond one frosty morning early in December 1863, I cautiously looked over the low wall that divides the sandy links from the cultivated land as soon as there was sufficient light to make observations on the dark swampy ground below. Ducks had been the object of my search, and though the air was thick with slowly falling snow a rapid glance revealed the fact that none were present. After waiting a few minutes, however, several dark spots became invisible, apparently moving slowly over the moss now partially white with snow. Though doubtful in the first instance, I was convinced at last that birds were in view, a small group of at least half a dozen having gathered where but one had been discerned a few minutes earlier. Large numbers of Golden Plover had been heard at flight-time the previous night, calling loudly round the duck-pits*, without offering a chance, and these I concluded, after passing the night on the sands and muds of the bay, had now betaken themselves inland. Without a sound to disturb the unsuspecting flock, the gun was raised, though for a time I hesitated, so motionless were the objects. A wing slowly raised at last attracted attention, and the trigger was instantly touched, the second barrel being discharged almost at random, owing to the smoke and haze caused by the state of the atmosphere. The well-known call of the Snipe uttered on all sides left no longer any doubt as to the species, between one and two hundred birds having risen at the shot along the course of the stream. After picking up three or four couple from the moss and following a few small wisps lower down the links, my ammunition began to be exhausted. Under such circumstances, it was by no means consoling to watch the birds, after wheeling round, alighting about every piece of water where the mud was unfrozen, exhibiting the greatest disinclination to rise on wing from even the very smallest amount of cover. No preparation in the way of cartridges having been made for securing a heavy bag, and being distant also between five and six miles from home, I was forced to quit the spot with fourteen couple of Snipe and a Mallard. The following morning the weather was more open and birds were far less numerous; though the whole of the links as far as Aberlady Burn were thoroughly searched, only ten or a dozen couple were flushed.

Snipes, when plentiful, rise at times so thickly and fly in such close company that I have repeatedly seen three or four birds brought down by a single shot. While shooting on the rounds round Heigham Sounds in November 1871, a wisp of five birds rose wild at the distance of at least one hundred yards. After wheeling high in the air for a few minutes the whole party swept down to the level of the marsh, and expecting that their line of flight would bring them within range, I raised my gun just in time to stop the leader as they came in view through the reeds over the marsh wall; on proceeding to the spot, one bird alone retained sufficient strength to flutter a short distance, the remainder of the wisp lying lifeless or helpless on the bank.

The slades and sloppy rush-marshes in parts of Pevensey Level formerly attracted large flights of Snipe; of late years, however, their numbers have greatly decreased. On two occasions I happened to be on the spot shortly after the arrival of the birds, and the immense numbers seen on wing will not

---

\* Shelters dug out near the pools on the links in which to await the Ducks.

readily be forgotten. On the 6th of December, 1860, a stretch of marshes, known as "Barnhorn Ponds," extending well inland between the cultivated grounds, was perfectly alive with Snipe. Though twenty or thirty birds would rise at a time, they flew for the most part singly; in no instance did I notice more than three or four keeping in company. But few shots had been fired, when from three to four hundred must have been on wing at once, soaring high in the air and, after a time, settling in the more remote patches of rushes. Having been in pursuit of Wild Geese, I was by no means prepared for Snipe-slaughter, my weapon being a ten-bore muzzle-loader, and wire cartridges forming the greater part of the ammunition. Early in March 1866 the weather was excessively cold and wintry. On arriving one morning at Pevensey, I learned from a keeper who met me at the station that while crossing the marshes in the dark he had heard Snipe calling in all directions. During the early part of the day we searched the slades in the neighbourhood of the coast, finding few birds and bagging but six couple; it was not till the afternoon, on arriving at "Barnhorn Ponds," that the Snipe were discovered, the scene being precisely similar to that previously described. On this occasion I was well provided with all necessaries, though an unlucky mishap considerably interfered with the prospects of the bag. Before entering the first marsh in "the ponds," Snipe commenced to rise from the rushes, and three fell to the first double, a bird in the act of crossing the line of the second barrel being knocked down at about sixty yards. On attempting to make my way across the wooden footway over the dyke the plank slipped round, and though escaping a ducking, thanks to a pair of long boots, both barrels of my breech-loader were stopped up with mud. While sorting out a pocketful of cartridges partially soaked by the splash of the water, the man, who carried a muzzle-loader, turned his attention to clearing my barrels with his ramrod. Using, unfortunately, more strength than skill, the rod snapped, and another delay occurred while the nearest hedgerow was searched in order to procure a suitable ash-plant. During the whole of the time we were engaged with the gun Snipe continued rising and settling in every direction as far as the rush-marshes extended, many flying round and offering most tempting chances. On resuming operations the birds, after lying well for a time, grew by degrees more wary, many extending their flight to distant parts of the level. After working hard while daylight lasted, twenty-five and a half couple of Snipe were counted out at dusk; there were, however, among them three couple of Jacks. On the following day I discovered, to my great regret, that the flight had moved on, leaving behind scarcely a straggler, a long tramp producing only eight couple, Jacks and full birds equally divided.

A week later, while shooting round the "crumbles" (a piece of swampy marshland near Eastbourne), I found several Snipe on the shingle-banks. The birds were scattered here and there, rising for the most part from below the stunted thorn bushes that grow in patches on the open beach where the gravel is fine and small. A few low tufts of grass and moss were the sole signs of vegetation, with the exception of the bushes, on this wide expanse of shingle; still the spot evidently possessed some unknown attraction for the birds.

Occasionally Snipe collect into large flocks, flying in compact bodies and wheeling in the air after the manner of Golden Plovers, Dunlin, and other small Waders. A flight consisting of three or four hundred were to be seen in the vicinity of one of the broads in the east of Norfolk during the latter end of September 1879. I had many opportunities of watching their actions, the birds appearing exceedingly restless, settling now and then for a few minutes, but seldom remaining for a sufficient length of time on one spot to allow an approach within gunshot. I often remarked that these large bodies exhibited a great fancy for the "floating hovers"[*], where they would settle at times in such numbers that many

---

[*] On many parts of the broads in the east of Norfolk the large water-plants occasionally die off in patches, the roots after a time rising up to the surface with a portion of the soil. The stalks of the rushes gradually rot away, and the masses of debris formed by the decaying stems and the soft mud prove favourite resorts for Snipe, such spots being known to the natives as "floating hovers."

were forced to alight on the small patches of surrounding reeds. A punt carefully worked is the only means of approaching one of these large flocks marked down on a hover; though repeatedly obtaining a view through the rushes of wisps numbering from twenty to thirty resting on these spots, I met with but one chance of examining a large flock quietly settled. A light breeze was blowing, and the rustle of the reeds prevented the sound of the punt slowly quanted through the cover from raising an alarm; some suspicion of danger had, however, apparently put the whole of the birds on the alert[*]. A few Snipes at the outskirts of the throng could be detected standing or moving slowly near the water's edge, though the main body were packed so thickly, squatting on the hover, that the rich brown colouring of their backs appeared like a fur rug stretched over the ground. An attempt to make use of the glasses attracted the attention of some of the outsiders, and rising on wing with shrill calls the assemblage broke up. Though alighting in company, these large bodies when disturbed usually go off in small parties, each following its own course. On this occasion, after the departure of the first flights the punt was worked up to the hover, when several more birds were flushed; for some minutes the shooting was fast and furious as the latest stragglers sprang out one or two at a time from the outlying clumps of rushes. This is the only instance where I found the birds composing one of these large gatherings so confiding, though it is frequently a matter of some difficulty to put up small parties when scattered over the more rush-grown portion of the ground. Owing to the amount of mud and ... brought into the boats, I seldom used a dog on such spots. The full birds can generally be flushed by splashing the water with a stroke of the quant; Jacks, however, occasionally drop on the ...... and by no means easily forced on wing. Having learned by experience that the attempt to ......... one of these floating hovers on foot was not unfrequently followed by a ............ in the ........ swamp, I have latterly taken up a position in the punt where the ............... by high reeds, and despatched a man to brush the cover with a quant. The safety ............ a native will make his way across the waving crust, avoiding dangerous spots and ......... as well as recovering any number of birds knocked down, would scarcely be credited by those ..... have never witnessed the proceedings. A few shots may be lost by this plan; but a somewhat lighter bag is decidedly preferable, in my own opinion, to the chance of getting one's boots filled and garments saturated with the slime and filth of the decomposing vegetation.

When the tides are high, very fair Snipe-shooting may be obtained from a punt about the hovers and marsh walls on many of the Norfolk broads. The birds seldom rise wild and, owing to the absence of all inconvenience as to standing-ground, usually present exceedingly easy shots. A well-built and roomy craft, however, is needed, and a man well up to his work, otherwise little success can be expected.

In addition to the well-known "scape" uttered on wing, the Snipe gives vent during the breeding-season to another call consisting of two notes. This somewhat monotonous cry is often repeated loudly for several seconds, the bird at the time being invisible among the rushes on a marsh. Pages without number have been written on the drumming of the Snipe and little remains to be added concerning this strangely deceptive performance. I have passed hours in watching the birds during the still evenings of early summer while soaring and darting through the air, and it appears obvious that the tremulous sound is produced by the feathers of the wings or tail. The names of "Air-Goat" and "Heather-bleater" bestowed on this species in the Highlands indicate the notion formed by the natives concerning the sound emitted by the bird. The Norfolk title of "Summer Lamb" is also by no means inappropriate.

In spite of the almost universal reclaiming of meres, bogs, and waste lands, there are still many out-of-the-way districts in which fair Snipe-shooting can at times be obtained where the ground is either free or permission is readily procured. As the birds found in such quarters are principally, if not entirely,

[*] I frequently remarked while watching Snipe searching for food on a bog or by the water-side that on the first signs of danger the bird would immediately squat, to most instances disappearing from view as if by magic.

migrants from the north of Europe, the date at which they may appear is so uncertain, and their departure for the most part so sudden, that it usually happens, unless one is on the spot at the time of their arrival, that the chance is lost. Floods or a rise in the tides will in some parts draw immense numbers, while in most localities the fens and marshes are alive with longbills for twenty-four or thirty hours previous to the setting-in of severe frost or snow. In flat districts, where little running water is to be found or few springs exist, scarcely a Snipe will be seen during the continuation of the frost, though the storms of westerly wind and rain that usually accompany the breaking-up of the ice will be safe to bring back several stragglers to their old haunts. Without some previous knowledge of the localities as well as of the resident natives, it is, however, improbable that the wandering sportsman will meet with any great success. The accommodation to be procured at several of the wayside inns in the more remote parts of the eastern counties, as well as in many other districts, is exceedingly scanty. There are, of course, exceptions, and passable though humble quarters may now and then be secured at even a lowly beer-shop; the dirt and discomfort, however, experienced on more than one Snipe-shooting expedition are still strongly impressed on my memory. Tramps, drovers, or itinerant pony-dealers appear to be the only class of wayfarers whose custom is anticipated. A single instance will suffice to show the reception accorded to visitors at some of these establishments. Having received word late one night in the end of February 1871, from a marshman at East Ruston, that several Snipes had arrived on the evening, I started before daybreak and after a twelve miles' drive found myself, as soon as it was fairly light, in the midst of a country that seemed to have been fashioned by nature simply and solely for the convenience and comfort of the Snipe tribe. Full birds and Jacks were in sufficient numbers to satisfy even the most exacting of shooters, and a heavy bag might have been obtained had not a small bunch of fowl claimed my attention for at least a couple of hours during the best part of the day. After circling round a few times the strangers settled down in a broad water-dyke, and a long and circuitous tramp had to be undertaken before I was able to identify the unknown as a couple of pair of Gadwall. After several hours' sport, as squalls of wind and rain were following one another in rapid succession and rendering the birds excessively wild, a move was made toward the inn to which the conveyance had previously been despatched. A glance at the exterior of the dilapidated building was by no means assuring, while an inspection of the interior proved still less inviting. In answer to a demand for refreshment we were informed that beer alone could be supplied on the premises. In consequence of a warning as to the unhospitable nature of the country towards which we were bound, our conveyance luckily contained a supply of eatables and drinkables, and the inquiry had simply been made in order to do something for the good of the house. Plates and tumblers had, however, been omitted or forgotten, and the loan of these articles was politely solicited. Three or four half-pint glasses, foul and dirty as lifted from the tap-room, where a party of sots were boosing, having been placed in the parlour, the grimy attendant declared it was utterly impossible to provide us with plates. At length, after considerable delay and not till borrowing from a neighbouring cottage had been resorted to, the landlady was induced to ferret out a sufficient amount of crockery. Luckily the driver had discovered a pump in the yard, as the plates when produced and placed on the table bore strong evidence that the last meal at which they were employed had consisted of herrings. An unlimited supply of water soon put plates and glasses into working order, and being well able to wait on ourselves no further difficulties were encountered.

Every sportsman retains his own ideas as to which breed of dog is most serviceable for Snipe-shooting. Two animals, as perfect as any I ever met with, were a lemon-and-white setter and a liver-coloured pointer, both bitches. In their looks there was little to commend them; but their work in the fens and marshes was undeniable. Neither was the occupant of a well-kept or fashionable kennel, nor had the lash of keeper's whip ever descended on their unbrushed coats. The setter found what shelter she could in the corner of a fenman's cowshed, while the sly old pointer had seldom any difficulty in securing quarters when the day's work was over in front of the tap-room fire of a cosy country inn.

Judging from many of the sporting pictures published some years back, a wild and noisy spaniel that ranged unchecked was the sort of animal that accompanied the gunner to the fens and marshes. If any faith is to be placed in these artistic efforts, Snipe and fowl must, in those good old times, have been far more confiding than at the present day, otherwise the shooters' bags must have been light indeed.

Many years ago I possessed a red Sussex spaniel, a quadruped much after the fashion of some represented in the old plates; being somewhat rash as well as jealous, his performances on the Snipe-bogs may be passed over, but one of his exploits is worth recording. After a fair day's sport on the fens of one of the eastern counties, I was returning homewards between eight and nine on a fine November evening; a low basket-cart was my conveyance, with a fast-trotting pony in the shafts, and the milestones flew past in rapid succession. The spaniel, having dried his coat after his day's work in the marshes by a snooze in front of the tap-room fire while a dinner of ham and eggs had been discussed, was, as usual, stretched out on my feet. In consequence of the garroting scare, now at its height, and also of several attacks on the highway perpetrated by footpads in the neighbourhood, a loaded revolver had been placed within reach between the cushions of the seat and the right-hand side of the trap. Though a few passing clouds occasionally obscured the moon, the night was fairly light, and the few travellers I met or passed could easily be distinguished at the distance of forty or fifty yards. The road was for the most part flat and good, and after leaving a long-standing turnpike ran for two or three miles across a piece of open land. When about halfway across this dreary stretch, two figures came in view, apparently following the same course as myself. As they persisted in keeping the centre of the road, I was forced to ease for a moment when they suddenly separated and, allowing the pony just sufficient room to pass, rushed one to each side of the trap with a loud request for a lift. The chestnut mare never needed the whip, and my right hand being at liberty, the pistol was grasped before the fellows laid hold of the trap. Startled by the noise the mare dashed off at a gallop, and the man to my left was immediately shaken off, while his companion losing his balance pitched headlong towards the bottom of the conveyance. The muzzle of my six-shooter was touching his left side as he sprawled across my knees, but no cause had as yet occurred to justify its use. What might have happened it is impossible to say, had not the old dog, with a savage growl, sprung up and seizing the man by the arm caused him, with an oath and a yell of pain, to throw himself backwards and roll heavily to the ground. Both of my assailants having been thus summarily disposed of without the slightest exertion on my own part, I proceeded quietly homewards, and imagining the whole affair to have been a drunken spree for which the perpetrators had suffered sufficiently, no further thought was given to the matter. On the following morning, however, on entering the stable-yard of the inn where I had put up, the ostler, who held in his hand a large butcher's knife sharpened on both edges, inquired where I had picked up such an elegant piece of cutlery. On demanding an explanation, the man stated he had found the knife lying with the rugs at the bottom of the trap. There was now no doubt as to the character of my two friends, one of whom must have dropped the knife when pinned by the dog, as I subsequently learned that having been balked in their first attempt, they had later on the same night attacked a poor old farmer, whom they relieved of a silver watch and the sum of seven shillings.

After a long continuation of frost Snipe, if not driven entirely from the country, occasionally succumb to the effects of cold and hunger. During an ordinary winter, however, the birds will usually ... in the finest condition on the approach of cold weather. My notes contain the weights of ... on which they were killed; to give the whole list would answer ... a ... will indicate the extreme weights attained. The heaviest couple I find under date of January 1st, 1872, when two birds bagged on the Holmes Marshes in the east of Norfolk turned the scale at 12¼ oz.; when tested in the scales one against the other there was not the weight of a feather between them. Snipe at the time were exceedingly scarce in the district; I learn by my notes that not a bird had been seen for over a month. In November 1880, a Snipe shot near Lancing, in Sussex, is recorded as 5⅞ oz.; there are also several entries of this weight during former years. In the early part of the season Snipe are often scurfy and in poor condition, the young are also not unfrequently light. In a list of birds bagged between the 15th and 30th of September, 1879, in the east of Norfolk, the weights vary from 3 to 5 oz. If the weights of Snipes were regularly taken by sportsmen at the commencement of a frost, I believe the average of the birds would be found much heavier than is usually allowed. While passing through the market of a town on the east coast during the severe weather in November 1879, I was requested by a game-dealer to inspect his stall, which contained a pile of from three to four hundred Snipe. The salesman then pointed out a smaller heap, all of which he declared would go three to the pound. I tried a few birds in the scales and found his assertion perfectly correct; there were at least thirty Snipe of this weight.

Though statements to the effect that this species occasionally alights on trees have appeared in print, I never met with a chance of recording a single instance of the fact. During spring in the Norfolk marshes I have repeatedly seen Snipe quietly resting on the notice-boards that warn trespassers to beware, paying little or no attention to boats quanting past at the distance of thirty or forty yards. On more than one occasion in May 1883 a bird was watched settling for a few minutes on the thatched roof of a boat-house; several instances have also come under my observation, about the broads and river-sides of the eastern counties, where the stakes employed to dry the eel-nets, and even the empty fish-trunks, were resorted to. When shooting during the summer of 1869 in the marshes near Rye, I often noticed a Snipe perched on a post-and-rail fence running across a gravel-pit that contained large pools of shallow water as well as rank vegetation.

The snares or springes formerly set for Snipe have been so frequently alluded to, that no description is necessary. Twenty years ago I repeatedly saw large baskets of birds taken by these means sent up to market from Romney Marsh in Kent; this method of capture, however, I believe is now but little followed. In Pevensey Level Ducks and Teal as well as Snipe were often taken by means of small steel traps placed in the open grips and slades frequented by the birds.

Unfortunately for the interests of sport, Snipes are exposed to much unlawful persecution, every lazy vagabond who can command an old musket waging at the time of frost and snow a war of extermination against the luckless birds, utterly regardless of license for either gun or game. The numbers killed by flight-shooters, professional punt-gunners, and loafers would appear incredible to those who have not closely watched the proceedings of those worthies. In the south of Scotland I well remember that a small boy, who was employed as a bent to scare the Wood-Pigeons from the turnips, killed regularly for a time one or two couple a day. The laddie was furnished with a gun and a supply of powder, with strict injunctions to discharge his piece whenever the flock of Doos threatened an attack. The strange feathered creatures that dropped at two or three springs on the outskirts of the loes near the field on which he was posted excited the curiosity of this precocious youngster; and having procured a charge of shot, he waited patiently concealed in the long grass with the barrel pointed till the unknown settled by the water-side, when a successful shot was made. I shall not readily forget the grin of delight with which the urchin produced his first prize (which he had previously described as "a beastie wi' a lang neb") for identification.

Every sportsman must have remarked that though the marshes occasionally bore evidence to the fact that Snipe had recently been present in numbers, scarcely a bird would be flushed during a long

homewards in a punt at dusk, or waiting for fowl at flight, I have
frequently seen Snipe after […] for a time in […] settle quietly down and commence boring along
the edge of some open pool; […] the birds would collect in small parties on ground I was well aware
[…] deserted by […] Wind and weather have an influence on Snipe that we can scarcely
expect to fathom; though the […] part of their movements may be understood and anticipated, they
partake at times a change of quarters that is utterly unintelligible.

The large flights of Snipes that cross the North Sea […] and then lose several of their numbers
through […] of the lightships. I was informed by the crews of some of
the vessels that these […] had been frequently taken on board, though during the two seasons of 1872
and 1873 […] and […] on the floating lights off the Norfolk coast.

[…] on inland marshes, I have frequently met with Snipe resorting, even in
open […] A few are now and then to be seen on Breydon flats in autumn,
and both […] are not uncommonly flushed on the saltings in Shoreham Harbour. The
small grassy […] at the head of the Cromarty Firth near Dingwall possessed some years ago great
attraction for Snipe at low water. During July and August 1868 I repeatedly put up from fifty to one
hundred birds by simply following the rising tide in a boat. Snipe being of little value so early in the
season, and the weather too hot to allow of their keeping beyond a day, I seldom molested them: on
one or two occasions ten couple were bagged; twice that number could, however, have been obtained
with the greatest ease.

During protracted frost Snipe at times are forced to betake themselves to situations where, under
ordinary circumstances, they would seldom if ever be expected. While the train was entering the
station at Tain in Ross-shire one evening in March 1869, I noticed a Snipe spring from the side of the
line and, rising straight in the air, strike the telegraph-wires with such force that it fell disabled to the
ground. As I was returning from shooting in the neighbourhood my gun was at hand, and proceeding
at once to the spot, four and a half couple of Snipe were bagged during the few minutes of daylight that
remained. The birds rose from a small brick drain of water that ran from the station, two or three
escaping through flying off in a line with the telegraph-wires; the station-master happening to be
present, I declined to fire lest some damage might be laid to my charge. On the journey from Dingwall
during the early part of the afternoon, I had noticed Snipe flying up more than once from the vicinity
of the large iron pumps employed to supply the engines. On the shores of the Highland firths where
the tide was perfectly salt, I have also watched these birds busily engaged in searching for food. While
punt-gunning one winter on a river in the north of Scotland, I noticed that Snipe were collected in
numbers along the banks where the mud was kept soft by the action of the tide. As a novel proceeding,
I tried one shot at them with the big gun; the birds, however, were so tame that it could hardly be
considered sport, and fowl being plentiful on the water at the time, I left them in peace, hoping to renew
the acquaintance on some future occasion[*]. During the day the puntsman knocked over three or four
birds with the setting-pole, and these as well as eight couple stopped by the shot of the punt-gun were
in fairly good condition, having apparently suffered but little from the severity of the weather.

A ridiculous mishap that occurred the same evening shall bring to a close the notes on *Scolopax
gallinago*. I was stopping at a most comfortable hotel, which, as is commonly the case in the Highlands,
was situated in a remarkably wild and, during winter, deserted region. Having finished a capital dinner,
and being tired of my own company, I strolled into the kitchen to see what was going on. Here I found
the punt-gun propped up on a couple of chairs in front of a roaring fire, with two or three keepers

---

[*] A few days later, when the weather changed, I discovered that my chance was lost; and after the breaking up of the frost not a Snipe could
be found within a mile of the spot.

sitting smoking beside it. As I noticed that several sparks from a lump of peat with which one of the men was lighting his pipe fell over the lock, I inquired if the charge had been drawn. "Yes," remarked John the puntman, with the air of one who thoroughly understands his business and has properly performed it; "she's washed out, loaded and primed ready for the morning." On inspecting the lock I discovered that the covering to the nipple was simply a piece of brown paper such as Highlanders use for tinder, and consequently extremely liable to ignite from a spark; so I suggested that the gun should be placed in the far corner of the room where it would still be protected from the frost\*. As nothing, however, would satisfy the landlady, who came in at this moment, but the immediate removal of the dangerous weapon, I ordered the men to take out the gun and draw the charge. In less than two minutes there was a deafening explosion, followed by a fearful crash; the glass was blown in, the lights blown out, the landlady fainted, the lassies screamed, and the dogs barked. On rushing out to see what had happened, I learned that after cleaning out and loading the gun, the men had carried the rods down to the punts when they had gone to see that all was snug for the night. Having no means at hand for drawing the charge, they placed a cap on the nipple, and holding the muzzle in the air with the butt steadied on the bricks corner of the yard had fired the charge, with the result described. On subsequent inquiry I found out that John, who had rather a spite against the landlady (as that stern matron had reprimanded him for some unbecoming levity she had detected between him and one of the damsels of her establishment), had done it in hopes of giving her a fright, without having bestowed a thought on the panes of glass that would be blown in by the concussion and naturally fell to my share to pay for.

\* Some gunners have an idea that it is dangerous to allow the frost to get into the barrel of a punt-gun.

# JACK SNIPE.

## *SCOLOPAX GALLINULA.*

On the approach of autumn the Jack Snipe is to be met with in all parts of the British Islands, more plentiful perhaps (according to my own experience) in the southern and eastern counties of England, though an annual visitor to every suitable locality from north to south. The occurrence of this species has been frequently reported in various counties during the summer months, and it is probable that birds weakened by wounds or other causes may occasionally be found after the usual date of their departure has passed; in many instances, however, I am of opinion that there has been some mistake as to the species. But a single statement that appears trustworthy has come to my knowledge; in this instance I was informed by a Norfolk marshman that while attending a net in 1876, which he fished every morning, a Jack Snipe was flushed regularly for ten days or a fortnight in the beginning of June, at a small slade in the marshes near Heigham Sounds: having passed his life in the district, the man was perfectly acquainted with Snipes, "double," "whole," and Jack.

There is, so far as I am aware, no reliable instance of the species remaining to breed in this country. Judging by the entries in my notes, jotted down in many parts of England and Scotland, the main body of Jacks take their departure in March; still stragglers are to be seen in April. In 1861 and '62, and again in 1864, I repeatedly met with a few couples in Pevensey Level in Sussex, early in the month, the latest entry in my notes referring to this species being dated April 18th, when a couple were flushed on "Barnhorn Ponds." In reference to the late stay of the Jack in the east of Norfolk, I find the following in my notes for 1873 :—"April 23. Cold north wind, frequent squalls of snow and hail. While looking over the traps set on the rondes round the Sounds, a Jack Snipe was flushed; not a single bird had been seen for the last two months. I learned, however, on the following day that a keeper who had been hunting for Plover's eggs on the marshes near Hickling had put up at least two or three score."

No great numbers show themselves before the beginning of October, and the larger flights are seldom encountered till a few weeks later in the season. When living in the west of Perthshire, I noticed for two successive years that the first couple of Jack Snipe were found at a small rush-grown pool on the low ground near the Lyon on the 29th of September. The third season I was anxious to ascertain if the Jack had reached the glen at their accustomed date. The day being exceedingly wet and stormy, I took no dogs with the exception of a retriever, old and steady. The rushes round the pool and a small stream that ran from it were thoroughly explored without starting the expected Jack, and at last I turned back somewhat disappointed at the want of success. Before proceeding many yards, my attention was attracted by the retriever shoving her nose into my hand, and on looking down I discovered old Nell was carrying a Jack in her mouth. As she had not stirred from my heels, it was evident the bird must have been walked over. Thinking that probably this Snipe was not alone, I returned at once, and hunting the bitch round the pool, she made straight for the side of a small drain near which we had passed, and immediately picked up a second. It was obvious this bird had been previously detected, but the living mouthful already secured would have rendered another capture impossible*. Glenlyon was by no means a favoured resort of the Jack Snipe, some ten or twenty couples being the utmost brought to bag during any season I remained in the district. The birds, however, put in an appearance as early as in any locality I am acquainted with. But a single Jack has been entered in my notes as observed in advance of the Glenlyon birds (September 20); this was shot September 18, 1879, near Hickling in Norfolk.

Large flights make their appearance in the east of Norfolk early in October, the 7th and 9th being dates on which I have found them particularly numerous in the neighbourhood of the broads. On one occasion (October 21, 1871), while shooting on the rondes round Heigham Sounds, twelve birds were dropped in rapid succession without stirring a foot, as fast as the cartridges could be inserted in the gun. Between forty and fifty Jacks must have been flushed within gunshot, the birds rising in some instances two or three together, but for the most part singly, each striking out a course for itself. Snipe, both "whole" and Jack, were in immense numbers on that occasion, and, strange to say, by well, which is seldom the case when found in wisps or thickly scattered over the ground. A rough morning with heavy showers had been succeeded by a soaking rain, which continued without intermission till after dark. I only became aware of the arrival of the Snipe late in the afternoon on my way towards the broads to learn if the storm had driven in any fowl from the coast. There was little more than an hour of daylight after I reached the spot—added to which my small stock of cartridges was speedily shot away, and all chance of further sport effectually put a stop to. Twelve and a half couple of Snipes (principally Jacks) were obtained; but a heavy bag might have been secured, notwithstanding the inclemency of the weather, had I commenced operations earlier in the day, well supplied with ammunition. A few days previous (October 9th), I met with a party of Jacks on a small marsh known as Ludham Hover; they were twenty in number, and every bird was brought to bag. In this instance "whole" Snipe were conspicuous by their absence; though at various times I have seen from fifty to one hundred collected on this piece of marshland, but a single bird was sprung on this occasion and (both barrels being empty at the moment) he escaped.

Pevensey Level in days gone by was a great resort for Jacks, immense flights being occasionally met with. The first week in December 1860, and early in March 1866, these birds as well as "whole" Snipe were especially plentiful. The numbers visiting this locality have, during the past twenty years, fallen off, and the same may be said concerning certain parts of Romney Marsh in Kent. Early in 1855, the "whole" Snipe were apparently driven from the county by the severity of the weather in the east of Sussex; Jacks, however, were little affected, being found in more than usual abundance scattered along the course of any open water or running streams. During the long-protracted and bitter frost of that terrible winter, I was handed over to a keeper in my father's service to be initiated into the art of shooting Jack Snipes—broken in, as the old man termed it. As the plan he followed was decidedly effective and, to the best of my knowledge, original, it may not be out of place to devote a few lines to a description of his mode of tuition. A Jack Snipe, my instructor truly argued, was almost invariably missed through firing too quickly, both barrels being usually discharged before the bird is five and twenty yards from the muzzle of the gun. This error was expressly pointed out, and I was forced to repeat aloud one, two, three, four, five, six, after the Snipe rose on wing, before bringing the gun to the shoulder. The first lesson being duly impressed on my mind, the antiquated muzzle-loader

## JACK SNIPE.

was ......... attempted. ......... in finding birds during ......... of running water ......... to congregate. ......... was ......... shooting even ......... the gun was ......... before the six was reached, no ......... claimed the gun ......... and practically ......... his ......... followed, the ......... of these ......... birds might be accomplished. It ......... hard on thirty years since I profited ......... lessons, but ......... now the well-remembered one, two, three, &c. frequently rises to my lips ......... the inevitable Jack appears, and ill luck invariably attends the bird that is patiently waited for.

On a cold wintry evening in March 1869, while shooting near Tain, on the east coast of Ross-shire, I watched a Jack, which flew in from the direction of the sea, alight on the shore of a small frozen burn. On being closely approached, he strutted slowly up to the soft and freshly fallen snow covering the banks, and deliberately thrust his head out of sight in the drift. For several minutes this singular bird retained his position, making, indeed, not the slightest attempt to escape till a stick was inserted in the snow and a portion of his hiding-place crumbled away. He then went off in the habitual perplexing fashion of his ......... had occurred. This is the only instance I have witnessed of a Jack conducting himself in such a ......... The bird might doubtless have been picked up, so deeply did he bury his head in the ......... That he was previously wounded was improbable, having been observed on wing for a longer flight than is usually undertaken by this species.

The Jack, unlike its larger relative the "whole" Snipe, is seldom wild and unapproachable. I never met with them gathered into flocks, flying and settling in company after the manner of those birds. Ten or a dozen up to even forty or fifty may frequently be found scattered over a small space; but on rising on wing the company break up and separate. Though usually dropping after a short and erratic flight, I have often seen Jacks go off strong on wing, with an evident intention of leaving the locality.

The difficulty of finding and putting up these strange birds is well known to all sportsmen; without a steady dog accustomed to their habits, large numbers must invariably be passed over. Jacks may frequently be detected squatting on the moist ground, the attention usually being attracted by the eye or the yellow stripes on the back. On one occasion, while cautiously making my way across a waxing bog * over which my weight was causing the water to rise rapidly to a depth of three or four inches, I noticed three floated off the short herbage and rushes on which they were squatted and swept down to my feet by the force of the current before they attempted to take wing, one of the birds being carried by the rush of the water a distance of three or four yards. The poor little fellow made no attempt to swim, the legs being kept perfectly still, and the head remaining drawn back between the shoulders, with the beak pointed forwards in the position into which they subside when danger approaches.

In one instance where a dealer in birds attempted to effect a capture, a net was placed completely over the small patch of rushes to which a couple were accustomed to resort. The ground having been brushed over with a switch without result, it was imagined the birds were absent; the moment, however, the net was withdrawn, up started the two Jacks.

In some remote districts in the fen countries there is, or used to be, an impression among the old gunners that the Jack and the "whole" Snipe were one and the same species—Jacks being the males.

* The ground to this tredded was exceedingly dangerous in many parts. A thin cake of sod had formed over the rotten swamp, interspersed here and there with luxuriant clumps of rushes. Bare patches of mud being left at intervals where only a strand or two of vegetation showed through. The whole surface waved and sank over a space of several yards when crossed, the water gradually rising. On such spots, when a commencement has once been made, the roots of the water-plants usually gain strength in a few years, and a firm bottom is established.

A well-known sporting writer* stated some years back that, for edible purposes, the Jack was far superior to the "whole" Snipe. For my own part, I consider the small bird decidedly inferior in this respect to his larger relative. While shooting in Norfolk in 1879, I kept the weights of about fifty or sixty couples of Jacks killed during the season. The birds varied from $1\frac{3}{4}$ to $3\frac{1}{2}$ oz.; the majority ranged from $2\frac{1}{2}$ to 3 oz., the lighter birds being for the most part the first arrivals in the autumn.

* "Hawker on Shooting," eleventh edition, p. 263.

# CURLEW SANDPIPER.

*TRINGA SUBARQUATA.*

---

Norfolk, Sussex, and Kent are the only English counties in which I have met with this species. On the Scotch coast I never recognized this Sandpiper in spring, though the young are far from uncommon in autumn along the sandy shores of the Firth of Forth, between Gullane Bay and Dunbar. Adults exhibiting the full breeding-plumage appear from my own observations, as well as from the information gathered from the punt-gunners and shore-shooters I encountered in my travels, to have been at all times somewhat scarce; in autumn, however, numbers of old birds, their feathers worn and the colours faded, as well as large flocks in immature plumage, are to be seen on the southern and eastern coasts. So far as I have been able to ascertain, but few of this species remain long enough on our shores to assume the winter dress.

The numbers arriving in spring vary considerably; in 1870, though I was on Breydon mudflats daily for the greater part of May, I did not meet with a single specimen, while on the same water at least a score were noticed the following season. In most instances the birds were flying singly, though occasionally in company with small parties of Dunlins and Knots. The first was seen on the 12th, leading about forty Dunlins; and the flock having settled on a part of the flats to which the punt could not approach within sixty or seventy yards, the specimen, which proved to be a male in perfect plumage, was secured by a charge from the big gun. On the 15th a single bird flew round the boats in answer to the call of the Plover, and on falling to a shot from the shoulder-gun was discovered to be a female. The colouring was by no means so rich as in the male, diminutive white markings pervading the feathers (much the same as in the female Sanderling) and giving at a short distance a mealy appearance to the whole plumage[*]. Several single birds were noticed during the day flying high in the air; though wheeling round in response to the call, they never ventured within range, and in every instance finally went off, holding a due north-east course. Unless one is well acquainted with the call, which somewhat resembles that of the Dunlin, only possessing more power and consequently audible to a far greater distance, many of these birds will escape notice, the elevation at which they fly being, as a rule, considerably higher than that of the other small Waders. The note of the Grey Plover is the call to which they usually respond; during spring, however, these Sandpipers are for the most part wary, seldom remaining long in one locality, apparently bent on making their passage to the far north. On the 16th a few Curlew Sandpipers were again seen on wing. I detected two or three dark red birds flying over the punts, and as many either females or in backward plumage, the distance being too great to identify their state with any certainty. Though constantly on the water from daylight till mid-day and occasionally till dusk, none were observed again till the 24th, when a fine red male was found feeding on the muds near the channel in company with about a dozen Dunlins and a Stint. Busily engaged in searching for food in the ooze, little or no regard was paid to the presence of the punt, only some twenty yards distant. The bird running

---

[*] From the mottled state of the feathers on the back it was evident that a considerable change had still to be undergone; I can, however, offer no opinion as to whether the plumage on the throat, breast, and underparts would have become darker as the season advanced.

rapidly across the flats apparently secured the small worms and other insects usually extracted by the majority of Waders. After a stormy night large quantities of Plovers, a few Godwits and Knots, together with several parties of Terns were on the water early on the morning of the 26th. I did not recognize a single Curlew Sandpiper; but on picking up the results of a shot with the big gun into a flock of Knots, a specimen in full winter plumage was discovered in the midst of the slain. This bird, though exhibiting the winter dress, would shortly have moulted, being thickly covered with red pin-feathers, a few of which had burst, but were invisible till carefully looked for. No other Curlew Sandpipers were seen this season, though Breydon flats were closely watched till the end of the month.

In the spring of 1872 I was on the Sussex coast and failed to recognize this species among the flocks of Waders frequenting Shoreham Harbour and the flat coast-line on towards Worthing.

Though the whole of May 1873 was passed on Breydon it was only on the 16th that this species was observed. The day was cold with a fresh easterly breeze and several Plovers and Godwits made their appearance on the flats. One Curlew Sandpiper which had partially acquired the summer plumage was shot and another (a dark red bird in full dress of the adult male) passed the punt so rapidly, flying due east, that there was not even time to snatch up the shoulder-gun.

Being absent for some years during spring on the Scotch coasts and various parts of the country apparently out of the usual range of this species, it was not till May 1881 that I again fell in with an adult Curlew Sandpiper. Several small parties of Godwits, Grey Plovers, and Knots having arrived on the muds in Shoreham Harbour on the 10th of May, I was on the spot early on the 11th. A cold breeze from the north-east blew over the flats soon after sunrise, the wind being especially suitable at this date to bring Waders along the coast. A flock of some twenty birds were soon made out on the flats, feeding gradually before the rising tide towards the embankment enclosing the river. This small gathering proved to be a mixed party composed of Godwits, Grey Plovers, Knots, Dunlins, and a single Curlew Sandpiper. The latter, I soon discovered, was a male in the finest stage of summer plumage; and the whole number being utterly unsuspicious of danger, there was not the slightest difficulty in examining them thoroughly by means of the glasses. In addition to this handsome specimen two brightly coloured Knots fell to the shot. As the survivors were not molested, they remained about the flats all day, betaking themselves at high water to the shingle-banks.

To record every instance where the adults (changing from summer into winter plumage) have been met with in autumn is unnecessary. In 1871, 1872, and 1873 I noticed numbers on Breydon during August and September. Several exhibited the transformation of plumage in a most singular manner, the breast at times retaining its red colouring, while grey and white feathers had made their appearance on the back. In these stages Curlew Sandpipers are not uncommon in Shoreham Harbour and other flats on the Sussex coast.

With the exception of the bird showing the grey feathers of winter, shot on Breydon on May 26, 1871, I have met with but one other specimen in the same state of plumage; this was obtained near Shoreham early in November 1875, being at the time in company with a small flock of Dunlins.

The young of the year usually reach our shores in autumn, much about the same date as the adults. I find the earliest arrival on the coast of Sussex is recorded, in my notes for 1859, under date of August 30th. This season birds in immature plumage were especially numerous about the Nook at Rye, and also on the flooded marshes stretching towards Winchelsea. The following year large flocks were also met with in the same locality, the birds being especially plentiful on September 14th. Though occasionally intermixing with Dunlins, they showed their predilection for the company of Stints (*Tringa minuta*), flocks numbering from forty to fifty composed entirely of these two species being often seen. In 1861 a considerable portion of the flats forming the Nook were drained; after more than one failure a sea-wall was built that successfully held back the flowing tide. The change from mud-banks to grass-marshes was evidently but little relished by the Sandpipers; the first autumn after the alteration I happened to be present when a large mixed flock of Curlew Sandpipers and Stints, after wheeling round two or three times, settled down among the sheep, which were now the occupants of their former quarters; after running about in the grass for a time, evidently bewildered by the transformation that had taken place, they appeared at last to comprehend the state of affairs, and uttering a succession of low cries, the whole flock took wing in search of more congenial feeding-grounds \*. After this date the flocks of Curlew Sandpipers resorted for the most part to the pools in the marshes, where a constant overflow from the dykes caused a muddy bottom, affording an abundance of food whenever the water fell.

On again visiting the district in September 1890, I found most of the old haunts of these birds about the Nook and the adjoining marshes deserted, improved drainage having rendered the nature of the soil utterly unsuitable to their requirements. Though I failed to detect the spot † to which they retired at high water, Curlew Sandpipers came in view soon after the tide commenced to ebb. On the extensive sands to the east of Rye Harbour, parties of small Waders were noticed, as the tide fell, gathering into one large body; on examining them carefully through the glasses and procuring a few specimens, I ascertained that the flock, numbering at least five hundred, was composed for the most part of Curlew Sandpipers with a sprinkling of Sanderlings and Kentish Plovers. Though feeding together on the flats, the various species separated when disturbed, alighting again, however, in company and at no great distance, and immediately spreading out to search the soft mud in the channels in the sand. Most of the birds were exceedingly tame; though watched closely through the glasses, I could not identify a single adult of this species, the whole number exhibiting the immature plumage.

I remarked that there appears but little difference in the dates at which these Sandpipers make their appearance in autumn on the Norfolk coast and the flats in the east and west of Sussex. As a rule, I gather from my notes and the information from the coast-gunners that the earliest arrivals are noted on Breydon. To the best of my knowledge, none were seen about Shoreham in 1882 till September 29, when a small party, all immature, passed along the coast about a mile at sea, flying west. In the season of 1883 I observed about half a dozen young birds feeding on the flats, in company with Dotterel and Dunlin, as early as the 15th of September.

\* The actions of these birds were exceedingly strange when the fact is considered that the whole of the Curlew Sandpipers were undoubtedly birds of the year, and consequently could not have visited the marsh in its former condition. Though I cannot speak with certainty, the Stints also appeared to exhibit immature plumage. On no other occasion have I noticed either species to alight on soil so hard and dry as this stretch of marshland recently reclaimed.

† Probably some soft muddy pool, at no great distance from the shore, in Romney Marsh.

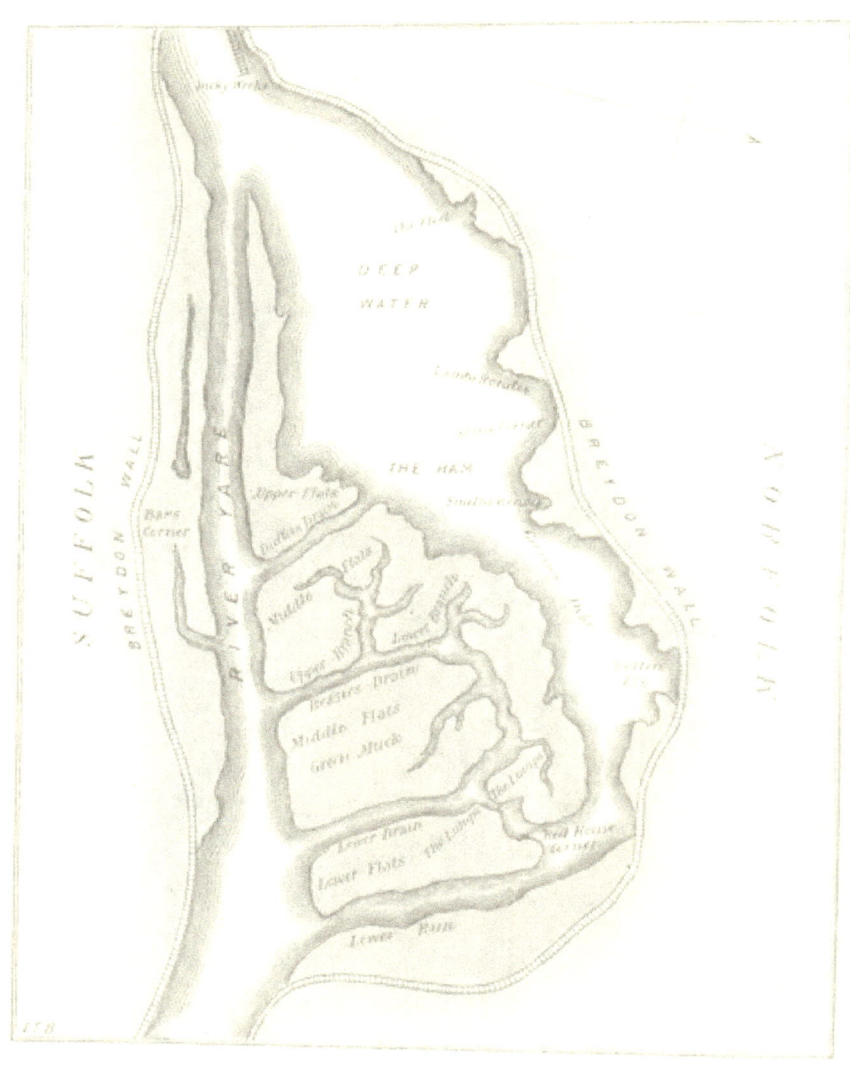

## BREYDON MUDFLATS AT LOW TIDE.

THIS SMALL MAP, DRAWN IN 1872, MAY BE OF SERVICE BY INDICATING THE WHEREABOUTS OF THE FLATS AND DRAINS SO OFTEN REFERRED TO IN THE ARTICLES ON THE WADERS AND WILDFOWL.

# KNOT.
## TRINGA CANUTUS.

---

Slowly but surely for the last twenty-five years * the number of Knots making their appearance in spring along the southern and eastern counties of England have gradually decreased. This falling off is somewhat unintelligible taken in connection with the fact that on the return journey from their breeding-grounds immense flocks still arrive at the usual season, the first comers striking the land as far north as the flat shores of Ross-shire and Sutherland. As autumn advances, the multitudes, for the most part in immature plumage, spread southward, till early in September the sand-banks and muddy estuaries bordering on the Channel are reached. In winter the movements of Knots are somewhat uncertain, wind and weather frequently compelling them to make a sudden change of quarters. From personal observation I am unable to give any particulars concerning the distribution of this species along the western shores of England. On the northern and western coasts of the Highlands and also among the Outer Hebrides I failed to detect a single specimen, though continually on the look-out when on shore and afloat. Only small parties, according to my own experience, find their way to inland waters or marshes, the extensive sands and mudflats round our coasts forming the favourite resorts of this abundant species.

There appears to be no certainty as to the date at which these birds assume the full breeding-plumage in the spring †. While shooting on Breydon mudflats I occasionally came across Knots in the grey garb of winter as late as the end of May. The following is an extract from my notes for 1871:—"May 30. Soon after daybreak made out a flock composed mainly of Grey Plovers on the flats by the channel. Being unable to identify the whole of their number, the big gun was fired, when the unknown proved to be a couple of Knots; one showed the full winter plumage without a sign of a red feather, while the other was but slightly advanced. The Plovers also were exceedingly backward, only a single bird exhibiting a perfectly black breast."

So late do some few stragglers (probably weak or backward birds of the previous year) remain that it is doubtful whether they quit our shores to start for the far north; wounds also may cause others to delay their journey if not entirely disabling them. In June 1868 I visited the Dornoch Firth on several occasions in pursuit of broods of Shelldrakes; on the 20th, and again on the 23rd, a small flock of about a score of Bar-tailed Godwits and Knots were noticed resorting to the sand-banks in Edderton Bay. Not having a punt on the water, I was unable to approach sufficiently close to obtain specimens for examination; there was, however, no difficulty in ascertaining that the half-dozen Knots were by no means in full summer plumage, but few red feathers showing among the grey of winter.

* My notes referring to this species go back to 1858. I have repeatedly ascertained that my own experience is corroborated by the evidence of many of the oldest coast-gunners.

† The same irregularity is also shown by Bar-tailed Godwits, Grey Plovers, and Curlew Sandpipers.

Knots making their way from the far north appear on our shores as early as the middle of summer, the first flocks being composed of young birds. Under date of July 8, 1808, while on the east coast of Ross-shire, I find the following in my notes:—" Left the Meikle Ferry early and pulled down the firth towards Tain, afterwards crossing over to the Dornoch shore. Several large flocks of Knots were seen during the day flying over the water as well as pitched on the sand-banks. The birds, as usual, were exceedingly tame, ample opportunities being obtained to examine them closely with the glasses. After repeated observations I at length came to the conclusion that there was not an adult in their ranks. Between twenty and thirty knocked down at one discharge, in order to ascertain their condition, proved to be in the juvenile plumage, their breasts coated with fat, and their legs and beaks exceedingly soft and fleshy. Many hundreds might have been obtained with the shoulder-gun alone; to slaughter them, however, at this season was simply useless destruction."

Though the young, according to my own experience, invariably show first on the north-east coast of the Highlands and also in the south of Scotland, I have on more than one occasion remarked adults arriving on the Norfolk mudflats in advance of the immature birds. While shooting on Breydon in the autumn of 1873, an adult Knot, partly red, though plainly exhibiting the change into winter plumage, was killed on the 1st of August. No young had as yet been seen, and it is seldom they are met with in this part before the middle of the month. In 1871 the first flock, numbering about a score, was seen on the 26th during a strong gale of wind from the west; these were all young with the exception of a single adult that appeared in perfect plumage till picked up, when its feathers were found to be much faded and worn. In 1872, on the same water, I noticed a few old Knots in company with adult Grey Plovers on August 24th. On the 27th it blew a hurricane from the north-east, rendering the work of navigating Breydon in the punts utterly impossible. On scanning the flats at low water from the North Wall, I made out a large flock of Knots, apparently all young. On the following morning at daybreak young birds were met with in large numbers, several, intermixed with Golden Plover, being bagged with the punt-gun. August 27th is the earliest at which I noticed the young so far south as Sussex, a pair being killed in the Nook at Rye Harbour on that date in 1858.

Though immature birds, according to my own observations, make the land towards the north of Scotland, the course followed by the adults appears to point more to the northern and eastern counties of England. For a couple of months from the beginning of August 1874, I carefully watched the arrival of Knots along the shores of the Firth of Forth, and during this season not a single adult came under my notice. About the middle of September a large addition to the birds previously observed was remarked; the following extract from my notes refers to the fact:—" September 16. While pulling slowly back from Gullane Bay, during a dead calm, immense numbers of Knots were observed resting on the slabs of rock round the island of Ebris. On making an examination through the glasses, they appeared, so far as I was able to judge, to consist entirely of young of the year. There were also a few Bar-tailed Godwits, Turnstones, Oystercatchers, and Purple Sandpipers scattered here and there over the lower ledges. As we approached, a couple of Ruffs showing immature plumage flew round the boat, and after circling for a few moments over the swarm of birds on the rocks, continued their course towards the south-east. No rarities being visible, we were about to leave the Waders unmolested, when one of the crew remarked that a few of the Plover (Knots) would prove most acceptable to some of the old folks at Canty Bay. The boat was consequently dropped quietly within range, and the birds drawing into a compact body as they rose from the rock, I was enabled to discharge a couple of 10-bores with good effect into the flock. In addition to the four hands from Canty Bay, we carried to-day two sturdy young fishermen belonging to one of the North Berwick boats, to assist in pulling the long oars in case of hard work in chasing wounded birds. These laddies proved extremely useful, though the eagerness they displayed while overhauling a brood of Eiders somewhat disconcerted the elder portion of the crew. This was probably their first experience in shooting, and the quaint remarks they uttered, as well the excitement shown in the sport, was most amusing. 'Eh! but yon's a bonnie slaughter!' exclaimed the leader, when despatched to collect the slain, as, springing on the rocks, they started in pursuit of the cripples rapidly making their way among the broken ledges. After a few minutes' search, between fifty and sixty, all in immature plumage, were gathered, several having been carried away by the tide, and others escaping, owing to the roughness of the ground."

On the northern and eastern coasts a heavy gale during autumn and winter frequently causes the movement of large bodies of Knots along the shore, the course held being usually head to wind. The following lines are from my notes in Norfolk in 1872 and East Lothian in 1874:—"November 11, 1872. Gale of wind with squalls of rain from north-north-east. Knots in flocks of from fifty to one hundred, intermixed occasionally with Grey Plover and a few Turnstones, were flying all day to the north along the Yarmouth beach. Though this gale, commencing on the 11th, did not abate till the evening of the 16th, I remarked that but few Knots were seen after the first day." "September 18, 1874. Blowing a gale from west and south-west. While on the shore between Canty Bay and North Berwick, I noticed immense flocks of Knots flying along the coast in the face of the storm. There were also thousands of Dunlins and a few Grey Plovers and Turnstones."

On the coast of Sussex I have repeatedly remarked that dirty weather setting in, with rain and wind from the south or south-south-west, about the middle of September, brings large numbers of Knots into the muddy harbours and saltwater estuaries. Immature Bar-tailed Godwits, clouds of diminutive Waders, and Terns of various species usually accompany them into the sheltered waters, all parties seeking to escape the buffetings of the raging storm outside. No sooner do the drifting squalls abate and the weather gives signs of moderating, than with the first gleams of sunshine breaking through the clouds the weary fugitives appear to pluck up strength and, winging their way across the dreary shingle banks, again betake themselves to the open coast-line.

Unfortunately for their own welfare Knots, and especially the young birds, are the most unsuspicious of the feathered tribe. Occasionally in winter and early spring I have met with large flocks as wild and unapproachable as the watchful Curlew; but, as a rule, continued persecution will be required to put them on their guard. They may commonly be seen in company with almost every species of Wader that frequents the mudflats; it is seldom, unless wounded, that a solitary Knot is observed. On the south coast I have often remarked a single bird or a pair the most conspicuous figures in a small party of Dunlins, while on the shores of the Highland firths flocks of hundreds, if not thousands, commonly join in company with immense bodies of Bar-tailed Godwits.

When shooting on any extensive mudflats, I have often decoyed small parties of Waders, and occasionally even large flocks, by placing out a number of wooden dummies*: Knots and Dunlins were usually the first to gather, and their presence would speedily attract the more wary species. A short extract from my notes while gunning on Breydon during the autumn of 1874 will give some idea of the actions of Knots after alighting to the decoys, as well as an account of the various Waders to be met with at that season on those well-known mudflats:—"The weather turned exceedingly coarse during the afternoon (September 8), and several Wigeon and Curlew were bagged. September 9: on reaching our former station shortly before daybreak, a large flock of Waders were detected feeding on the

---

* The dummies I employed were carved out of wood, and painted to represent Godwits, Plovers, and Knots. Their beaks and legs were of iron, the latter screwed securely into small pieces of board from four to six inches square, according to the size of the bird. When arranged on the mud, head to wind, it was impossible to detect the imposition at any distance. Unlike stuffed birds, these decoys were never injured by wet or weather, and the damages caused by a charge of shot were easily effaced by a small application of putty and a fresh coat of paint.

flats; owing to the imperfect light, it was impossible to identify the whole, though Redlegs and Knots were evidently among their numbers. Being well aware that other punts were on the water, and in all probability the birds would be disturbed before a chance occurred to make a clear examination through the glasses, I fired the large punt-gun* in hopes of some rarities falling to the shot. After collecting the dead and wounded, we counted out about a score each of Redlegs and Knots, a dozen Ruffs and Reeves, and a few Curlew Sandpipers. The Knots were all young, and the Sandpipers adults in somewhat curious stages of plumage, the breasts being still red, while the upper parts were mottled black and grey. On attempting to load the big gun it was discovered that the nipple was blown out; and the necessaries for repairing the mishap having been accidentally omitted from the punt-box, I was forced to send her back to Yarmouth. After changing into the second punt, as two or three small bunches of fowl had been seen through the mist flying west, we made our way slowly towards the upper part of the water. Several flocks of Knots were observed, and a pair of Spotted Redshanks flew past, declining, however, to venture within range, though one of my men was the best imitator of their call I ever heard. On reaching the 'ronds' near the deep water, two punts were discovered to have already taken up their stations, so turning round we dropped back towards the spot lately quitted. Not a dozen yards had been passed over when the two Shanks† again came in view, holding a course that would have brought them within a fair shot of where our boats were concealed below the banks, when a gun (as so frequently happens on Breydon) was discharged, and the birds at once veered towards the south. On this occasion one of the gunners stationed at the 'ronds' had fired his shoulder-gun at a range of considerably over one hundred and fifty yards‡. While passing the lower branch of 'Dessies drain,' a single Knot in company with a small Wader I could not clearly identify, owing to the drifting rain, flew round in answer to the Plover-call, and the stranger (proving when recovered to be only a remarkably diminutive Reeve) was knocked down. As several scattered birds, disturbed from lower down the flats, continued making their way towards the exposed muds near the river-side, the dummies were placed out, and the boats withdrawn a short distance. Almost immediately a single Redleg, rapidly followed by a Ruff and Reeve, was attracted, and hovering round for a moment alighted within a few yards; about a score of Knots (all immature) were the next arrivals. After calling and twittering in a low tone to the unconscious dummies for several minutes, they one by one turned their heads over on their backs, and carefully buried their beaks in the plumage, then puffing out the feathers of the breast and belly, and in most instances lifting one leg, comfortably resigned themselves to repose. For over an hour and a half, during which a drifting rain continued, the whole party remained almost motionless; to say, however, that they slept, would scarcely be correct, as powerful glasses revealed the fact that every few moments one of the eyes of any bird I was enabled to examine were slowly opened. Shortly after midday the weather cleared, and a view of the whole of the flats was obtained; as the greater part of the flocks seen in early morning appeared to have taken their departure, I resolved to knock off work for the day. Our movements in the punts speedily attracted the notice of the Knots, and rousing up slightly, a few commenced to stretch themselves in a lazy and indifferent manner; it was not, however, till the men approached to remove the dummies that the unsuspecting birds exhibited the slightest alarm. At first they merely ran a few yards, uttering

* In order to be prepared for all chances, a man with [...] of wader-shooters, especially when in pursuit of Waders [...] under such circumstances a second gun often proved exceedingly handy.

† In this district the Spotted Redshank is generally known as the "Shank."

‡ The distances at which some of the Breydon gunners will occasionally "strike a light," as these characters term the act of firing, is often positively ridiculous. Jealousy, of course, at times has much to do with such mistakes, as well as overanxiety to obtain a few shillings to keep the family not a-hoking [...]

a low note, evidently unwilling to quit the spot, as the decoys showed no signs of shifting their quarters. At last they got on wing and flew a short distance, returning, however, immediately and sweeping round with repeated calls, attempting to induce their late companions to make their escape. In order to obtain a further insight into the proceedings of these infatuated birds, I recalled the men towards the boats; though the main body continued hovering round, three or four settled at once, and the unmistakable signs of perplexity they exhibited were comical in the extreme. Turning their heads with necks outstretched to at least twice the ordinary length, they intently regarded for a few moments first the immovable dummies, and next the occupants of the punts; then after a few low calls had been exchanged, they rose on wing, and joined the remainder of the flock."

I often noticed that other Waders which had remained in company with the dummies exhibited great reluctance to seek their own safety without giving ample warning of impending danger; Knots, however, were invariably the last to move away.

The seductive marshes round the broads in the east of Norfolk, after the manner of other districts, do not appear to possess any great attractions for this species; at times I recognized a few straggling parties of from two or three to half a dozen, the largest flock that came under my notice being seen on Rush Hills, near Hickling Broad, on the 3rd of March, 1873. These birds, numbering about a score, were in company with some half-dozen Curlews, and exhibited, of course, at this season the full winter dress. Though seldom visiting the inland broads of the eastern counties, Knots, together with Bar-tailed Godwits, usually resort during the winter to Breydon mudflats. This favourite feeding-ground would undoubtedly draw a far larger number of birds were it not for the constant persecution to which they are exposed.

Though frequenting the southern and eastern coasts during winter, these Waders do not entirely desert the shores of the Highland firths at that season; occasionally, however, they disappear for some weeks. Early in March 1869, and all through the month, I found immense flocks of Knots about the muddy creeks and harbours on the northern shore of the Dornoch Firth. Owing to the absence of gunners the birds were unusually fearless for this time of year, and had slaughter been my object, innumerable chances for heavy shots were presented.

It is only on the Norfolk and Sussex coasts that I have met with opportunities for carefully watching the arrival of the spring flocks. With a north-east breeze Knots that have passed the winter further south often commence flying over Breydon mudflats as early as the first week in May, a few small parties occasionally showing themselves in the latter end of April. The first arrivals seldom exhibit any great amount of colour, and birds in perfect red plumage are not to be looked for before the 8th or 9th of the month. All through May they continue passing; the numbers seen, however, vary considerably, the wind, as with all Waders, greatly influencing the course followed.

In 1870, though on Breydon daily (with the exception of the first week) throughout May, I only remarked one bird, which was shot on the 9th, in full summer dress. In 1871 a few fine specimens were obtained on the 12th, 16th, and 26th; while in 1873 only half a dozen, in company with a small party of Bar-tailed Godwits and Grey Plovers, made their appearance on the mud-banks. These birds were discovered on the flats early in the morning of May 15th, and no specimens of which I was in need coming in view, the flock was left for a time undisturbed. Spreading out at last over the mud in search of food, the Knots gradually approached to within about forty yards of the punt, when, by the help of the glasses, I ascertained that one of their number showed a particularly dark red colouring. A shot fired on the upper part of the water put the whole party on wing before there was time to aim the big gun. For some hours they remained absent, and on arriving again in the vicinity of their old quarters evinced considerable mistrust; in all probability a warm reception had been accorded them elsewhere, as a couple of Plover were missing. Though attracted by the dummies, which had been placed out, they declined to settle, and continued sweeping round, the Plovers calling loudly. Doubting whether a better chance to secure the specimen previously noted would be obtained, I waited for a time, following their movements with the big gun, till at last they drew together in the act of turning at the distance of about seventy yards. The trigger happening to be pulled at the exact moment, every bird, when the smoke which had drifted into our eyes cleared off, was discerned stretched out on the sand; but a single cripple succeeded in regaining its legs. Though the whole number (three Godwits, five Plovers, and six Knots) were in full breeding-plumage, the Knot far exceeded any specimen I had previously seen in the richness of the tints on the back and the deep colouring of the underparts. As I had passed during the two seasons of 1871 and 1873 on an average between ten and twelve hours a day on the mudflats all through May, it is unlikely that any large number of Waders escaped notice.

On the Sussex coast for several years this species has been exceedingly scarce in spring, the greater number probably passing at sea. Fishermen frequently reported large bodies of Knots as well as other Waders having been seen at some distance out in the Channel making their way due east. While fishing on May 13th, 1880, wind light and easterly, six or seven miles off Shoreham, I watched several flocks flying east shortly before dusk. On the 11th of May, 1882, a few remarkably fine specimens were noticed on the beach between Shoreham and Lancing, in company with a mixed party of Bar-tailed Godwits, Grey Plover, Curlew Sandpipers, and Dunlin, the majority showing full summer plumage.

I cannot speak from personal experience concerning the edible qualities of the Knot; that the species, however, is held in some estimation for the table, may be judged from the fact that when Plovers are scarce these birds bring in to the fowlers as much as four pence, and occasionally even five pence, a head [*].

Unless needing specimens (either for preservation or to ascertain their plumage and condition) I invariably felt a certain amount of compunction in slaughtering these confiding birds. Though the Knot is at all seasons one of the most accessible of our Waders, the young on their first arrival in the autumn occasionally suffer themselves to be shot at time after time without making the slightest attempt to escape, the survivors of the flocks simply rising on wing at each discharge, and after a short flight alighting with the dead and wounded.

From the crews of the light-ships off the east coast I ascertained that Knots were well known; on some of the vessels they appeared to have been frequently captured. These Waders were described as flying in large bodies, numbers falling at once on deck; and one of the men declared that the last flocks he observed had suddenly shied when close to the lantern, and but one or two had been taken.

[*] An old acquaintance, frequently met with on the Scotch firths, was my authority for this statement. The latter price he obtained for a number killed (212, if I remember right, being the heaviest shot) during the winter of 1867.

# LITTLE STINT.

## *TRINGA MINUTA.*

Though the Little Stint appears, from the information given by certain writers concerning its distribution, to be of not uncommon occurrence on even the north-eastern coast of Scotland, it is only in the southern and eastern counties of England that it has come under my observation in any numbers. On two or three occasions I met with small parties in autumn on the sands at the mouth of the Tyne near Dunbar in East Lothian, and early in June 1867 a flock of ten or twelve, flying north, skimmed past within twenty yards of the boat halfway between North Sunderland and the Fern Islands. Though several years were spent on the coasts of Ross-shire, Sutherland, and the adjoining counties, much time being passed on the shores of the various firths and muddy harbours, I failed to identify a single individual of this species.

While arrayed in its summer dress, the rich chestnut and warm brown tints on the back contrasting with the snowy white of the underparts render the little bird as it flits over the mudflats or runs by the waterside especially attractive. In this plumage the visitors to our shores are but few in number; I have, however, occasionally noticed small parties of two or three birds on the saltings near Shoreham all through May, and a pair were obtained in the harbour in the first week of June 1880. On Breydon flats flocks numbering from three or four to ten or a dozen are commonly to be seen from the middle to the latter end of May, all at this season exhibiting the finest plumage *. During the spring of 1870 and the following year I had ample opportunities for watching the habits of these active little Waders; towards the close of the latter season they were especially plentiful; on the 26th of May several small parties appeared on the flats shortly after daybreak, followed towards midday by a flock of at least twenty birds. At this time of year our visitors usually remain but a few hours on the flats, evidently intent on making their way towards the far north.

Though the Little Stint usually frequents mudflats where the water is salt, a few birds occasionally make their appearance inland during summer and autumn. Early in 1870, after a long continuation of dry weather, the water on Hickling Broad, in the east of Norfolk, fell exceedingly low, large masses of green weed usually submerged being exposed to view. For several days from the 9th a party of twelve or fourteen Little Stints, in the brightest plumage, were to be seen alighting on the patches of weed round the edges of the broad, where they eagerly searched for food †. For the most part the Stints were observed by themselves, though they occasionally joined in company with parties of Dunlins and Wood-Sandpipers, the whole of these small Waders having doubtless been attracted by the unusual extent of feeding-ground left dry by the falling water. A few stragglers also show themselves

* Unlike the Knot, Godwit, Grey Plover, and Curlew-Sandpiper, I have never at this time of year remarked specimens in the garb of winter.

at times during autumn on the hills round the broads in the eastern counties. I remarked two or three small parties in winter plumage resting on one of the hills on Hickling Broad after a gale of wind and rough weather towards the end of September 1879. Dunlins were also present in numbers, together with Knots, a few Curlew, and Greenshanks. The tiny Stints, evidently exhausted by the storm, presented at a short distance the appearance of balls of white down as they rested on the dark green grass of the hills, their heads turned over on their backs and the feathers of the breast puffed out to the fullest extent.

Previous to the draining of a part of the flats known as the Nook at Rye, these birds were exceedingly numerous during autumn; since 1861, however, when the sea-wall was built, they appear to have gradually decreased in the district. At this time of year Stints usually joined in flocks with Curlew Sandpipers, and for a season or two both species still continued to resort to the reclaimed land, evidently reluctant (though the ground was now sufficiently firm to afford grazing for sheep) to quit entirely the vicinity of their old haunts. In September 1860 I obtained many specimens of this species showing autumn plumage on the marshes and on the mudflats round Rye, and remarked a great difference in their size and weight.

A heavy gale of wind from the south and east not unfrequently brings numbers on the coast of Sussex so late as October. About the middle of the month, in 1869, Grey Phalaropes, many in the last stage of exhaustion, were found for over a week in hundreds along the shore from Shoreham towards the west; I also observed several worn-out parties of Stints and Grey Plovers. During the continuation of the rough weather Dunlins and other Waders were conspicuous only by their absence. In all probability these northern breeders had been on the passage in company from their summer-quarters when overtaken by the force of the storm, and driven by the protracted buffetings of the squalls from their accustomed course.

The fact that Dunlins (especially in autumn and winter plumage) are known in some localities as Stints, has, I am of opinion, in many instances led to their having been recorded as specimens of this species.

# TEMMINCK'S STINT.

## TRINGA TEMMINCKI.

NORFOLK and Sussex are the only counties in which I have met with opportunities for observing this elegant little Sandpiper; the species, however, judging from the numbers occasionally seen, is by no means so rare as is generally supposed.

Though this Stint resorts commonly to the saltwater mudflats and the banks of tidal rivers, it is seldom if ever found on the sands of the sea-shore or the open coast-line. Unlike *Tringa minuta*, which is generally to be seen in flocks of Curlew Sandpipers, Dunlins, and others of the family, feeding and flying in company with them, this Stint appears to prefer the society of its own species. I repeatedly noted that small parties or single birds were feeding at no great distance from, or even intermixed with, other Waders would join company at once when driven up.

I have noticed but few of these birds during spring and summer, the course by which this species makes its way towards the breeding-grounds in the far north lying probably to the east of the British Islands. Early in May 1873 two or three single birds, that rose from the marsh-dykes or the pools of water on the hills, were met with about Hickling Broad in the east of Norfolk. Though unable to procure a specimen, the birds in every instance springing unexpectedly while working the punt, I was sufficiently close to ascertain that all appeared to exhibit the dark dress of the breeding-season. On the 25th of July, 1878, the diminutive size of a Wader running actively along the edge of one of the mudflats in Shoreham Harbour attracted my attention, and on shooting the bird it proved to be a male of this species in the dark summer plumage. Its actions while feeding on the ooze by the water-side much resembled those of the Common Sandpiper; the light and wavering flight when on wing, however, at once proclaimed the species. During August and September a few Temminck's Stints (for the most part exhibiting immature plumage) are commonly to be seen frequenting the harbour and the saltings for a mile or so up the river Adur.

I have seldom been on Breydon mudflats during autumn without noticing several of these Stints; they fly, however, for the most part singly or in small parties, and are extremely likely to escape observation. A few extracts from my notes for 1872 will show the regularity with which, at certain states of tide, the various species that frequent the flats approach their feeding-grounds. On the 2nd of September, while stationed in the punts at "The Lumps," a light-coloured Stint, evidently in immature plumage, settled about a hundred yards lower down the run; the boat, however, had taken the ground, and the bird was again on wing before a chance for a shot occurred. In the expectation that it would revisit the spot at the same time of tide on the 3rd, I was on the look-out, and the muds were no sooner exposed than it flew round, alighting after a couple of turns. A juvenile Rook, feeding on dead fish and other refuse by the water-side, instantly made a swoop at and drove up the small stranger. This portion of the flats appeared to possess some strange attraction for the species, as, after a short flight, the bird again approached and, passing within a fair distance, was secured. It proved to be in the immature plumage, the brown feathers on the back being edged with a lighter shade; legs and feet a dirty olive-yellow; base of upper and lower mandibles olive-yellow, darkening into brown towards the point. On the 4th (large numbers of Waders had been heard flying over the town the previous night) I was again on the water, and after shooting round the flats all the morning, made my way towards "The Lumps" shortly after the tide commenced to ebb. The Ruff noticed on the preceding day (easily distinguished by a feather cut from the wing) put in an appearance at the accustomed feeding-time, and, fearing he might again disturb any wandering Stint, I availed myself of an early opportunity, and, while hovering over the drain, dropped him on to the falling tide, when he speedily disappeared from the scene. While removing the gun from my shoulder a small Wader, skimming rapidly under the shelter of the bank, came in view just in time to be stopped by the second barrel. This bird showed precisely the same plumage as the specimen procured on the previous day.

The full winter dress is occasionally assumed before the end of summer; while shooting on Breydon towards the latter end of August 1873, I met with several specimens in this stage of plumage. On the 26th, after a stormy night and severe thunder storm, during which immense numbers of Waders attracted by the lights remained flying over Yarmouth for several hours, Redshanks in thousands were found on the flats at daybreak. Towards midday, after the tide flowed, flocks of Redshanks and Greenshanks, together with about a couple of hundred small birds, came down to "The Lumps," where a score or so of young Common Terns had already settled. I had been for some time watching several young Kentish Plovers, intermixed with Ringed Plovers and Dunlins, when half a dozen Temminck's Stints were recognized sitting quietly within twenty yards of the boat. These little Waders had been so densely surrounded by the throng that no chance had occurred to detect them earlier. The next moment a shot fired on the upper part of the water put the whole body on wing, and I only succeeded in stopping a couple with the shoulder-gun. Later on in the day I obtained a third, on the edge of the reeds round the mudbanks close to the town, and for the next week or so a few stragglers frequented the flats. Two of the specimens were adults in perfect winter plumage, while the third still exhibited a few of the dark feathers of summer, intermixed with the grey of winter, on the back.

# DUNLIN.
## TRINGA ALPINA.

Those desirous of ascertaining the English counties in which the Dunlin breeds must consult other pages than those of 'Rough Notes.' Having ascertained during my wanderings in the Northern Highlands that this species was widely distributed and plentiful in the summer months, and that any amount of specimens in all ages and stages might be obtained, I did not explore the districts they frequented in the south.

Rough weather in autumn is sure to move Dunlins along the shore; I have watched them scores of times flying head to wind while a heavy gale was raging. A couple of extracts from my notes will give some idea of the numbers of this species that may be brought together and put in motion by the approach of a storm.

"September 18, 1874. Blowing a gale from west and south-west. While on the shore between Canty Bay and North Berwick, I noticed immense flocks of Knots flying along the coast in the face of the storm. There were also thousands of Dunlins and a few Grey Plovers and Turnstones passing; Skuas continued flying along the shore all day, and those I was enabled to identify were Arctic, but others were too far off to be clearly distinguished."

During the terrible week in November 1872 more Dunlins than I should have imagined to be in existence in our part of the world were seen off the Yarmouth beach.

"November 11, 1872. The wind was from the north-east, and a frightful gale blowing with terrific gusts and squalls of rain. Large bodies of fowl and Dunlins in innumerable swarms were passing, all bound to the north. A few flocks of Knots and Golden and Grey Plovers were now and then distinguished, and Turnstones and Purple Sandpipers settled in some instances about the puddles in the road that runs to the harbour mouth." On the 12th, the following day, some thousands passed, holding the same course, though the wind had shifted to east-north-east; the numbers seen, however, were not to be compared with those of the previous day.

Dunlins did not breed in Glenlyon, in the north-west of Perthshire, where I had the Innerwick moors for three years, commencing in 1865, though further north they proved abundant, as might have been expected. At Tain, in the east of Ross-shire, where I hired the shootings over the "Fendom," a flat stretch of sandy ground surrounded by the Dornoch Firth on one side, and the open sea on the other, I discovered that they sometimes leave the heather-clad moors and rear their young on the sandy flats adjoining the briny ocean. While at lunch one day in June 1869 on a small grassy slope in this uncultivated desert, a pair of Dunlins were noticed fluttering round and occasionally alighting close at hand; soon after, a downy youngster was observed under the shelter of some rough herbage within a yard or two of where we were sitting, and the remainder of the family were speedily detected when a search was made. Before leaving to return to our boats drawn up on the shores of the Firth, we spread out and, examining all the likely ground, disturbed three or four pairs, all evidently having either eggs or young, in the immediate vicinity of where they were first discovered. Their haunts were not intruded on, as we secured as many downy mites as were required for specimens from the first pair observed. Since that time I have never molested this species during the breeding-season, with the exception of removing a couple of eggs that remained unbroken in a nest on the flat moors of Caithness, that one of the keepers put his foot upon while we were watching the movements of the Arctic Skuas breeding on the floe. While making observations in Caithness and collecting in that and the adjoining county of Sutherland, I received great assistance from the late Mr. W. Dunbar, who hired a great extent of ground for sporting-purposes in that part of the county. During a residence of two or three weeks at Strathmore Lodge, I noticed that in the evening Dunlins were repeatedly seen on the lawn in front of the house, which was unenclosed towards the open moor-land. On every occasion they were in attendance on one or two Golden Plovers, standing on the short green turf about a yard behind. On account of this curious habit of following the Golden Plover, alighting at the same time and retaining their position if an advance was made, I ascertained they were known in this part of the country by the name of the " Plover's Page "*.

Dunlins do not show a partiality for the Norfolk freshwater Broads, but few, except on rare occasions, visiting these localities, the absence of the food on which they usually subsist being doubtless the cause of a move being made to other quarters. I can find but one or two entries in my notes where the species is referred to during the many years spent on Hickling Broad, Heigham Sounds, and the adjoining pieces of water, and in only one instance are they mentioned as being met with in considerable numbers.

"April 28, 1883. A cold breeze from the east-south-east. Grasshopper Warblers heard for the first time in the season, and Ring-Ouzels observed. The whole of the Ruffs and Reeves were gathered together on one of the hills, and proved utterly unapproachable. There were many Black Terns, exhibiting a great difference in plumage, and also several Common Terns beating about over the water; Greenshanks, Curlew, and Whimbrel were flying round in small parties or singly, and for the first time on this Broad a large flock of Dunlins attracted my attention, sweeping in a cloud here and there over the water, and finally alighting on the grassy point of 'Swimcents.' There were swarms of various species of Waders and Terns, and all proved exceedingly unsuspicious of danger with the exception of the Ruffs and Reeves, which rose on wing at once if the punt approached their quarters."

In the summer of 1873 I witnessed a rather amusing mishap that befel a juvenile of this species on Breydon mudflats; and a short extract from my notes will give an account of the affair:—

"August 11, 1873. Wind west. While watching some young Dunlins running about feebly in the shallow water about the *** I noticed one make an attempt to rise on wing, but was immediately dragged down again by a large cockle firmly fixed on to one of its toes. The poor little bird flapped helplessly on the surface of the water for about a minute, but succeeded in getting free just as I came to the spot, leaving all the bait to go to its assistance."

The first year that the preservation of Waders and other species came in force I was on Breydon, and the effect it had on the flocks gathered together on the mudflats was remarkable. A short extract from my notes refers to the subject:—

"May 8, 1873. Wind north. Up Breydon soon after daylight with the Batchels. *** a few Grey Plovers in the intermediate stage between winter and summer plumage, their breasts sprinkled with black and white. There was also a flock of about two hundred Dunlins associated with a few Ringed Plovers, as well as half a dozen Sanderlings, which kept together. These little Waders (thanks to the new Act) were perfectly fearless, allowing us to work the punt up within a few yards. Nearly all were resting on one leg with the head covered with the feathers of the back, and so it lasted till a few yards on the approach of the punt, when crossing the smaller drains they still kept the leg drawn up, and on alighting again launched idly on the one leg."

On the following day, May 9th, there were again in active numbers of Dunlins, Ringed Plovers, and a few Sanderlings. A Dunlin suddenly started from sleep hopped such a distance that I chose to my astonishment till at last, when at a distance of about three yards from the side of the punt, he too I stood out quickening the resting leg, lowered his neck and deliberately scratched the back of his head.

* I never noticed this behaviour elsewhere; ***

# PURPLE SANDPIPER.

## TRINGA MARITIMA.

The Purple Sandpiper is one of the most confiding of the feathered tribe; such slight regard do they pay at times to a near approach that, feeding quietly in some dark pool or crevice among the rocks, their presence might easily be overlooked. More fearless even than the Dunlin, a charge of shot through their ranks does not appear to instil the accustomed dread of their natural enemy, usually so soon acquired.

In May 1865, I found a large flock of some hundreds in the finest stage of summer plumage resorting to the range of rocks on which the beacon stands below Seacliff, on the coast-line of the Firth of Forth between Canty Bay and Dunbar. The conspicuous red-brown tint on their backs *, shown off to the fullest advantage by the bright sunlight, at once attracted my attention, and imagining, from what I had previously learned concerning the species, that their presence at this season was unusual, no time was lost in procuring specimens. In such dense and compact order did the whole mass wheel round when driven up, that the single shot fired proved far more destructive than I anticipated. Not more than a couple of minutes had passed before they were back almost on the same spot, running, apparently unconcerned, within the distance of a few yards while the victims that had fallen were still being collected. This was the only occasion in spring on which these unsuspecting birds were molested, though several parties were met with here and there along the ledges of rock as far as I followed the coast-line towards the east. The numbers decreased early in June; a few, however, remained till the following month and, indeed, all through the summer; these were, for the most part, in worn and dingy plumage, and usually in company with Turnstones. As far south as the Fern Islands, and on many of the straggling rocks composing that dangerous group, I frequently recognized the two species during May and June. In no instance could I learn, from personal observation or any trustworthy source, that they remained and bred on our shores. I am aware that eggs strongly resembling those of the Purple Sandpiper are reported to have been procured at various points round the British coasts, but in no single instance have they been taken and the birds identified by a competent judge. I have noticed small parties in May on the low reefs of rock that fringe the shell-strewn beach † in some of the bays and creeks between Thurso and Duncansby Head and round towards the south; these all exhibited the full summer dress, and were, in all probability, on their way towards the north, as, with few exceptions, they had departed by the following month. Among the rocky islets off the west coast of Ross-shire, and also in the Outer Hebrides, a few small parties were met with early in May every season I visited the district.

Though both old and young in mixed and variegated stages of plumage may be observed along the east coast of Scotland so early as the beginning of September, it is not till a month or six weeks later that any number are usually found along the shores of the eastern and southern counties of England.

* This bronze tint on the back disappears soon after death. No coloured plate I have seen gives the faintest idea of the living bird.
† To the casual observer the shore along the coast, particularly near Elgin (the spot where the traditional Jonah of Infant's house was supposed to stand), would present the appearance of a fine white sand. If closely examined it will be found to consist entirely of particles of broken shells.

During the heavy easterly gale that broke over the Norfolk coast on the 11th November, 1872, and continued without intermission for the five following days, I repeatedly remarked small parties running round the pools of rain-water on the drive at the south end of Yarmouth, just opposite the Nelson monument. There were also several single birds, or pairs, seeking what shelter they could obtain about the wooden landing-stages in the harbour. On one occasion (November 2, 1872), when going on board a steamboat from the north side of the river close to the pier, I noticed that two or three, which were peeking about on the seaweed and slime collected on the steps, only fluttered a yard or two on to some of the adjoining piles.

On both the Bass and the Isle of May, and many of the small rocky islands (Ebris in particular) in the Firth of Forth, I remarked a few of these birds at almost all seasons running fearlessly on the ledges close to the water's edge, making way but a few yards when approached. Along the Sussex coast these birds resort at times during autumn and winter to the salt-water creeks and inlets to the west of Brighton, though their favourite quarters in this locality appear to be the pools and small channels among the blocks of chalk scattered broadcast below the cliffs between Brighton and Rottingdean. Here seaweeds of various kinds grow strong and rank, harbouring a constant supply of their natural food. At one piece of water only (a brackish pool just inside the ridge of shingle that holds back the gradually encroaching waves between Shoreham and Worthing) have I met with this species engaged seeking for food unless in the immediate wash of the salt water.

The winter plumage exhibits a decided purple or, rather, a neutral-tint shade, the rich red-brown on the back, as well as the gloss, having entirely vanished. The colouring of the legs and beak, especially in the younger birds, is more dingy than in summer, and the general appearance is by no means so conspicuous or attractive.

The food of this species, according to my own observation, must be procured for the most part, if not entirely, from parts of the coast exposed to the influence of salt water, small crawling insects and minute Crustacea probably forming the chief part of their diet. Though I have repeatedly watched large numbers while busily engaged hunting for a meal on the dripping rocks at the distance of only a few yards, the prey they captured was in almost every instance so diminutive as to escape detection by the naked eye.

# LAND-RAIL.

## CREX PRATENSIS.

The Land-Rail or Corn-Crake is widely distributed over the British Islands, being remarkably plentiful in the cultivated portions of many of the remotest Highland glens; in the west of Perthshire I found this species exceedingly numerous, also in the east of Ross-shire and even still further north. It occasionally happens in certain parts of the Highlands that the hay is not cut till well on in September; in such localities these birds commonly take their departure unnoticed, unless attention is attracted to their presence by the monotonous croaking note, which may usually be heard soon after the beginning of May.

On two or three occasions in the autumn of 1867 I met with downy nestlings, that could hardly have quitted the egg above a couple of days, so late as the first week in September. In all probability these were second broods, large numbers of full-grown young resorting to the same piece of land—a stretch of rough marshy ground (that furnished a scanty crop of hay) adjoining the course of the Lyon in the west of Perthshire. While making a few casts for trout in June 1866 I was somewhat surprised to see a Land-Rail, which had been disturbed by a retriever, run down the sloping bank towards the river and without pausing a moment drop quietly into the water and strike boldly out for the opposite shore; in less than a minute the dog arrived on the spot and immediately sighting the bird, now in mid-stream, plunged in and captured it before gaining the land. This Rail, which I examined alive, had not received the slightest injury, being blessed with the full use of both wings and legs, so that its taking to the water was entirely a matter of choice.

Fishing being evidently looked upon as an exceedingly dull pursuit by old Nell (the black retriever frequently alluded to in these pages), I always allowed her to hunt over the rough ground in the immediate vicinity, and many broods of young and nests of eggs, that would otherwise have escaped my observation, were detected. On no occasion was the least damage done to the downy mites she offered for inspection; juvenile Oyster-catchers, Sandpipers, Redshanks, and Ducklings were frequently captured and afterwards returned to the care of the old birds. The pursuit of Land-Rails, however, appeared to afford her the greatest amusement, and specimens in all stages of plumage were at various times brought from the hay-field to the river-bank.

I have never met with any statements as to whether this species crosses the Channel in flocks; it is, however, evident that they occasionally arrive in large quantities, though possibly not in company. While searching round the hedgerows in the vicinity of the coast of West Sussex early one morning during the first week in May 1867, to ascertain what migrants had reached our shores during the night, I noticed immense quantities of the smaller Warblers and also several Land-Rails, no less than twelve or fourteen of the latter being put on wing from a rough bank not more than a couple of hundred yards in length; scattered birds were also found in the adjoining fences and the coarse grass bordering the plantations. On searching over the ground the following morning not a single specimen of this species was seen.

Previous to making a move towards the south in autumn Land-Rails frequently collect in large numbers in the neighbourhood of the coast. In September 1860 I rode into the midst of a party of at least thirty or forty that were crossing a lane with steep banks near Crowhurst in Sussex: the birds had probably been alarmed by a wild and unbroken spaniel rushing through a piece of clover adjoining the roadside; some fluttered as if wounded, some ran in the usual skulking fashion, while others flew boldly towards some cover across the track. While shooting near Battle early in September many years ago, I assisted in bagging eight and a half couple in about two acres of clover; had breechloaders been employed at least double the number must have fallen.

Though this species is occasionally almost overloaded with fat at the commencement of the shooting-season, there are few better birds for the table when dressed with care.

It is asserted by some writers that young Land-Rails are at first covered with a black down; I should rather be inclined to term the colour a dull dark sooty brown.

# SPOTTED CRAKE.

## PORZANA MARUETTA.

---

Though the Spotted Crake is said to be distributed over the whole of the eastern counties of Scotland, I have only on one occasion identified this species to the north of the Tweed, a very strongly marked specimen having risen at my feet in May 1864 from the water-plants growing round the swampy portion of the ground on Gullane Links, in East Lothian. This stealthy bird is doubtless plentiful in most suitable localities in England, though escaping notice in many instances, owing to the inaccessible nature of its haunts and the difficulty of forcing it on wing. On certain boggy spots on Wicken Fen, near Ely, I discovered two or three nests some five and twenty years ago, and more recently, in the east of Norfolk, the species has been met with in considerable numbers; in the marshes of Sussex it also makes a short stay in spring, and a few are occasionally killed during the return journey in autumn.

To state accurately the date at which the Spotted Crake leaves our shores on the approach of winter is well nigh impossible; though the majority evidently take their departure before cold weather sets in, a few stragglers are occasionally seen even as late as the new year, wounds or weakness probably accounting for their incapacity to undertake a lengthened passage. My notes for 1871, while shooting in the east of Norfolk, contain several entries relating to this species: on the 9th of October a couple shot on Ludham Hover are alluded to; on the 11th six and a half couple were bagged by two guns round Heigham Sounds, and several more might have been secured had I taken all the chances falling to my share*. During the remainder of the month many were seen on the various Snipe-grounds. On the 15th of November a single bird was killed at Reedham, near Ludham; and on the 21st of December, while crawling over a marsh near Hickling to obtain a shot at Geese, I drove one from the shelter of some rushes, broken down by the effects of frost and snow, under which it had sought refuge on my approach—creeping stealthily out within the distance of a foot, there could not be the slightest doubt as to its identity. So recently as the winters of 1879 and '80 three more specimens, fresh killed, came under my observation; a couple were secured by shoregunners in the marsh-dykes near Shoreham harbour, and the third was picked up disabled near the banks of the Adur, having probably struck against some obstacle while on flight.

In Sussex I failed to discover the nest of this Rail, though a pair were obtained in a portion of Pevensey Level known as Barnhorn Ponds early in April 1866. The first bird was sprung on the open marsh and easily killed; the second, rising shortly after, merely topped the coarse herbage for a yard or so, and immediately dropped into a thick bed of rushes near the edge of a dyke. All attempts to discover its whereabouts having failed, I came to the conclusion that the bird had succeeded in making its escape. As usual, when shooting in this part of the country, I had engaged the services of one of the natives residing on the marsh, who was followed by the most villanous-looking representative of the genus *Canis* that has ever come under my observation. This ungainly quadruped (apparently a cross between a Sussex sheep-dog and a rough terrier) having taken up an attitude intended for a point by the side of the dyke, intently regarding the surface of the water, its master "the looker"* declared that the bird was concealed near at hand, and, turning up his sleeves, groped into the weeds at the bottom, bringing up the object of our search at the second attempt. These Crakes, I learned from the man, were by no means uncommon in this locality at certain seasons; he also described another species, somewhat similar in colouring, but not above half the size, of which his dog had at different times brought him three or four specimens. Not having the slightest doubt that the unknown would prove to be Baillon's Crake, I requested the man to let me know immediately any of these diminutive Crakes were met with, giving him special orders not to destroy them. The following spring I was again shooting over the level and adjoining marshes, and on making inquiries concerning these birds, the "looker" stated that, shortly after my last visit, his dog turned savage, and he was forced to shoot it; since that time not a single Crake (large or small) had come under his observation†.

On the rondes and hovers of the flat marshy districts of the east of Norfolk I occasionally met with nests of eggs or broods of young belonging to this species. On the 28th of April, 1873, a nest containing eight eggs was pointed out by one of the fenmen, four or five inches below the surface of the water; the tide had risen suddenly, and the floods must have proved destructive to immense numbers of eggs.

Though I was not so fortunate as to secure a specimen, an undoubted Baillon's Crake rose at my feet on the rondes round the west side of Heighams Sounds in the autumn of 1872. Both barrels of my gun having just been discharged, the bird escaped, disappearing from view round a patch of reed before a cartridge could be inserted; to start it again proved an utter failure, though our endeavours were continued for a couple of hours. On carefully scanning the runs in the soft mud and comparing the footprints undoubted signs were found that at least two of these Crakes had lately resorted to that portion of the swamp. Two dozen and a half small traps were set as speedily as possible, but owing to the numbers of Coots and Moorhens frequenting the spot, it was impossible to keep them in working order. On our first visit but two traps out of thirty were unsprung, no precautions having been taken to secure captives so strong as Coots, these powerful birds had in many instances dragged the pegs and made off. Even after working over the adjacent reedbeds and hovers with the assistance of dogs for several hours, three or four traps still remained undiscovered, a second setting having also resulted in a failure from the same cause, the attempt to secure the bird in this manner was relinquished.

---

* Large numbers of cattle, often from some distance inland, were annually sent down to fatten on Prensey Level, while feeding on the marshes they were watched over by natives of the district, who were known as "lookers."

† In out-of-the-way parts of the country the natives frequently express their ideas in a comical and singular manner. The "looker" informed

# WATER-RAIL.
## RALLUS AQUATICUS.

---

Water-Rails appear far less abundant throughout Scotland than in the southern and eastern counties of England; in the Highlands this species has come under my notice only in Strath Tay, in the vicinity of a few small reedy lochs near the Spey, and about Lairg and Altnaharra, in Sutherland. While residing in East Lothian I remarked that a pair or two regularly took up their quarters on the approach of winter about a small stream, known as the Eel Burn, falling into the Forth a couple of miles to the west of North Berwick. Shortly after daybreak, one cold and bitter morning in the winter of 1864, when the sands immediately congealed with ice as the tide receded, I watched a pair peeking about on the shore round a small pool of open water at the mouth of the burn; the poor birds had evidently been driven from their usual haunts by the severity of the weather, and appeared sadly cut up through want of food.

Rails evince a decided partiality for low-lying marshy ground, though in the east of Sussex I often met with scattered pairs along the course of the small trout-streams meandering through the densely wooded portions of the county. The extensive reed-beds and trackless swamps that abound in the neighbourhood of the broads of the eastern counties are admirably adapted to the habits of this species; on the slightest signs of danger they betake themselves to the thickest cover, and, unless driven out by a dog accustomed to their skulking habits, usually escape observation. Though but seldom seen, their strange cries may be heard at certain hours, almost continuously, in fine still weather during the summer months; the peculiar squeaks and grunts, however, that are emitted would never be supposed, by any one unacquainted with their note, to proceed from the throat of a bird.

On the 27th of June, 1873, while passing through a slade near Hickling, I walked over a nest of this species in a bed of sedge where the bottom was exceedingly moist and sloppy; the old birds, evidently close at hand, kept out of sight, expressing their disgust or alarm at our presence by a succession of noisy, though far from melodious, sounds. Noticing that several of the eight eggs were chipped and evidently just on the point of hatching, I returned on the following day, being anxious to obtain the downy young as specimens. On reaching the nest but two eggs remained, with a few portions of broken shells lying scattered around; the old birds proved still more vociferous than on our former visit, and while examining a small patch of grass and sedge in which they were concealed, one of the juveniles was detected squatting on a bare spot. After a careful search, the whole six were secured within a radius of eight or ten yards. How these tiny mites had reached so great a distance was somewhat puzzling, unless conveyed by their parents, their limbs appearing scarcely strong enough to sustain their weight. The youngsters were covered thickly with a glossy black down, possessing, when viewed in the bright sunlight, a metallic lustre, exhibiting much the same bottle-green tints as the plumage of the Black Guillemot or White-winged Tern when fresh-killed. The legs and feet were of a dull brown; bills dirty white, tip black, with a small white speck near the point. Having previously obtained specimens of adults, I did not molest them, and, in order to lessen their bereavement, returned one of the brood to the nest. A few days later, the two old birds, accompanied by their reduced family of three, were encountered on the same marsh, though their quarters had been removed to a part where the soil was firmer. The young had rapidly gained strength, running actively across the open and hiding themselves so securely in the cover, that without the assistance of a retriever there would have been but little chance of alighting on their place of concealment. On the 7th of July, while quanting up one of the adjoining dykes, I again came suddenly on this small party, when the youngsters at once betook themselves to the water, swimming boldly across a shallow pool, and, on making the shore, instantly disappearing in the coarse herbage.

Though Water-Rails remain in Great Britain throughout the winter in considerable numbers, it is obvious that many arrive on the south coast during spring from across the Channel. Along the shore near Rye and Pevensey, and again, further west, about Brighton and Shoreham, I occasionally fell in with these birds in the coarse grass about the brackish pools near the coast, or in the ditches intersecting the adjoining marshes. Shortly after daybreak one morning in the spring of 1859, between twenty and thirty were put out from the beds of samphire and other salt-water weeds growing on the mud-flats in the Nook at Rye.

A Water-Rail that I kept in confinement would occasionally mount to some height among the branches of the shrubs and bushes in the garden, being able apparently to grasp strongly with its claws. After remaining in captivity for a couple of years, it was at length killed by a combined attack of three Herring-Gulls, who surrounded the poor little bird and pecked it to death before assistance could be rendered.

# MOORHEN.

## *GALLINULA CHLOROPUS.*

This            short        John         over the British
      the                                   endless task; the
           on         or              on the most extensive lake or loch

            this species becomes exceedingly fearless, scarcely quitting the roadside pond on the approach of traffic, and feeding regularly with poultry in the farmyards. In company with Coots they resort in numbers to the water collected in the excavations adjoining the embankments of several lines of railway, regarding the passing trains with the greatest unconcern. In most situations these birds are in all probability perfectly harmless, though the game-preserver in charge of young Pheasants will do well to keep an eye on any chance visitor that may approach his coops.

In some localities in the Highlands these birds gather in large numbers round the moorland lochs, breeding almost in colonies, so thickly are their nests placed in the more favourable situations where dense cover and waving bogs afford the necessary security for bringing out their young. The extensive reed-beds surrounding the broads and meres of the eastern counties also harbour countless Moorhens; in many parts the swamps to which they resort, as the only chance of safety, are utterly impassable to any one except a native fenman. Towards the end of April 1878, the water on Heigham Sounds and the adjoining broads rose rapidly, owing to the high tides caused by a continuation of strong westerly winds. The overflow being sufficient to float a light punt through the bushes * and over many dangerous parts of the roads, the immense losses suffered by Coots, Moorhens, and Rails were easily ascertained, scores of nests with the full complement of eggs being seen from three or four to half a dozen inches below the surface of the water.

Throughout the neighbourhood of the broads and in marshy districts in all parts of the country these birds construct their coarse and roughly built nests among the flags, reeds, or sedge, employing solely strands of rushes and other water-plants. When resorting to small ponds or streams in wooded localities, they avail themselves of the shelter afforded by the stubbs and twining roots of the willow, alder, or hazel overhanging the water. Though statements are recorded by various authors to the effect that nests have been observed in trees at an elevation of twenty feet, I have never noticed one at a greater height from the ground than between three and four feet. On one occasion I examined a most picturesque site for a cradle that had been chosen at about this height among the twisted limbs of an old and weather-beaten alder, thrown down by the winter gales across the bed of a mountain burn in a desolate Highland glen; though the gradually rotting stump exhibited no signs of foliage, the luxuriant fronds of endless spreading ferns sprouting from the peat-mould on the surrounding slabs of rock afforded ample concealment.

* A reed-bed is always termed a "bush" by the natives of these dreary wastes.

On first leaving the egg, the downy Moor-chick exhibits most conspicuous red and bright blue tints about the head; as these bright shades are for the most part confined to the skin, they rapidly fade after death. In order to give a good idea of the appearance presented by the juvenile during life, a coloured sketch ought to be taken from a living specimen.

The young during their first autumn may readily be distinguished from the adults by the brown and grey tinges of the plumage on the back and breast being less pure, a dirty white also shows on the lower portion of the breast and belly. Beak a dull olive-brown, with a green tinge; legs and feet a dull greenish yellow; claws horn-tint.

Though almost every writer on British birds with whom I am acquainted gives the title of Dabchick to the Little Grebe, this name is invariably bestowed on the Moorhen by the country people in the east of Sussex.

# COOT.
## FULICA ATRA.

the ............ by scenery of a totally ............ in ............ greatly resemble those in the flat ............ of the east of England; ............ bottom with shallow ............ the pools that prove so attractive to diving fowl in both localities; large beds of ............ other luxuriant water-plants spring up in a dense mass round the edges and afford a retreat in ............ utterly impenetrable. A stretch of swamps and rush-grown marshlands, interspersed here and there with small patches of alder and osier, will be found in the vicinity of the broads; while waving bogs, rank heather, and coarse grass, with an occasional straggling thicket of fir or birch, for the most part form the immediate surroundings in the north.

The shores of the majority of the Highland lochs do not offer suitable breeding-quarters for Coots, and consequently this species is by no means common, though widely distributed, in the north. There are, however, on the Tay, the Spey, and some of the branches of the Shin, as well as on most large rivers, still and reedy pools where at all seasons (except, probably, the depth of winter) a few pairs of these birds may be noticed. In addition to the great nurseries of Coots in the eastern and one or two of the southern counties of England, this species is found in all parts of the country where sheltered ponds and sluggish rivers or streams affording sufficient cover are met with. When free from persecution these birds become remarkably fearless, though a sharp look-out is usually kept. Passengers on many of our lines of railway must have noticed the contempt with which the passing trains are treated by the Coots and Moorhens resorting to the pools of water within only a few yards of the rails.

In open weather Coots may usually be seen during the whole winter in the neighbourhood of their summer haunts; a long spell of severe frost, however, drives them to the coast or the tidal rivers. On the large broads of the eastern counties the water immediately surrounding the reed-beds is generally first affected by frost; as the cold increases, the open water gradually diminishes, leaving only here and there a few "wakes"[*], in and around which the starving birds collect. At times when the whole broad is "laid"[†] I have watched the Coots gathered together in a silent and desponding manner in one or two large parties—each unfortunate standing frequently on one leg, with the feathers puffed out and the head drawn back, every member of the group presenting a picture of patient and helpless misery. Should the frost continue, the whole body are shortly forced, through want of food, to change their quarters and make a move for the nearest open water, whether fresh or salt.

[*] A "wake" is the local name given to a piece of water either kept open by the action of the wind, or broken and cleared by the keepers for the accommodation of the same species.

[†] The broad is termed "laid" by the natives when entirely frozen over.

In some localities, particularly in parts of the eastern counties, the Coot is highly esteemed for its edible properties. Though a few were tried and proved, when properly dressed, decidedly preferable to any of the diving ducks, with the exception, perhaps, of the Pochard, I never avail myself of the chances that the immense flocks of this species occasionally offer to the punt gun. It is decidedly bad policy on preserved waters to harass these birds, as large bunches of fowl are occasionally attracted to the spot where Coots are feeding. If hitherto unmolested they will quietly regard the approaching punt, possibly gathering slowly and paddling quietly away, though without exhibiting the slightest signs of alarm. If constantly fired at, they rise on the wing at once as soon as threatened, and flying round for a time in a confused mob, give warning to every fowl or wader within view, and destroy all chance of a shot. On waters open to the public, or when driven to the coast in winter, it is useless to spare them on the score of spoiling future sport, as the loafing shore-shooter will blaze at every feathered creature passing within a quarter of a mile, while the professional punt-gunner, as might be expected, invariably makes the attempt to possess himself of any fowl he thinks will pay for the charge of powder and shot in his old-fashioned and too often unserviceable barrel.

One or two regularly organized Coot-shootings used formerly to be got up annually on many of the Norfolk broads, and the same style of battue has been mentioned by several writers as taking place in the south-western counties. For some time past the Coots in the broad districts have been slowly but surely decreasing in numbers, and these shootings, which for years were looked forward to by all the countryside, have now gradually fallen into disrepute. A few lines with reference to the manner in which the proceedings were usually conducted and the circumstances that led to their being discontinued may not be out of place.

The meet was usually fixed for an early hour; but long before the appointed time the company were to be seen arriving in craft of every description, those who were unable to get afloat contenting themselves by taking up a position on the various hills or on the banks. When all was ready, the boats, numbering usually from thirty to fifty, formed in line and worked round the birds so as to enclose them in a corner of the broad. As soon as they found themselves hemmed in and the space gradually contracting, they rose and flew in all directions, always at last making for the open water beyond the line of boats, affording great sport and still greater confusion for several minutes. If the line was well kept, the Coots appeared bewildered and continued flying round and round for a considerable time before attempting to break through, though if only a single boat fell out of its appointed station the whole of the birds in a body made for the gap and the drive was spoiled. Those that escaped the first round settled on some remote corner of the broad and were again attacked in the same manner. So long as Coots were plentiful and order maintained, a good day's sport was usually insured. Since the falling off in the number of the birds less interest has been taken in the affair by the proprietors of the water, and naturally no discipline is now enforced. Boatloads of strangers, either utterly careless or not understanding the regulations, are frequently present, and there is little wonder that the attempt to drive the birds proves a failure. Instead of endeavouring to keep in line, the crews of the boats appear only anxious to secure what they imagine the best position, and consequently all order is speedily lost. Some years back I joined on one occasion in the drive; latterly, however, the sport has only been watched from a safe distance, the reckless manner in which much of the shooting was conducted preventing the slightest desire for a nearer view*. Small and well-organized parties are still, however, got up by the owners of some of the waters.

Wounded Coots are often lost should they retain sufficient strength to dive. The frequency with which they escape has impressed many of the old gunners in the east of Norfolk with the idea that a broken-winged bird invariably grasps the weeds with its claws and remains fixed to the bottom when dead. That they become entangled in the water-plants and are unable to free themselves is probably the true state of the case.

Coots commence breeding early in the season, their first nests being for the most part exceedingly conspicuous, owing to the scanty vegetation. Large quantities of eggs are taken by the marshmen among the reed-beds during April, but few of the earlier clutches escaping. I have, however, met with two or three newly hatched broods in the east of Norfolk by the 20th of April. The nest is a large and coarsely built, though strongly interwoven, structure, composed of the dead stalks, strands, and leaves of many water-plants. The eggs vary in number, four, six, or eight being at times the full complement, frequent robbery at the commencement of the season probably reducing the number of the later broods. The bright colours on the hairy down about the heads of the young contrasting with their otherwise sooty covering render them exceedingly conspicuous. Though scores of newly hatched birds have come under my observation, I never detected one in the nest if perfectly released from the shell; it is probable that they take to the water almost the first hour of their existence. The orange tints soon fade, and by the time the young have reached rather more than double the size at which they quitted the egg their appearance is far less attractive. The first feathers on the lower part of the head, neck, and breast are a dirty white; a few long and curling grey bristles or hairs at this stage still show among the black down on the crown. The pale slate-grey feathers make their appearance on the lower part of the belly and flanks while a long sooty down covers the back. ................ first autumn and the early part of the winter may easily be recognised by their ................ on the head, and generally slighter build than the adults. There seems ................ female when the mature plumage is assumed.

................ the beginning of June 1873 (weather cold, with a thick ................ the ................ my attention was attracted by a most singular piebald fowl making ................ from ................ land. This stranger was rapidly followed by ................ any of the others. On examining the ................ were a pair of old Coots with their young, each ................ completely covered ................ the ................ lying thickly on the banks, having been blown in ................ water by ................ northeast wind. After swimming a few yards the ................ roosting.

................ distance on the marshes from its parents, does not escape ................ the ................ meddlesome Peewits. In order that its portrait might be taken from life, a juvenile of some four or five weeks had been captured and released on the completion of the drawing. Confused by the ordeal through which it had passed, the helpless youngster strayed on to the rush-grown portion of the hall instead of towards the water where the remainder of the brood were concealed. In a few moments the strange appearance of the long-limbed fledgeling, rushing hither and thither with extended neck and clumsy legs stretching out behind, had attracted between twenty and thirty Peewits and half as many Redlegs. Screaming loudly, dashing down and sweeping round and round, a tremendous uproar was created, which lasted till the object of their solicitude was again captured and returned to the water.

The usual note of the Coot is a shrill scream, which may occasionally be heard in the vicinity of their haunts; the birds, however, are by no means clamorous. When on wing during the night they proclaim their presence by frequent cries. Though seldom moving far from their quarters by day, unless disturbed and alarmed, Coots make extended flights by night. In fine still weather in July and August I have repeatedly listened to their notes uttered high in the air during the hours of darkness, the birds being at the time at least a mile or two distant from the waters they frequented by day. The sounds that break the stillness of night in the midst of the extensive marshes of some of the eastern counties are extremely varied, the strange whistles and cries of many of the denizens of the swamps being exceedingly puzzling to identify with certainty.

## COOT.

Towards the end of the summer of 1873 the weather in the east of Norfolk was exceedingly hot and sultry, and the eels in the rivers and broads, being in some manner affected by the water, crowded in immense numbers into the small channels and dykes before the rising tide, to escape its influence. In such spots they were caught in incredible quantities by the natives by means of "bobs"[*]. In order to ascertain if the reports were not exaggerated, I resolved to pass the night on the water and visit the localities where the best takes were declared to have been obtained. A short extract from my notes referring to the expedition will show how frequently Coots passed over during the night:—

"Shortly before the darkness set in, a few 'colls'[†] of Teal and two or three couple of Mallard were noticed sweeping low over the marshes to some favourite feeding-grounds. The Peewits were exceedingly noisy, and continued wheeling and tumbling over their haunts till the daylight had entirely disappeared. A Short-eared Owl or two flapped across the rushy ground, their long-eared relative also came in view, and the screech of the Barn-Owl was distinctly heard from the neighbourhood of the plantations. Though invisible owing to the height at which they kept, the cries of Coots were audible soon after dark, the birds evidently flying singly without any settled course, their calls occasionally being answered by others at a distance. For the first hour or so after dark numbers flew past; the cries were then less frequent, but between 10 P.M. and 2 A.M. on the following morning the notes of at least two or three were recognized during each succeeding hour. The night proved excessively close and still, even the rustling murmur of the reeds was hushed, not a breath of air stirring their feathery heads or lifting the wreaths of fog off the stagnant flats. Shortly after 10 P.M., while quanting from one spot to another where the eel-fishing was being carried on, a mile or two of the river having been passed over and the silence broken only by the hum of the insects and the occasional slashing of a fish, the scream of a hare caught our ears, which, coupled with other sounds, left little doubt that poachers were taking leverets on the land adjoining the Martham marshes. I was rather surprised at the fact of the poaching fraternity being at work to-night. On my way to the boats just as day was closing in I had passed the door of a waterside public-house, and attracted by the chorus of one of the popular airs of the day chanted in a slow and faltering manner by a single beery voice, had peeped round the corner of the door and detected a well-known poacher, seated by himself in front of the dying embers that smouldered in the kitchen grate. Not another soul appeared about the premises; but here sat 'Spurgeon' (the title by which this character was known in the district), beating time to his melancholy dirge with the bottom of his quart pot on the top of the range. At last his voice grew fainter and fainter and finally ceased, the mug was drained, and a fresh supply demanded in almost inaudible tones. No response being obtained, the pot was hammered on the hob till dashed to pieces, when sinking back in his chair after a few muttered sentences his head dropped forward and a long-drawn snore proclaimed the stupified sot in the land of dreams. About 11 P.M. a bird with a note I was totally unacquainted with crossed rapidly over, high in the air. The call was somewhat similar to that of the Spotted Redshank, though it differed materially in many respects. At 11.30 P.M. several Peewits were disturbed on a distant marsh, and remained flying about and calling for nearly a quarter of an hour before again settling. Shortly after midnight a couple of Greenshanks passed over Heigham Sounds in an easterly direction, their notes being audible for several minutes. About an hour later a heavy thunderstorm broke over the country towards the south-east, and, though some miles distant, a fire, probably caused by the lightning, was clearly visible and continued burning brightly for a considerable time. With the exception of Coots, Peewits, and a solitary Curlew, no other birds gave evidence of being on the move. Shortly before daybreak a drenching shower came down, when the drip of the rain on the water, and the wind rising in gradually increasing gusts, put a stop to all chance of further observations."

[*] To "bob" for eels is a most deprecable style of fishing. The fish is a bunch of worms threaded on worsted held in the water close to the boat's side by means of a stout rod. The fish usually taken are small, but now and then a 2-lb. eel is captured.

[†] "Coll" is a local name for a brood of the young of any of the web-footed tribes.

# GREY PHALAROPE.

## *PHALAROPUS FULICARIUS.*

---

The first Grey Phalarope I met with was discovered, one stormy evening in September 1866, swimming in a pool of water in a marsh adjoining the banks of the river Lyon, in Glenlyon, in the west of Perthshire. This part of the country is nearly fifty miles from the sea-coast, so the poor little bird must have been driven a long distance inland by the gale, which would account for its weakened condition, as it paid little or no attention when approached within a yard or two. I was anxious to procure the stranger as a specimen, and as the daylight had rapidly faded into darkness, it was by no means an easy matter to get a chance of securing it; with the assistance of a keeper, however, I soon met with success. The man remained near the pool, while I took up a position about twenty-five yards off, and he then pointed out to the best of his ability where the bird was resting and withdrew a few yards. Aiming at the spot as well as I could judge, both barrels of the gun were discharged, and the unfortunate wanderer was found dead, floating on the surface of the water, when we reached the pool.

On the 23rd of September, 1870, while fishing for silver whiting about a mile from the shore off Brighton, during a strong breeze from the east, I caught sight of a lightly marked Grey Phalarope swimming and drifting over the waves at a great pace with the tide. The breaking of the surf now and then forced the bird to rise and hover on wing for a moment and alight again on the surface of the water. Drawing in the line that held our small boat, we went on board, and soon came up with and secured the little bird, which proved to be a juvenile in plumage of the first autumn.

On a stormy morning after a very rough night during the first week in October 1870, I happened to be over at Shoreham soon after daybreak, and met with a great number of Phalaropes along the shore between the Norfolk bridge and Lancing. Several were swimming in the oyster-ponds and moving about on the grass fields inside the shingle-banks; others paddled about in any small puddles they could find, where the rain water had collected in the fields and marshes within half a mile of the shore. There were also hundreds passing along the coast, flying towards the west, alighting now and then among the breakers, where still unruffled water could be met with, and resting for a few moments to recruit their strength. Many were so fatigued by exposure to the long-continued gale, that they were utterly unable to press on their journey; several I picked up were in the last gasp, and about half a dozen were dead and cold. This large flight, performing their annual migration, must have been passing the south coast for a fortnight at least; on fine days with a light wind few would be seen; should the breeze freshen, and a gale of wind set in, they would again put in an appearance, exhibiting signs of distress from the effects of the severity of the weather.

The two most handsome specimens I secured at this time were discovered flitting over and alighting occasionally among the breakers rolling on the beach at Brighton, just to the west of the new pier, on the 16th of October, 1870. Several fishermen and boys were flinging stones at them, but the fearless birds took not the slightest notice, unless the spray of the water was driven over them, when they only fluttered a yard or two. Shortly after, the pair got on wing and moved a few hundred yards further out to sea; and having ascertained that they were in excellent plumage, we again hauled down a boat belonging to a friend in which I had previously been afloat and shot a Long-tailed Skua sheltering from the gale in the smooth water near the pier. The flag at the signal-station on the esplanade prohibiting beach-boats that ply for hire to put out had been hoisted on account of the gale to prevent accidents, and we could not have gone afloat had we not taken possession of and used a private boat. The birds were both turned over by the first barrel, and proved to be in very handsome clear grey plumage. Nearly the whole of the Phalaropes obtained at this time were in very poor condition, and these were the only pair, with the exception of two exceedingly large birds shot in the marshes between Lancing and Worthing, that could be considered up to the mark, these four being both plump and heavy. The immense flocks which appeared at this time seem to have been blown ashore along the whole of the south coast; they were mentioned in the papers as having been particularly numerous about Plymouth and still further west. It is evident that the Phalarope must pass our coasts regularly every autumn, though we only notice the species in any numbers after heavy gales from the south or east, when the greater part of the unfortunate travellers are disabled by the rough weather, and have not strength to continue their journey, being forced to seek shelter till the storm has blown over. On the evening of November 1st, 1873, while steaming past the entrance to Lowestoft harbour, our vessel nearly ran over one of these birds floating quietly on the long rollers caused by the strong tide rushing through the narrow channel inside the sands.

As daylight was closing in on a stormy night in November 1870, I detected one of these birds running round a small puddle of rain-water on the King's Road at Brighton, near the west end of the town.

The Phalarope feeds on tiny flies and small water-insects, which it takes while swimming or running over the muds or among the blades of grass. I have often watched them picking up their prey within the distance of a few yards, and they have taken not the slightest notice of our presence.

www.ingramcontent.com/pod-product-compliance
Lightning Source LLC
Chambersburg PA
CBHW030730230426
43667CB00007B/665